NEVER A SHOT IN ANGER

Col. Barney Oldfield, U.S.A.F. (Ret.)

BATTLE OF NORMANDY MUSEUM EDITION

CAPRA PRESS / SANTA BARBARA

*To all war correspondents
all the military public relations crews,
and all the brave men they knew,
whether they like it or not,
this book is dedicated.*

Second printing October 1956.
Battle of Normandy Museum Edition, September, 1989.

ISBN 0-88496-306-3 (cloth)
ISBN 0-88496-307-1 (paper)

Other Books by the Author
Vol. 1, *Those Wonderful Men in the Cactus Starfighter Squadron,*
with Tom Rhone, 1976.
Vol. II, *Those Wonderful Men in the Cactus Starfighter Squadron,*
1984
Operation Narcissus, novel, 1978

Contributor to:
How I Made the Sale Which Meant Most to Me, 1981
Yanks Meet Reds, 1988

Published by Capra Press
Post Office Box 2068 / Santa Barbara, CA 93120

Contents

TAKE

FOREWORD

This book, NEVER A SHOT IN ANGER, about the war correspondents of World War II in Europe, has been going in and out of public and reference libraries ever since it was first published in 1956. Countless books, monographs, and scholarly dissertations list it as a "source." It endowed at least one scholarship, and has been an ever-popular "auction item" on fund-raising occasions for educational TV stations, and has been placed in four time capsules in the cornerstones of buildings. The British Imperial War Museum in London, and the Portsmouth D-Day Museum on the south coast of England have copies.

As it was about the men and women who wrote, voiced and photographed the evolvement of the victory through the Normandy threshold to the continent—those who processed their accounts through whatever media was their individual specialty—it was due to eyewitnessing intrepids such as these that the war came to homes and families oceans away. There were fifty-eight of these war correspondents accommodated in what was called "first wave" slots with the surface invasion force for Normandy's D-Day. In late May, 1944, all were asked to casually "wander up" (no groups, please!) to a block of mean flats in Edgerton Gardens, near Brompton Oratory, in London's Knightsbridge and knock on the door of No. 38. Once inside they were asked for their current office and home telephones and addresses, given their bare minimum requirements to be taken with them when they would be called to join the units selected to take them—and as a last thing, to sit down at one typewriter on a field table and write their own obituaries! That was no macabre ploy, but a way of cementing in their minds the hazards of their commitment and how carefully they should guard the highly secret nature of the D-Day enterprise. There was censorship, of course, but secret-keeping became an individual imperative as war correspondents could bleed from indiscretions as well as soldiers. Sharing in a developing story with a whole world waiting they would be, but they could also suffer in a debacle if the invasion were signaled in advance.

i

WWII was the last time military press censorship was used by the United States at war.

The man who always opened the door at No. 38 Edgerton Gardens knew everyone personally who would come calling and they all knew him—(then) Major Barney Oldfield, a paratrooper, and a former newspaperman himself—before the "active duty" call in 1940. He wrote NEVER A SHOT IN ANGER as he felt it should be put down somewhere, in human interest story style, telling tales about those whose job it was to tell human interest stories about others. These correspondents were surrogates for all those at distance from battle who could not have—and probably didn't want—the catbird seats they had for conflict.

It seemed to us at the U.S. Committee for the Battle of Normandy Museum that this book, from its unusual perspective, and dealing with those who chose to go close-up to the war of greatest magnitude in human history should be reprinted—with an update by the author, now a businessman, a consultant for International Relations with Litton Industries in Beverly Hills, California. He is a Charter Member of the U.S. Committee, and was selected by President Reagan to be a member of the Presidential Delegation to the inauguration of the Museum. I commend this account to you for enjoyment and for the thoughts it may inspire in readers of that other time when the Fate of the world was on the line—and a lot of what we accept so casually today would be decided from D-Day onwards in Normandy.

ANTHONY C. STOUT, *president*
U.S. Committee for the
Battle of Normandy Museum

January, 1989
Washington, D.C.

UPDATE, 1988!

The White House was on my phone!

Gerald Koenig, a staffer, said: "President Reagan has selected you to be one of his White House Presidential Delegation members being flown to Paris, June 2-7, 1988, for the unveiling of the Battle of Normandy Museum in Caen."

Shortly after, in the midst of all my reflecting on how incredible it would be traveling under such high level auspices after my first 1944 Normandy landfall in a battered C-47, there was another call from Leslie Lautenslager, of the Protocol Office of the State Department. She said she needed my passport to have a French visa affixed.

That was a statement all its own about the world affairs situation. "Surprise attack", that hoary specter, a leftover of our being catapulted into World War II with Pearl Harbor's devastation, had now evolved into *terrorism* as the new combat form. Now human targets were being struck down in busy streets, in airport ticket counter queues, among teams at Olympic Games, plus hijackings, kidnappings with proximity and horror added by television which found it could be played like an organ-grinder with his panhandling monkey. Proper targets were no longer munition dumps and marshaling yards, but anything that bled so transmission of the gory details could intimidate and horrify not only individuals, but governments as well. A visa issuance wasn't much, but it gave this France 44 years after D-Day some means of better knowing and controlling, and if need be, tracking down fanatics sent to harm, maim and even murder the innocent merely to get attention.

In my own interim post-Normandy, that 22-mile long stretch of beaches shaped like a giant hockey stick that was ablaze that awesome and awful June morning, events had piled on putting it increasingly to the rear. If mankind had learned lessons from its carnage, and some surely had, the difficulty to maintain the required will and persisting determination was not easy. Deterrence (enough strength in being militarily to back diplomacy), coalitions of nations built around common purpose (or, more true, common fear) capable of well-directed common effort—had been pursued diligently. That learning had taken a long time, surely, as people who kept such records knew there had been more than 14,000 wars in one form or another. Even in a lifetime, I found, something as big as World War II could become "one of." As an 8-year old I'd whooped with joy when World War I ended. Mine had been World War II, and the Korean "police action," and I had retired just as the Cuban Missile Crisis was coming to a boil. President John F. Kennedy who had said we "would bear any burden" was about to tell U.S. Military Advisers in Viet Nam they could "shoot back." While I was still in uniform, though, in Viet Nam Army Specialist 4 James Davis, of Livingston, Tennessee, became the first American killed out there in the rice paddies, the initial name eligible to be engraved on that later Viet Nam Washington monument[1]—and in two years, almost to the day, Kennedy knew an assassin's bullet. Some of the young who mourned and idolized him would later "bear any burden," but others turned their backs on his admonition and those among them who wore the uniform.

As our Presidential delegation flew the Atlantic, Viet Nam's messy end was almost a generation back. Europe, that unbelievably repetitive abattoir throughout the ages, had known 43 years of peace and the rewards of economic cooperation. The glowering face of the Soviet Union changed with General Secretary Mikhail Gorbachev at its tiller, and it appeared as fatigued and weary by the perpetual standoff as the alliances and other wary hostiles at its borders. The North Atlantic Treaty, a perpetual credit to western statesmen who were its architects, had actually been glued together by the frowns of Josef Stalin and his dour, heavy-handed successors before emergence of this fresh new whiz on the world's stage after he'd meteored out of the Stavropol-'Region into the Big Picture like some bottled genie biding his time. After three state funerals in three years, the Soviet Union had felt its already clogged arteries hardened at the expense of its own people. The Conference Table was now upstaging the War Room, it seemed, but the sophisticates knew it had been the other way around for a long time and necessarily so. Although happy with the turn of affairs, they were still guarded in their enthusiasms.

This was not happenstance and American names imbedded away back in the early '40s Normandy preparations had also hung around afterward to bring all their considerable powers of persuasion and victorious credentials to bear on the often fussing European states telling them over and over their togetherness would bring all things sought, while separateness could be courting disaster. Those names—General Dwight D. Eisenhower, who had agonized over pre-Normandy detail to assure his soldiers every conceivable support; his superb planning "altar boys," Alfred M. Gruenther and Lauris Norstad; Matthew Ridgway, who had jumped his 82nd Airborne Division near Ste. Mere-Eglise and had liberated the first French village on D-Day morning—were not only warring names, but NATO Supreme Allied Commanders to be. Norstad, the son of a Lutheran Minister whose family came from Stavanger, Norway, was to be in high European positions for twelve-plus years, probably the military service's most knowledgeable about Siamese-twinning politics and military power to gain objectives without a fight. To a man they had all gone the extra mile and had not entrusted entirely to civilian leadership the victory so expensively won. In their commitment and performance, if it could be said that war is too important to be left to the generals, they showed the other side of the coin, and equally valid, that peace attained after mortal struggle is too dear to be left alone on the doorstep of politicians.

Lofty, inspiring, proud stuff, leadership examples to recall, and be thankful for, indeed!

As the White House Presidential delegation aircraft droned along over the North Atlantic, it was my 130th crossing since the first time in 1943, bound for the great adventure. The route was nearly the same—Goose Bay, Iceland's Keflavik, but on OVER London to LeBourget. In 1943, London was the destination, and LeBourget would have to wait. At such times ghosts walk, old shadows are freshened into life, and hindsight is total.

That Presidential delegation[2] invitation, for instance.

It dated from April Fool's Day 1939, just five months before Hitler would hit Poland. Warner Brothers studio in Burbank, California was having a press party launching a new movie, "Dodge City," in that old frontier cattle drive railhead. "West of Leavenworth," it was said, "no law; west of Dodge City, no God." The very film itself was part of a chain of improbables. Grad Sears, Warners' sales boss, and Charlie Einfeld, the company's publicity honcho, had some months before ridden the Santa Fe Chief all the way to California for a two hour harangue with Jack Warner, the executive producer, and now were on the long train trip back to New York. They were grousing about their inconvenience, the waste of time it had been, and what SOBs bosses could be with egos added. One of those sudden plains' snows that blow down over the flat lands from Canada piled train-high drifts over the railway, and they found themselves stuck. The club car was old stuff by then, so they waded uptown and found there was a ballroom, no patrons, the orchestra trapped just as they were. Being on expense accounts, they hired the hall and the band, then invited all the train's passengers to be their guests and literally "have a ball," which they did. The local theater manager joined in, and told them delightful stories of "when Dodge was young." When the train was finally able to go on east, Sears and Einfeld wrote a memo to Warner, undoubtedly self-serving to excuse their delay and showing they had the company always on their minds. That memo said Warners should make a movie called "Dodge City" starring Errol Flynn! Press invitations went out to film columnists and editors of which I was one, and we were to board an "eastern train" which would take us all to Dodge City where a "western train carrying 26 stars and featured players" would join us for the film's launch. Mentioned by name were Errol Flynn, Ann Sheridan, "Little Caesar" himself, Edward G. Robinson, Humphrey Bogart and his (then) wife, Mayo Methot (he called her Sluggie, which she did to him a lot). The rest of the promised 26 were "also rans", no identification. It was a fun day and the staid Kansas City Star interviewed Slapsie Maxie Rosenbloom, after introducing the New York "East sider" to a horse, that seeming only fair as it was a western picture. Sitting in my compartment on that train in the late afternoon writing my story, and watching Errol out of my window as a winsome young Dodge City girl was offering, blouse open, her well-filled bra for autograph, there was a rap on my door. A young face stuck its head in with the not too surprising statement: "The publicity department said I should meet all you press guys on this train. My name's Ronald Reagan. Be sure you write something nice about me." We shook hands, laughed a little, he went on down the corridor banging on other doors and I finished my story. That's how it started—and since the order has never been rescinded, I have continued to write and say nice things about him. When that World War II that included Normandy was ended and my uniform hung away, my post-war payroll attachment was the Warner Brothers publicity department. In those days, publicists were assigned players about whom to generate comment and glamorous tales, and unbelievably, my list included Errol Flynn,[3] Ann Sheridan (the stars of "Dodge City"; Janis Paige, whose real name was Tjaden and she'd been a plumber's helper in Tacoma, Washington but was rounded generously in such ways as to be thought promising star material; Jane Wyman, a one time dancer who was becoming a big screen presence and not too far from an Academy Award;—and for one picture, a teen named Elizabeth Taylor, whose interests in chipmunks were fast waning in favor of boys—and that former Iowa sportscaster, who had come to Catalina with the Chicago Cubs for spring training, got a screen test, and stayed—Ronald Wilson Reagan.

Errol Flynn and Humphrey Bogart always called him a "boy scout." They were surely not, knowing far more interesting ways to start fire than by rubbing two sticks together. The studio bosses' orders to me, however, were always to take any visiting government or foreign potentates who came on the studio lot to the sound stage where "Ronnie Reagan is." Unlike most actors who "uh-uh," "you know" and "I mean" a lot unless there's a script, he was an easy and amiable conversationalist and all people were comfortable with him. He was a liberal, some said "left-wing" Democrat then, had idolized and grown up admiring FDR and how with that voice and a microphone—even though tethered to a wheelchair—had led a nation through the several valleys of shadows, war and peace. There was the kinship of being a "fellow broadcaster." A politics junkie, he talked it all the time. His affable counterpart was over at Metro-Goldwyn-Mayer in Culver City, the song and dance man, George Murphy. They were the institutionalized "good guys", and Hollywood's "ambassadors of good will." They made the movie environs respectable. On the other end of my spectrum was Errol Flynn, who used to regale me with stories about how his first boudoir experience had been with his sister Rosemary's babysitter, and that she had introduced him to his idea of "the promised land." One of my chores then was reading his fan mail, looking for some swashbuckling angle, but most of it was beyond the pale. The mothers-to-be of what were Hugh Hefner's centerfolds sent along specimens of mammary-minded appeal in self-shot photos in explicit detail with "come and see me" invitations. It led me to tell people later that all I knew about love, I had learned "by correspondence", doing Errol's mail![4] Ronald Reagan is a great story-teller. An every morning ritual on the set was to put together three or four one-liners which the columnists loved to quote—habit which has endured unbroken between us ever since. When Hollywood, for whom he'd made 50 movies and only once had been a bad guy, decreed his film days behind him, he swung to TV, the real "mass" medium, then there was the run for governor. Having been with him when he was becoming disillusioned with liberalism, I found myself on the itineraries of eastern writers who came west to "do a job on Reagan." Telling them I didn't like their language, as he was a friend, and had been a credit to the film business, had served well as head of the Screen Actors' Guild and as "ambassador," I was sure he could only raise the level of politics in public esteem—which wouldn't be too hard. They always came unbelieving, knew little of his long interest in politics and political figures, and his instincts which adapted him to such requirements as might present themselves. After each session, I'd send him a brief memo of the questions asked and the answers given. One day he was on the phone: "I think I'll go up to Lake Arrowhead," he said, "and stretch out in the sun—you're defending me better than I am."

He always had an admiration for the military service. In the mid-30s, he'd taken CMTC (Citizens Military Training Corps) courses at Fort Des Moines, and that eventually got him his cavalry commission—and a fondness for horseflesh which never left him. When he transferred to the Army Air Corps in the early '40s and was with the motion picture unit making those training films, many of his critics labelled him a "Fort Roach commando," as the Hal Roach studio was the place the films were made. He took his lumps, never defended himself, and it wasn't until 1981, when his old military overcoat was enshrined at the U.S. Air Force Museum in Dayton, Ohio that he allowed Curator Royal Frey to exhibit his medical records as part of the display. They show him as lucky to have even been allowed to serve as his eyesight was so bad, and he was restricted to the continental limits of the U.S.[5] "What kind of a guy is he, anyway?" questioners always ask. What you see is what you get. If there was a street in town named Normal Blvd. he'd live on it. In the studio days, if a publicist had lunch with one of his "stars," it was a business lunch and the tab could be signed there in our Green Room (dining hall). As many as four times a week, when the set would break for lunch he'd come over and say: "How about letting Jack Warner pick up our tab today?" And off we'd go. It was a boyish thing, like stolen watermelons always taste better, which we had both known as country boys. When we decided to make a grant of money to his old Eureka College, he included me in the meeting with the fund-raisers and he told them to address any mail to him through me, otherwise it might get lost in the "fan mail department"— and delayed. That made me a kind of "hollow tree" where trusting lovers leave notes. Unlike so many, fortunately, who rise to high places, he has never jettisoned or pigeonholed anybody because he "doesn't need them any more." He's hung onto us all. Perhaps that's one reason why I was included in that White House Presidential delegation.

On our Normandy-bound plane that day, sitting across the aisle from me was Jack Thompson, the Chicago Tribune's "jumpboot journalist" who'd gone by parachute into Africa with Col. Edson Raff and the 2nd Battalion of the 503rd Parachute Infantry, and later repeated with Col. James M. Gavin's[6] inaugural combat jump with his 505th Parachute Infantry Regiment into Sicily. Because there were so few who would take a risky route like that just for a story, airborne operations were spottily dealt with in press accounts. As one of the "early day" paratroopers, Class 23 at Fort Benning, my 1943 reason for going to England was to somehow talk war correspondents into taking parachute and glider training, ending by making five jumps and taking five glider rides.[7] Jack had always been my "for instance," as he was a gentle and soft-spoken man, appeared a little like the prophet Moses as portrayed by Michelangelo, but it masked an inner toughness. He was respected, and known to every paratrooper affectionately as "Beaver" (from the kid game in which the first to see whiskers on a chin so hollers out). A true "warhorse," he was a sort of William Howard Russell of the old London Times re-visited, who once started covered little else but conflict. Jack, in World War II, became easily one of the most celebrated of his craft, respected by every General and private first class he ever met, and he'd even done Viet Nam time, although his hair and his beard made him look more like Santa Claus than an inquiring, sensitive reporter.

It was in Viet Nam that Barry Zorthian, as Chief spokesman for that 11-year long effort, had a battery of public information people that included 119 civilians and 128 uniformed people from U.S. sources, plus another 370 Viet Namese, all engaged in "explaining" that "out of inventory" struggle. The media—peaking at around 550 in-country at one time—probably reached 4,000 including the short-timers, in-and-outers, who came and went. About 65 of them, because of that war's fuzziness, were killed and more missing.[8] Credibility was not high, reportage was un-censored, position-paper accounts were plentiful and military security not a big concern, especially among the rookies—where if there was debate at all, the "evening news nearly always won." The days of our Eisenhower instruction, which appeared in so many pre-Normandy papers and memos, that he wanted all war correspondents treated as "quasi-staff officers, rank of captain," seemed long ago. With field press censorship, there were STOPS and PASSES with which copy was read before transmission—and it was mutually beneficial. He recognized their stories as helpful in sustaining public support back home, and they could write up to and against the censor guidance.

In severe contrast to Normandy and World War II where all accredited war correspondents wore uniforms of their country, General William Westmoreland, a straight arrow if there ever was one, who had the U.S. Military Assistance Command, Viet Nam (MAC-V, for short) once said ruefully: "IN World War II... they all wore the same uniforms we did... they went through the censor so as not to give the enemy information... all the troops knew they were on our side and they wanted us to win. In Viet Nam... they didn't wear any uniforms... they could have been beer salesmen for all we knew. Instead of a pen, they had TV cameras... there was no censorship... and their stories relfected the prejudices they represented, the soldiers were very disillusioned with the media. Their attitude was that the media didn't want us to win... and I think they had an adverse effect on morale." Vice President Hubert Humphrey, on a trip there, asked the media "to give the American side... the benefit of the doubt when speaking to our people." President Kennedy tried to get New York Timesman David Halberstam transferred as he was the doyen dissenter. He did a book, "The Best and the Brightest" about Camelot gone astray. Secretary of State Dean Rusk was always asking of media people "... whose side are you on?" Once at dinner, seated across the table from him, I asked him if he had read "The Best and the Brightest". He said he had and just for the heck of it had made annotations on pages of quotes and incidents as *he* had remembered them. "I made the mistake one night at a reception," Rusk told me, "of telling someone about it. In a few minutes, a man I didn't know came up to me and said he'd give me $50,000 for my copy of that book with my penned observations and clarifications. I think what has been a parlor game with me has now become an *estate matter!"*

Jack Thompson, brooding there and looking down on the ocean below, knew a lot about the soldiers' points of view. For such men, those "First Amendment rights," and "right to know" are remote to a man with a rifle in hand crawling in the dark, or a pilot combat-loaded and streaking toward a target—the *right* he's interested in mostly is the "right to somehow live through this and go home—whole" Cocktail prating and press club bar observations where the greatest hazard is rush hour traffic don't really refer to the same world. Jack Thompson might argue with censors a lot, and did, but had no wish to be an unwitting, or worse yet, uncaring conveyor of information which would "give aid and comfort to the enemy." In Viet Nam he saw many who were young, on the make, who were cavalier about this. "Obviously," he said, "some intelligent form of press censorship[9] should have been in use in Viet Nam."

Will there ever again be journalists willing to bend a little from ritual dogma about a free press, in the interests of winning rather than placing the highest priority on "getting the story out." Both Jack and I had been with the United Press War Correspondents trek to Normandy on the 40th anniversary of D-Day—that time when Ronald Reagan, the President and Commander-in-Chief—attended the many ceremonial observances up and down the Normandy beaches and added the ring of his emotional oratory to the now much older attendees awed at still being alive to hear it. On our tour bus that day, the several United Press oldsters compared notes on who was the highest salaried United Presser on D-Day. Just down the beach, doing a special was one of their alums, Walter Cronkite, who had been in a fighter aircraft over the tumult below him. It was finally determined that the highest pay for that reporting group had been $67.50 a week—and Walter Cronkite was NOT the most highly compensated on D-Day! It caused some amused conjecture that in some future great power confrontations. Department of Defense accredation credentials will not be as important as a rating by Dun & Bradstreet.

Ghosts DO walk on occasions of this nature. In my mind's eye, crystal clear, was summoned recollection of a lunch one day in 1943 with Edward R. Murrow. His was probably the most convincing, leading American voice (he was on the scene enduring, sharing the Battle of Britain with those courageous people and Roosevelt was afar in Washington) arousing U.S. sympathy for that suffering nation standing and bearing alone—a people who had given us the very language we used—with alterations. Our conversation over that sparse meal was about how to put the voice variety of war corresponding in proximity to the action of our invading forces once the continent was breached. My job then was writing the Tables of Organization and Equipment for (until then nonesuch) military units to be called Press Camps. They were to be the war correspondents "home away from home," with everything on the premises—transport, housing, communications, feeding and collective administration while on the move following the field armies across Western Europe as the Axis was being done in. I told him I couldn't see him or his colleagues comfortable with staying back in London where the undersea cableheads were reading into microphones teletyped reports of the wire services, even if rewritten for individual style. He shuddered at the thought. From that exchange came inclusion of those so-convenient, mobile 400-watt radio stations which could bounce a voiced signal strong and clear enough to be fielded by BBC's London monitoring service, then transmitted by cable to networks in America. It was a monumental moment when JESQ (Jig Easy Sugar Queen) arrived in Normandy so his CBS people like Larry LeSueur, Charles Collingwood and Bill Downs, plus others could be heard with their own commentaries.

All that contrasted sharply with a 1983 gathering at Murrow's alma mater,

Washington State University in Pullman, Washington. His widow, Janet, had asked me to serve on the board of their Edward R. Murrow Symposiums, WSU that day, quite a feat, too—had assembled every living head of CBS News since Murrow into an eye-popping power panel, no small tribute to what a long shadow he still casts and how much they all owed the foundations he'd laid for them. It was there in Pullman that his voice teacher, frail and infantile-paralysis-twisted Ida Lou Anderson had told him how to phrase his dramatic signature and broadcast opener, "THIS ... is LONDON!" The panel[10] included all those who'd built what insiders called "the treehouse of the 800-pound gorilla" (said "gorilla" being the anchor). Nothing then equaled it in weight, reach and influence. So, what was the game they played in editorial decision making for a goggle-eyed student body filled with fledgling journalists?

YOU, a reporter, hear rumored there's to be a secret military operation, even its code name, and are searching for confirmation, in the office of a high Pentagon official. Right there on his desk is a big folder with the code name stamped on it, and with the classification TOP SECRET. The squawkbox summons him down the hall for a quick answer only he can supply, and YOU are left alone in his office. Question! Would YOU take advantage of his absence and give that document a quick read with the intention of breaking it on the evening news?[11] As the "what if" game unfolded, little concern was evidenced about the military force itself, doing a mission regarded as necessary by elected government, depending on surprise to minimize losses by shock effect of catching the adversary with defenses relaxed or down. It was mostly "evening news time". Every so often, as if in church, intoned was "What would Ed Murrow do?", leaving the clear implication he would read the document and shift gears into kiss and tell mode. But the Murrow they were talking about had gone on such life-endangering outings as the first bombing run on Berlin, and up there with fingers of flak reaching for them all, told listeners from the intimacy of his high risk platform about the crew-converted farm boys and urban ghetto youth with precision and coolness did what was required of them "for their country."

BUT, even more than that, with the free world in a serious head-to-head with a great power, and the special location of Pullman, Washington, in relation to that, it seemed to me that future journalists in Edward R. Murrow's name should see signs of thought about "how to" address that. It's easy to dismiss any such happening as "unthinkable", but that doesn't erase any requirement to think about it. Future journalists could have to make greater value choices than they were given that day. Why? When Soviet

Major and Cosmonaut Gherman Titov did his 17 orbits of the earth 185 miles out, Aug. 6-7, 1961 in a 24-hour period he passed over four locations in the U.S. *twice*—one of them, Pullman, Washington! If he had had with him proper instruments and photographic equipment, he could have recorded every square foot of the earth's surface. What was to be called the Strategic Defense Initiative had many of its roots planted at that time when Gen. Laurence S. Kuter said "we have now entered the era of requirement for an anti-satellite satellite, one which can detect, intercept, identify and if need be, destroy an armed enemy satellite!" With all the remarkable technologies on the march, and this Pullman affair 22 years later, there was no attempt, inclination or desire for the mind-expanding exercise which could come from addressing a "... worst scenario such as all-out war—how and who would cover it ... hopefully in the public interest and expectancy ... or *'need* to know')?"

Simple things? Who would be the war correspondents? What story decisions would they have to make? "All out war," big as it would be, would be in multiples of community disasters, so wherever a reporter was would know instant conversion, if he or she lived, into a war correspondent. Big story? Rebuke government leadership for having let this happen? Hardly. But where are there surviving clusters of doctors and hospitalization. The weather and prevailing wind direction would tell which way fallout was taking. What medium would be most important? Most newspapers are downtown in cities, and that's where Ground Zero is for atomic attack. Even if the structure was missed and still operable, who would be at the rewrite or assignment desk to take a call? Or to roll the presses? Or deliver the newspaper? Or be there to read it when it was thrown on the veranda? With radiation, TV screens would be seas of snow. Perhaps, and what a lovely occasion to bring it up, it would be Edward R. Murrow's first medium, radio! People would be trying to escape in cars and would have the dashboard radio on, wouldn't they? That had occurred to me at the North American Air Defense Command 5 years before Titov's orbits and for our regular exercises of the air defense system, I'd asked war game planners to include space for the redundant communications net to be called into service of the President of the U.S. and the Prime Minister of Canada, those statements to be recorded and passed through NORAD's lines to every subordinate unit and copies made to be handed to still-operating radio stations. There was laughter among the operations people—all out attack, and we have to make room for political speeches? Not likely. Next time in Washington, in the office of Presidential Press Secretary James Hagerty,[12] I asked him his opinion. He said: "There will be no announcement of greater importance under such circumstances than that the leaderships of countries are alive and doing what they are supposed to be doing. Make no mistake about that and we'd go out of Washington by every communications means available, including a barbed wire fence if that's all we had." Not long after that he became ABC News President, a journalist before government service, and a wiser one after government service. Unhappy as was the transition from CBS News for Edward R. Murrow to direct the U.S. Information Agency starting one week after the Kennedy inaugural, even he learned a lot. When we all went to the Protestant Episcopal Church on Madison Avenue in 1965, just up the street from where he'd won and lost his CBS News battles, the head usher was Howard K. Smith and he took me to the "family pew" for the goodbye. When will there be his like? Not ever. Firsts only come once, others copy.

"The Moose," they always called Lt. Col. Bertram Kalisch, a former newsreel man with News Of The Day, in New York. He used to brownbag and walk across Central Park, saving a subway nickel, to get to his office. He was not well paid, had a wife and two kids to feed. Yet most of those often seen films of the Normandy D-Day landing and troops splashing ashore would not be available except for his stubborn, imaginative persistence. "Persistence" used to describe Kalisch is rather inadequate. On one of those Central Park walks, he was suddenly confronted with a beggar who'd hung himself from a tree-limb. Flashing into Kalisch' mind was the $10 offer of a New York tabloid for picture tips. He ran to the nearest kiosk, phoned the photo editor breathlessly explaining what he had. "Stay there," the man said, "I'll have a guy over right away." Kalisch ran back, and faced disaster. In his absence, a mounted policeman had come by and cut the hanged man down. Kalisch saw his $10 flying off unclaimed unless he could change things. He got on his knees, and in the name of his near starving wife and kids begged the cop to help him re-hang the dead man until the picture was taken—and he'd split with him. The cop did it—he had a hungry wife and kids, too!

Kalisch before D-Day actually stole (moonlight requisitioned, as it was called) 115 RAF gun cameras, each loaded with 100 feet of film. Once switched on, the cameras ran all the way through the spool. Kalisch wanted to mount one on each of 115 landing craft to be used in the invasion's first wave. Placed next to the tiller and rigged to switch on when the ramp went down in the water and the troops jumped out to wade ashore, they would last just long enough for the disembarkation, raising the ramp, and for the empty craft to scram. The Navy said NO. Kalisch had graduated from the U.S. Naval Academy, and even that didn't change things. He said he wanted to do it because he'd heard Army people saying they were sure if the beach approach was met with heavy fire, the Navy skippers would dump them in deep water and run—the cameras would be their proof it wasn't so. On that argument, the Navy agreed to the installations. Of the 115, for one reason or another only a handful worked—but what they recorded is ours forever. If Kalisch were alive and in the Pentagon today, he would be awash in satellite dishes and how to bring back the in-flight details of Strategic Defense Initiative launches to play in whatever media available. Let others have headline fun with procurement gaffs but his mind would be working—as always—on the Big Picture.

Those Normandy days going in and coming out in the Victory March with the 82nd Airborne Division on Jan. 12,1946 up Fifth Avenue in New York would hardly set me on course toward ore of the most unusual leadership figures I ever knew, but it did. He had gone by Normandy, too. But the circuitous way it happened, crazy! It started on the set of a Warner Brothers musical, "Romance in High C", which starred a new studio hopeful Doris Kappelhoff (make that Doris DAY). A grip answered the set phone, took it away from his ear, and said it was Washington—for me. Maj. Gen. Floyd L. Parks, for whom I'd worked in Berlin, was calling. "I want you to do me a favor," he said. "Go over to March Field at Riverside—and take the regular Army exam." Telling him that exam was undoubtedly too much for me, he kept talking as I looked out over the costumed sea of make believe on that sound stage. He kept pressing, and I finally agreed. On a dull studio day, I drove over to get it behind me. The crusty old sergeant handed out the questions, said he'd call time in a few hours, and after that each of us would have an oral. It was a True-False, which meant even the dumbest guy had one chance in four of being right. Going through it quickly as there was no wish on my part to pass it, I was ushered into the presence of several musty colonels, each seemingly within weeks of retirement, and probably dismayed thinking what they saw before them were the inheritors of the Army they'd loved and served seeking entry. They studied my filled out personal questionnaire, which asked that names of five officers familiar with my military service be listed as references. Being a blithe spirit, I'd put down General of the Army Dwight D. Eisenhower, Lt. Gen. Omar N. Bradley, Field Marshal Sir Bernard Law Montgomery, Maj. Gen. James M. Gavin and Maj. Gen. Floyd L. Parks.

One of the colonels cleared his throat, looked over his half-moons at me and said: "Do you seriously mean to tell me that if I called any one of these five senior officers you've put down here—which I'm not about to do—any one of them would know you?" Nodding, I said I'd worked for all of them. He put his folder down, and looked away. My next inquisitor asked what the job was "at this place, Warner Brothers studio." He was told about publicity, getting stars names in stories and columns to increase fan interest and box office returns; sometimes to keep the names out, if that was best. He wanted an example of the last kind, and I asked him if he'd heard of Errol Flynn. He had. "Well, if Errol gets in, I try to keep it from getting out!" All the folders closed sharply and I was told to go. Enroute back to Warners I was as happy as a hummingbird in the lilac bush, as most assuredly I had bombed on both oral and written exams. The security guard at the studio gate asked if the news had gotten to me yet, and what I was going to do—the studio was going to be closed for the indeterminate period, vacations with pay to be allowed if not yet taken, and I hadn't taken mine. Coming to work the next day was like entering a funeral parlor, everyone stunned, and I only half noticed the telegram lying in the middle of my desk. Probably from some movie editor wanting a gag for a feature. But when opened, it read:

CONGRATULATIONS! YOU HAVE BEEN ACCEPTED AS A REG-ULAR ARMY OFFICER, REPORT TO THE NEAREST MILITARY INSTALLATION TO TAKE THE OATH. YOU HAVE 72 HOURS TO COMPLY!

When I laughed, my colleagues thought I'd gone bonkers. It suddenly dawned on me if I took the oath, I'd be the only one in the whole studio on TWO payrolls. It also told me about the Army, if one goes through the required motions—taking that entrance exam—it didn't matter how it turned out, as long as someone wanted that individual.[13]

Schools have remedial reading, but in the Army, my remedial was the Command & General Staff College at Fort Leavenworth, Kansas. My next door neighbor and classmate was one picked early for top Army leadership for which this was a way station. He'd gone over Normandy's beaches with an armored command. On reaching the banks of the Moselle river, dark, cold and flecked with an occasional snowflake, XII Corps Commander General Manton Eddy asked him if he could get his tanks over. "Sir," he said, "the way I see it—over that river is the shortest way home," and over the river he went. He'd been the one to break through and relieve the surrounded 101st Airborne Division in Bastogne. The German always tracked him in their Order of Battle chartings as where he was something explosive was bound to happen or might already be in progress. His name was Creighton Abrams, "Abe" to everybody.

Thoughts of him, also, paralleled with Normandy. In the same class of 36 officers, it was the custom to set aside one hour each week when a provocative, controversial or arguable premise would be thrown out for each member to do a mental wrestle with—a thought processes checkout of sorts. Once it was "pre-emptive strike"—a hostile power doing a buildup of menacing speed and size, the U.S. the target, on a superiority kick aimed to do America in—do you go to him while the odds are still in U.S. favor, or let the opportunity go by and have to deal with him when he's ready? Thirty-four of the class said to strike. Abe and I, invoking past history when it took great public outrage and bloody encroachment—Boston Massacre, Boston Tea Party, impressing of American sailors on the high seas, firing on Ft. Sumter, blasting a hole in the Battleship MAINE, unrestricted submarine warfare and downing of the Lusitania, Pearl Harbor—in order to set up the emotional resolve to sustain a war effort, said no leader could safely go to the battlefield without that kind of "we're all in it together" determination. Clauzewitz called it pursuing "policy by other means." "Abe" and General Westmoreland were the ones who inherited just such a situation in Viet Nam. Westmoreland described it as "...limited war...with limited objectives...prosecuted by limited means...with limited public support. Therefore...it was destined to be a long war (and was)...a war so long that public support waned and political decisions by the Congress terminated our involvement...resulting in a military victory for the North Vietnamese Communists. The Military did not lose a single battle of any consequence. The war was lost by Congressional actions withdrawing support to the South Vietnamese government despite commitments..."[14]

One night at dinner after General Abrams came back to be the Army's Chief of Staff, he told me how often he had remembered that 34 to 2 decision against us at Leavenworth and how the Fates had picked him to prove its correctness. It was a conflict being "thought out" by whiz kids and dilatantes in Washington while being "fought out" in the Viet Nam rice paddies by soldiers he knew and respected, and they bled a lot. Suddenly, he asked rhetorically: "Ever thought about who really wins our wars? It sure isn't politicians, or generals or admirals, either. It's three or four soldiers in an untenable position and they know it. Every bit of common sense tells them they should get the hell out of there, but they don't. They HOLD. Others who are running see them holding, and come back to help them—and they win the day. Those soldiers are the ones who win our wars." His clear implication was that a few Congressmen with the guts to hold wouldn't be all bad, either.[15]

It was a different Army I'd come back to find, extraordinary for a peacetime one—if one could call it peace when there was a requirement to stabilize a chaotic world by what was called "presence" in many lands. Because it was big, having to be that way to do all the chores being assigned to it, it had a whopper budget. It became a kind of piggy bank to some in Congress, a place to cut to line a pork barrel. And as always happens in corporate life—when people transfer who had the idea one is working on, successors want to disassociate or advance ideas and projects of their own. The "idea" had by General J. Lawton "Lightnin' Joe" Collins and General Parks had been to get into uniform a professionally experienced public relations nucleus to help with the burgeoning public accountability tasks. With them gone, the Air Force came beckoning, as it was a brand new separate service as of September 1947, and my transfer was on July 25, 1949, the very last day inter-service switches were allowed. That Air Force to which I was a stranger, decided to start me "from scratch" which was the Warner Robins Air Material Area in swamplands near Macon, Georgia. Ticket to oblivion, my old Army friends said, as this was a Sears, Roebuck nuts, bolts and parts depot which hired jillions of civil service people and Congressman Carl Vinson wanted something in his district to do just that. I must admit I was thinking of what Gracie Allen had once told George Burns in her malaprop responses: "All right, you have buttered your bread—now lie in it."

What made their hoots at my flawed judgment wrong was a Washington call from the office of the U.S. Air Force Deputy Chief of Staff, Plans & Operations. The instructions were to "get to Washington for a Tuesday 8 A.M. appointment" with no less than the holder of that exalted position, Lt. Gen. Lauris Norstad! It was a Friday afternoon and with no further explanation, it sent me back over my checkered past trying to think what transgression suddenly surfaced causing me this level of rebuke. My longtime belief in the aphorism " ... never ask permission, but be prepared to ask for forgiveness ... " had surely run aground. It was not the most pleasant weekend of my memory, but at 7:30 that Tuesday, there I was in his waiting room. Gaye Holladay, his secretary, couldn't enlighten me and could only offer sympathy. "He does things like that all the time," she said in no way lessening the small beads of perspiration I could feel at the roots of my hair. When he came in, he nodded to her, took no notice of me and went into his cubicle. I was not reassured, but consoled myself that drawing-and-quartering and death-by-a-thousand-cuts were no longer considered reasonable punishment. When summoned I did my best heel-clicking roundhouse salute and said those formal proper words that I was "reporting as ordered." He was cleaning his pipe, and without looking up from that said: "Stand there a minute! I want to look at you." By physical construction, I am not knock-kneed but I came down with a case of it nonetheless. Then he looked up, smiled disarmingly, and told me to sit down in a chair next to him. To this day, there's no way I could swear "sit down" was what I did, more to the point, "collapsed." Behind that ever boyish face lay one of the greatest steel-trap minds in any of the military services.

Casually, he said: "You may have read in the papers that I'm going to command a joint Army-Air Force exercise called SWARMER this spring down in North Carolina. (I hadn't). It's to test what we've learned in the Berlin Airlift to see if a position deep in enemy-held territory can be combatable and sustained entirely by air re-supply . . . " My eyes began to focus, and what he was saying made sense. He said that just the week before he'd assembled the joint planning staff of generals and colonels who'd been sketching out this "war game", and as a diplomatic ploy said on checking the troop lists, he noticed he'd have far more Army than Air Force strength, so he would take the Army's nomination of one of their own to be the public information explainer if there was press interest—and he knew there would be. He said he had viewed a miracle—that nothing like it had ever occurred before—to him, anyway. (He had been the key strategist who had pried a separate Air Force out of the Army, so knew how raw the edges could be firsthand and over a long time).

"An Army General," he said it slowly as if still making sure it was true, "told me the Army would waive that if I'd get the Air Force officer they would prefer! They said to get you, so I put my exec on your trail—that's why you're here. I want to transfer you here to the Pentagon at once. You'll have an office next door until we go down to North Carolina. You'll have to share the office, I'm afraid, but the other fellow isn't around much." That tossed-off line was instructive about the Norstad manner as the "other fellow" did occasional consultant jobs for him and his name was Charles A. Lindbergh! At the end of SWARMER which went very well, making him visible in a command rather than staff way for the first time, many things totally unknown to me were on the horizon—a multinational military force within the North Atlantic Treaty's 12 signatory countries, and a North Korean adverturism ever so close. There was a requirement for an after-action report and in it I suggested a permanent 25-man "flying squad" fully equipped with cameras, still and reel, recording capability, writing skills, voice broadcasting experience—have it all available for use anywhere in the world for maneuvers, or real situations and that unit be the foundation of media handling as correspondents were fed into the coverage of any U.S.

xx   NEVER A SHOT IN ANGER

commitment. That report, turned in on May 20, 1950, was considered by Maj. Gen. Sory Smith, the Secretary of the Air Force Director of Public Information as "interesting and a good idea" but was shelved the same day. "A unit like that, in being for such stated purpose," he declared, "would prompt a Congressional investigation." Then Secretary of Defense Louis Johnson was on the speech circuit saying he "was cutting the fat and saving the muscle" of the military forces. A little more than a month later, on June 25th, after Secretary of State Dean Acheson had stated the Korean peninsula—a forever fought over nose-like appendage to East Asia, eyed covetously by Russians/Soviets, Chinese and Japan—said it lay outside U.S. defensive concerns, so the North Koreans struck.

Across the 38th Parallel they flooded, the line where hostilities had ceased in 1945. Dictator Kim Il-Sung had decided on unification and as the surprised occupation garrisons fell one by one, it looked as though he was going to do it. As we all came rushing into the Pentagon that day, there was General Smith with a Red Line Urgent message from Gen. George Stratemeyer, the Far East Air Forces commander in Tokyo. It read:

URGENT. NEED ONE FULL COLONEL COMBAT EXPERIENCED. PUBLIC RELATIONS IMMEDIATELY.

The full colonel meant parity with General Douglas MacArthur's ranking information officer, Col. Pat Echols. The Personnel punchcard sorter whirred and one—just one—fell out. Col. William P. Nuckols. He'd gone by Normandy, too, but at that moment had finally escaped military public relations and was enroute to Mexico City to be the Air Attache in the American Embassy. All points messaging pursued him and caught him lying in the sun on the beach at Panama City. He was "not pleased," with profanity added, but as ordered flew to Washington. While he was still airborne, General Smith said for me to begin reconstructing that Exercise SWARMER "flying squad." Nuckols was in a black mood, as for his constancy in dealing with media matters, all his peers had passed him by, were wearing two, three and even four stars. He told General Hoyt S. Vandenberg, the Air Force Chief of Staff, and Norstad, who was temporarily vice chief, that he'd taken his lumps and wanted no more of it. They told him sternly as long as he was wearing those eagles on his shoulders, he'd go where sent—and Tokyo and Korea would be where he would be getting his mail. Then, the official part behind them, they took his arms, companions in trouble, telling him to do well and they would take care of him. It was in that glowering demeanor that he appeared before my desk.

"YOU," he said, in remembrance of our long ago startup for Normandy, "know exactly what I'm NOT going to have when I get out there. Nothing to work with, people or equipment. Up to now, coverage of the Officers' Wives Club, and the softball leagues, the bowling—they don't know zilch about a communique. Don't leave me hanging out there. I don't know how in the hell you're going to do it, but do it." He marched out. He'd made his speech for all the good that might do him. But, there IS a fraternity of those of us who have known "being out at the end of the line", and he had been speaking loud enough that General Smith heard it all. "Poor guy," he said, "get what you can and take it out there to him." Few people get to know what it's like to be centered as the "last straw" when chaos is evident. To clear my head a little, and with the knowledge that the "flying squad" was coming together, it was equipment that was the problem. Whatever had been mothballed, forget that. For no apparent reason I headed over on the E-Ring for the Norstad office. Very close to his door were two lieutenant colonels talking excitedly, and as I came up alongside I heard one say there was a new code for procurements related to the Korean "police action." He said: "If you state THIS IS A *HOLD OFF* MESSAGE, and send it to Wright Patterson in Ohio with your list of needs, they can buy on the open market without bid-letting!" Running back to my typewriter, I put together the grandest wish list I could think of, sent the message, and asked that all stated equipment be sent to Travis Air Force Base, near San Francisco to be picked up by the "Flying Squad" which would rendezvous there to Fly ASAP (As Soon As Possible) to Tokyo and Korea. Our Tokyo arrival even had theme music as we picked up the Far East Network station at sea playing "Put Another Nickel In." We arrived at 3 A.M. "under cover of darkness" and using commandeered trucks were caught in the act of unloading as Nuckols arrived that morning. "My God," he said clapping his hands to his head seeing all the bright, shiny, new, totally unexpected pile of goodies, "we're all going to Leavenworth (the federal prison), I'm sure, but we'll go happy!" Placed in Korea, quickly grouped military people supplemented coverage[16] and took the same risks as the war correspondents along that fluid perimeter where correspondent casualties ran high. A monument to their memory was later erected in Freedom Park (halfway between Seoul and Pan Mun Jom).[17] First there was going to be no censorship, just guidelines, until finally action to impose it was about to be taken—then the Inchon Landing, and the North Korean rout kept it from happening.[18] It was after Inchon, in rubble-strewn Seoul, that a courier came along on a truck. "I was told to tell you if I found you, you are supposed to return to Tokyo and Washington!" The Chinese "volunteers" were just beginning to pour in, winter was coming on—it was not the worst news I ever had.

There Norstad told me that he was taking me with him to Hq United States Air Forces Europe, that President Truman was recalling General Eisenhower to active duty and nominating him as Supreme Allied Commander for the NATO military forces, that he would probably get some allied job under him. "Whatever he needs that we have," he said seriously, "we'll give him. If he asks for something we haven't got, we'll get it and give it to him." Later he "loaned" me to him as an "advance man" for his highly successful pre-command assumption survey of the 12 countries.

The Norstad/Eisenhower relationship was almost father/son in a professional way. In his book, "Crusade in Europe", on page 119 were two lonely sentences. Eisenhower said that it was in North Africa on an Oran air field "I first met Lt. Col. Lauris Norstad, a young Air Force officer, who so impressed me by his alertness, grasp of problems and personality that I never thereafter lost sight of him. He was and is one of those rare men whose capacity knows no limit." How prophetic that statement was!

Norstad had been in on the Operation TORCH planning for North Africa, but with Normandy as a next step. While in England, he had often gone on ABSIE (American Broadcasting Station in England) and broadcast to Norway, the land of his ancestors. As is almost always the fate of long range planners, those skilled in placing themselves out ten, even 20 years or more in time and seeing what will be required, they are seldom there to see how accurately their forecasts were—and if they were, to savor vindication. He was to be one who did—in spades. On January 20, 1951 "advancing" the Eisenhower party, I was about to take off for the next stop, Iceland. Norstad's pilot called in for landing instructions at Y-80, near Wiesbaden. Neither of us knew then when we shook hands and I updated him briefly that this was the beginning of more than a decade that he would be the consistent top military shot-caller in Western Europe, and that respect for him would grow and grow. In international security terms, he has to have been one of the most valuable genealogical "returns on investment" in this often troubled 20th Century. He was an architect first, then a presider-over and holder-intact of the beyond Normandy fate of the European continent. He was an applier of political intuitiveness, organizer of coordinated effort from which the achievement was sustained and enduring peace. He gave confidence to the movers and shakers to erect behind the military protection a European Common Market, impossible without the sentry-like umbrella he managed. He could be cool as a broken-off Greenland iceberg while moving just as inexorably.

As our Normandy delegation was traveling by bus to Caen along the Seine, there was La Roche Guyon. It had been Field Marshal Erwin Rommel's headquarters, the "Desert Fox" transplanted from shifting African sands and fortunes to make German propaganda's "Atlantic Wall" just that. He, and his chief of staff, Lt. Gen. (also Dr.) Hans Speidel had been deeply involved in the plot to kill Hitler, July 20, 1944. Speidel was a paradox, a man who genuinely loved France, yet was under orders to occupy it—ruthlessly, if that was needed—and defend against its liberation. He eventually knew arrest, merciless interrogation, torture, imprisonment, saw Rommel murdered for his part in the conspiracy against Hitler, yet somehow stayed alive.

He had always been a prime example of the pin-setter type mind of General Lauris Norstad. When Truman had sent a handwritten note in October, 1950 to Eisenhower at Columbia University in New York, asking him to come see him the next time in Washington, it was during that chat that the President told him he intended to nominate him to be Supreme Allied Commander. Eisenhower recommended some means of including the Germans in defense of Western Europe as it "doesn't make sense to attempt to do it without them." Politically, that was bad medicine even if good sense. The role Germany would play once there was an agreed treaty was subject of heated debate, and a military version of the Tower of Babel—multinational units, a European Defense Community hodgepodge—precautioned that shoulder to shoulder in ranks, they could be watched, couldn't go adventuring on their own. In the French Chambre the speeches were emotional, and a one-armed veteran asked how he could be expected to "link arms" with the Germans when they'd been the ones who'd cost him his. "Out there", though, it was inevitable, but how.

In 1952, when General Norstad's Allied Air Forces Central Europe was in Fontainebleu, unexpectedly, there was Dr. Hans Speidel calling. He was carried as an "observer" at NATO's proceedings in Paris, had no voice, but could monitor. Not until May, 1955, would the Federal Republic of Germany become a restored member of the "family of nations." It made the scalp prickle a bit to be talking with someone who had tried to bring Hitler down, and had lived through the aftermath of vengeance that was carried out. He said there were two German reporters, a man and a woman, from a publication in Dusseldorf, driving from Paris to see me. He said they would be with me in less than an hour, with allowances for French traffic that day. "I thought you should have some advance knowledge of what they want," he was saying matter-of-factly. "They hear rumors that one day our country— once more a nation—will have some military forces, and it will have to be to

NATO stipulations, but when this happens, they wonder if German soldiers and their officers will be welcome in allied formations and headquarters on staffs. A headquarters such as yours, as example."

In that time, that was a gulper—first class. Every attempt and suggestion about such an eventuality was subject to spirited argument around tables as well as highest government circles. Once the phone was hung up, I dashed up to Norstad's office. "To what do I owe the honor of this visit?" he asked looking up from his papers. At the mention of Dr. Speidel, the smile went off his face. "I have not heard anything you're saying. I'm not interested in YOUR problem." Avoidance of the subject was his stance, guidance NO. In the public relations field, this is "walking the plank" time and "deniability" is the vogue. Or, the go until you hear glass syndrome.

Before the arrival of the Germans, I picked one man from each of the six nationalities on our staff—Canada, Belgium, The Netherlands, France, Great Britain and the U.S. Using a "worst case" criteria, each had had a bad WW II German memory—shot down, wounded by, chased by, known Gestapo surveillance, or Prisoner of War. And I told them to express themselves honestly. Germany was still under four-power Occupation, after all, and reluctance would not be improbable. The German media duo came, were told the nature of the group they would talk with, and they thought it a good idea as they wanted an honest reaction. It would never have been my forecast, but every one of the nationalities said if the Germans brought professionalism and numbers to help with the common goal of the headquarters, they would be welcome! The reporters drove off on cloud nine. It had gone so well, I went to Norstad's office again to tell him so. He waved an imperious index finger at the door and said: "Out! I don't want to know anything about it." Tail between legs, I left.

When the Federal Republic of Germany was born in 1955, its allowed military forces could only be locked into NATO. The first 4-star General commissioned was Dr. Hans Speidel. After Supreme Commanders named, the fourth was General Norstad. That Dusseldorf publication aroused no ripples at all, although it was generously upbeat about NATO's acceptance of Germany's rightful—and helpful—place. After Greece and Turkey, Germany became the 15th NATO member, but astride that historical invasion route of the ages. Not only an ally, but a crucial ally. In 1957, General Lauris Norstad appointed Gen. Hans Speidel Commander of NATO's Hq Allied Forces, Central Europe in Fontainebleau.

Long looker, Norstad truly was. But his "how to" instincts were fascinating. Politically savvy, he would know exactly how to sow seeds of acceptance by floating a trial balloon with an off the mainline publication to see if someone picked up on it, made a fuss—a toe in the water testing for temperature. And I have always believed that he probably called Speidel sketching out a means of getting the debates off dead center, and advancing the inevitable—German participation. There had been no fuss, no bother— but even so, after those two notable strikeouts and I was then in Colorado Springs, Colorado at the North American Air Defense Command. I did not write to him again of my Speidel 1952 phone call—and all that jazz! Once bitten, twice shy; twice bitten, let sleeping dogs lie!

But for President Kennedy's unease with Eisenhower friends and leftbacks, as far as Europeans were concerned, General Lauris Norstad, boyish looking when he came and boyish-looking when he left, probably could have stayed Supreme Allied Commander until the 21st Century, had he been allowed to live that long. Of all those who studied Normandy and France in those old planning days, his was surely one of the most dedicated passages, cerebral, calculating, constructive, consistent, cajoling or commanding as required, yet for all of that, he had mystique about him, liked obscurity, being withdrawn until he wished to emerge, and truly a man of the century, deserving of scholarly probes and study in our long history to come.[19]

Caen—again!

Once it was my daily curse as one of the writers of the twice-daily communique from Hq 21st Army Group, when Field Marshal Montgomery was the overall invasion ground forces commander . . . On D-Day, reading from Operation OVERLORD plan and phaselines, Prime Minister Winston Churchill said " . . . there is fighting in the streets of Caen . . . " Truth was, the invaders were stuck with and before Caen until July 11th. They were held outside by the tenacity of the German 716th Infantry and elements of the diehard 12th and 21st SS Panzer Divisions. Caen, 80% destroyed, was reduced to rubble before what Churchill said was correct. All that time, our communiques and bolstering censor guidance protected his statement. Our word alternatives brainstormed were akin to a scrabble game, covering terms such as "outskirts," "suburbs," "around," "encircling," "penetrating," "increasing pressure on," "carrying the fight to the enemy in," and as the late Yul Brynner put it " . . . et cetera, et cetera and et cetera." Pundits oceans away, nearby war correspondents and generals fretted about that left flank having taken root. If all the brimstone Lt. Gen. George S. Patton, Jr. had lavished on the situation had seen print, the coalition could have been shredded. Yet the machinery of the communique and press censorship applied in review of written reports and commentaries kept public opinion patient and supportive[20] and dismembering did not occur. How effective this was was hinted in the book written by Theodore (Ted) Koop, after his background with the Associated Press and as a CBS newsman, was assistant director of U.S. Censorship and the title he chose was "Weapon of Silence." Leadership can't be all charisma, and while it's important to entrust it to optimists, it is not indestructible. It is far too important to be tested by casting doubts about it when what its being asked to do has victory as its goal.

When General Eisenhower was on that swing around the NATO countries in January 1951, at his stop in Brussels, one who came to see him was the old out-of-office Prime Minister Paul Henri Spaak, he spoke gloomily of NATO's prospects. "General," he said, "every continental Army in the west was defeated in World War II! Do you expect us to rally around such leadership again?"

"I don't care if you have to go back to your great, great-grandfathers to find someone to be proud of—if you have to, do that!" Eisenhower said it quickly, sincerely. Spaak's dull eyes lighted, his face wore a big smile and he left that meeting in high spirits.

And there in the Battle of Normandy Museum on June 6, 1988, my seat for the dedication was in the section set aside for military attachés, near the representatives of the Soviet Union and the Federal Republic of Germany. Had the western allies been turned back at Normandy 44 years before, it is possible that with the relentless momentum post-Stalingrad achieved by the Soviets in pursuit of Hitler's retreating armies they would have pressed on to the Atlantic. The Redoubt that was feared their last stand in Bavaria, which never materialized, might have been in Spain with remnants crossing into North Africa.

But that didn't happen. As they lined the delegations up for French President Francois Mitterand to pass by, my position was to the right of a French Cardinal. Mitterand came along, shook hands with the high churchman, chatted briefly, then shook my hand asking where I was from. "California," I said, "and I'm sorry I am not as powerful as he—who can forgive you all your sins, if you have any. I can only wish you well." He smiled, and his interpreter said: "He needs that, too."

That night after a big reception in Deauville, I drew a girl taxi driver for the return trip to my Caen Hotel Malherbe. She was in her '20s, spoke some English and had been to New York once—otherwise had lived all her life in Normandy. She got out of the taxi, opened the door for me, took my hand and kissed me on both cheeks. Suddenly, I felt young again, and she said:

"Eet ees for my grande-muzzer. She knew *soldat Americain.* She still veesets heem at Colleville-sur-Mer." Colleville-sur-Mer is the American Military Cemetery. He had been a country boy, had helped her milk the family cow. Then after the war, she married, had a daughter, and a granddaughter who drove a taxi. She had told them both about him often. To her, he was always 24, the birthday he had before he was part of the breakout at St. Lo—where the bullet ended his life.

Truly there are many reasons why Normandy is remembered and should be, and noble as it is, the Battle of Normandy Museum will never be able to accommodate all of them! Some will always be in the hearts of human beings, and rightly so.[21]

NOTES

1. Museums and monuments are means by which nations attempt to "do right" by the dead left in wars' wakes. Those who live through it, not always whole, are compensated by pensions. In U.S. conflict participations, those "dead" numbers are: Revolution, 25,324; Mexican war, 13,2843; Spanish-American War, 2,446; World War I, 116,708; World War II, 407,316; the Korean "police action", 54,246, and Viet Nam, 58,302. WWII produced the "GI Bill" encouraging de-mobilized veterans to get on with interrupted educations, which was to pay back the nation handsomely in abilities to assume leadership in business and the professions.

2. The White House Presidential delegation included: Rear Admiral John D. Bulkeley, USN, who spirited General Douglas MacArthur and Philippine President Manuel Quezon to safety before the Phillipines fell, and transitioned to Normandy with his PT Squadron, where on the night of June 4th, spaded up sand samples on UTAH beach for determination as to whether the beach would allow passage of heavy vehicles. A German sentry confronted him, and Bulkeley threw a spadefull of sand in his face, jumped on him and choked him to death there on the beach, took his sandpails back to England; Lt. Col. Thomas Collins, a seven-year POW in North Viet Nam; Robert Evans, Detroit industrialist; Maj. Gen. Calvin Franklin, D.C. National Guard commander; H. Miller Hicks, pilot, small business expert, developer, Austin, Texas; Kathryn Morgan Ryan, widow of Cornelius Ryan, author of "The Longest Day" and other World War II books and herself a writer of renown; Paul Sheeline, hotel executive, who ran the Hotel Meurice in Paris as an Officers' billet, after it was vacated by German General von Choltitz, who disobeyed Hitler's orders to burn Paris; John "Jack" Thompson, President of the War Correspondents association, first paratrooper journalist, formerly Chicago Tribune; General James Collins, Jr., Chairman, Board of Historians; Congressman Samuel Gibbons, who landed D-Day in Normandy with the 101st Airborne Division; and White House staffers, Robert Tuttle, Charles Dutcher, Nancy Kennedy, Charles Rostow, Jackie Wolcott, Catherine Murdock, Leslie Lautenslager, Clark Wurzburger, and the delegation head, Anthony Stout, President, U.S. Committee for the Battle of Normandy Museum.

3. One of my first Warner Brothers assignments was researching and interviewing stars in connection with the company's observance of the 20th Anniversary of Talking Pictures. Once I took a TIME magazine writer to interview Jack Warner and he was recalling early times and said: "We used to send Rin Tin Tin, the dog star, in over the transom to save the girl. Now we send Errol Flynn. She was a helluva lot safer with the dog, I might add."

4. AUTHOR'S NOTE: Rosemary, later married to a U.S. Air Force Colonel, was stationed in Wiesbaden, Germany the same time I was. Her mother came to visit and stood in the receiving line at a party in her honor at the Officers Club. Rosemary introduced me as one who "used to work with Errol." Her mother looked at me and said: "Errol was a very naughty boy." It always seemed to me that was one of the understatements of the ages!

5. The day following his election as President the U.S. Air Force Museum rang up. "We have really goofed," Curator Royal Frey said. "You helped us get our 'Celebrities in Uniform' wing of the Museum going (Jimmy Stewart's flight jacket, the oil painting of Clark Gable in uniform, the cap and baton of Glenn Miller). Today we have a movie-star President who was in the Air Force and we don't have a damned thing of his. Can you get something." Sent a note, he responded that all he had left was his overcoat. It has been enshrined in the Museum, and an album called "One Old Overcoat" is sold in the Museum's gift shop.

6. The Gavin "fan club" ranged extensively, military, political, business. After the Army he became chairman of the respected "think tank", Arthur D. Little, Inc., was President Kennedy's Ambassador to France, and with "seed money" contributed by the author, a James M.Gavin Preparatory Scholarship is fully endowed and working at the U.S. Military Academy at West Point. There were 126 givers to that endowment, 15 of them Generals, 19 Lieutenant Generals, 39 Major Generals and 18 Brigadier Generals. Gavin, who had fibbed about his age, enlisted in the Army without having gotten even a high school education, took the West Point entrance exam offered enlisted men—and went on to glory.

7. Parachute battalion commanders wanted war correspondent "qualification" by experiencing jumps and glider landings prior to being slotted in a military operation. Sixteen took such training before Normandy, though not all went that way. Paratroopers were fearful that one who might volunteer to go with an airborne operation with only the "story" in mind might "rethink" the whole thing, freeze at the moment of commitment and screw up the whole operation.

8. One of them was Sean Flynn, Errol's son.

9. A Dept. of Defense aftermath paper reads: "To say the word "censorship" is to raise eyebrows of the American people and to bring rantings of protest from the American press." From December 1941 to August, 1945, the U.S. operated in what probably was the most completely controlled-news atmosphere ever in the nation's history. During that period, the American people not only accepted, but seemed to demand censorship of war news. Military press censorship is a *wartime* practice that can only be invoked by Executive Order of the President. It involves not only clearance of passable information viewed no violation of security of troops and plans, including direct and indirect steps applied by the military. Operating under virtually the same guidelines is "voluntary press censorship", but this leaves to editors' and reporters' judgments whether security is at stake, and is generally found to be akin to carrying drinking water up a steep hill in a sieve. In WWI, the British kept war correspondent accreditation to 50, the Americans to 31—British were "treated like pariah dogs" subject to arrest for General Staff ideas of indiscretion. By the last days, the American ranks had swelled by nearly 400 non-accredited press types with minimal access. The American Civil War was a triangular conflict, the North, the South, and the press, partly because denial of information was attempted for government or political actions as well. Serious censorship action first surfaced in 1907, puttered along until Congressman Edwin Y. Webb, in 1916, introduced a Bill to punish with life imprisonment any unauthorized person, who in time of war should collect, record, publish or communicate certain military information, or should publish or communicate false statements intended to cause disaffection in or interfere with success of military and naval forces! It became the Espionage Act in June, 1917, was coupled with the Trading-With-The-Enemy Act and became the underpinnings for first Censorship Board in U.S. history. It wasn't until 1935 with Hitler, Mussolini and the Japanese warlords on the move that old papers were re-studied, and on Feb. 21, 1941, FDR put the "voluntary press censorship" floater out there, Military Intelligence was given the responsibility in June with Presidential approval. On Dec. 7, 1941, almost in stride with Pearl Harbor's devastation Brig. Gen. A.D. Surles, of the Army's Chief of Public Relations, announced censorship was on because "the time has come when any failure to protect any information which comes to your possession can mean the loss of American lives." It has never been applied to that extent since, but it has been forever interesting as a discussion topic about its lack in those un-declared "wars" called Korea and Viet Nam.

10. Panel members were Sig Mickelson, Fred Friendly, Richard Salant, Bill Leonard and the then CBS News President, Van Gordon Sauter. It would be Walter Cronkite himself, a longtime "gorilla" who referred to the exaltation of the giver of the news who overwhelms it and is bowed to, and that was when his old CBS Evening News producer, four-square integrity himself, Burton "Bud" Benjamin, died. He'd been the one called up to do an in-house investigation of that highly controversial "The Un-Counted Enemy: A Vietnam Deception" which raised a firestorm about what viewers SEE as NEWS is arrived at. Benjamin sighed one day and told Cronkite that sometimes he felt "like the towel boy in a brothel!" Walter guessed that would make

him the equivalent of the "madam"—which put reporters in the same perspective as the "girls." He said it in his eulogy at Benjamin's funeral in September, 1988.

11. Something very close to this "hypothetical" involved CBS News John Gilligan who was in the Pentagon Public Affairs' office of Russ Wagner. A Navy gob came in, paid no attention to him, and began posting on the situation map the blockade lines around CUBA at the time of the "missile crisis" of 1962. Wagner returned, saw Gilligan watching the fascinating inadvertent disclosure. "You reach for that phone, now or later," Wagner said, "and there'll be hell to pay." President Kennedy was set to address the nation that night, and Gilligan chose to let him make the announcement of what was up. At WSU that day, he would probably have been "flunked" for not favoring the "evening news."

12. The remarkable Eisenhower rapport with the media, un-equalled by any high military commander before him—or since, really had only two major dis-illusionments: 1) The Merrill "Red" Mueller incident— Eisenhower knew him well as the NBC member of the pool covering his headquarters, had him in for dinner as he was preparing to leave. Enroute to Moscow at the time was Air Chief Marshal Arthur Tedder on a highly secret mission to talk with Stalin and his generals about mutual strategies to hasten the war's end. Tedder called in during the meal saying he was weathered in Rome, and Mueller listened to the Eisenhower end of the conversation—and his first broadcast when beyond reach of the censors was about that secret mission. As FDR was even then steaming toward Yalta to talk about just such things, Mueller's broadcast seemingly pre-empted a head of government. 2) The celebrated Kennedy affair: AP's Paris bureau chief, Ed Kennedy, with the pool which had agreed to an embargo on their stories until a release time set by the Eisenhower SHAEF headquarters, witnessed the actual surrender signing by Hitler's Field Marshal Alfred Jodl at the "little red schoolhouse" in Reims. Kennedy, with a priceless journalistic gem which would *always* be a story, chose to circumvent his own word—breaking the fact of the surrender before the embargo was lifted. The embargo (or hold was there 1) because Eisenhower wanted the fighting fully stopped as communication to isolated German pockets of resistance was difficult and casualties coming in after the war was said to be "over" could be devastating to prematurely relieved families back home and 2) ending of hostilities announcements belonged to political leadership. Overall, though, his memories of the many media pluses he'd received by cooperation led him to be the first President to permit filming/taping of White House press conferences, edited before release. The print media squawked, and Hagerty explained: "Why not? HE lives in the 20th Century—last half."

13. As I left Warners, Ronald Reagan said: "Coward! Leaving Warners to join the Army." Humphrey Bogard, morose as usual, declared: "NOBODY *leaves* Warner Brothers—he goes 'over the wall.' "

14. AMERICAN HERITAGE in its Spring 1988 issue had a story WHAT SHOULD WE TELL OUR CHILDREN ABOUT VIET NAM, and got a quick answer from one who'd been there—Richard B. Smith, who commanded the 9th Marine Regiment, wrote " . . . it was a just cause and a winable war; it was lost by irresponsible news media, and an irresolute government."

15. When the media protests were lodged about being left out of Grenada's first phase, it was understandable as many of those officers planning and executing that quickie righting in the Caribbean Basin had reached top positions carrying bitter Viet Nam memories of media. To ask them to make slots for media accompaniment was like requesting one who had been snakebit to carry a black mamba in his shirt, keep it warm, and risk it biting him later. Joint Chiefs Chairman John Vessey asked Maj. Gen. Winant Sidle, retired, to head a panel, sort out the complaints, make recommendations. None of the media umbrella organizations would provide panel participants, but would "cooperate fully," which meant would present their positions. Sidle said he felt it "must be stated emphatically that reporters and editors covering military operations must exercise responsibility," meaning in terms of the military security required. One of the military testifiers said "The media must cover military operations comprehensively, intelligently and objectively." And right at the beginning his memo stated: "In the matter of so-called First Amendment rights, this is an extremely gray area and the panel felt it . . . was for the legal profession and the courts and that we were not qualified to provide a judgment." With the military, the media is learning it has "a public relations problem." When the country was young Alexander Hamilton, a founding father, linked freedom of the press with a responsible press. He went so far as to content that no friend of liberty or order could believe that the press was *wholly* free . . . and he didn't think truth was an ironclad defense. Anything SECRET is to the media both a challenge to render it not so, and a gnawing sensation as long as it is. Illustrative is the story of the ecumenical conference during which a priest, a rabbi and a protestant minister got to be very good friends. One night at dinner the protestant said now

that they had known each other so well, why not tell each other of sins they'd known. The priest mentioned a girl. The rabbi said he ate ham and called it veal. They looked to the protestant who said: "My sin is gossip and I can't wait to get out of this room!"

16. General MacArthur often took with him on his swings around the Far East his own version of a media "pool". It consisted of Russ Brines, AP; Ernie Hoberecht, UP, and Howard Handleman, INS, the three bureau chiefs. Other media hands, not accorded this special privilege, called the retinue "Jesus Christ and his THREE Disciples!" When our "flying squad" began its work, our main story was effectiveness of "close tactical air support". The U.S. Marine philosophy was to have aircraft tied directly to units, and the USAF preferred the greater flexibility of air power, especially interdiction, catching enemy on back roads before they got to forward positions. It seems impossible now, but we were depended upon for two features a day, morning and night, by each of those agencies—and INS, hard put to keep its stateside bureaus customers supplied with "local angle" stories with its own limited staff, took as many as could be provided them.

17. The names on that monument to the 16 KIA Korean War Correspondents are: Corporal Ernie Peeler, Pacific Stars & Stripes, July 10, 1950, and Ray Richards, INS, who was riding with him; Wilson Fielder, TIME-LIFE, July 22, 1950; Maximilian Philonenko, Agence France Presse; Albert Hinton, Journal-Guide, Norfolk, Va.; Stephen Simmons, Picture POST, London; James O. Supple, Chicago Sun-Times; Jorge Teodoro, United Nations Public Information, from the Philippines; Charles Anderson, and Ken Inouye, INS, all on July 27, 1950, when the North Korean surprise attack was blazing and the 'front' unknown; William O. Moore, AP, July 31, 1950; Ian Morrison, London Times, and Christopher Buckley, Daily Telegraph, on the same day also, Aug. 12, 1950; Frank Emery, INS, Sept. 7, 1950; Jean-Marie Premonville, Agence France Presse, Feb. 11, 1951; William A. Graham, New York Journal of Commerce, Mar. 3, 1951, and Derek Pearsey, Reuters, May 25, 1951. About 100,000 Korea visitors go by Freedom Park enroute to and from Pan Mun Jom, and the De-Militarized 151-mile long and 4,000 meters wide separation of the opposing forces neither at war nor peace. No one ever seems to pick up on the ninth name on the list, Ian Morrison, but he was the enamored of Han Suyin, indefatiguable apologist for the Peoples' Republic of China, and Communist guerrilla movements in southeast Asia, who wrote of their romance in "Love Is a Many-Splendored Thing", which became a movie starring William Holden and Jennifer Jones, and for which Songwriter Sammy Fain wrote his great musical hit tune of the same name. In happier days when the romance was on, Morrison's irreverent colleagues used to describe Han Suyin as "in her politics she's to the left, but her love life was just about right." That Sammy Fain tune won him an Academy Award.

18. In his book, "Reminiscences", published in 1964, General Douglas MacArthur mentioned WWII censorship only once suggesting its value in running a war as a kind of psychological weapon, a fixer of priority attention. He had ordered release of the horrible details of the killing "Bataan death march" that cost 25,000 American lives. He was overruled by Washington and a STOP was put on it, he thought to concentrate public attention on Europe's war first—a confirmation that censorship, well beyond "First amendment" dimensions—is, indeed, a means of focusing public attention and marshaling it behind the step-by-step strategy with victory as the goal. Directing it, not frittering it away. When Korea's "police action" broke, assuming it was going to be quickly dealt with, he told some 80 correspondents then based in Tokyo there was no intention to invoke censorship, but gave them some guidelines to observe 1) nothing on troop movements, 2) no unit, base, headquarters or other installations locations, 3) no unit identifications in combat until officially released, and 4) never to assume phones were secure. Every one of the restrictions was violated so often that Congress and the Pentagon so distressed by the flow of military security endangering information, planning for its use began. The success of the Inchon landing averted some rigid form of media review. Korea, had it been studied in that regard, was a beacon light on what would later bedevil commanders in Viet Nam.

19. In 1976, the Iron Gate Chapter of the Air Force Association endowed a General Lauris Norstad Falcon Foundation scholarship to give prep school assistance to aspirants for appointment to the Air Force Academy in Colorado Springs, and on his death at 81, September 12, 1988, a General Lauris Norstad Scholarship in Political & Military Science was endowed at the University of Nebraska, available to a political science major in ROTC who intends on being commissioned to serve in uniform.

20. Professional football's top prize is the Vince Lombardi Trophy, given annually to the winner of the Super Bowl. He said: "Confidence is catching, but lack of confidence is, too."

21. The daughter of a Richmond, California hospital scrubwoman started in Normandy what would

eventually make her America's "most decorated woman." Unable to afford a babysitter, she took her toddler to work with her every day and the small girl visited wards—and in this association with illness and pain decided to be a nurse. She became one, United Airlines recruited her when RNs were necessary to be stewardesses and the author first met her in the spring of 1943 when she graduated in the first class of Air Evacuation nurses at Bowman Field, Louisville, Ky. Her name was Lillian Kinkela—and her airborne ambulance aircraft was first to land in the initial operational airstrip in Normandy. Through WW II and Korea, she picked up 450 combat loads of wounded, and compiled the amazing record of never having lost a man, no matter how seriously wounded, under her care in flight to hospitalization. She rode with jerricans of gasoline to replenish Patton's fuel tanks, took wounded back. In Korea, she went all the way to the Yalu. When Ralph Edwards honored her on his next-to-last THIS IS YOUR LIFE program on NBC-TV, it was one of the ten greatest mail-draw response producers of them all, letters pouring in from wounded men still alive who remembered her. She was the inspiration for the movie, "Flight Nurse", starring Joan Leslie and was its technical adviser. There is a Capt. Lillian Kinkela Scholarship in Nursing in the Nebraska Medical Center, in Omaha, Nebraska, in her honor. She, and her Air Evac colleagues, contributed significantly to the greater percentage of wounded who recovered from their injuries and lived on to full lives.

"The First and Greatest of War Correspondents"

"If the Danish people want their Lion back," said General Eisenhower over the phone, "by all means, let them have it." He was talking to Major General Floyd L. Parks from Frankfurt, and Parks was in Berlin with a Danish war and foreign correspondent, Henrik Ringsted, sitting across the desk from him. All Ringsted wanted was a little help to move a monument.

It was September, 1945, and no one in military public relations by this time could have been startled by anything asked of him by a war correspondent. Henrik Ringsted had come into my office only a few minutes before. The Danish people, he had said softly and with some emotion, were greatly interested in a monument in Berlin, a fifteen-foot, 2,500-pound bronze statue of the Isted Lion. The request was appropriate, he ventured, in that the Allies had won their last battles of World War II, and the Isted Lion belonged to the last battle ever won by tiny Denmark, one fought near Flensburg on July 25, 1850.

For eight decades, the Lion had suffered the indignity of being a German war curio, and all that while had been revered by the Danes in song and history book. "We think it is time he came home," Ringsted said firmly. "Through the years, we made every kind of appeal to the Germans, but got no satisfaction. My newspaper, the *Politiken,* wonders if the American Army can help us."

As of that moment, he continued, the Isted Lion was less than a half mile away, in the former SS officers' school—the Adolf Hitler Barracks—which was now serving as our motor pool.

We walked together down the corridor to General Parks's office, and he beckoned for us to come in. Ringsted told him all about the Isted Lion. It was a memorial which had been erected over the men who fell in the decisive Battle of Isted when the Danes put down the attempt of German-sponsored Duke of Augustenberg to wrest the province of Schleswig-Holstein from the Danish crown to which it had belonged since 1460. When the Germans came back again in 1864, the Danes were overcome and, besides taking Schleswig-Holstein, the Germans had hauled the guardian Isted Lion to Berlin as a showpiece for the victors.

If General Eisenhower had been somewhat surprised by the Danish request for their Lion, it was nothing to the British guard's reactions a few days later when I came up to the German-Danish border in the middle of the night with a 10-ton trailer hitch covered with a tarpaulin.

"And what official reason do you have for entering Denmark?" he asked, while busily writing on a form mounted on a clipboard.

"I'm taking a Lion to the King!"

"Oh, I sye now," said the sergeant, "let's not have any bloody American nonsense. You have to have an *official* reason." We beckoned him out to the trailer, lifted the tarp, and flashed a light onto the bronze face of the Isted Lion lying comfortably on his back on a bed of sawdust. The immensity of the statue staggered the sergeant. He waved us on.

King Christian X himself made the formal acceptance speech in a ceremony in Copenhagen, and it was a day of national celebration.*

* The return of the Isted Lion was emotional in more than one way in Denmark. It was first proposed to King Christian that it be mounted in some large public area, and he was in favor of it until Poul Riis Lassen, the Danish resistance leader during the German occupation, was killed in the street of Aarhus. Lassen's death made the king fearful that die-hard Danish Nazi sympathizers might use such a focal point as the Isted Lion to collect a crowd target for a bombing, or other dangerous demonstration. He chose the Tojhuismuseet, which was enclosed, and the witnesses were by invitation only. The statue was put under guard the minute it arrived, and the erection of the pedestal was carried out under armed protection and bright spotlights during the hours of darkness. There was no incident at the ceremony. Although the Danes decorated some Americans for the homecoming of the Lion, none of the public-relations crew who actually brought it off were included by their own choice. By the end of 1955, more than 1,300,000 Danes had made pilgrimages to see

The hospitality and graciousness of the Danish people toward those of us who participated in the return of the Isted Lion were bountiful, but there was a significant fact about Isted which was never mentioned. Twenty-eight war correspondents from seven nations and four Army public relations officers were present that day, and all of us were the offspring of a development in that Battle of Isted, too, for that climactic struggle in the old Danish rebellion was the first to be covered by a professional war correspondent—William Howard Russell of the *London Times*.

At the Battle of Isted, where Russell sustained a flesh wound, was born the descriptive reporter of wars, and as his profession increased in numbers, the armies of the world introduced the public relations officer to work with him.

If the Isted Lion had escaped his shackles by World War II's end, so had the war correspondent become a full partner with military effort, not a little of his achievement being due to the 3,000 officers who accumulated from a little to a lot of public relations experience in this liaison duty.

For Russell it all came about as a sort of editorial accident, in that the *Times*'s editor, John Thaddeus Delane, merely told him to go to the scene and do a descriptive job on it. Forty-three years earlier the *Times* had missed a chance at this "first" when Henry Crabbe Robinson sent it "letters from the Elbe" about Napoleon; Robinson had never bothered to see a battle.

In America, some twenty newspapermen, led by George Wilkins Kendall, the New Hampshireman who edited the *New Orleans Picayune,* chased after Generals Zachary Taylor and Winfield Scott in the penetration of Mexico in 1846-47, but they were mostly one-shot campaigners.

From the day that Russell moved up with the troops at Isted, for many years he scoured the world for wars to write about, and nobody is inclined to debate the truth of his marker in St. Paul's Cathedral in London which says: "THE FIRST AND GREATEST OF WAR CORRESPONDENTS."

The armies, even of his own country, spread no welcome mat for Russell, and he first encountered their disdain when Delane sent him off to the Crimea in February, 1854, for a "few weeks' work," promis-

the statue, and the guides nearly always say, "... and the Isted Lion is home today because of the American Army."

ing him he would be "back by Easter." Britain had decided to throw in with the Turks against Czarist aggressions, a business which was to be settled in short order. But it was three Easters before Russell came home, and in the meantime he had had to fend for himself for food and lodging, had seen his tent demolished with military sanction, had been insulted, and had been ordered off the battlefield by the British commander, Lord Raglan, on more than one occasion.

Not a military hand was lifted in his behalf until the morning after the Battle of Alma on September 21, 1854, when he wearily seated himself on an artillery parapet overlooking the carnage to write his story for the *Times*. A British officer came along, noted his uncomfortable working conditions, and secured a bit of planking for him to lay over two wine casks as an improvised desk.

This must have been the original military public relations gesture, but nowhere in history do we find that man's name listed.

The doorways of enlightenment opened by Russell were many. "How many English captains," he once wrote, "were slain in times gone by in distant fields whose names were never heard by English ears? When Marlborough or Granby won, who heard of Brown, or Jones, or Robinson—of Lloyd, or Campbell, or of O'Hara who fell dead in Flanders?"

A hundred years later, the U.S. Army's policy of sending back the home-town or individual story reached such cherished proportions that eight out of every ten dead in Korea carried a faded, folded clipping from some newspaper back home. Today a great effort is put into destroying the anonymity of those who really fight the battles—and die in them. Their stories may not be important, in the sense of far-reaching effect, but they are important enough to the men themselves. "I know of no thing which so improves the morale of the soldier," said General Eisenhower as late as 1951, "as to see his unit or his own name in print—just once."

When Russell wrote movingly of the miseries and privations of the ill and wounded in Crimea, "Are there no devoted women among us able and willing to go forth and minister to the sick and suffering soldiers?" it produced the dedicated and immediate response of Florence Nightingale, who came with thirty-eight other nurses to the hospital in Scutari, a converted Turkish barracks, roofing 18,000 stinking, dismembered, maddened men, a human house of horror.

h.

From his writings and Florence Nightingale's response have come our military medical services of today, and the remarkable degree of recovery of human life after the scourge of conflict.

The only man surprised by his fame on his return home was William Howard Russell. "Billy" of the old "on call" days at the *Times* was now "Crimean Russell"; later, when he covered the Civil War in America, he was "Bull Run" Russell; finally he was made Sir William. Dublin-born Russell was a great wit and raconteur and he became a confidant of Sir Colin Campbell, a cherished companion of the Prince of Wales, and an intimate of Thackeray and Bismarck. As a veteran of hundreds of battle actions and eighty years, he appeared one day before the same prince, now King Edward, to have the ribbon of the C.V.O. slipped over his head. The king whispered to his old friend, "Don't kneel, Billy, just stoop," and his handshake was strong and warm.

William Howard Russell ran the full gamut of the press relationship with the military, from the arrogance of Lord Raglan in the Crimea to the cordiality of Sir Colin Campbell in India. Campbell briefed him on every move, with the proviso that Russell say nothing in India and confine his information to "letters to the Times." The sailing time to and from London would protect Sir Colin's maneuvers.

One factor inherent in military operations throughout recorded history was brought to a more reasonable and honorable status by him and the people who emulated him—the use of censorship.

At first the use of the censor was generally to control the public portrait of the monarch or war lord, but it slowly developed as communications improved, until it was solely an instrument of security, although war correspondents have always debated the purity of the censor's motive.

Some of the bitterest antagonists of the censor, however, will change sides when acquiring a new point of view. This was the case with a Boer War correspondent who wrote, "Alas, the days of newspaper enterprise in war are over. What can one do with a censor, a 48-hour delay, and a 50-word limit on a wire?" When this critic became a world figure, with a war on his hands, he appointed a Navy admiral as his chief press censor! The critic was Winston S. Churchill.

The press played an increasingly active role in wars. At Buena Vista, the coverage of the V-formation, which Jefferson Davis used, produced the oft-quoted statement, "A little more grape, Captain

Bragg!", an important element in Davis' choice as President of the Confederacy.

General George Meade, of Gettysburg fame, rode a *Philadelphia Inquirer* man, Edward Crapsey, out of camp backward on a lop-eared mule while the band played the "Rogues' March," whereupon the whole press corps put him under blackout and probably deprived him of the presidency.

In the Russo-Japanese war, correspondents rode to Chinese ports to get their material out. The Japs were notorious for behind-lines entertainment, but reluctant to let war correspondents get anywhere near the battle or file what little had been learned. This may have been where some military professionals got the idea that a public-relations man had to be one who "could drink with the boys."

The only telegram William Howard Russell ever used in his first fifteen years was the one sent on the fall of Sebastopol. Although Matthew Brady introduced the war photograph in the Civil War, most of his pictures waited until long afterward to be published, making him more historian than news man.

The Spanish-American War offers two outstanding examples of the extreme latitude given the press in the field. The first was the *New York Herald Tribune*'s George Bronson Rae, who broke for publication a copy of Captain Charles Dwight Sigsbee's handwritten report of the sinking of the battleship *Maine*. And a colleague on the same paper, J. L. Stickney, a Naval Academy graduate, offered himself as an aide to Admiral Dewey in time to be accepted and be on the bridge of the command ship, *Olympia,* when Dewey said, "You may fire when ready, Gridley," opening the Battle of Manila Bay. Stickney dispatched his exclusive through Hong Kong on May 5, 1898, a dual use of position which would well cause a Congressional investigation today.

Richard Harding Davis, the flamboyant chronicler of fighting, thought Rae of the *Herald-Tribune,* Major Grover Flint of the *New York Journal,* and Sylvester Scovel of the *World* were the most courageous of war correspondents, and Stephen Crane was called by him "the coolest man, whether an officer or civilian, under fire at any time during the war."

World War I started for Americans with ringing slogans to make the world "safe for democracy," and it was the biggest news story in a generation, but the press was slow to respond and never did get going in great numbers. The "local story," the Civil War, had drawn several times as many writers.

General John J. Pershing mentioned the press only three or four times in his memoirs, but the U. S. war theater public-relations officer was introduced by him. Pershing's intelligence officer was Maj. Gen. Dennis E. Nolan, and under him were four subsections dealing with enemy information, counterintelligence, maps and press and propaganda. The latter, called G2 (d), was the bailiwick of a professional soldier, Brig. Gen. Walter C. Sweeney, and his successors, Brig. Gen. E. R. W. McCabe and Major A. L. James, Jr. Their executive officer from August, 1917, to September, 1918, was an artillery captain from the *Chicago Tribune,* Mark Watson.

When Watson attempted to escape the job and get back to the artillery, he was told to produce a replacement, which he did, in the person of an infantry lieutenant from the Eightieth Division, Steve Early. There was hell to pay when Early found out who had done this to him, but he finally relaxed and took it as best he could, just as he did when he became Roosevelt's press secretary in the White House.

The American entry into France at Chaumont, the GHQ town, attracted only three U. S. wire services, and a handful of special writers from the *New York Times, New York World, New York Herald, Philadelphia Ledger, Chicago News* and *Chicago Tribune.* When Eisenhower came, another war later, he had 943 correspondents accredited to him at one time. One of them was Mark Watson, now with the *Baltimore Sun,* who remembered what a dog's life it had been handling such roisterers as one-eyed Floyd Gibbons.

The cavalcade of war correspondents, service supplemental writers, photographers and broadcasters reached the peak in World War II, probably for all time. This great carriage-load of noncombatants was frowned on by some commanders, but Eisenhower directed that they be considered as "quasi-staff officers." By all they were to be treated and thought of as valuable links to the citizens of their homelands. Those were the orders.

His ability to rationalize this relationship paid General Eisenhower well throughout a war which was as loaded with political pressures as with purely military problems. As a result, the second world conflict was best covered in Europe, both as to accuracy and detail.

k.

The official U. S. record, carried by the Office of the Chief of Information, Department of the Army, names 1,828 people who were accredited by the War Department during World War II. There were actually more people than this who wrote, broadcast, and made photographs, but apparently many operated as "specials."

An astounding thing about the British and the French, normally meticulous about recording everything, history or trivia, is that they did not consider this journalistic activity in the rear of their armies, navies and air forces sufficiently important to keep any accounts of it. In fact, when Brigadier A. Geoffrey Neville, who was Field Marshal Sir Bernard Law Montgomery's chief of Publicity and Psychological Warfare at the Twenty-first Army Group, found that I was asking each war correspondent headed for Normandy to write his own obituary, he was appalled.

"Whatever for?" he asked. An explanation of the way by-lines were followed in America, and of the fact that by-liners were interesting to readers, left him completely unconvinced. "A lot of bloody nonsense," he said.

There isn't a chance that any major war in the future will allow time for accreditations, airlifts and boat rides to distant geographic points, and for the correspondents to live snugly in press camps behind the front in the wake of a creeping, ground-bound Army. Only in the "brush fires" like Korea, where engagements are fought by a rule book, after which the umpires retire to Panmunjom or Geneva to check their respective points, can the professional war correspondent carry on, and even in those cases he will degenerate into a political reporter before he knows it.

The old approach to war reporting, which flowered so fully in the 1939–45 period, was affected like everything else by the first self-sustaining nuclear chain reaction produced at the University of Chicago, December 2, 1942, and its later manifestations over Hiroshima and Nagasaki. The speeds with which modern weapons can be carried and dropped make everything instantaneous and total.

Many of the last great gathering of the followers of William Howard Russell in that last maximum, or world, effort were my friends and associates. They were lined up on both sides of the fence, and there *are* two sides of the fence even today—the military and the correspondents. They agree on one thing—the need, the desire, and the aim for ultimate victory—when war comes, or is in progress.

Both have ways of pursuing their callings in the direction of that victory, and often they do not coincide. This is understandable, because the military element, its officers and men, must deliver the victory. The correspondent sees a war as beats told in flashes and cables which box up nicely somewhere in the eight columns of a front page; or as a recorded or filmed interview with drama packed into it.

Between them is the public-relations officer, and to say that is just another way of saying he is the man in the middle. In this middle position, with which I have had considerable experience, nothing is ever dull.

NEVER A SHOT IN ANGER

... TAKE 1 ———————————————

Early Maneuvers

So far as I know, only one public-relations officer ever won the Congressional Medal of Honor, and he wasn't working at public relations at the time. This doesn't mean that he was the only brave one, because the profession is a no-man's-land, mined, booby-trapped, under constant fire, littered with irretrievable casualties.

The name of this recognized hero often cropped up afterward, but very few ever asked him what he was doing from June of 1916 to September of 1917. He was the first of the regular Army officers to be beached away from line and staff assignments in a strange berth called the Bureau of Information of the Office of the Secretary of War. Here designated as Chief, he set about his task in masterful style—a characteristic of the man who, in June 1916, was known as Major Douglas MacArthur.[1]

[1] When General MacArthur was asked recently whether it was increasing press interest in the Office of the Secretary of War or the conflict in Europe which caused his appointment as the first Chief, Bureau of Information, War Department, he wrote me that, "I can only give you my conjecture that the action of Secretary [of War, Newton D.] Baker was influenced by both the reasons advanced by you. In addition, it was perhaps somewhat to relieve himself of the pressure of his own time. I was then the junior member of the General Staff consisting of 22 officers, and without any previous discussion was directed by the Secretary to assume the duty in addition to those I was performing." With that remarkable fidelity to an established precedent which is typical of the military service, the public-relations or information officer to this day tends to be "the junior member," and to be "directed" to take on the job, more often than not "in addition" to other duties, "without any previous discussion" or experience.

Just thirty years later, in 1946, a distinguished division and corps commander of World War II, Lt. Gen. J. Lawton "Lightnin' Joe" Collins settled into the immediate postwar period with one of the most troublesome tasks of his life. The Pentagon, so recently ringing with global decisions, was now presiding over a global debilitation. It was trying to create some sort of military posture for the United States after the "bring Johnny home" campaign had all but wrecked its armed forces.

At this moment General Collins became the Chief of Information. As Major Douglas MacArthur had been the low-ranking beginning of the Army's consciousness of a public-relations requirement, Lt. Gen. J. Lawton Collins was the high-water mark of emphasis given the activity after two world conflicts. This change represented a lesson learned the hard way, like many battlefield lessons.

Under General Collins, a trio of generals were harnessed to help him pull the informational load. Two of these had participated in the fighting in Europe as he had, and the other had been a long-time specialist in the climate of Washington pressures.

In the battle days, Maj. Gen. Floyd L. Parks had been chief of staff of the First Allied Airborne Army. For General Collins he ran the public-information operation, the avenue through which passed the mainstream of news of the Army, its policies, needs, and day-to-day life. To hard-bitten combat veteran Brig. Gen. C. T. "Buck" Lanham, went the information and education chore. Lanham had had to make a choice when he was a lieutenant—a choice of whether to pin his hopes to poetry or a platoon. He chose the infantry, but never lost his facility with words. Through "Buck" Lanham went the Army's route to the mind of the soldier, telling him why he was necessary and something about the vast world in any part of which he might suddenly find himself.

General Collins inherited Maj. Gen. Wilton B. "Slick" Persons, and no better or more adroit tactician had ever mounted guard over the Army's interests before Congress on the "Hill."

No man ever made more powerful friends for any service than General Persons, whose liaison job found him responding to Congressional inquiries with alacrity or, in Army terminology, "on the double."

These men were not to be last heard of in these jobs, either. Like

MacArthur, Collins, when he took the information post, was on the way to becoming Army Chief of Staff.[2]

General Parks had been well tuned up in the patience and persever-ance trade. He came to his new job directly from being the first American member of the Kommandatura—the four-power city coun-cil of Berlin—where American idealism cut its first teeth on Russian realism. This soft-voiced but firm graduate of Clemson, by the specifics and speed requirements of his job, had direct access to, and was the spokesman for, the Army Chief of Staff, General of the Army Dwight D. Eisenhower.

General Parks was quick to determine that the armed forces, with their world-wide commitments to stand, watch and wait, would need a lot of explaining to a tax-burdened and uniform-weary public. This could not be done by lofty pronouncements from starred shoulders in Washington, but was going to depend heavily on public understanding. Prior to 1939, the Army had been content to carry on quietly at its posts, a rather clannish society to which few people paid attention. Seldom did top commanders make utterances which would muster headlines, nor did any want to do so. In almost any emergency the policy was to play dead or dumb, or both. In all those easy, delicious years, the intelligence officer—by profession and nature the most secretive and non-communicative man on the staff—was considered the logical man to meet the press, if and when they came calling, God forbid! The main function of the intelligence officer in those days was to draft the enemy situation when maneuvers and exercises were being held, and he frequently treated press queries as the field manual said he should answer enemy interrogation—by giving only name, rank and serial number.

But in 1946, a new feeling was in evidence in most quarters in sup-port of public relations at all levels—high and low. General Parks went to General Collins with a proposal. His research of the World War II records had shown him that some three thousand officers in the Army (which then included the Air Corps) had had public-rela-tions experience, both in uniform and out. Almost without exception,

[2] General Persons later became the presidential trouble shooter with Congress when the Eisenhower administration took office, while General Lanham was General Eisenhower's public information chief at SHAPE, in Paris, before he retired.

they had either become civilians or were hanging on precariously as reservists.

The problem, as General Parks stated it, was one of guaranteeing that come what may, the Army would be assured of a hard core of professionals who would bring with them not only their understanding of the Army, but a knowledge of mass communications. He wanted to start a program immediately which lined up a picked thirty of these former practitioners by offering them regular commissions.

First, they would have to pass a stiff examination. The knowledge that such a program had been put into motion came to me in a letter from General Parks, whose public-relations officer I had been in Berlin. The letter asked that this regular Army exam be taken at March Field, the nearest point to the seat of my employment of the moment, the publicity department of Warner Brothers' Studio in Burbank, California.

The exam was a tough one, and it was said that about 100,000 former Army officers were trying it against a quarter of that number of vacancies. If successful, each man had then to face a rather rough board composed of regular officers for a personal grilling.

My former connection with General Parks had been one to convince me that when the Creator was drawing up the design for a gentleman and a general, a sort of celestial package deal, he must have had Floyd Parks in mind. He was a hard man to turn down, so I didn't try. After all, there was nothing wrong with taking the treatment. The chances were I would bust anyway. If the exam didn't cut me out, that personal interview with the board was bound to do it. How could they approve anyone who made his living as a sort of flank-protector for Errol Flynn?

It was off to March Field, and a run at the gauntlet, then come back to work as if nothing had happened. And nothing did, for three months. Then Western Union caught up to me with the startling message that I had been "selected for the regular army." It further stated that the appointment must be accepted or rejected "in 72 hours." The job was to be special projects officer for General Parks in Washington.

This was 1947 and, almost fifteen years to the very day, the pendulum for me had swung from one wild extreme to the other. Military trappings caught on with me at the University of Nebraska, where, after four years of ROTC, on June 6, 1932, they pinned on the bars of a reserve second lieutenant. As such, eleven days later, I went to

Fort Crook, Nebraska, for two weeks of training. There bloomed my first mistake, and I learned a slateful.

Our commander that summer was Major Hardin C. Sweeney, a dashing figure and young to shoulder the gold leaf of his authority. The camp was made up of ROTC officer material from several Midwest universities, and at that time etiquette was more important than marksmanship. This may have been because cartridges were severely rationed from leftover World War I stocks. Army appropriations were meager, but social life was not.

One of the rituals of the period was the formal call on the commanding officer, which had to be attended to before a newly arrived officer had been on station more than twenty-four hours. Four of us were to go that first evening, but the afternoon duty roster had made me officer of the day.

A tour of the tent area was required and by the time I had prowled the tent-rows, turned up a couple of poorly constructed dummies in cots where college boys should have been, and made out the reports, it was very, very late.

On arrival back on Officers' Row, I was told that the "formal call" was long since ended, and that explanations and apologies were due. While debating this dilemma, I headed for the nearby officers' latrine to wash up before going to bed. As I came through the door, there was Major Sweeney, shirt off, busily scouring his teeth over the long communal sink. My rather gay "Good evening" brought his brush to a momentary stop, and he eyed me balefully, his mouth full. I, too, took off my shirt. Seeing that the major was gagged for the time being, and feeling that someone should carry on conversation, I made a rather grand gesture, I thought, of expressing my apologies for having missed his tent-side tête-à-tête, adding that this meeting might make up for it. All this was offered in a lighthearted, not to say bantering vein.

Well! My part of the conversation terminated abruptly. The major spat into the sink, straightened up, braced me, and the latrine literally rocked with his recital of the facts of military life. Part of his tirade was delivered while he was still in his undershirt, more of it as he put on his OD shirt, and still more when he crushed on his campaign hat. After he had stalked out, there was still enough of an echo in the place that I held onto my brace and the toothpaste tube. Evidently my grip on the latter was firm because there was a full yard and a half of toothpaste on the floor in all sorts of fanciful curlicues.

It was front and center for me first thing the next morning. The adjutant counted off on his fingers all my sins. There was no elasticity in Army etiquette at any time, he said. My name was Mudd with the major. Nothing official, he assured me, is ever done while officers are in the latrine.

Few have ever seen an efficiency report like mine for that two weeks. There was one line which floated before my memory fifteen years later when the tap came for me to join the regular Army. On the old forms of 1932 there was a question which asked if, in the opinion of the then rating officer, the one being rated had any ability or adaptability for public relations. Major Sweeney not only dismissed this alarming possibility, but added that it should not be allowed to come about under any circumstances.

In the years since 1932, however, other military men had used me on their public-relations staffs—such general officers as George V. Strong, Ben Lear, Jacob L. Devers, Omar N. Bradley, William H. Simpson, Floyd L. Parks, James M. Gavin, and the redoubtable Field Marshal Sir Bernard Law Montgomery.

Perhaps that wrath-provoking characteristic which had been frowned on by the major—a sense of humor—was more important than anything he had offered in its place. At any rate, I have come to believe that every public-relations officer, if he would survive the whirlpools which toss him daily—and nightly, too—must have a sense of humor.

The regular Army was never much of a place to nurture the public-relations officer, and his growth as a staff factor was largely in the realm of the reserves and the National Guard. Both of these had a genuine use for public attention, and both were newsworthy because of their community roots. Their home activities and their annual summer encampments made lively material, and there was a press ready to print reports of these annual conclaves.

Many of us, in newspaper and radio fields, actually got our starts in them. It was not then too popular with newspapers and broadcasting stations to cover the encampments, because it would tie up too much manpower. Instead, they relied on craftsmen in these professions who took their summer holidays in the role of militia or reservists. The most popular material was the column full of names, low on strategy, and with a feature twist, a type of journalism which later made Ernie Pyle a household word and a reading must. This news service arrangement was all right at times, particularly when some of the papers paid for the columns delivered.

For eight years I was a faithful reservist attending the usual two-week summer camps and usually glad to get back to the sanctuary of civilian life. Suddenly in the fall of 1940 word came from Washington that all reserve officers would have to take on a year of extended active duty in their basic branches, mine being infantry. Never one to duck the dentist in the hopes of outlasting an aching tooth, I walked across the street from the *Nebraska State Journal,* where I worked, into the Lincoln, Nebraska, post office to make my application for the "year"—to get it done.

In November, 1940, orders came sending me to the scene of my latrine rout at Fort Crook, Nebraska, for duty with the First Battalion of the Third Infantry Regiment. It was commanded by Lt. Col. Koger M. Still, a heavy-handed, somber man who wore the responsibility for a few hundred men like a sack of cement. Smiling was for other people, not for him.

Each of the new arrivals, many of them still in their civilian clothes, had an audience with him to determine any military possibilities, and my time came to present myself, a very newly promoted reserve captain.

He looked at my papers, frowned a bit. "Just what was it you did in civilian life?" he asked.

"I was a newspaperman . . . gabbed on the radio."

"What did you specialize in?"

"The movies. . . . I was a motion picture editor."

"What do you do on a job like that?"

"I saw every film that came to town."

"*Every* film?" he asked, in some awe. "You must have seen a lot of those B pictures."

"That I did, sir."

"Well," he said with the air of a man struck by a bright idea, "I've got just the spot for you. I'll give you B company."

But it was not for long, and inexorably my past experience drew me forward through a series of public-relations hitches, culminating in June of 1941 with temporary duty in Manchester, Tennessee. This was the field headquarters of the Second U. S. Army and its fiery-tempered commander, Lt. Gen. Ben Lear.

General Lear, so the rumor had it, was the reincarnation of the commander of Caligula's Praetorian Guard. New stories of this roaring cavalryman were circulated around the mess tables every day, and none doubted their truth. General Lear had a way of seeming capable of them all, and used to tell some of them himself.

These tales were great mental hazards for all the junior officers who were in positions of vulnerability around the headquarters, i.e., that of being in jobs where contact with the commander was inevitable. Public relations was one of these, and particularly so was my special responsibility, the radio section. This involved scripts and statements which had to be written and checked through him, and microphones which had to be placed so close to him that, if he felt like it, he could bite the arm off the man who pushed it toward him.

The Tennessee maneuvers over which he was presiding were the biggest feel of America's military muscle since the end of World War I. Inevitably this led to arrangements to broadcast the findings over the stations of the National Broadcasting Company. The scripting chore fell to me, and it appeared at the outset that there would be a tug of war between General Lear and a very new, very junior brigadier general who bossed the "Hell on Wheels" Second Armored Division—name of George S. Patton.

Not having the least idea what generals find out about seventy thousand men who are being moved around a dusty landscape day and night, it was going to be impossible for me to get the material for a broadcast without getting some personal expressions from the generals. General Lear agreed that mine was a logical request, and arranged for a recorder to be set up in his office when he, General Patton, and others, would hold forth. From the recording of their talk, a script could be born. Almost immediately after the conference began, Patton stung General Lear with a derogatory reference to the cavalry. General Lear sprang to the defense of the mounted service against Patton's highly vaunted armor. As determined as General Lear, General Patton maintained that his rumbling, iron-treaded, freewheeling monsters would be the deciding factor in any future land battle.

The meeting broke up eventually, neither man having been convinced, with the room unusually warm even for that time in Tennessee.

The recording proved to be highly informative—and colorful. The script had to be written anyway. It was to be submitted to the principals in the early afternoon before they were scheduled to go on the air. All hands were to be in General Lear's office for the initial run-through.

After several rewrites, with touches here and there by various staff officers who insisted they knew what this or that general would want to say, the script was finally in hand. At the time set, we all went to General Lear's office and laid out the scripts. The quorum was complete except for General Patton.

"Where's Georgie?" General Lear asked.

Major Johnny Snowden, of Memphis, Tennessee, and Lear's aide, held up his hands. He had phoned the Second Armored, he said, but General Patton was not there. A twinkle crept into General Lear's eye, and he seemed well satisfied, rather than upset. "Okay," he said, rubbing his hands, "let's get on with it. Georgie can see it later."

When the meeting was over and the script revised, General Patton was left with a few affirmative, respectful, monosyllabic answers, not at all in keeping with his previous stand. General Lear was delighted. I was handed the now official version and told to have clean copies ready before broadcast time. Being last out of the schoolhouse door, I was somewhat surprised to see General Patton's car come around the corner of the building and stop in the graveled roadway.

"Hey," he called, "I'm sorry I was late, but I suppose you've got the script there?" He was not just supposing; he knew very well he had his target in his sights. He hadn't been waiting in back of the school for nothing. He came bounding over to me, reached for the script, sat down on the school steps, and began to read. He knew he couldn't win in the general's office, but here he was in command.

He got all the way to the middle of page three, and he had had enough. I felt he was about to offer a succinct opinion, and he did. "This," he said, "is the goddamnedest hogwash I ever read."

He then reached in the pencil pocket of his Flash Gordon tanker's coveralls, came up with a stub, and began furiously editing and building up his lines. Under his fast-moving pencil, the polite affirmatives disappeared, and in their places grew Pattonesque assertions that the Tennessee maneuvers had proved the Second Armored Division invincible and victorious over all.

With the script being butchered in this horrible way, charges of insubordination for having violated the trust of General Lear loomed before me. As I paced nervously, trying to remember how the script had read before he had gusseted it, Patton went through it again from front to back. Sensing my urgency, he nevertheless refused to give it to me when he was through.

"Where were you going with this when I came up?" he asked. It was a disarming question, but my heart sank.

"The general told me to clean it up and get the copies reproduced in final shape for the broadcast."

"Fine," said General Patton. "Let's do it." Without letting the script out of his hands, he walked with me to my small office where a typist was poised to get the stencils cut for the mimeograph machine. It gave me a lot of class that afternoon to have a brigadier general helping me by turning the crank on the mimeograph machine, but I would have preferred doing it alone, and with a chance to put those scripts right. All the while, the specter of General Lear's volatile temper hung over us—with this difference: Patton was happy as a hummingbird in flowers. As the machine coughed up the pages, he even helped me collate them. Taking all of them under his arm, he then buddied up some more, offering a ride in his car to the broadcasting site.

Miserably, I went along. There was no escaping. He left nothing to chance. I found myself brooding about the five months still left of that year of active duty I was doing. It took no imagination at all to see my buttons being pulled, and me being drummed out of the service.

Patton, on the contrary, gained in gaiety as we went along. He was like a youngster who had lit up a hotfoot for the sleeping town marshal and wanted to get to a vantage point quickly to view the effect. Because World War I had ended in a railway car at Compiègne, France, our radio station—WSM in Nashville—had arranged for a Pullman car to be sidetracked in the rail yards of Manchester and for the broadcast to originate from it. Soon after Patton and I arrived, General Lear came up in his car. Before taking to the air, a runthrough was planned for engineering and time tests. General Lear looked up suspiciously when he took his seat, noting that Patton was distributing the scripts. As this scene progressed, I grabbed Major Snowden, General Lear's aide, pulled him aside, told him all, and then stood off discreetly out of range in the Pullman vestibule.

As the reading got started, at every one of Patton's refurbished lines General Lear would flush to his collar and look wildly over his shoulder trying to locate me. It appeared sure there would be an altercation, but there was no time after the rehearsal to get into it. The announcer held up his hand for silence. From General Lear's side of the table, it was a sulphurous one.

"Thirty seconds," said the engineer, then brought down his hand in the signal that all of NBC had opened before the group. The moderator, Will R. Manier, Jr., began.

In spite of everything, the show went very well. The minute it was over, General Patton took up the initiative. "I sure want to apologize," he said, "for not being there at that first script reading this afternoon, sir—but the way it looks, you fixed me up much better than I could have done had I been there."

Lear put his best gimlet eye on Patton and was about to let him have it.

"Let's have a drink," said Harry Stone, of WSM, who had originated the broadcast for NBC. "It was a fine show." On that note, a tense situation ended—even though armor had outrun the horse among the kilocycles, coast to coast.

These Tennessee maneuvers, which had just introduced me to the fabulous Patton, also gave us a close-up of the military expert caught with his predictions down. The occasion was late June, and NBC had once again agreed to have WSM pick up a special event from Lynchburg, more than twenty miles from Manchester. The village had lined up a street dance for the soldiers, and the townspeople, particularly the girls, were in a generous mood.

NBC had allotted a quarter hour. As I wound up office affairs I came upon Hanson Baldwin, hammering away at his typewriter on a think piece for the *New York Times*. On being told about the street dance, he asked if we would mind holding the car for a few minutes so he could join us. Not long after, he handed in a sheaf of paper to the Western Union operator with instructions to move it out fast.

"Sorry to hold you up," he said. "I was getting out a piece for the Sunday edition."

We were bouncing along the rough country road by this time, and he continued talking. The piece, it developed, was his analysis, based on the best Washington sources, showing why the war in Europe was developing into a super-standoff. That night in Tennessee Hanson had come to the reasonable conclusion that Germany would never attack Russia, or vice versa.

About an hour later, we arrived at Lynchburg, and it was already humming. A hillbilly orchestra was providing the rhythms, and at times it appeared almost a jug band, so often were its members taking whets at the brew, which seemed to be of purely local origin and to be plentiful.[3]

NBC's pickup was set for 10:45 P.M. The announcer, Jud Collins, finally put the show on the air, and ran through his ad lib descriptions of the setting, the maneuvers, the soldiers, the Southern girls, whereupon the orchestra swung into "Chicken Reel." The thunder of a thousand feet in the town square left no doubt that a time was being had. But the announcer began to act oddly. He would stop his talking, seemingly in mid-sentence, then press his headphones to his ears and listen intently.

Slipping around in rear of the orchestra, I approached the engineer, Johnny Campbell, who was concentrated at the dials, in a listening attitude.

"Anything wrong?"

"They're breaking in on us from the NBC studio in New York," he said.

"What for?"

"A news bulletin."

"What about?"

"They're reading Hitler's orders to his armies in the East. The Germans are invading Russia."

By this time, the strangeness of behavior had attracted Hanson Baldwin, too. "What's up?" he asked. And we told him.

He gurgled like a man who had gone through the trap and snapped to at the end of a rope. "Where's a Western Union office?" he asked frantically, when he could speak. "The telephone office?"

But the village, except for the soft-drink dispensaries, was closed tighter than a clam and the telephone operator was somewhere in the stomping, swirling mass jitterbugging with a sergeant from upstate New York. Even if she could have been located, nothing could have prevailed upon her to swap the time she was having for a stint at the switchboard.

No one but Hanson Baldwin, the distinguished military expert, could know how horrible it must feel. As Western Union was stream-

---

[3] The evening's enthusiasm that June 21 night was in no way hindered by the Jack Daniels' distillery being on the outskirts of Lynchburg.

ing his words in from Tennessee, the German short-wave radio was feeding New York verbatim reports of Hitler's exhortations to his field marshals. Of course, his story was never printed, but colleagues have a way of remembering such things for years and at the worst of all possible times.

There was a public-relations postlude to the Tennessee warmup, when the exercise was being broken up and the units were heading back to home garrisons. A quartermaster unit, normally the last kind of an outfit in the world to make headlines, was to mobilize American public opinion, very lukewarm at this point, in behalf of the common soldier, and it was General Lear around whom this situation swirled for days.

The unit, at the end of June, headed out of Murfreesboro, Tennessee, en route to Camp Robinson, near Little Rock, Arkansas. As the truck column passed a golf course on the outskirts of Memphis, some of the tailboard Romeos zeroed in propositionally on a couple of girls who were wearing shorts and about to tee off. Coming up on the fairway, in his civilian clothes and relaxing after the maneuvers, was General Lear.

He dashed out in the roadway, flagged down the convoy, and instructed the commander and his officers to report to him at his headquarters in downtown Memphis the following morning which was Sunday. They were to hold their organization ready to do penance, too.

So was born the famous "Yoo-hoo" incident, which got nationwide attention. General Lear laced the whole command section of the unit up and back, then instructed the officers to truck themselves with their troops to the outskirts of West Memphis where all of them were to dismount and march fifteen miles toward Little Rock.

Memphis photographers and reporters clambered aboard this story, and the news dearth of summer found it being snapped up all over the country. General Lear became a national monster. At one time, the Memphis newspapers had to lay open two entire pages to accommodate the printable "Letters to the Editor" which poured in. After the order, repeated requests to the General for comment were met with flat refusals. The men made their fifteen-mile march, and went off into that special pedestrian darkness which usually surrounds the QM.

Old ladies who hoped that somebody would make an example of

General Lear never knew that the call of "Yoo-hoo" had never been uttered, and had they heard the ones which *were* addressed to the girls on the golf course they would have fainted flat-out.

Since we were in the first year of the military build-up, there was an extra, extremely advantageous dividend to this event. Nobody seemed to notice at the time, but it could not have come at a better moment. Until this incident the soldier had been regarded pretty much as a second-class citizen. Suddenly he became everybody's hero.

Now he was welcome in homes in towns where before he had had only the street corner to stand on. A great wave of public sentiment and sympathy for the man in uniform crept in behind this "Yoo-hoo" affair. And it was all the result of the stand taken by General Lear, who could have told the press at the outset exactly what the soldiers had said and exactly why he had been prompted to resort to punitive action.

"I can take it," he said once in his office, when we were pressing him to tell his side of it. "I will not vindicate myself at the expense of the American soldier. He's going to be needed for bigger things than this." And he was right. The American people were soon to have something bigger to think about, too. Less than a year later, another march was to take place—the Death March from Bataan.

Deception at Alexandria

People who make history usually have it sneak up on them unexpectedly. Although it had been many years since Marconi had nailed down the principles of wireless, we had to go all the way into World War II before its full versatility was developed. It then became a two-bladed vehicle—a route to public education and morale of the military forces when used one way, and also a real weapon against an enemy for his confusion and subversion. Partly because of the latter, there was a rash of traitor prosecutions after the fracas was over. Among those who got their rewards were such sorry figures as Lord Haw Haw, Axis Sally and Tokyo Rose, all of whom had acted as radio mouthpieces for the enemy.

If any of them had bothered to ask me in the beginning, I could have told them they were courting great danger. This is because the first use of radio as a psychological warfare weapon on American troops with a misleading intent came through the efforts of a crew of mine. No court action was ever inspired by it, but it caused no end of trouble for me. Two generals almost popped blood vessels, and a colonel named Dwight D. Eisenhower had me thrown into a prisoner-of-war enclosure in a swamp, where, after an inhospitable night, a cottonmouth water moccasin dared me to wash my face in a nearby stream.

As a sequel to those first maneuvers in Tennessee, the scene had shifted to southern Arkansas and western Louisiana where far greater numbers of troops were to be involved in large-scale exercises in the field. By this time, the Army was getting used to its role as a first-rank newsmaker, and public relations, as a staff function, was now being taken as a matter of course—even gaining some respectful attention. General Lear reached out for an old friend, Major R. A. Griffin, a Monterey, California, publisher, to head his information staff, and after my service in Tennessee he bracketed me for the top hand in the radio section.

The needs of a public-relations establishment were already mushrooming and it was no longer a simple matter of having someone to answer queries asked by correspondents. The administrative tasks in their behalf were mounting daily, and taking proper care of the press, radio and pictorial people involved a great deal of transportation, a communications filing point open at all hours and places to feed and house the correspondents. In addition to the physical facilities to make it easy for correspondents on the spot, there was the responsibility of providing regional and home-town coverage and interview recordings for radio and press outlets which could not afford their own correspondents.

There was extremely limited guidance available from the remainder of the military staff, so any and every kind of activity could be made to seem reasonable for the public-relations people. One staff officer once instructed us, "Go 'til you hear glass."

General Lear put it another way, but made the same point. "If you know what you're doing, I'll not bother you," he said. "If you don't, I will."

The professional soldiers felt they had been providentially handed a situation which, properly managed, could be made to cancel itself out. Just as the Army was becoming real news, it was inheriting from the reserves and from the dragnet of the draft, a wide range of experience in the very section now dogging the Army's trail. Former newspaper and radio people, now in uniform, wound up as interpreters —explaining the needs of their craft to the military, and explaining the military to ex-colleagues.

The classification system of the Army was a great leveler, however, and was inclined to lump all newspaper talents under one occupational heading; with radio, the same was true. A lot depended, too, on the glibness of the interviewee as he passed along the line. It was not unusual for a former newspaper boy to get himself tagged as a newspaperman and be classified as a writer. A janitor in a radio station more than once made the climb to program director with only a few minutes of fast talk. Classification would pass them on, and let someone else worry it out.

When Jimmy Stewart, the movie star, came into the service, some of the clerks were waking up to the fact that they were being had from time to time. "Whadyuh getta week?" the clerk asked him, not recognizing the actor.

"About $2,700," said Jimmy, quietly.

"Wise guy, eh? All these twenny-five-a-week guys get rich when I ask 'em that question. Just where'd you make this pile?"

His honesty impugned, Jimmy insisted that the clerk call the number of the cashier at Metro-Goldwyn-Mayer. The clerk took up the phone. Did they have a James Stewart who was formerly employed there? Yes, they did.

"Whadyuh pay 'im?" The receiver squeaked a bit, the clerk's eyes dilated, and he almost dropped the phone. But this was an unusual classification clerk, and an unusual type reporting in. Most of the clerks would settle for whatever they were told.

As the time came to build up a radio section as a unit capable of script preparation and production of recorded programs in the field, the results from personnel requests were uneven, to say the least. Some of the men I drew had actually been in radio, others knew about radio only from listening to it, but somehow we managed to form a radio staff which was to make its limited beachhead on history.

The starting blocks [1] for the maneuvers were first set in Prescott, Arkansas, and the public-relations spot was a deserted creamery building just across the street from the headquarters. Our best-known correspondent was Richard Hottelet, of the United Press, with us by courtesy of Hitler's dread Gestapo. While with the UP bureau in Berlin, he had been snatched up on a spy charge and thrown in the hole for writing letters to a girl friend in England which the Germans thought were too revealing. He had gotten about quite a bit in the wake of the German armies on all fronts, which gave him a valuable

[1] The Arkansas–Louisiana phase of the 1941 maneuvers was to start with a "border incident" for the press in the town of Texarkana, which lay half in Texas, half in Arkansas. The "incident" was to include locking the Texas police chief in his own jail and taking some local girls (willing ones, that is) as "hostages." It was called off at the last minute, which put the soldiery in mourning. Nobody was concerned about the sheriff, but there were some mighty fine-looking potential hostages around there.

yardstick with which to assess what he could see of General Lear's Second Army, much of it involved for the first time in a major exercise. We were to be pitted against Lt. Gen. Walter Krueger's Third Army eventually, an engagement of well over 400,000 troops.

Also at these maneuvers were the *Chicago Tribune*'s representatives, Max Corpenning and Clay Gowran. Since the determined Colonel Bertie McCormick wasn't choosing to have any of President Roosevelt's great citizen Army, his representatives naturally did *not* look upon or write of the fledgling armed forces with great favor.

The Columbia Broadcasting System had its weekly "Spirit of '41" to fill, which kept Burgess Meredith on the go constantly, but the networks generally were beginning to think of maneuvers as more of a news story than a source of special program material. Reporters like John Charles Daly, Bill Slocum and Dave Garroway were roaming the bush looking for tales which would hold an audience.

The extreme range of the public-relations officer was brought into focus when Metro-Goldwyn-Mayer sent a second unit into the maneuver area to get as much background action with tanks as it could lay lens on, all to be worked into an upcoming production which would star Wallace Beery.

Colonel Robert B. McBride, the Second Army intelligence officer and supervisor of the public-relations operation, turned up very troubled one morning. General Lear was more and more in demand for speaking appearances, and McBride was not at all sure Lear was as good on the podium as he should be. Major Griffin and I were called in, and McBride laid out the problem, while we waited patiently for him to get to his point. "Somebody," said McBride, "is going to have to find a way to give General Lear some elocution lessons." And they both looked at me.

"You work it out," McBride said. Nothing direct would do in tackling this problem, so an oblique course seemed advisable. The best way, then, would be to get the general in a position where he could recognize his own weakness and want to make his own corrections.

The radio section laid its hopes on our primitive recording machine, which had a limited playback capacity. The machine was set up in a church a block away from General Lear's office, and we had been doing our recording there because it was quiet. We actually used a little room where the youngsters normally attended Sunday school classes. Should the experiment fail, the general couldn't very well blow a fuse in such a setting, and it was even possible that the atmosphere would make him tolerant of what he might consider a foolish proposal.

The timing could not have been better for our purposes, since he was committed to make an address to the troops in about a week and this was to be picked up by NBC. Knowing that General Lear already had a rough draft of the speech in hand, I got the equipment all rigged, had the engineer at the ready, then sought an appointment to make the proposition.

He thought it a capital idea, was in an affable mood, and appeared to welcome the proposal, which was that, since he was faced with an appearance before the troops and a simultaneous appearance on a coast-to-coast radio network, he might like to record the speech. On the playback, he would be able to hear his own delivery, check his voice for any little adjustments he might want to make, make switches in emphasis, and time himself for pace. He said he'd be at the church at eight-thirty in the morning.

Promptly on time, General Lear's sedan stopped in front of the little church and he came striding in. The microphone was quickly placed in front of him, and he read an opening paragraph so the engineer could get the voice level. Then the needle was set, and the engineer signaled him to start. He went all the way through the speech without stopping.

The coils of thread-like acetate, dug up by the needle, were carefully swept away and the playback began. The effect on General Lear was electric. He was sitting in a chair when it started. With the first dozen words, he hopped to his feet. At the end of the first paragraph, he was all the way to the door. When a minute had elapsed, he was pacing the corridor outside, seemingly trying to escape his own voice. "Do I sound like that?" he asked of no one in particular. "That's awful."

We went over it together. Underscoring would help; also he tended to gallop here and there. He agreed to take it slower. Three times that morning, he recorded the speech, and each time it showed improvement. When he finished, he was satisfied and headed for the car. "That was a good idea," he said, and drove away.

An interval between phases of the field problems found us with some time on our hands, and it was decided that we try some experimentation with radio and "take over" a station as a stunt. The station which lay in our path was KELD, in El Dorado, Arkansas, and this it was that put us on the threshold of history. Fletcher Bols, the station manager, readily accepted our offer to intrude for a day, and agreed to keep it to himself. We were shooting for maximum listener surprise.

As long as we had the open door to KELD, we wanted to make it mean something prophetic in a military sense, wanted our test to tell us whatever it could. It takes a great deal of planning to take over management and programming of a station abruptly, without being able to size it up in advance, and we had to make the entire operation go with eight people, many of whom had only been on the listening end of radio before.

The "take-over" was slated for 6 A.M., September 2, 1941, which gave us five days. First, we had to plan the fifteen-minute news periods, which meant taking the scissors to the constant stream of teleprinter copy which poured in. This chore was split between John Conrad Sarber, a little private with a deep voice, a radio professional, and Sergeant James D. Asher, a one-time corset salesman in Lawrence, Kansas.

A recent addition to our small force was Brooks Watson. He had been a civilian radio consultant in the War Department Bureau of Public Relations. A tall, dry microphone smoothie, who had all the ether savvy anyone could ask for, he could step into any breach, be it the professional reading of a snuff commercial or a full half-hour ad-lib interview.

A New York advertising agency lad, Sergeant Sam Dobrans, was not at all terrified at having the radio engineer's console thrown to him, and he had a nimble line of patter along with a great deal of knowledge of popular records and the men who made them. He was a dual-threat gap-filler.

There were two dreadful program periods, one in the morning and one in the afternoon, which were regular station features, quite popular. They had to be done. They also would require soldier voices, if the integrity of our capture was to be maintained. They were women's programs, one devoted to the care and feeding of babies and the other to gardening and flowers. All we were told was that the regular contributors of these programs would provide the scripts. Somebody in our crew had to do them.

On the staff in a clerical capacity was Sergeant William Duncan, an Ozarkian who was called "Oinee", after the popular character in the cartoon strip, "Draftie." His resemblance to "Oinee" was remarkable, both physically and conversationally. Because he was so naturally funny, Duncan was elected for the women's programs. He was horrified, never having faced the mike before. He begged and he pleaded, but with some wheedling and a promise that we would put him in the studio alone and close the curtains so the others couldn't laugh at him, he agreed.

After these people were set as mainstays, everyone else was on a firehouse basis, ready to go in wherever needed. The detailed organizational headaches at no time overshadowed the wish on the part of Watson and myself to see whether, in a tactical situation, it might not be possible to overrun a radio station, then put it to purposeful use. We had to find out whether we could hold the existing regular audience, or would lose or gain. If we could hold or gain listeners with soldier programming, it could be important, indeed. It would mean that the way was opened into thousands of noncombatant homes where instructions about their behavior could be given before our troops arrived, and it could also be used to confuse enemy forces.

In order to maintain the secrecy required, none of our crew went near KELD until just before it was to go on the air that second day in September. The program director, Wilfred McKinney, and the chief engineer, John Riley, were there to meet us and unlock the station doors. We had a quarter hour in which Riley showed Dobrans the console. Sarber and Asher took over at the news teleprinter, and Watson, with the aplomb of an old hand, seated himself expectantly at the studio mike.

McKinney and Riley put the station on the air in the usual way, and promptly they were confronted with military rudeness before an open mike. They were told that the station had been captured by the Second Army. The interrupted commercial was picked up immediately by Watson. It was done in its entirety in his best sales voice.

El Dorado awakened that morning to a whole new kind of radio. Every half hour, I went to the microphone to announce that the station had been captured by the Second Army on maneuvers. The day was phenomenal as it wore on. The studio transmitter and studio were lumped in one very small building at the outskirts of the town, but the local citizens of all ages, on foot, on bicycles, in their cars, came out to see what was going on. This turned out advantageously, since, in our haste to get going that morning, we had overlooked the necessity for eating, hardly a normal GI trait. A mention of this on the air started a non-stop parade of sandwiches, cakes, cold meats, cheeses, and pie, threatening to bury us. We started without a cracker and began to look like a commissary.

In the middle of the morning came the crucial moment when we had to put Duncan on the air to explain the care and feeding of babies. He was almost as nervous as an expectant father. The routine prepared that morning by the kind lady broadcaster was one dealing with babies and their diapering in hot summer weather. She had even brought a wax doll to the studio, which she had intended to use as a model to keep her timing right. She gave script, doll, diaper, and safety pins to Duncan, and he was on.

All of us were extremely glad that she had brought a doll rather than a real baby, because Duncan might have been very lethal armed with a safety pin. He had once been a bayonet instructor. The serious spontaneity with which Duncan applied himself had the gang outside the studio rolling. His asides and departures in times of frustration were startling and refreshing, and he sounded for all the world as man always has when hit with this emergency for the first time. Immediately good southern ladies were on all the phones to the studio. "Please, oh, please," they begged, "put him on again." We promised him for the afternoon to talk about gardening, and as far as the women's audience was concerned that afternoon, their dials were set in cement.

One of our standbys was Larry Sanford, who had worked for a small station, WDZ, in Tuscola, Illinois, and he was constantly pestering me for a chance to go on. When not badgering me, he was trailing Brooks Watson. "If I can get a guitar somewhere," he promised, "I can lay 'em away." Finally he disappeared, and in half an hour came back with a guitar which he had borrowed at a downtown second-hand music store. Larry had had an accident before joining our crew and appearances were against him. In a car crash, his face had smashed into the steering wheel and he had lost two upper and two lower front teeth—none of which had been replaced. He had to talk with his mouth tilted slightly skyward, else he would have had a tough time putting a dam on his saliva.

Meantime, Fletcher Bols, the station manager, was listening contentedly in his downtown office, and getting calls from friends about his having been upended by the Army. He decided to have some fun, too, so he composed a wire to International News Service and had it fed back in over the station teleprinter. Sarber was standing guard with the scissors, when this "news item" came in saying that the Second Army had suffered a sudden reverse in the El Dorado area and was in full retreat. The "enemy penetration," the story said, was heading between the KELD radio station and El Dorado.

At the particular moment, the Thirty-fifth Infantry Division band was set to go on the air for a half hour. Each member immediately grabbed his instrument and cleared the studio. A half-hour hole suddenly yawned before us. Larry, like the dreaming waterboy of the football bench, came rushing into the breach with his trusty guitar. He had been making mournful backyard noises to its accompaniment for some time. Shrugging to Watson through the glass, I waved Sanford in.

Watson, as suave as if doing a remote from the Rainbow Room in New York, made a flowing introduction of this new talent from the never-ending sources within the Second Army. With not a single clue as to what would come next, the contrast between Watson's polish and what happened when Sanford went on put a look of absolute terror on Watson's face.

With a demonic gleam in his eye and the poorly tuned guitar at high port, Sanford, in a terrible, cracked falsetto, offered a grotesque parody of all hillbillies before and since. His patter was somewhere south of nonsensical, and his singing was pure late Saturday night. In audience appeal, however, we had guessed him wrong. Larry had been right. He ran neck-and-neck in popularity with Duncan, the women's broadcaster, and the phone calls were equally heavy asking that he be re-scheduled. They all thought Larry was kidding. Anyway, we now had two hits on our hands, and would not have to worry about hole-filling materials.

We gave the station back to its ownership at ten o'clock that night, after sixteen straight hours of broadcasting. We had drawn more than 1,800 phone calls during the day. Duncan and Sanford appeared three times each, and they could have stayed on that station for life. About 2,500 people made the trek to the station during our air time, and once on the lawn around it 800 people were standing to watch.

Fletcher Bols wrote a long letter to General Lear telling him about it, and how successful it had been from his point of view as the station manager. Major Griffin and I immediately were called into General Lear's office. The letter had given him an idea, which he might want to try during the final phase of the maneuvers when he had to tackle a numerically superior Third Army.

"Could you take over another station like this again?" he asked. "One in Alexandria or Shreveport, Louisiana?"

It seemed reasonable, but I asked to be allowed to make a check and tell him for sure in an hour. I quickly made contact with E. R. Capellini, of KALB, in Alexandria, and with John McCormack, of KWKH and KTBS, in Shreveport. Both agreed, given a day's notice, to let us come in as we had in El Dorado.

"I want to use you as a decoy," General Lear said when he was told. "We've decided we want your unit to go into Alexandria." He hastily sketched the plan. The main weight of the attack was to be well north of Alexandria, but he wanted to create the impression he was going through Alex in force in a flanking attack. This was to be no entertainment venture. Our strategy was to take over the station very quietly and run its programs exactly as the station had had them scheduled. Our sole departure was to make use of phony news and bulletins. It was common knowledge that intelligence officers constantly had their portable radios tuned to local stations in the "enemy territory," listening for man-on-the-street broadcasts, special-event shows, and news periods which were extremely handy in providing stray bits of information of Order of Battle value. We were going to give them exactly what they were listening for—the only difference being that our offerings would be deliberately contrived to delude.

In advance, we recorded the voices of several correspondents known to be with the Second Army, particularly Richard Hottelet, whose United Press by-lines were getting a good ride, and Lewis Sebring, of the *New York Herald Tribune,* who was always on maneuvers and a well-known military authority. Their recordings spoke of what an overwhelming spectacle the armored crossing of the bridge at Alexandria had been, and speculated on the chances of rolling up General Krueger's south flank with this surprise development.

We carefully segmented a road map of the Alexandria region, and wrote a series of advance bulletins presumably from "the state highway department of Louisiana." All of them were motorist warnings asking in the interests of safety that they avoid the routes north and south through Alexandria because of "enormous numbers of armored and half-tracked military vehicles on all these roads heading south."

"Hostilities" were to open before dawn on that mid-September D-Day, so my contingent was brought to the Second Army end of the bridge by car under cover of darkness. We had had the addition of Lieutenant Rankin Roberts, from the Illinois National Guard division, the Thirty-third. In the darkness, we scooted on foot over the bridge into Alexandria and furtively approached radio station KALB.

"Just don't blow it up," said Capellini, when we came in, and then, with a good businessman's afterthought, admonished, "And don't miss any commercials."

Again at 6 A.M., we were on the air, but this was not for fun— a definite tactical advantage hinged on how well we were able to pull this off. There was no departure from the station's legitimate programming for the first hour, though we knew that the "war" was on. At seven o'clock, there was a news broadcast and here we intruded our own version of the maneuvers, presumably from the wire services. In the text was a reference to heavy troop concentrations on the river bank opposite Alexandria, striking forces of Second Army. Twenty minutes later, in the middle of a record program, Brooks Watson broke in with the first of the false highway warnings. His voice rang with authority. He repeated this announcement each quarter hour.

The streets outside the station suddenly began to be active with Third Army scout cars, and a formation of reconnaissance planes came over low. Not long after ten o'clock, by pre-arranged signal, we got word to announce that the "Second Army has captured the radio station in Alexandria" and "is passing through the city in force."

This was the kickoff for playing the transcribed interviews. All of them had been interviewed by Brooks Watson, so this hooked up grandly with the voice that had been giving those highway bulletins all morning. Watson was on the air when our time ran out. Two half-tracks and a staff car drove up in front of the station and stopped. The men, fully armed, dismounted and came clumping up the stairs. Noting that the game was up, Brooks put his finger to his lips as he read all the way through a commercial, after which a rough voice rasped out, "You're under arrest." Watson closed by saying that the reign of the Second Army at KALB was at an end, and gave the station back to the staff. He very painstakingly said nothing about it having been a ruse, leaving the impression that the town was still being fought for.

The ultimate in ignominy of arrest was mine. They caught me trying to slip out through the ladies' room window! Usually in things of the kind we had tried to pull off, it took a long time to assess the success which had been attained. In our case, a panorama of it was spread out before us the rest of the day.

A prisoner of war in maneuvers has to spend at least twenty-four hours in the evacuation chain, a necessary part of training for his captors. It was obvious we were going to get the treatment. Taken to the outskirts of Alexandria on the south in the half-tracks and staff car, we saw a full regiment advancing on the town in a skirmish line. This was the leading element of a full brigade which was coming up. The rest of an infantry division was on its heels rushing in to blunt the "enemy" advance through Alexandria.

The enormity of our offense began to dawn when the brigadier general commanding the advance forces came rapidly over a plowed cotton field toward us. He began shaking a menacing finger before he was close enough for us to hear him. His name was never learned by any of us, but he was livid, and the size of his temper was only an indication of the completeness of his deception.

"You have broken the rules," he said, leveling the finger at me. "There is nothing in the rules which says you can use a radio station, a civilian radio station, in this way in connection with a maneuver."

Watson, a civilian, spoke up. "Do the rules say that you can use radio information you pick up by monitoring civilian stations?"

This almost brought on apoplexy, and the general whirled on him. "I'm going to report this whole thing to Third Army," he said, "and I'm personally going to see that it is brought to the attention of the Federal Communications Commission. What you have done should never be condoned, it's unorthodox, and whoever did it should be punished severely."

His complaint about violation of the rules was a scant eighty days before Pearl Harbor. He turned his back and walked away toward the ever-advancing elements of his division.

"What'll we do with 'em?" asked the officer who made our capture.

"Take 'em back to division," said the general's aide.

This time we were loaded on a passing truck, and instructions were given to the driver to take us to the division Command Post then only two miles down the road. He shifted gears on the truck and we bounced away southward. After passing slowly along roads choked with trucks and foot troops converging on Alexandria, we were deposited with the intelligence officer. He said that the division commander was so angry that he was going to send us to the rear without bringing us to the general's attention. We gathered that the intelligence officer had been one of those who monitored our radio show and had turned in the tip that big doings were up Alexandria way. He probably didn't want to face the general either.

He called the intelligence counterpart at Third Army, who said to hold us for a moment until he could speak to the Third Army chief of staff to see what disposition he was inclined to make of the case. The eight men of my doughty crew were getting somewhat apprehensive now, and the elation over their deception achievement was beginning to wear off. It would have been fine among friends, but not among these embarrassed "enemies."

Third Army called back. "I talked to the chief of staff," the caller said, "and he says just to send them all over to the PW cage near Lake Charles."

And so, Col. Dwight D. Eisenhower, then chief of staff of the Third Army, cast us into the swamp, deeper, it seemed, than the one which had enfolded Chloe. As night fell and we went slowly back along the road, we never seemed to be away from units moving endlessly north along the route over which we had just come—a full seven hours after we had been captured. A whole division, and some special separate supporting artillery units were involved—a total of about 20,000 men. In exchange, General Krueger had eight tired radio hands lying on the floor of a slow-moving truck, almost the only vehicle headed south. In the early evening one artilleryman leaned out over his truck's endgate and hallooed. "Hey," he said. "Ain't you guys going in the wrong direction?"

"We sure as hell are," piped up Duncan sleepily, "but so are you."

"How come?"

"You don't know it yet, but you're on the way up to get *us*—and we're already here."

The artilleryman gave him a Bronx boo, and his truck lurched into motion, taking him forward toward KALB in Alexandria—that strong point which had now become a Third Army sore point.

. . . TAKE 3

Organizational Agony

No matter how many honors the world may lay at the feet of Winston Churchill, there will never be any dissent from me. He doesn't know it, but he's my friend. When he came to the United States in 1942, we were well up to our armpits in the war, and I was in Class 23 of the Parachute School at Fort Benning, Georgia. Churchill made it possible for Class 23 to be graduated with only four, rather than five, prescribed jumps.

A demonstration drop had been planned for Churchill at Fort Bragg, North Carolina, and there were so few troop-carrier planes there that the Parachute School's training aircraft had to be employed. Otherwise, there would have been no chance to provide the Prime Minister with any kind of a spectacle.

My need for his intercession at this time was drastic and the press was responsible for it.

For a long time Joe Wing, editor of the Associated Press feature service in New York, had had a request in for a "first person" story from someone going through parachute training. They had been waiting for the first newspaperman with enough rocks in his head to volunteer for parachute duty. When I came along the mouldering writing job was given to me.[1]

---

[1] AP Features circulated the by-line story with pictures, which was used by more than 400 newspapers the same day the German tanks were crossing the Russian Don river, and said, in part: "FORT BENNING, Ga.—We were 1,000 feet above Lawson field when the jumpmaster commanded: 'Stand in the door!'

In going off the thirty-foot tower for a picture to illustrate one phase of the rigorous curriculum, my arresting harness snapped on one side, letting me crash into the ground and giving me a severely bone-bruised ankle that promptly swelled to the size of a grapefruit. To report to the medics would have automatically set me back about six weeks, so the medics were avoided while I tried to numb the pain with an elastic bandage under heavy socks inside my jumpboot.

The following week we began daily drops from a plane, and I was having a miserable time worrying out each jump and trying to land in the most comfortable way. The fourth of these falls had been a hair-raiser, nerve-wrackingly compounded. The chute of the man behind me as we came out of the door in very close order was suddenly robbed of its air and collapsed. He fell like a plummet, through my

---

First up was Lt. Leonard Anglin, of Lumpkin, Ga. He planted his feet and let the prop blast roar in his face as he stuck his head out the door. We were all hooked up, our static lines fastened to a long cable in the roof of the transport. It was graduation day for paratroopers. Then the jumpmaster swinging the flat of his hand hard up against the underside of Anglin's leg yelled, 'Go!' As in an unfinished, old fashioned two-step, left foot in the lead, right coming up but never passing, we shuffled to the door. Pivot on the right foot, left to the ledge, a push and we hurtled through space, turning a quarter turn left and dropping fast under the tail of the plane. '1,000, 2,000, 3,000,' we said. That's three seconds. If that snap of the chute opening hadn't been felt by then, we were instructed to pull the reserve ripcord on '4,000.' Mine opened in the middle of '2,000.' I said it something like 'two-umph-thousand.' I looked up and the canopy was over me like a tent, suspension lines taut. Below me was the field like a well kept lawn. There was no feeling of falling or height, but I was swinging a little so grabbed the right front and left rear risers, chinning myself to check the oscillation. We were about 800 feet up. Somebody yelled. It was Lt. Rodger Meadows, of Akron, Ohio. 'Nobody in Akron would believe I'd ever do this,' he said. An air current hit me at 100 feet. I grabbed the risers, rocked them hard to keep oscillation from setting in again. Twenty feet up, I looked down praying I'd land lightly on that week-old sprained ankle, then suddenly realized I was coming in backward. The ground! I spilled backward, did a complete roll and never touched the ankle. The chute collapsed, and as I unstrapped the harness, I looked for the next groups already in descent. Meadows lit fairly easily. Lt. Henry Buchanan, late of Anderson, S. C., came in on a slight knee bend and stood up without a roll. There was a puddle of water off to the right, and Lt. Robert Carlson, of Utica, N. Y. plowed it up like a motor boat. What kind of a man does it take to become a paratrooper? I would say it takes a man who can conquer his fears, grit his teeth, and do what's expected of him in any pinch. Like no other soldier, he proves his courage every day of his training . . . it takes a man who is original, individual, and who believes he can take command of his own destiny. . . . The paratrooper has no illusions about fear. He doesn't brag that he's never afraid of anything. He brags rather that he is often afraid, but he goes ahead and does what he is asked to do, no matter what it is."

shroud lines as I swung momentarily in range of his descent, and he remained entangled with me. This meant my canopy was holding the weight of us both, and we tumbled into the turf about twice as fast and hard as normal.

Such accidents, although far from unusual in parachuting, are always dangerous, even when one is able to use all his physical powers to cushion the landing shock. This smashing fall sent lightning all the way up. It had my ankle palpitating, my knee twinging, while my hip felt as if someone had struck the pelvic socket with a heavy hammer.

Surely, I thought, it will never be possible to endure that all-important fifth, or "graduation," jump tomorrow. This unhappy possibility tortured me as my group rode from the drop zone back to the flight line. Weary and in great pain, I let myself down cautiously on the cement apron in front of the hangar which served as a parachute packing shed.

"Pack your chutes," the sergeant said. "and turn 'em in."

"Turn 'em in?"

"You guys are unlucky," he said. "They're takin' the planes away tonight. Four jumps will qualify you and they'll pin the wings on you just as you are now."

I don't know how much relief the other battered members of my "stick" felt, but that sergeant, hitherto known only as a torture artist, suddenly looked like a pal. Limping into the packing shed, I spread the pile of rumpled silk which had just transported two of us safely to earth, separated the shroud lines, and began stuffing and stowing mechanically, but with growing elation. Unlucky, indeed!

Normally inspections are the last of military functions to enjoy, but that Winston Churchill was making one at this particular moment was celebration material for me. In the years to come, on the many occasions I was to see him, the timeliness of this great man in both a global and individual sense always impressed me. The world was lucky when he came along as he did—and so was I.

About a year passed and another Englishman taught me something of the fast footwork of adjustment needed when a V.I.P. was not exactly on time. In 1943, Brig. Gen. E. G. Chapman, boss of Airborne Command at Fort Bragg, asked me to shepherd a special writer named Walter McCallum of the *Washington Evening Star* and Mrs. Lillian Harlow, a North Carolina newspaper woman, during the visit of the British Foreign Secretary, Anthony Eden.

Eden was of the highest V.I.P. order, and he was conducted on this tour by no less a personage than General George C. Marshall, the Army's Chief of Staff. For his appearance that day, two separate airborne landings had been programmed, and timed to the second. One involved the release of a flight of gliders, which were to deposit their loads of armed infantrymen just a few feet from the Eden reviewing stand in one location. After this, the V.I.P. convoy, preceded by MP's on motorcycles, would be rushed to another reviewing site about a mile and a half away to watch the mass drop of a parachute battalion.

Eden had barely taken his seat at the first point when the tugplanes appeared in the distance and the gliders were released. The kite-like craft came careening in, touched down and rolled gracefully up to their positions, tilted to their noses and stopped. The fully armed and packed infantrymen bolted out into assembly areas, and phase one of the Eden show was complete.

Hoping for a word of praise that could be relayed to my press charges, I moved nearer to the official car which now had its door open waiting for Eden and the general. The MP motorcade was fretfully sputtering, ready to roll. Eden stepped halfway into the car, and with one foot still on the ground, turned to General Marshall. "I wonder," he said musingly, "if it would be possible while I'm here to see one of those portable chapel organs such as your chaplains use when conducting services in the field."

If General Marshall was flabbergasted, he did not show it. He was in full knowledge that the planes, loaded with paratroopers, were even now only minutes out, but he cast about quickly for the MP in charge of the convoy. He asked if there was such a piece of equipment in the area. If the MP had been quick-witted enough, he could have said he did not know of anything like it, but this was an MP who knew Fort Bragg. There was one, he said, in a chapel about two miles away.

"You," said General Marshall to me, quietly but urgently, "go to operations and have them turn those planes around until we can call them in again. We won't be long." To the MP, he said: "Lead the way."

The cavalcade roared off, and I ran for operations. The formation was caught just fifteen miles out. The pilots had drawn in tightly, leveled off at eight hundred feet, and were ready for a closely packed, quick drop. All the paratroopers were on their feet, static lines hooked, and had counted off their inspection. All that was left was that nape-of-the-neck-tingling command: "Stand in the door!"

Suddenly, they all swayed on their static lines like Brooklyn strap-hangers as the subway curves them into Manhattan. The planes were banking, spreading, and turning away from the landing field. Crew chiefs came back in the cargo compartments to tell the paratroopers to unhook, and go back to their bucket seats. "There's delay," one of them said. "Time for tea, maybe."

Meanwhile, as this was going on in the air, the British Foreign Secretary was entering the small chapel. He seated himself at the organ and began to pump, then tested the keys. Later, I asked the MP what he played. "I'm not sure," he said. "Noises, mostly."

Apparently satisfied, Eden then rejoined General Marshall and the procession headed for the reviewing stand. In a few minutes the recalled paratroopers came over and did their drop, and the show was completed.

Increasingly, circumstances were drawing me toward that Britain from which came these two men to look over the burgeoning strength in this country. Public-relations assignments, so common in the first days of my military service, had become almost unknown. For more than a year and a half, the traditional chores of a paratrooping infantryman had been mine.

One of the old maneuver correspondents of 1941, Jack M. Redding, then representing the *Chicago Herald-American,* now had a commission in the Air Corps. He was berthed in the HQ European Theater of Operations in London (ETOUSA), deputy to Colonel Tristram Tupper, a writer of books and brother-in-law of General Marshall. Colonel Tupper devoted the bulk of his time to the public-relations needs of ETOUSA's commanding general, Jacob L. Devers, and he left the running of the remainder of the office to Redding.

Major Redding was like the long-time top sergeant suddenly commissioned as an officer. Having been a newspaperman who would howl for all he could get and steal the rest, he was very difficult to sneak up on from a blind side, and the fact that he once considered all legerdemain legitimate did not alter his own indignation at the first hint of the unethical when someone tore a page out of his old book.

He had a ferocious scowl, which he wore in various styles for various occasions. The one for mornings could curdle cream. It was in the presence of one of these moods that Major Reavis O'Neal of the

Eighth Air Force once asked Redding if he had time to be "mad" at somebody.

"Who?" Redding asked with surging belligerence.

Somewhat startled with having inspired this turn of events, Reavis pursed his lips, then snapped his fingers and said: "Jock Lawrence?"

Lt. Col. J. B. L. Lawrence, late of the Sam Goldwyn school of publicity and now fronting with the press for Maj. Gen. John C. H. Lee, was keeping up a home-town news saturation mill in behalf of the Services of Supply. Redding dialed the extension and got Jock on the phone. The tongue-lashing lasted for about five minutes, started nowhere and ended inconclusively. Lawrence was not altogether surprised, but he was slightly mystified. Redding put the phone down with a crash, creased his face uncertainly into a smile, and Reavis fled.

With the needs for the second front made fairly transparent by the North African sideshow, it was Redding who was dispatched to the United States in the autumn of 1943 to pick up a crew of public-relations specialists from any and all sources. The preference was for those who had had backgrounds in press, radio and pictorial lines, but who had been absorbed and schooled in the Army's various branches. They were all to be gathered in ETOUSA for the time being, then to be placed in slots apportioned to First U. S. Army Group, slated for command by Lt. Gen. Omar N. Bradley.

Redding's net was thrown across all the commands in interior U. S., and about twenty-five people were drawn up in it. My selection came up partly because of my organizational work with mobile press installations, and partly because he wanted a paratrooper who knew the Eighty-second and 101st Airborne Divisions and the Second Airborne Brigade, all of which were being placed in England in readiness for Normandy. In October, 1943, orders sent me to England.

The only activities running off the British Isles were provided by the Air Forces, busily applying the principles of strategic air power to the sinews of the Axis. The rest was build-up, clouded in censorship. Billeting and training bulged the countryside and every city with British uniforms, American, Canadian, and with extra clusters of exile units, the Poles, Czechs, Belgians, Dutch, Norwegians, Danes and French.

The day-to-day life of these military forces provided some news, and there were names floating in and out on side-bar wartime missions whose disclosure would hurt nothing. This caused special press arrangements to be necessary from time to time, and the so-called "press facility visit" was common, in which tours were set up for various installations.

There was an overhanging "Remember Rover" slogan which always came out when these public-relations ventures were undertaken, recalling a debacle during a visit to England by Mrs. Eleanor Roosevelt. This foul-up occurred before the first Christmas Americans were to spend in Britain, and it was used as a warning signal to anyone who assumed, rather than made sure, that everything was nailed down tight.

Mrs. Roosevelt was to follow an itinerary touching some half dozen RAF stations at which American Air Force units were in residence while hammering away at Germany. The public-relations officer who arranged the tour came up with the idea that it needed something special to provide a story snapper, and he suggested that Mrs. Roosevelt be confronted at the last station by her son, the Air Force's Elliott Roosevelt. This would give the ride a strong climax, with a homespun, or human-interest, angle far above the usual. He thought this mother-son reunion would offer a vicarious, pre-holiday lift to every mother who had a son in the ETO.

The day of the trek was a miserable one, such as can be guaranteed in England's winter season. The fog was in, it was cold, and to no one's surprise, but everyone's discomfiture, Mrs. Roosevelt's schedule began to lose ground.

All V.I.P.'s had to travel under some code name in the war days, and the Eighth Air Force had tagged the peripatetic Mrs. Roosevelt with the not too inappropriate label of "Rover." All the plans teletyped to RAF stations on the tour asked that certain things be accomplished for "Rover" and indicated that "Rover" was to arrive at each RAF site at a stated time. The day wore endlessly on, and the press, never reluctant to extend blame for weather to the public-relations attendants, became more and more restive, and more and more articulately unhappy. The PRO could only cross his fingers, act mysterious about upcoming rewards, and hope that his day would be saved by the grand climax at the last RAF station.

When it hove to in the fog, the reception committee greeted Mrs. Roosevelt warmly, but one of the commander's aides approached the PRO to tell him that Mrs. Roosevelt's Air Force son had not shown himself. It was a combination of fog, the mixed-up schedule, and a rather loose handling which had not explained the urgency of the requirement fully.

The PRO, who felt he must produce Elliott or the day would be lost, ran to the communications building. Throughout the Eighth Air Force network, the teletypes suddenly cracked into life with the gong message: "Need urgently whereabouts information. Rover has lost her pup."

When Irving Berlin brought over *This Is The Army,* or rather came over with it as one of its actors, the great soldier show was in the first stages of bringing more than $10,000,000 into armed services relief funds. His was one of the offbeat Army-arranged press conferences, and for the first time in my life I heard a man sing at one. The tune, of course, was "White Christmas," and he sang it in answer to one newspaperman's query about the reason for its success. Berlin couldn't explain the song's popularity very well himself, and after the press heard *him* sing it, neither could they!

But Berlin's presence in London, and in *This Is The Army,* turned into one of the most moving theatrical experiences of all the war for the displaced American GI, a little homesick, tired of the inevitable sameness of life in uniform, and with some dread about the uncertain future.

One of my beginning tasks was the press end of the Command Performance of *This Is The Army* at the Palladium. As is customary on these occasions, those who constitute the "theater staff" line up to receive the Royal Family. King George VI looked very tired, but eager for the few moments of escape the show would give him. Queen Elizabeth stopped to ask a question, and I answered her with a "ma'am" finish, which appeared to be a *faux pas,* though the British protocol expert said it was "better than average" for an American. Princess Elizabeth, at seventeen, was turning into a poised, beautiful girl, and Princess Margaret looked as if a game of hopscotch was about to start.

When Berlin's turn in the show came up, he walked on slowly in his too-skimpy World War I uniform, his precision-wrapped leggings accenting his pipestem legs. With his campaign hat in his hands, he sang through a medley of old tunes in that painfully small voice of his. The applause reached out to him when he finished, curled in rear of the stage tormentor, and brought him back for bow after bow, hanging onto him until he signified his intention to stay. He looked up at the Royal Box, then out to the audience, "Are there any of my old songs you'd like to hear?"

The response of the packed house was deafening, and almost in unison. From all the national voices and accents came the clear call: "Alexander! Alexander's Ragtime Band."

Almost thirty years before, the singing waiter of "Nigger" Mike's Saloon had put this simple tune together. Now, in the uniform he had worn twenty-five years before, he stood in front of the Royal Family of another country and heard this noisy, deeply moving testimony.

Irving Berlin swung into it with an accompaniment of the soldier orchestra, and the Royal Box applauded as loudly and unrestrainedly as the U. S. Army privates up from a Salisbury depot on a three-day pass.

The strangest of all the wartime press conferences involved an American sergeant who had leaned too hard into his goodnight kisses when courting a British girl in the midlands. She gave birth to quadruplets.

The sergeant was married to a girl back home, and when the midlands press asked him what he thought his wife was going to do about all this, he intrigued them considerably by saying that he had written her a letter of explanation, and that he was certain "she will understand." Such assuredness of wifely devotion under what seemed to be great duress made the sergeant extremely interesting to the London-based correspondents, who promptly applied pressure to have him brought into the British capital.

The sergeant didn't seem to mind. After all, what more could happen to him? The family of the girl who had contributed her share of this four-ply disaster from doorway dalliance seemed philosophical about the whole thing, so up he came to London.

It was an exceptional gathering of the press, a certain hilarity of spirit prevailing. At another extreme, it was somewhat like the first showing by Phineas T. Barnum of Tom Thumb.

Ruth Cowan, the women's angler for the Associated Press, paced the floor outside the room where the meeting was being held, craning her neck to hear.

"Why don't you go in and take a seat?" I asked her.

"No, thank you!" she said, shying away. "I wouldn't risk breathing the same air with him."

Behind all these doings, there was the long-range planning—planning necessary to put a major portion of the press, radio and pictorial contingent in nearness to, and provide subsistence and other guarantees for them in, a series of highly mobile situations. It would start with Normandy, but the organization had to be able to roll under its own power from the beaches all the way to the heart of the Reich.

Not long before this planning was undertaken, Ernie Pyle had recounted his experiences in trying to get his stories out and meet deadlines thousands of miles away. His story was based on the facts of life as he had found them in Africa and Sicily. The weakest point, he said, was in communications, no matter how expert their performance may have been under normal conditions. Ernie said he made as many carbon copies of every story he wrote as he could, sometimes a dozen or so. He filed one to the recommended medium of communications. After that, every truck, jeep, liaison plane, or other conveyance heading in the direction of radio terminus or cablehead would be given another copy with instructions for personal delivery.

Even with all this precaution, there were times when a good story would never reach the U. S. offices of his syndicate.

It was expected that Normandy would have to accommodate at least 150 correspondents of all kinds, writers, voice broadcasters and photographers in the first week, and more thereafter. Three armies would figure initially, American First, British Second, and Canadian First. From the American point of view, within less than sixty days, there would probably be two armies (First and Third) in action, over which would be an Army Group.

The correspondents not only had to be protected in a communications sense from the Continental side of the English Channel to the cableheads in London, but must have transport, messing facilities, briefing arrangements, plus a guardian flock of uniformed people who understood their wants and what they could get and pass through censorship.

Major Redding tabbed Bruce Fessenden, an Ohioan with a fierce mustache, and myself, to start the organizational job. In the Army, all such tasks begin on paper, and the experience of days and nights on the move in Arkansas and Louisiana two years before now came in handy since it had been the Army's biggest experience in handling the needs of correspondents behind a field force. The big difference was in the sorest region, communications, because we could in no way depend upon the Western Union office or the telephone callbox. Getting the story was no longer the hardest part of the operation. No profession is without its myopia, and in journalism and radio it is usually found in advanced stages. Men who have worked in an office, gone to the corner lunch counter for a snack when hungry, used the telephone in any callbox for instant tie to a rewrite man, or grabbed a cab by merely raising a hand to get from one place to another are inclined to oversimplify the problem of processing a war story—until they have been initiated. Then it is learned that everything—from paper and pencils to intercontinental radio transmitters—must be packaged and carried along.

Such was the problem facing our small staff. Redding's instructions were simple, too simple. He first asked for a "publicity service company," which was to be "breakable into three separate, self-sufficient platoons" which could provide "messing, transport, and administrative services" for fifty war correspondents each. He set a ceiling of 100 for the whole unit!

Assuming 150 correspondents as the total overhead, at the rate of two to a jeep, we required seventy-five drivers and seventy-five jeeps. This gave us no overages in equipment and left us with only twenty-five people from whom to draw cooks, motor-pool specialists and administrative help in the supply and clerical fields.

The two of us chewed up pencils, scratched out, reworked, erased, added and subtracted. With an absolute minimum, no-loss-contemplated unit, we came up with a first draft requiring 100 men and eight officers, knowing in our hearts it was not enough.

Redding's reaction was pained and profane. He charged us with having tried to scuttle him before we were well started, and said that the manpower allocations group of the headquarters would never agree to such a great number. With much misgiving, however, he finally agreed to doing it the Army way. This got us on the safe ground of "the Book," the organization and equipment manual provided as a guide for setting up all special units. With "the Book," it became easier. Starting with the number of men to be supported, "the Book" lays out the number of cooks, second cooks, kitchen help in general. Given the number of vehicles, "the Book" tells how many specialists and what kinds will be in the motor pool, and so on through the maze. A new set of problems loomed on the horizon when other agencies which dealt in information began to descend upon this small unit, trying to fit their specialists into a package with us—the Office of War

Information, the Office of Strategic Services, Psychological Warfare and others.

On a grand scale now, we turned more and more to building a structure which would do big what we had done in a small way with the Second Army in 1941. In three and one half weeks, there was a draft for a "Publicity and Psychological Warfare Battalion" of nearly 600 officers and men—which excited nobody, and promptly became possible by being approved.

The unit was prepared to support the correspondents of the Army Group under General Bradley, but it also contained mobile radio transmitters which could move either voice or text, mobile printing presses which could turn out propaganda and surrender leaflets in the thousands, mobile public-address systems, interpreters, writers, commentators, special-events announcers, cooks, drivers, mechanics, clerks and all the array of specialists who would have to be available to a unit of this kind which must maintain and repair itself in the field— be it from normal wear and tear, or from battle damage.

One of the contingents was to be assigned to First U. S. Army, then couched in Bristol on England's West Coast. The second would go to Lt. Gen. George S. Patton, Jr.'s Third Army. The remainder, and the administrative overhead, would stay with the Army Group.

London was straining at its seams with officers and men who were carried as casuals until they could be slipped into the sprouting new organizations. Redding's crew, gathered on the U. S. trip, had now been added to the crowd, and it was embarrassing to him to have them leaning unoccupied against the walls of the Grosvenor Square building which housed ETOUSA.

Colonel Tupper, a tidy man, summoned me to his office, told me to go to Bristol, get with a housing and billeting British civilian there and locate some village site in the west country just big enough to house our unit. He wanted something which would take about 700 men, and into it the replacement depot stream would be sluiced until it was filled with the P&PW Battalion.

A few miles south of Bristol I found Clevedon. It was on the Bristol Channel, not far from the place where Robert Louis Stevenson's Hawkins, the future cabin boy, met the piratical crew and started the story of *Treasure Island*. It was the professional Englishman's retreat for summer holidays, a mecca of leisure for doctors, lawyers and the like in peaceful times. Straight across the Channel were Newport and

Cardiff, in Wales, within vision on clear days, but always blacked out completely at night. A dismal, somber parade of white hospital ships coursed down the Channel empty, and up that Channel full of their loads of pain from the battlefields all over the world as men came back to Old Blighty, some for long convalescence, and some to die— but to die at home.

Clevedon had everything we needed. There were rolling hills, a minimum of traffic which would allow us free run for training exercises, and the population was used to soldiers. Their own territorials, the Somersets, had been billeted there early in the war. So Clevedon became the base for one of the oddest of all collections of diversified humanity, the P&PW Battalion. By its very nature, a mixture of straight-line duty men, expert linguists, truck drivers, newspaper editorial writers, radio program directors, and cloak-and-dagger men, it was bound to cleave in dozens of ways and be as explosive as a disturbed atom—it was truly Babel revisited.

Redding's idea of useful employment for the public-relations element during the waiting period was a refresher course in basic military activities, and Clevedon became a boot camp. The mile run to breakfast, calisthenics, the practice march, the sleeping bag on the hard ground, elementary map reading, and other soldiering foundations were to be relaid.

To bring this about Redding sent Captain Jack Widmer, a Colorado horse rancher, into Clevedon to be the field marshal responsible for the hardening-up. Widmer had once written a book called *How To Train a Horse,* and he fell in with the scheme with fervor. Using the whip method, he paced the men relentlessly.

"I'd feel a lot better about this," grumbled Lt. Charles Rhodes, a member of this coterie of confusion, "if I knew which end of the horse he trained back there in Colorado."

The members of this group were on the way to being remembered by more war correspondents than some generals, and they will never be forgotten by Clevedon. Included among them were such captains as Casey Dempsey, an Illinois newspaperman; Ray Craft, who had been one of the ink-stained wretches in California journalism; Ernie Deane, an Arkansas professor whose mirth-making saved many a situation, and a string of lieutenants; Charlie Rhodes, once a Hollywood fan magazine photographer; Jack Hanssen, a radio program director from Mankato, Minnesota; Jim Campbell, a veteran of United Press in Tennessee who clung tightly to his cavalry boots (wore them to sleep in, the British thought); Ross Hazeltine, of the *Indianapolis Star;* Sam Brightman, a cynic from the *Louisville Courier Journal;* two *Herald Tribune* men, wire-haired Roy Wilder of Gourd Hollow, North Carolina, and a lover of "chitlins" which came to him in the mail and sent his colleagues in search of fresh air, and serious Ken Kilbon; likable George Fuller, who had done radio in Baltimore; and steady, suave and tall Bill Drake, once an editor in Chillicothe, Missouri. There were others, but these were to be the press hinges on the doorway into Normandy.

Clevedon's Royal Pier hotel, operated by Mrs. Ellen Coles who had come originally from Cardiff, and her son, Jack, and daughter, Maizie, became the official turning-in spot after the drill grounds. The Simms family held the town together in a communications sense, since they were the local monitors of the telephone switchboard, a manual operation. They could find anyone in town with a few calls, and Clevedon 90 was a phone number to reckon with for anyone who wanted a little action. There was always someone at Clevedon 90 who had a good line into any division, corps or special unit. As the London element of First U. S. Army Group (FUSAG) knew its way around the higher headquarters strata, the Clevedoners knew the rank-and-filers who would shortly be doing the fighting. They grew into this knowledge as they went out on special projects to pave the way for the press.

This was the period of tension, when GI's did not sleep well, dreaming nightmarishly of the fiery welcome which awaited them at Hitler's Atlantic Wall. In response to this disquiet, Generals Eisenhower and Bradley, Field Marshal Sir Bernard L. Montgomery, and even the British Prime Minister began to walk among the troops and talk to them, to allay a portion of their fears by inspiration and by giving them an idea of the firepower which would back them up.

These visits were always security-ridden, and every segment of the arrangements was closely watched. This meant that anything done for the press in advance was bound to create uneasiness among the counterintelligence elements, who would be down our throats at every turn.

It was always the same. Instructions would come down to move into a given town, or area, and contact the local General Post Office manager. He was asked to keep a full crew on for transmission via his telegraph lines to London on the appropriate date. If it went past

5 P.M., it meant overtime, and he could never authorize overtime on his own. Every time we came to this impasse, we could only sigh and brace ourselves for the inevitable.

The local GPO would contact GPO in London. But the latter would trust no one about expending His Majesty's funds, so he would verify. This meant calling Number 10 Downing Street, the official residence of the Prime Minister, or one of the major military headquarters. This always put the fat in the fire. Either of these would know the projected V.I.P. movements, and because they knew would always put the worst possible interpretation on what must be going on down in the obscure village asleep and unaware until now. Each of these crises would eventually simmer down, and we would go on with our special projects.

Ernie Deane, Charlie Rhodes and I worked several of these, one of them in Newbury, the old race-course town not far from London on the Bristol road, temporary home and training area for the 101st Airborne Division which had a brand-new commander, Maj. Gen. Maxwell Davenport Taylor.

The visitors in this case were the Prime Minister, General Eisenhower and General Bradley. A regimental airborne drop and a review were the main fillips, with an extensive walk-around for a look at specialized airborne equipment. We had run the gamut, been in the soup with the London GPO as always, but were cleared in time to put our twenty jeeps and drivers at the disposal of the press retinue.

General Eisenhower chose to escort Churchill around the static display, which attracted a covey of photographers on whom Charlie Rhodes was somewhat desperately riding herd. The Prime Minister stopped before an 81-millimeter mortar, on either side of which stood two ramrod-stiff corporals, while racked behind them were some of the new finned mortar projectiles. These caught the Supreme Commander's eye. "This 81," said the general, "using this new ammo has a range of about 3,000 yards."

One of the soldiers rippled visibly from foot to head, then broke in. "Excuse me, sir," he said, looking straight ahead. "It's 3,250 yards."

A twinkle rose merrily in Churchill's eye, and Eisenhower looked with paternal sternness at the corporal. "Look, soldier," he said, "you wouldn't make a liar out of me in front of the Prime Minister for 250 yards, would you?"

Churchill laughed loudly, and so did his escort. The corporal was set for life in the 101st, and was a tourist attraction pointed out to strangers. "He's the one who keeps Eisenhower on the ball," his squadmates would insist.

As the two moved on, Charlie Rhodes kept close to the cameramen and had one eye on me. Using Churchill's aide for that day, his WAAF daughter, Sarah, I kept counsel with her on how her father's temper was running as he was close-upped by so many, so often. When she thought it necessary to restrain the photographers a bit, a relay of signals to Charlie would have him going for their collars to drag them back.

With Sarah on this day was Kay Summersby, the Supreme Commander's driver, and upon spying her, the Prime Minister suddenly broke from the line of inspection, raised his hat from his almost naked pate and, reaching to shake hands with her, huskily betrayed inroads of his recent illness. "My dear," he said, "I never did get to thank you . . ." and then his voice trailed off. She accepted his thanks graciously and stepped back.

Pierre J. Huss, of International News Service, sensed a great feature, which smelled of intrigue somehow, certainly of mystery. He bored in to get details. Kay shied away, saying it was personal, and the press corps became further titillated.

Later, because the pressure began to envelop me, I told her curiosity was about to bust their buttons, so, with an air of a conspirator, she confided, "He's been ill. He just thanked me for some lozenges I had loaned him for his throat." It seemed better that it stay a mystery.

Few have ever equaled Churchill in ability to roll up a neat sentence, and this review was provided with one, which in a few words summed up his remarkable career. As a climax to the day, he walked to a jeep which was centered before the tough troopers as they stood rooted at attention. After he was helped up on the hood and had firm footing, he waved for them all to break ranks, come forward, and cluster around him. He took off his bowler hat and removed his cigar from his mouth. The wind gently blew a wisp of his hair forward into his eyes, but he paid it no attention. He looked intently for a moment out over this sea of faces of America's finest fighting men.

"I stand before you," he said slowly to let it all sink in, "a man with no unrealized ambitions except to see the Axis wiped off the face of the earth."

The fullness of that capsuled sentence, spoken by a man who had packed so much richness into one long life, placed his career in

perspective. A cheer went up from his listeners. The paratroopers recognized themselves not only as a part of the American hope for victory,
but as the keys to the remaining ambition of this man who had been
the architect of the Anglo-American alliance about to bring its weight
to bear on tyranny.

... TAKE 4 ————————————————

Going Over the Jumps

The pioneer wartime jumpboot journalist was bearded Jack Thompson of the *Chicago Tribune*. On November 15, 1942, he took part in the second jump of Lieutenant Colonel Edson Raff's parachute battalion at Youkes-les-Bains, near Tebessa, Algeria. Since Eddie Raff's outfit carried the banner of America's new airborne force into battle for the first time, some of the glory naturally reflected on Jack Thompson. Always calm and unruffled, he got along well with the unorthodox paratroopers and they adopted him as their Boswell, giving him a reputation and standing which stayed with him. His flowing beard gave him the appearance of a House of David baseball player, and he was easily the most readily identifiable individual among the ranks of Raff's highly refined cutthroat artists. In electing to jump with Raff's battalion, he opened one more gateway by which an enterprising reporter could get a story. What Jack got he had pretty much to himself because there was no competition from his colleagues.

One jump was not enough for Thompson, either. When the time came for Colonel James M. Gavin to spearhead the Eighty-second Airborne Division's landings in Sicily with his sharp 505th Parachute Infantry Regiment, Jack showed up ready to go, his beard freshly trimmed.

Gavin found that he had not one, but three guests who wanted to go with him to Sicily. The others were Lieutenant Colonel Charles Billingslea of San Francisco and Lieutenant Colonel William T. Ryder of St. Louis. Ryder had been the long-time commandant of the Parachute School at Fort Benning and had been the first man to jump in the Army's original test platoon. Since both Ryder and Jack Thompson were, in their ways, parachute pioneers, Gavin set them to chaperoning each other.

Jack's beard had long since earned him the name of "Beaver" and he was the reason for one of the two security violations which occurred early in the Sicilian campaign. The first had nothing to do with him, but was caused by a radio operator wanting to be sure he was among friends that black night.

Radio silence was to be in force in the first stages of the landing, and the challenges for the night had been agreed upon. When it came time for this paratrooper to switch on his walkie-talkie, he was afraid someone might have worked his way into the backfield, so to speak, and learned the signals. He made up his own call, going on the air with a brisk, unexpected salute: "Come in, Beechie Howard!" [1]

And in that darkness, filled with spasmodic gunfire and with paratroopers scattered all over southern and eastern Sicily, he felt completely sure of anyone who would answer *him* back. While the call might have been extremely mysterious to any German or Italian, it had a comforting sound for paratroopers. Beechie Howard's in Phenix City, Alabama, was known far and wide among the jumpers as a place where all things fair were available at a fair price.

"Anybody who'd answer on 'Beechie Howard,'" the radio hand said in justification, "could only be a friend."

The other security break came after Ryder crashed into a hillside olive grove. He struggled quickly out of his harness, checked his weapon, and started a whispered hunt for Jack Thompson who had been in the jump stick with him.[2]

The challenge for that night was "George Marshall." If any move-

[1] Historically, this had been laid to PFC Lindsey Prescott, of the Intelligence Section. Among other things, he was a cartoonist of style, who did the art work in the Eighty-second's postwar book, *Saga of the All-American*.

[2] It was Friday, July 9, 1943, at 2030 (8:30 P.M.) that the 505th Parachute Infantry Combat Team plummeted into Sicily, making the initial assault in Hitler's Festung Europa. General George C. Marshall later said, "The aggressive fighting of the 82nd ... throughout the war from Sicily onward was an inspiration to all fighting men." German General Kurt Student, the foremost Axis authority on airborne operations, said at the Nuremberg trials: "It is my opinion that if it had not been for the allied airborne [82nd] forces blocking the Hermann Goering Armored Division from reaching the beachhead, that the Division would have driven the initial seaborne forces back into the sea. I attribute the entire success of the allied Sicilian operation to the delaying of German reserves."

ment was noted, a man would ask nervously but quietly, "George?" And if anyone so challenged valued his life, he came back quickly with "Marshall!"

So Ryder began his quest. "George?" he'd say.

"Marshall!"

"That you, Beaver?" When the finding was negative, he went on. After about five minutes he became disgusted. He got up off his sore knees and rose to his full height. Slinging his carbine over his shoulder, he cupped his hands and roared through them into the night: "Beaver! Where the hell are you?"

Thompson had landed with a crushing sideslip and the breath was knocked out of him. Ryder actually searched within a few feet of him, but his call went unanswered.[3]

Ryder, in addition to chaperoning Thompson, had two other responsibilities. He was the parachute liaison officer for the Fifty-second Troop Carrier Wing, which had made the paratrooper haul that night, and he was an "extra lieutenant colonel" available to Gavin for command assignment if need arose. He set about collecting strays from other jump sticks, figuring Thompson had done his own linking up.

Jack regained his powers of speech and locomotion to find that he was in the most terrifying of all positions—alone.[4] Starting off blindly with no weapons, he was not even in possession of his typewriter. He was startled when two figures loomed ahead of him. They all took cover. There was no firing, but Thompson, without anything to defend himself, was reluctant to say "George!" for fear the answer would be a fusillade. He finally did, got a whispered "Marshall!", and everyone breathed again.

"Boy, am I glad to see you," yipped Thompson running forward to be included in their armed protection.

[3] Said Jack Thompson of the jump: "I was the last out of Gavin's plane, just behind Ryder. I crashed through an olive tree and lit on one knee, busting two ribs, and gashing my leg. Had a hell of a time getting out of the damned harness. Then, like a dope, I started rolling up the 'stick' the wrong way from Ryder and eventually wound up with the medics. They gave me the Purple Heart for my unskillful crackup."

[4] Thompson was not the only *Chicago Tribune* correspondent to have a frightening time in the Mediterranean area. Later, William Strand, teamed with stuttering Homer Bigart, of the *New York Herald Tribune* was in a command post when it was receiving heavy shelling. "C-c-could you g-g-give m-me s-s-some idea of w-w-what's b-b-been g-g-going on around h-h-here?" asked Bigart of the commander. "For God's sake," said Strand, ducking as each shell whistled over, "let me ask the questions, or we'll never get out of here."

"Shut up, you noisy bastard," hissed one of his discoverers, "we're medics, and don't have any guns!"

The doings in the Mediterranean sector seemed clearly, almost from the very first, to be side-show in nature, pinning down forces and holding them away from the main invasion area close to the British Isle along the northwest coast of France.

The prevailing joke among all the professional military men, British or American, was that there was only one place a serious thrust could go—off the British south coast toward Normandy. The water obstacle was narrowest there, the supply dumps were the closest, and, for any military college problem treating with invading the continent from a British base, both the British and American staff colleges had nearly always used Normandy as the school solution. Anyone, the wags claimed, who had ever attended a military school and had picked up the proper respect for the school solution would dread going against that "school solution" even this far away from the campus and the ire of the commandant.

One of the troubles in the mounting up for Normandy was the great number of war correspondents who wanted, or professed to want, to be in the so-called "first wave." In it was the lure of the front-page by-line and the established reputation for all time.

Soon after arrival in England, along with the others on the staff, I was caught in the tangle of drawing up quotas of words per correspondent and quotas of correspondents for the wire services, news agencies, and radio networks. The photographers were another category and were to have their product pooled for common use.

The spaces in shipping were scarce, and on landing craft they were even harder to come by. The precedent established by Jack Thompson in the Mediterranean gave Redding an idea, as a result of which he handed me the toughest of all sales tasks, to wit: Use the space shortage on ships as a clincher in persuading correspondents that the next best thing was the airborne route to the continent.

The way was mine to provide. It required first that these war correspondents be talked into accompanying the troops, either by parachute or glider. Having gotten them into this lineup, a not inconsiderable feat, we next had to have some way of assuring the airborne commanders that these newsmen would not freeze on the jump and jeopardize operations. The only insurance for this, of course, was to condition them for the ordeal, test their powers of determination and self-discipline, get them qualified as paratroopers or gliderists through practice jumps or rides. The best that could be said for this original scheme was that there was no quota to worry about. Come one, come all, there was plenty of space for the ride in the air.

Truthfully, it can be said that there was no whirlwind of enthusiasm for the honor of emulating Jack Thompson, or for the distinction of being among the vanguard to touch down behind Hitler's Atlantic Wall. Perhaps there were too many of those aerial photographs showing the pointed stakes and rugged posts that stood in every Normandy cleared area, ready to impale jumpers or to rip the wings off a fragile glider. The *Tribune* even counted Thompson out, figuring two such ventures should be about par for the course.

To start with it was essential to have the training lined up, and it was to the 101st Airborne Division we turned for help, this division being spotted all along the London-Bristol road between Reading and Hungerford. The 101st was commanded by the father of U. S. airborne forces, Maj. Gen. William Carey Lee.

In the small thatched village of Chilton-Foliat, consisting of about a dozen houses and north of the main road, General Lee had marked off a portion of the Whitelaw Reid estate and had improvised a parachute school which turned the willing into the brave in two acute weeks of physical torture. This school accommodated soldiers based in England who volunteered for the parachute troops, and Navy and Air Force people who were being groomed as D-Day observers and artillery spotters. Chilton-Foliat would provide the correspondents who elected to come along not only the necessary training but a minimum cooling-off period.

General Lee agreed to allocate two spaces in each two-week class to war correspondents. Should we not be able to take up these spaces, he was to be informed so that he could give them to others on the long waiting list. The Chilton-Foliat curriculum was not for those who felt any aversion to exercise or to enduring muscular aches compounded by shooting pains and fatigue. Any given day of the grind invariably produced in all participants the desire to crawl off somewhere about 7 P.M. and die. The school staff had been broken in by Sergeant Bill "Red" King, a one-time professional fighter from Nashville, Tennessee, who joined the army and got to be one of its colorful champions in the ring-brawling prewar sports life at Fort Benning. "Red" was Mr. Paratrooper himself.

When General Lee, then a mere major, had gotten the bug about vertical envelopment and had begun to talk it up in the War Department, he got nowhere until the morning of May 10, 1940. That morning one thing and two phone calls came about. The "thing" was the quick fall of Belgium's prize Fort Eben Emael to Hitler's airborne troops when the Germans crashed into the low countries. The first phone call was from President Roosevelt, who asked the Chief of Infantry what our Army was doing about airborne troops. The second was from General Marshall, asking the same question.

The result was a directive to convene a test platoon of forty-eight enlisted men and two officers from the Twenty-ninth Infantry Regiment at Benning. William T. Ryder, lieutenant in charge, who later chummed it with Thompson in Sicily, and Red King were one-two out the door in the first parachute jump made by this test group. An extremely hard man, Red had wrung all tendencies toward softness, if any had ever existed, out of his system. It was to him and his brutes and bonecrushers that I had to lead each of the somewhat reluctant new pupils to begin each new term. At first it would be easy to avoid the subject of King and his helpers, but once the word got back to London, it would soon be buzzing around the Dorchester, the French Club, Grosvenor House, and the bar at 8 South Audley Street. The picture painted would suggest that Heinrich Himmler himself might profitably cross the English Channel and enroll to get a postgraduate course in sadism. As if volunteers were not hard enough to get anyway, this would make it well-nigh impossible.

No sooner had we set up shop for this special project than sex began to cloud the atmosphere. Women, who had fought a bitter, but mostly losing, battle for D-Day spaces, began to pry for airborne places once they heard that the field was wide open. Nearly everyone learned early in World War II that there are women and women correspondents. They may look the same, but they are not. The latter had a better arsenal of weapons, and greater versatility in their use, than any man. Most of them could hold their own in any league.

One of the seasoned American veterans of deadlines had come to England during the Battle of Britain, and had elected to live on an RAF station where scores of British youth, barely up to regular shaving, were swatting back the Luftwaffe day and night. Her stories were well written, and well read, so much so that the local British housewives invited her to tea one afternoon. This American woman had one aversion, and it was British women, but she decided to be big about it and go through with the tea if it killed her, as well, she thought, it might. All went well through the introductions, and the tea was poured, whereupon the conversations wandered off into village gossip and women-talk, very pale fare for the hard-bitten typewriter feline who was guest of honor. Her girlhood long since behind her, she was still living a life those ladies could neither know nor understand. She became restive, and this attracted the attention of her hostess.

"Oh, I say," said the hostess, signaling the rest of the room to be quiet, "I have been dying to ask you something." The woman correspondent turned a wary glittering eye toward her questioner. "It must be so exciting," the bellwether continued, "living out there on the station—the only woman and all those young men. Tell us about it."

The correspondent figuratively spat on her hands, picked up the bat, and eyed the left-field bleachers. "Oh, it's exciting, all right," she said seriously, "but their youth is embarrassing, too."

"So?" pursued the hostess. "In what way?"

"Sometimes," said the lady correspondent, "after a few drinks, I just can't be sure whether I'm laying 'em—or having 'em." Teacups crashed to the floor all around, a hush fell over the room, and the lady correspondent left the premises, never to return.

Women, no matter how rough and ready they claimed to be, continued all through the war to be the subject of a great debate. Every time allocations for spaces came up, someone was bound to suggest that the women stay with field-hospital units where nurses were already provided for or not go at all.

It was no particular wonder, then, that we viewed with some trepidation the pressures the girls were now putting on to get into our paratroop enterprise.

The three most persistent candidates, who never lost interest as some of the others did, were Dixie Tighe, a still attractive woman of some years who had been a Hearst sob sister and was now with the International News Service; Judy Barden, a British girl who worked in the London bureau of the *New York Sun* and North American Newspaper Alliance; and petite Betty Gaskill, who represented *Liberty* magazine and would have had hardly enough weight to pull a parachute down after her.

Sidestepping their persistence as best I could, it was my job to keep telephoning, or treeing in bars, those male war correspondents who

were the best prey because they were unlikely to be drawn for the
waterborne quota to Normandy. First efforts were concentrated on
the representatives of the wire services. International News Service
was a tough one, because Dixie Tighe was in a mood to protect her
priority with that agency. It was hard work to scout for a male nom-
inee without alerting her. I ran into Pierre J. Huss at Grosvenor
House, who said he was not interested himself but asked that the
agency not be counted out because Richard Tregaskis was soon to
report into the theater. This was a maybe, at best.

The check at Associated Press found the bureau manager, Bob
Bunnelle, referring the matter to Wes Gallagher, who was already
slated to be AP's field marshal along the western front. Wes had nobody who was interested, he said. Trying to work up competitive
spirit, I told him that Pete Huss had just tentatively nominated
Richard Tregaskis and asked us to hold a place for him. Gallagher,
tough as hardtack, was not to be goaded. "All that means," he said,
"is that Pete Huss is going to be INS's top hand in this theater—if he
has to kill Dick Tregaskis to do it."

United Press was not in the market at all. Reuters turned out to be
a gold mine, because, though British, it had an eager-beaver American
named Robert Reuben from Omaha, Nebraska, who hankered for the
paratrooper assignment. The agency had a second prospect in Marshal Yarrow, who said that he was favorably disposed to a glider ride.
Yarrow was a carefree Canadian, one of the finest and funniest.

When we swung to the radio field, the American Blue Network
produced Tommy Grandin. Edward R. Murrow, boss of the London
office of the Columbia Broadcasting System and Mr. "This . . . is
London" himself, said he thought Larry LeSueur might be interested.
The National Broadcasting Company intended to put Wright Bryan,
editor of the *Atlanta Journal,* which owned NBC outlet WSB, into
one of the paratrooper planes for the round trip—he would accompany the jumpers to the Cherbourg Peninsula drop zone, cover their
exit and return to base. The British Broadcasting Corporation provided Chester Wilmot, who selected a glider of the British Sixth Airborne Division which would land on the extreme eastern flank of the
Normandy beachhead.

The news magazines liked the idea, partly because they had time
to play with. Even if their representatives got stuck for two or three
days, the material could still get back ahead of deadline. William

Walton of *Time,* a hardy, handy Wisconsin boy, was used to hazardous ventures, having made some Eighth Air Force time in a gunner's post, substituting a camera for the gun in his port. He was ready and eager for the parachute deal. *Life* had two uncertain nominations, Bob Capa, a nervy Hungarian who called himself "the enemy alien war correspondent," and Bob Landry. *Newsweek* was represented by another bearded type, lean and cadaverous-looking Joseph Evans. He volunteered for the Chilton-Foliat course even though he didn't look as if he could run across the room to a telephone. *Stars and Stripes* produced Phil Bucknell, a man who liked to hold down his end of the bar and who wore the uniform of the U. S. Army over one of those corpulent figures which always invited mayhem at the Parachute School—and did in his case.

Joseph Dearing,[5] a photographer for *Collier's*, set a record for enthusiasm, doing all five of his qualifying parachute jumps in one day. On the last one, he crashed into a tree trunk, dented his helmet, and knocked himself out for ten minutes. He was a great favorite in the school, and his acceptance of the challenge there was one of no holds barred. Walter McCallum, of the *Washington Evening Star,* had already elected the glider and was slated to go with the 101st Airborne Division.

The time came eventually to corral Bob Capa, Bob Landry and Larry LeSueur, since they had already missed several classes and time was getting short. There was a big party being thrown by Capa in his Knightsbridge flat on a Saturday night, a gay, mixed crowd of great color and dazzle, a coeducational assembly in honor of arriving Clark Lee, of International News Service, who had changed sides of the world to be in on the upcoming big show. The congeniality of the champagne bottle found me doing better and better as the evening wore on, and by the time the ice buckets were all at half-mast, it appeared I could have signed up the whole gathering then and there. In fact, some, overcome by the spirit of the occasion, entertained the

---

[5] There was some worry on the part of the war correspondents that they would crush their typewriters if they carried them along, so I had to seek the help of the 101st Airborne Division parachute riggers in construction of a sponge-rubber case into which a typewriter could be slipped. It was attached to the harness just below the reserve parachute. To test the case I had to jump with *my* typewriter since no one else wanted to risk his own. Noting the shape and location of my load before the jump, Joe Dearing observed, "You look pregnant—on the square."

notion of jumping out of the upper-story window without parachutes, so well had the motif of my visit permeated the party.

By midevening, when I took my leave, Capa, Landry and LeSueur had all put their signatures on the "release forms," the papers which said they were taking the training of their own free will and that, should anything happen to them, the government of the U. S. would be absolved of all blame. Pickup time was to be the next day—Sunday, at eleven o'clock, on Hyde Park Corner, an easy meeting place.

About a quarter to eleven, our car drove up and slid into the curb near the Hyde Park Gate. It seemed a dreadful thing to drag my roistering companions of the night before down to Chilton-Foliat for enrollment in the parachute school and its two weeks of assault on body and soul—to say nothing of what it would do to a champagne hangover.

My sympathy was wasted, however. By half past eleven I went into a nearby telephone kiosk and pushed Button A, dropping my tuppence on hearing LeSueur's sleepy answer, and reminding him of the appointment. "I'm sorry," he said, "but when I left Capa's last night, I stumbled off the curb getting into a taxi. Sprained hell out of my ankle. Can't even bear my weight on it. They boys told me they'd tell you. Didn't they?"

"They didn't make it to Hyde Park Corner either."

"Oh," said Larry, then hung up. Scratch one volunteer.

The next tuppence produced Landry, equally sleepy. "Boy, I'm in misery," he said. "When I left Capa's last night, I'd had too much, I guess. Fell off the curb reaching for a taxi, and have I ever got a sprained ankle this morning! Didn't the other guys tell you?"

"No," I told him, "but they're using the same script so far."

Scratch two volunteers. Next up in the batting order was Capa, but his phone didn't even answer. Later, he did do his qualifying jumps with members of the Eighty-second Airborne Division, and was pronounced ready, but that Sunday morning's roundup taught me a lot about champagne contracts!

The pressure by the women had never stopped through all this period, and it was becoming more and more imperative that we have some kind of an answer to turn them back. In desperation, a buckslip was sent rotating around each of the FUSAG staff sections asking whether, in the knowledge of anyone, there was any good, or even fair, reason why we should refuse the feminine trio the right of parachute descent into Normandy. The buckslip came back in two weeks, negative on every count. The only ray of hope was noted in pencil by a major in the office of the Surgeon General. He had a conversational suggestion, he said, but would not care to make it official.

"It may not be worth anything," he said, in response to an urgent telephone plea, "but I used to know a woman who was a stunt parachute jumper—knew her very well. She did free falls until she was about 500 feet above the ground and then pulled the cord. She was always falling real fast by this time, and the opening shock would give her a real snap-up." This didn't sound like much, but lowering his voice, he murmured a few more words.

"She did what?"

"Yes, sir, whether it was the right time of the month, or not!"

"Really?"

"Scout's Honor. I asked her about it, and she said it was like that every time. It might be useful to you, because if there is that kind of violence in the break-out from a free fall, think how much more drastic it might be with a woman who isn't used to it if she went through one of those 115-mile-an-hour prop-blasted openings such as the paratroopers get." He went on to say that he couldn't make it official, because he was sure it wasn't true in most cases, but we could talk confidently about what the sharp jolt of the exploding parachute canopy could do to the delicate female apparatus.

But how to use it? The easiest one to handle was Betty Gaskill, and the route to her was through her husband, Gordon, an accredited magazine correspondent in the theater. He took the explanation mirthfully and promised to call Betty off. He said he was sure that *Liberty* magazine would settle for her services in some less spectacular way, so that was one away. Gault MacGowan, chief of the *New York Sun*'s London bureau, Judy Barden's boss, was approached. He promised to take Judy out of the parachute picture and use her on a more mundane assignment.

Only Dixie Tighe remained, but the chances of getting her bureau chief to run the interference died with Charlie Smith's refusal to have anything to do with it. He was even ungallant. "This Dixie is no chicken," he said. "Do you think a little thing like that would scare *her?* Tell her yourself."

It was not an easy subject to talk over with a woman face to face, and it was embarrassing enough by telephone, but the latter was preferable, and Dixie had to be sold this bill of goods. She had had the best of them try that in her day, not any of them very successful.

She listened politely, and it became obvious that some bracing for a blast was in order, but she chose to be sweet about it. "Okay," she said, "if the Army doesn't want me to go, I won't go, but let me give you a bit of advice." She could almost be heard shifting gears. "You better keep what you've told me a secret," she warned, "because, if it ever gets out on this tight little island that a parachute jump will do what you say, you are in for trouble."

"Trouble?"

"If the girls ever hear of it, considering how many are in a fix from cozying up to you Americans—you'll have so damned many petticoat paratroop volunteers you won't know what to do with them."

... TAKE 5

Pigeons and Hot Flashes

Lieutenant George Fuller was always good at meeting girls. It was said that he could go farther on a shilling than any other American in England. Not that he minded spending money, but he had a sure-fire method of getting acquainted. His routine was simple, and so good he never varied it. He took up a stance in the middle of the street, held his shilling in his open palm, and scrutinized it closely, puzzling over it. When the first pretty girl approached, he would ask if she would mind helping him. "Could you tell me, please," he always said, "how many sixpences there are in this coin? I always forget whether it is four or two."

No woman could ever resist this appeal, and the conversations inevitably would drag on and cover many subjects. Sometimes they were very productive. But, good as he was in making the acquaintance of the fair, George never got around to meeting Joan Ellis. The two of them, however, figured in their own ways in wartime communications excitement.

On about the same day Joan was released after four years in the WAAF, where she had served as a teletype operator in MI (military intelligence) 5, George was out in the English Channel off Plymouth in a wallowing landing craft—alone with sixty carrier pigeons. George was there because it was felt that no communications opportunity should be overlooked, even the slowest and most ancient, if it had a reasonable chance of helping to move press material back across the Channel on D-Day. Joan was preoccupied with the Channel crossing, too, but her tragedy had to do with the speed, rather than the slowness, of transmission.

The overwater link of the Channel was such a great worry in public-relations planning that Maj. Gen. Francis Lanahan, the signals chief for General Eisenhower, later said he could not have remained at his SHAEF post if he had not provided for press needs with care equal to that given to military demands. The primary reliance was on mobile radio transmitters and teletype circuits provided by the military. Army support was also granted to a commercial radio installation, Press Wireless, slated for use by First Army (U. S.) and capable, it was hoped, of moving both censored voice [1] and text to New York from Normandy with no intervening relay. But it would take time to put this electronic gear across and into operation, at the very moment when the most pressing story material would be found in the crossing itself and the lodgment.

A speedboat courier system was laid on as an interim measure to gain a shore-to-shore channel through which early copy, undeveloped negatives, film packs and wire recordings could come from Normandy to the southern coastal ports. Teletypes were already installed to speed the copy from these sea terminals, and motorcyclists were ready to roar to London with the photographic and recorded materials. In addition, as soon as a landing strip opened anywhere on the continent, an air courier service was to be put in motion to gather copy and other material for delivery into London direct.

Bales of striped press bags, made of white canvas duck material with red or orange bars across it and imprinted with the word "Press," were issued to war correspondent clustering points, and it was published everywhere in the armed forces that, no matter where found, these bags had only one destination—London.

Time was closing in on the planners, who were none too sure that everything possible had been done, and the awful magnitude of the D-Day story was enough to make any planner check and recheck. At this moment a sergeant named Morris, a pigeon fancier, brought up his favorite subject, the carrier pigeon. The Army, he said, has about 54,000 of these carriers, which it had allocated for world-wide

---

[1] Initially, Press Wireless was geared only for text transmission, with dependence for voice on an Army mobile unit, JESQ, which could link with London. Press Wireless would add voice after the strength and adaptability of the signal was determined in France.

use. Carrier pigeons, he pointed out, were capable of 45 miles an hour in flight, and had been able to cover 700 miles in a twenty-four hour period. They had an altitude ceiling of about 20,000 feet. Despite the sergeant's enthusiasm and statistics, the planners were not stirred. Pigeons, no matter how anybody sized them up, had an uncomfortable antiquated look alongside the military electronic gear with its capacity estimated at 100,000,000 words daily.

How far back we would be reaching was there for anyone who wanted to look up carrier pigeons. Herr Paul Julius Reuter, born in Cassel, Germany, in 1816, laid the foundations for what was to become a great news agency by using pigeons to bridge a gap of about the same mileage we were working to span. His was the distance between the German telegraphic terminus of Aix-la-Chappelle and the end of the French-Belgian circuits at Verviers, and he pulled it off in 1849 by "pigeon post." His birds outpaced the fastest carriages by a good margin. It took Reuter nine years to get any newspaper to use his dispatches, and it took us almost nine weeks to face up to a pigeon experiment.

Just then the story of the pigeon, "GI Joe," a blue check-splash cock, came through from Italy and interest heightened. On October 18, 1943, he was credited with saving several hundred members of the British Fifty-sixth Infantry Division at Colvi Vecchia. An air strike had been called for to uproot a strongly held German position, and the Germans suddenly withdrew, letting the British into the town. It was just thirty-five minutes before the air strike was scheduled when someone remembered the unit was now in the bull's eye of the target. "GI Joe" was released with a message to hold the air strike, and he nipped the takeoff by five minutes after a twenty-mile flight. "GI Joe" put a floor under the planners, and George Fuller was picked to be the key man in the test.

There was something ironic about George Fuller, a specialist in radio voice-casting which had almost instantaneous reception no matter how far it had to move, now being assigned this pigeoneering task, but he entered it in all seriousness. A pigeon specialist was brought in, who gave George a thorough briefing, what the birds could do, and their peculiarities. He made the point that there were two kinds, overland and overwater varieties. The overland carriers cued themselves to their home cote by landmarks, while the overwater species set their course in a more instinctive fashion.

A corps-size landing exercise was being mounted down near Land's End, with all the enormous check list of invasion equipment to be loaded, but even to those inured to novelties and unexpected accouterments the sight of George with his wicker cages containing five dozen carrier pigeons raised a few brows. Some thought he was bringing live squabs to bribe the admiral of the fleet to put him down on a remote beach.

In spite of the catcalls, George took assurance from the glorious history of wartime pigeons, including one named "Cher Ami" who had saved the "Lost Battalion" of the Seventy-seventh Infantry Division in World War I. Carefully he tucked his charges away aboard the landing craft and, when the expedition set sail, George sat quietly among his baskets of cooing and slightly excited feathered messengers. These were guaranteed overwater pigeons, and his instructions were simple. They were to be released well out of sight of land, and he was to stuff a few of the aluminum leg band capsules with messages to mark them as the public-relations birds.

As his expedition moved on, George sat composing little gems on tissue-like squares of paper. Attaching the capsules to the birds, he did not notice exactly which direction land was when it disappeared. All that remained for him to do was to release the pigeons, time the departure of the first and last, then slip-slop in the landing craft back to Plymouth. His phone call upon arrival would give us a way of figuring the time en route, while the test itself would give us a percentage reading on the reliability of the pigeon service. This statistic would help us in approaching the war correspondents to offer yet another stop-gap service.

Solitary in the watery expanse, George finally reached in among his fluttering friends, pulling them out of their wicker cages and tossing them into the air. The birds flapped wildly a few times, got some altitude, then took a heading and disappeared. Having no idea now where land was, George could not swear that the way they went was correct, but he did note with some satisfaction that they all took off in the same general direction.

Redding and I were at Montgomery's Twenty-first Army Group headquarters at Southwick House, near Portsmouth, and had only a general idea of the time the release point would be reached. The pigeon cote was in London, and the keeper was instructed to call us as soon as the first bird came in. The experts said we should hear something within twelve hours.

The first twelve hours went by, and no call. The hours stretched to twenty-four, then to forty-eight. By this time, pigeons had been given up in disgust. Almost fifty-six hours went by before a toll call came from Rhyde, the capital of the Isle of Wight, a triangular chunk of land which stoppered the mouth of Portsmouth harbor. The caller was about thirty miles from our headquarters, but a good one hundred and fifty miles over land and sea from London.

"Are you there?" asked the British voice. He identified himself as the chief of police in Rhyde. He asked whether it was advisable to speak freely over the line about something which was troubling him. This was a time of extreme security care.

"Now—have you lost anything?"

"Lost anything?"

"Er . . . feathered things, I might suggest."

"Pigeons?"

"Right ho," he came back in some relief, "absolute bags of the bloody birds!" Redding grabbed the other extension. "My police station is full of them," the chief of police reported. "They are walking all through the gaol. They've been here since yesterday. We can't shoo them away. They won't leave, and they've dirtied up the place something dreadful."

"Are they carrier pigeons by any chance?" Redding asked him. "Do they have leg bands, or little message capsules on them?"

"That they do."

"Have you opened any of them?"

"No, not a one. We wanted to be sure it would be all right."

"If they are the birds I think they are," Redding assured him, "it'll be all right. Check a couple of them, and use your own judgment from what they say before you read them on the phone."

A silence fell at the other end of the line in which the sounds of scurrying about and violently flapping wings came through to us. Redding drummed angrily on his field desk.

"Are you there?"

"Yes, what do they say?"

"The first one says—ah—'Kilroy was here.' "

Redding grunted.

"This one says 'My Goodness, My Guinness.' " [2]

"That's enough," said Redding irritably. "How many of them got there?" The policeman estimated fifty or sixty.

"What shall I do with them now?"

"Anything you want," said Redding. "Kill 'em and eat 'em, they're no damned good to me."

After we hung up, the subject of carrier pigeons in the public-relations planning never came up again, except for laugh purposes, but it was not the last time the pigeon entered the picture.

Joan Ellis, the ex-WAAF, had gotten herself a job by this time with the Associated Press and was working in London as a "puncher" or teletype operator. If George's experimentation had failed to pay off, hers paid off too well. She was on her AP job only about four weeks when she participated in journalism's greatest wartime *faux pas*, even though she was far from new to the teletype or to the meaning of security and the penalties for its violation.

When she came to the AP, she was immediately engulfed in that steady, twenty-four-hour news mill, having entered its mainstream at the most trying time. The air was tense with invasion preparations. Press censors were on duty right in the AP bureau offices, and the heavy marking pencils and deleting razor blades of their craft were becoming more ruthless than ever. Everything possible was being done to preserve the elements of surprise which would give advantage to the Allies.

News agencies, on the other hand, work in the knowledge that some of their subscribers are either going on the air or to press every minute of every day, and there is a lively demand to beat the "opposition" which may be serving the same radio station or newspaper. A thirty-second lead on a hot breaking story can sometimes inspire crowing messages serviced back over the inbound printers, citing a job well done and recounting the play given the beat in key publications.

Under such pressures, it is quite natural for anyone in a position where crucial time can be lost to want to get his operational procedures down to fast, smooth, perfect timing. Joan Ellis, the teletype operator, whose fingers would have to fly, was in this category. At the same time, knowing this, it is understandable that an agency bureau chief is fearful of rehearsals, or "dry runs," and forbids them, espe-

[2] A catch line of the British firm making very popular ales and stouts, which conducts one of the best saturation advertising campaigns in England.

cially at crucial periods, because a teletype machine can be the equivalent of the "gun that wasn't loaded" in shooting down records for care and accuracy. On this point, there is still a difference of opinion.

The AP, whose London boss was Robert Bunnelle, contended that his employees were forbidden any run-throughs of sample copy on any pretext at any time. Joan is equally adamant to this day that she was "encouraged" to get up her teletype speed and reduce a D-Day "flash" down to split seconds in transmission.

In another part of London, it had fallen to me to handle a grisly job at 38 Edgerton Gardens, an unpretentious-looking block of flats. Every one of the fifty-eight invasion correspondents scheduled to go in on D-Day, or to follow up within the first week, filed in to go over a list of needed equipment, to be accurately listed as to correct address and telephone, and to be warned never to be out of reach from now on. Then, in a very final sense, I had to ask each man to write out his own obituary, so we would have it in our files, for use in case of necessity.

This last request never failed to get a reaction. Some of them took it in high good humor [3] to cover their real feelings, others straight, and some were shaken. Charles Wertenbaker, of *Time* and *Life*, chose to be facetious, listed each of his wives and their separate offspring, gave his own date of birth, and that was all. William Stoneman of the *Chicago Daily News* syndicate refused to do it unless his old friendly enemy competitor H. R. Knickerbocker,[4] the veteran International News Service circuit-rider who had gone to the *Chicago Sun,* turned in more than four pages on himself. Knickerbocker's piece ran four and half, whereupon Stoneman still balked. "Just say I was all the places Knick was," he said, "and usually filed first, too."

It remained for slightly built, wiry-haired Ernie Pyle to sober everyone, as it was well known that he lived with the premonition that he would not survive the war. He sat down at the office typewriter, wrote steadily for a few minutes listing the bare bones of his colorful life, then stopped and put his face in his hands. After a moment, he tapped out a last line to his obituary which spoke of his deep belief: ". . . and when it becomes necessary to release this information, please

[3] Bert Brandt, the Acme photographer, even gave "laying-out" instructions. "Part my lips in a smile," he said. "That's the way everyone would remember me." Then in afterthought: "If they ever find me."

[4] Knickerbocker was killed after the war in a plane crash in India.

inform my syndicate so it can break the news to my wife, rather than informing her direct."

There was no "if" for Ernie Pyle, only that gnawing "when."

General Eisenhower was known to be on the south coast in his own field headquarters, or "advance" location, a couple of miles from Southwick House where his invasion service chiefs were available to him—Field Marshal Montgomery with his three armies, Admiral Sir Bertram Ramsay with the Allied navies, and Air Chief Marshal Sir Trafford Leigh-Mallory, who controlled allied air power. Every indentation along the coastline was jammed with shipping of all kinds. Every wood hid masses of men, vehicles and stacks of equipment ready for transfer to Normandy. Paratroopers and glider-borne fighting men of the American Eighty-second and 101st Airborne Divisions and the British Sixth Airborne Division were charcoaling their faces at planeside. It was General Eisenhower and this weatherman, General Eisenhower and that weatherman, as the aircraft of the allies hammered away relentlessly and unceasingly at the cross-channel targets to isolate the battlefield. Decoy aerial forays were being persistently run into the Pas de Calais sector.

Major Bob Mack and his service cameramen had already asked Captain Frank Lillyman of Skaneateles, New York, to do a special parachute jump for them with a loaded camera strapped to him. The camera was focused on his face and mounted on a board to give it a steady surface. As he jumped out of the door, he pressed the button which set the camera whirring and caught his expression during the fall, the opening shock and the ride to the ground.

Lillyman, who bossed the pathfinders of the 101st Airborne Division, had the distinction and fearful assurance that he would be the first man to land in Normandy to light the way in for the paratrooper and glider skytrain set to join him about an hour later. Through this advance film, Lillyman, with the big black cigar in his teeth with which he always jumped, was certain to make all the newsreels. He did the jump as required, but he nearly invalidated the film. The board mount for the camera caused him to wrench his back and almost jeopardized his chances of leading the invasion.

Rear Admiral George P. Thomson, self-styled "blue-pencil admiral," was the chief press censor, by appointment of Prime Minister Churchill, to the British Ministry of Information, and he had actually been told on June 3 that the invasion was set for the following morning. The admiral set a few planned processes in motion without explanation, then was called in and told that General Eisenhower had put the landings off "for at least twenty-four hours." The press was watching Admiral Thomson closely, because his own movements might well serve as an alert. Knowing all this, his aides thought he was carrying his air of nonchalance a little far when he packed off home with announced intention of going straight to bed. Not wanting to give anything away, he chose not to cancel any of the arrangements, so the known top-flight censors took their chairs in critical places, and, of course, some of the ablest and most experienced showed up that night at the AP bureau.

By this time, one rumor was chasing another, reporters and couriers were dashing in and out, and phones rang constantly. Noting that the censor's first team was on hand, Joan Ellis was caught up in the fever and decided to do a little last-minute practice on an unconnected teletype machine. She began tapping the keys expertly, and this produced the usual perforated tape, which, when not fed into the transmitting device, fell harmlessly to the floor. If put into a live transmitter, however, it was in shape to move. Joan tore off the first strip, checked it, then threw it in the heaped-up office wastebasket. Again, with an attempt to improve her speed, she typed up the same "flash," checking her watch to see that she saved several seconds on the first time through. This was her critical moment, and she was about to become immortal in journalistic circles.

It was 10:38 P.M., British time, and one of the AP editors rushed up to her with a sheaf of copy paper which contained the latest monitored Russian communiqué from Radio Moscow. He told Joan to jam it through. Having just finished the second trial "flash," Joan was distracted by this unexpected urgency. She turned, forgetful of the tape, and began punching the keys.

"APL 91 PBC PSS ASD 12235 SOVIET MONITOR RUSSIAN COMMUNIQUE 'DURING JUNE 3RD NORTHWEST AND SOUTH OF . . .' "

The pseudo "flash" preceding the Soviet communiqué on the tape was then introduced into the transmitter and off it went to five continents. Desk men suddenly popped their eyes as they read: "URGENT PRESS ASSOCIATED NYK FLASH EISENHOWER'S HQ ANNOUNCES ALLIED LANDINGS IN FRANCE."

Tagging along came the Russian radio report.

Approximately half a minute went by during which the rest of the world did anything but stand still. Western Union offices in the United States, through which all these messages passed in transit to the New York office of AP, noted no AP log number, and no PBC (passed by censor) on the flash and questioned it. About the same time, veteran teletypist Irene "Chick" Henshall in the London AP office caught the error. She broke into all circuits with the familiar news-agency panic button transmission: "BUST THAT FLASH . . . BUST THAT FLASH . . . BUST EISENHOWER. . . ."

Barely six lines of the Soviet communiqué had moved when the mistake was being rectified. This meant the correction was easy for newspapers, reached long before the slip could have been jelled in type. But it was nowhere near fast enough for a full stop on radio, or at those places serviced by Western Union tickers such as ball-park press boxes, brokerage houses and horse parlors. Evidently every recipient at these points broke records doing something with it. At the Polo Grounds in New York, the Giants were embroiled with the Pittsburgh Pirates before a good Saturday crowd of nine thousand people. It was 4:39 P.M. when the public-address system, normally used only for statistics and line-ups, tolled forth word of the invasion. Buddy Kerr was just coming to bat for the Giants and the Pirates had gone ahead (they won, 7 to 6) by one run at the top of the tenth inning. The announcer, electrified with his news, called for the game to be halted for one minute, and for the 9,000 patrons to rise in silent prayer for the success of the Allies.

In Buenos Aires, mournful sirens wailed long and loud. In London, the furore coincided with BBC's documentary redoing the 1940 debacle of Dunkirk. Some people who heard about the "flash" tuned in BBC for "the word." When they came in on the Dunkirk story midway, they got the impression that the invasion was indeed on and that the Allies were losing it. BBC itself, however, was calm, for it did not receive the AP bloomer. This was lucky because the French underground was faithfully listening to BBC for the cue to rise in the rear of the Germans.

At Belmont Park in New York, the Belmont stakes were off at 4:40 P.M., and the track announcer had just sing-songed the name of "Pensive," with C. McCreary up, going into the lead at the far turn. WOR, the Mutual Broadcasting System's outlet in Gotham, dampered down the race and an announcer said: "The Allies have invaded France!" When Belmont Park came back on, the track caller was talking up "Bounding Home," leading in the stretch. Again the WOR announcer came in: "This is the greatest event in history, greater than the defeat of Napoleon." By the time Belmont came on again, the also-rans were being named and horse-parlor addicts were left in a state of suspended animation, literally chewing on their tickets. They had good reason because Jockey C. L. Smith, laying the whip on "Bounding Home," had come all the way in and paid $34.70 for each wagered $2.

Around the world, police and broadcasting stations, newspaper offices and government departments were being badgered for more news and clarification. On the scene in the London AP office, the impact hit Joan like a sledge. She folded up in complete collapse. The AP's night editor, soft-spoken and gentle Russ Lanstrom, treated her with great consideration, gave her a sedative, then sent her home.

Bob Bunnelle, the agency's London chief, was also president of the London-based foreign and war correspondents. Through him the gripes, real and fancied, were normally funneled. Now, with what amounted to a tremendous hole torn in the tight Allied security precautions charged to his own organization, Bunnelle found himself holding open house for stern-visaged intelligence officers who probed searchingly into his own operations. Joan was grilled by them too. Even the White House got into it. A "White House spokesman" said, "The President is in constant touch, but the announcement is untrue. . . . Such an announcement would normally come from the Office of War Information."

The degree of tension was indicated within AP by the "explanatory" statement published in some papers: "A mistake by an inexperienced operator caused the AP to move on its wires an erroneous flash announcing that General Eisenhower's headquarters has announced Allied landings in France. AP London printer delivered this urgent message which was immediately moved on all its wires. Less than two minutes later came the message to 'bust that flash' and a kill was sent out. The London bureau advised New York that an erroneous message had been sent by a new girl teleprinting a wholly unauthorized text on a teleprinter punching keyboard. Both editorial and traffic staffs were under strict instructions neither to prepare nor to practice with any such kind of copy against the possibility of precisely such an incident. The young operator who erred said she had been practicing on a disconnected machine and thought she had torn up the perforated tape which transmits the electric impulse on the teleprinter. However, she then started to transmit the first tape of the transmitter strip of tape containing the erroneous flash. . . ."

The journalese jargon lost most of the readers on the first turn, but the East Central No. 4 postal district of London was irked in another way. In this home of Fleet Street and its subsidiary publishing houses, it was being freely said that a big American agency should not so finger a new, twenty-three-year old employee, and a British one at that! Fleet street, center of British journalism, purpled at its collective collar and "unsporting" charges were being made in all the pubs. *World's Press News,* trade paper of the British fraternity, had a cable from its New York correspondent: "The explanation issued by the AP concerning the false invasion flash has not satisfied all newspapermen here. As for the general public, involved talk about unauthorized text on disconnected machines and punched tapes has just confused them. I was surprised to see the blame put on a 'young British girl' by a great American organization. One would have thought that this huge association would have taken the rap and the responsibility and would not issue the name and the nationality of this unfortunate girl operator. . . ."

Byron Price, a one-time AP man himself who had gone off to become the Director of the Office of Censorship in the U. S., was pulled into the ruckus. He was reported to have said: "There is nothing I can say, since the U. S. censorship had no part in it. This story came out of England in the regular channels over which the British censorship has control." Had he elected to spit on the foreleg of the throne in Buckingham Palace, he could hardly have picked a better way to rekindle the dying embers. There was an immediate rocket-burst of retaliatory statements from Britain reminding him that censorship in England was a joint American-British responsibility, both in manpower and instructions.

Fleet Street then heard that New York had advised London to "take necessary disciplinary action" against Joan, but the American press was rallying in her defense. The *Miami Daily News* cabled her: "Cheer up. All is forgiven. You didn't miss it by much." The *Frederick* (Maryland) *Press* was appreciative, too: "Joan Ellis should be thanked for putting us all on the alert." *New Orleans States,* with true southern gallantry, admonished: "Withhold anything against her. . . ." The European manager of International News Service, Joe

Kingsbury-Smith, stirred the pot a little with a wire of his own to Joan: "Can you call in and see me or telephone me to discuss the possibility of employment with us?"

Joan was afraid to stick her head out of the house, and when she did people pointed her out as the "one who shoved Eisenhower." Bunnelle called her to come back to work, and she replied, "I only want to crawl under a stone somewhere." "That makes us even," he said, "I've been thinking of jumping off the Thames bridge myself."

When it was necessary for me to call Capt. Harry Butcher the next day about some other matters, I asked him if General Eisenhower had heard of the furore. "I told him about it," said Harry, "and he sort of grunted. He has bigger worries."

Captain Frank Lillyman and his pathfinder paratroopers never knew about the slip until later. It might have been a great psychological blow for them to buck, knowing their small force could be falling into the laps of alerted German legions.

That evening, with Corporal Max O. Shepherd, of Nokesville, Virginia, my driver, we set out to promote some American food. We headed for the SHAEF advance camp in the woods nearby, and were stopped as we came to the entrance gate by two stern MP's, who asked for either SHAEF or Twenty-first Army Group credentials. While these were being looked over, two more MP's on motorcycles popped up on each side.

"Clear the gate!" This sharp order startled the two regulars, who held us by not returning the credentials.

"Clear the gate!"

As I looked back over my shoulder, a half dozen deep-breathing sedans were stalled behind us, so I grabbed the cards and told Shep to step on it. We dashed up the winding roadway, turned off at the first opportunity, and stood there as the cavalcade went by. It was Churchill and General Jan C. Smuts with General Charles de Gaulle, the latter coming to make a last-minute complaint, feeling by-passed and sensitive, while Churchill was there to make one more personal plea to land on the beaches. After the procession wound out of sight, we went on up to the mess tent, and found they were having frankfurters and sauerkraut. "Shep," with his mind still on the column of V.I.P.'s who had almost run up our back, remarked: "When we set out to steal a weinie, it sure causes a hell of a commotion."

About this time Joan Ellis received another comforting message from an American named Ben Jones in Pittsburgh, Pennsylvania, who cabled: "I have been a telegrapher for thirty years and I once saw an item like yours ahead of some telegrams. It said: 'I hate every G— D—— person in this office and I wish they were all dead.' This went out ahead of all the messages between Pittsburgh and Baltimore one day." But it was Joan's old landlady and friend, Mrs. Jones, of 14 Rochester Road, Camden Town, NW, in London, who put her whole affair in best perspective. When Joan was home, broken and nervous, she comforted her. "Don't you worry, luv," she said. "At least, you made 'em pray for the poor lads before they went—instead of after it was too late."

Down on the south coast, General Eisenhower left for Southwick House after the Prime Minister, crestfallen with his refusal from the Supreme Commander, and de Gaulle, still unhappy, had departed. As the Supreme Commander renewed his crucial session with the weathermen, checking the forecasts of one against the other, everyone was tense about the chances of severe tidal action hitting the early buildup. Without his knowledge, General Eisenhower had picked up a new ally in Major Lettau, the German high command's meteorologist. Major Lettau was telling Field Marshal Rommel and his staff that June 4 was the "magic date" for weather. "If the enemy does not invade by June 4," he informed his superiors, "bad weather moving in from the North Atlantic will make it impossible to conduct a seaborne operation for several days." As result of his forecast, many German division officers were on leave or on maneuvers well in the rear of the Normandy beaches.

Admiral Sir Bertram Ramsey said later that General Eisenhower [5] had used "some quaint American expression" to start the Allied fighting men on their crusade. "I believe," said the Admiral, "he used just three words—'Let her rip.' " [6]

[5] In Southwick House now there is a plaque in the room of General Eisenhower's ordeal, which reads: "In this room at 0415 (4:15 A.M.) on the 5th day of June, 1944, General Dwight D. Eisenhower, the Supreme Allied Commander, made the historic decision to launch the assault against the Continent of Europe on the 6th day of June despite uncertain weather conditions. Had this major decision not been made, the whole operation would have had to be postponed until the next suitable tidal period a fortnight later. Adverse weather conditions which then arose might well have altered the whole course of the war."

[6] Lt. Gen. Walter B. Smith, Eisenhower's chief of staff, later gave him credit for a more formal quote: "Well, we'll go."

D-Day and the Unexpected

The evening of June 5 a Negro truck company was leaving Bristol, headed out for the long drive to Southampton, and Tom Treanor of the *Los Angeles Times* was getting chummy with the Coast Guard crew with whom he was assigned to take a trip across the Channel and back. Treanor and the truck company were destined to meet in Normandy, where neither of them was supposed to be—but this was only one of many unexpected things which had been going on for hours, and would continue to happen.

Among the unusual developments was our issue of some eight gross lots of rubber contraceptives to press and Signal Corps photographers. Although there was a serious purpose for this, the explanations could scarcely be heard above the ribald roar. But history will always owe a debt to these contraceptives, at least, the ones used according to our directions. Each cameraman was advised to drop his completed film pack into one of these rubber receptacles and to close it tight with a knot or rubber band. This would provide the negatives with a rain-coat of sorts to ward off seepage or splashing salt water. This protec-tive idea had sprung as much from a cartoon by Bill Mauldin, the *Stars and Stripes* caricaturist of conflict, as from any other source. Mauldin had sent a spasm of mirth from one end of the ETO to the other when he sketched contraceptives over the muzzles of the rifles of his Willie and Joe. The rubber snood kept moisture from trickling down the barrels of their guns and rusting their innards. Bob Capa of *Life* told the cameramen the idea was worth trying, and Bob Landry urged it too. The past records of these two entitled their remarks to respect.

The photographic officer on General Bradley's Public Relations staff, Lt. Col. Bertram Kalisch, had already seen to the mounting and testing of dozens of small movie cameras on the tanks scheduled to hit the beaches and on the navy landing craft from which the infantrymen would scramble to shore. He triggered the tank cameras to roll with the first machine gun fire, while the landing-craft reels were set to turn as soon as the tillerman dropped the front end. There was no way to put cameramen ashore first, so all pictures of the first terrible moments of Normandy had to be of men's backs as they plunged into the fight.

Kalisch's job had been anything but easy, because there were many weird orders at the last minute and commanders were wary of these. One armored-combat boss, Lt. Col. Creighton Abrams, even had to sit still for the issue of instruments for a complete military band while he was waterproofing his equipment for combat loading. Nobody knew where the order originated. Somewhere on the floor of the Channel a salvage crew may some day stumble over a bass horn and wonder how it came there, and Abrams will be the first to tell them.

The movie-camera cause was in good hands with Kalisch, however, because he went serenely ahead and was a hard man to turn down, in fact, impossible to turn down. He literally beat down any armored or Navy objections with his wheedling rhetoric, usually with a firm hand on his subject's lapel. In the end, the movie cameras were bolted on and the handling crews briefed. Some of D-Day's pictures which will be dragged out again and again for decades in commemoration of June 6, 1944 are owed to the eight gross lots of waterproofing contraceptives and to Kalisch's long gamble with fixed-mount cameras.

Four of the original Clevedon contingent, by now referred to as "Redding's Rangers," were the spearhead of what was to grow as quickly as possible into the First U. S. Army's press camp. They were George Fuller, Bruce Fessenden, Sam Brightman, and Roy Wilder, lieutenants all. Since they had only verbal orders and were accompanied by their "first wave" war correspondents, the military invasion hands gave them a hard time, but they finally found spaces and places by pleading, promising and stretching the truth.

Brightman and Fuller were slated for V Corps, bound for Omaha Beach, while Fessenden and Wilder drew VII Corps whose destination was Utah Beach. The Brightman-Fuller entourage contained Don Whitehead, AP; John O'Reilly, *New York Herald Tribune;* Bert Brandt, an Acme photographer; John Thompson, the paratrooping pioneer of the *Chicago Tribune;* John McVane, NBC; Bob Capa, *Life;* Tommy Grandin, the Blue Networker, prepared as a paratrooper but switched by office edict to the seaborne assault; and an Australian named Harold Austin, *Sydney Morning Herald.* Charles Wertenbaker of *Life* and Ernie Pyle, the lucky ones, were already set for General Bradley's command ship, the *Augusta.*

The Wilder-Fessenden party included Larry LeSueur, CBS; Bob Dunnett, BBC; Bill Stoneman, *Chicago Daily News;* Clark Lee, INS; Henry Gorrell, UP; as well as Bob Landry, the *Life* photographer.

The first job of the lieutenants was to introduce their charges to the various commanders. The correspondents quickly picked it up from there by assurances to the units that their dispatches would make them famous. Wilder and Fessenden found upon arrival at Plymouth that VII Corps correspondents were not included in early landings, so they appealed to the chief of staff who carried it to Maj. Gen. J. Lawton Collins, the commander. General Collins authorized front-row seats and the correspondents were scattered through his shipping for the assault.

In his last briefing of the lieutenants, Colonel David Page, chief of the First Army's Publicity and Psychological Warfare section, instructed them that their primary duty was to see that copy and pictures got back to England. He said they would be judged for success only in terms of the chain established shore-to-shore, and that they would be damned by all hands if they were the missing links in this operation. Each twosome was equipped with a wire recorder, a generator, a jeep with radio transmitter installed, and a small hand-keyed Morse set. Their instructions told them of Navy courier speedboat plans. If all else failed, they were to make for the *Augusta* where some press messages might be sandwiched between military communications.

About the time the paratroopers were getting airborne, the Negro truck company, driving now with pinpoint lights, or "cat's eyes," was running into all sorts of maddening traffic snarls as it approached Southampton. None of the men in the convoy knew that D-Day was near or that they were approaching one of the big embarkation areas. They thought they were caught in one of the interminable night maneuvers. An MP suddenly appeared out of the darkness and the convoy was waved to the curb, where the whole string of trucks was to wait, kill engines and lights. The drive had been long and tiring, and this was a good chance to get some sleep. Nobody argued.

Captain Frank Lillyman was well out over the Channel by midnight, making the dog-leg turn which would bring him into the vicinity of Carentan at the foot of the Cotentin Peninsula. June's sixth day was only forty-two minutes old when his jumpboots thumped into the ground. With his detachment, he had less than an hour to get bearings in relation to the major drop zones, avoid capture, and set up the lighting devices for the hundreds of troop-carrying planes. This was one of the long hours of history. It was actually uneventful, though tense with the threat of disaster.

Over in Southampton, the MP came along the parked convoy and banged smartly on the windshields with his club, told the Negro drivers to get awake, start their engines, and go ahead as directed. They went down a line of MP's and were waved through. One of them said afterward he had a vague idea they had gone into a tunnel, but were stopped when only part way through, told to close up, bumper to bumper, turn off the engines and lights, and relax again.

The paratroopers were streaming out of England now toward the two flanks, and glider tugs were lined up, with men boarding after last-minute equipment checks. Along with the boys of Lancashire and Yorkshire was Leonard Mosley, a British correspondent from the Kemsley Newspapers who was writing for the combined press. He noted that his takeoff time was more than seven hours before the sea-borne elements were to scrape sand across the Channel. In a planeload of American jumpers of the 101st went Robert Reuben. Despite Fuller's sad test of pigeons, and alone among all the correspondents, Reuben had decided to gamble on carrier pigeons as part of his personal communications equipment. With the pigeons at his feet, Reuben looked back through his small porthole window as the planes [1] turned into the watery V between Brittany and Cotentin. As far as he could see in the upper darkness, the aerial armada was strung out behind him.

His lead contained that magic word, "Normandy" as the dateline, and all he had to do was touch down to make it good. The rest would

[1] There were 432 troop carrier planes in the 101st Airborne Division flight, carrying 6,600 paratroopers out of the total of 17,000 being dropped in Normandy that night.

be up to the pigeon to whose leg-band capsule his lead was consigned. Neither he nor his brave companions knew that this third-dimensional attack had been opposed with great eloquence for several days by none other than the Allied air forces commander, Air Chief Marshal Sir Trafford Leigh-Mallory. A courageous man himself, he had been arguing against the airborne plan with every statistical and logical resource he could muster. He was horrified that three divisions, with all their fine fighting men, might well be going to their collective deaths in what seemed to him a certain catastrophe. And while General Eisenhower's decision to go had been unflinching, a memorandum suggested that the airlift should be expected to have a 50 per cent loss and that its elements should be ready to be reconstituted on that basis on June 7. This was an extremely pessimistic view, but no one could be sure then. Had Reuben known about this, he would indeed have worried about making good that "Normandy" dateline. Touch down he might, but early guesstimates were that he might touch down dead.

Wright Bryan's strategic placement by NBC in one of the C-47 paratroop planes was a good stroke, in that he rode with Lt. Col. Bob Cole's battalion of the 502nd Infantry Regiment. Cole, from San Antonio, Texas, became one of the most courageous and spirited battle leaders, and Bryan's tense story revealed what men think about before commitment. He approached Private Robert C. Hillman, of Manchester, Conn., who held his hand possessively on his reserve parachute. "I know my parachute's okay," he said into Wright's recording mike, "because my mother checked it. She works for the Pioneer Parachute Company in our town, and her job is giving the final once-over to all the 'chutes they manufacture." Hillman's mother was unusual that night in that she had, in this way, given a final touch to her son's safety as he went into combat. Other mothers, if they sensed the impending danger, could only pray.

In the eleven minutes Bryan's plane was over France, he got the last minutes of drama before the unknown, and he took it back out with him, making it one of the early stories to get on the air. He could not say he was in Normandy, but 800 feet above it was sensational enough at that time.

William Walton of *Time* and Phil Bucknell of *Stars and Stripes* were with Colonel W. E. Ekman's 505th Parachute Infantry Regiment of the Eighty-second, the same escort Jack Thompson had had when he went into Sicily. Marshall Yarrow snuggled deep into his glider seat, with an Eighty-second landing-zone destination coming up. Yarrow communed with himself, trying to gain reassurance by repeating the "sales talk" which had gotten him there. "Be in early, that's what he said. Paratroopers will have the place in hand. Get the story. Pretty soon there'll be an airstrip. Transports will sit down to evacuate the wounded. All you have to do is hitch a ride back to England, and you can even get more story from the wounded en route. You'll have a big story, and be out with it." Yeah, thought Yarrow, that's what he said. Off in the distance, the sky yellowed and glowed with flashes of anti-aircraft fire. As they drew closer, the number and size of the bursts increased. Fingers of tracer bullets zipped up.

By 4 A.M. on June 6, all the airborne war correspondents had made the short distance from static or tow-line to the ground. Reuben released his first pigeon and it was so frightened it didn't know whether to fly low or high. Chances of its negotiating the hazards and the distance to England looked very slim.

Phil Bucknell came in swinging on his shroudlines and crashed hard to become the first war-correspondent casualty in Normandy. He netted a badly broken leg not far from Ste Mère. Église astride the Carentan-Cherbourg highway. One of the paratroopers propped him up against a tree, and Bucknell asked not to be left behind. The paratrooper was abrupt. "If I were you," he said in a rough whisper, "I'd just stay here real quiet-like. If you make any noise, you may attract someone you won't want to see." And he was gone.

Yarrow's glider nosed in at 2:35 A.M. and plopped into one of the many inundated areas back of Utah Beach. While his companions went bounding off, Yarrow chose to stay in a comforting ditch. The glider with Chester Wilmot came over the coast of France far to the east of Yarrow. It was right on course, identified by the river Orne and its canal nearby, but the pilot found it hard to distinguish between the landing lights and the anti-aircraft fire. He cut the tow, the glider seemed to brace itself in the air, then banked tightly to get in near the landmark church tower. Five posts, Rommel's "asparagus," were mowed down in the landing area, but nobody was hurt as the glider rolled to a stop at 3:32 A.M. By the timetable, Wilmot was two minutes late—probably the nearest on schedule of anyone that night!

Very much alone, Yarrow decided to set off in search of friends. He came upon Colonel Charles Shellhamer, a New Yorker and personnel officer of the Eighty-second, who had two riflemen and a medic with him. It was not a big task force, but it was something. Going along behind a stone fence, they came to a break. As the party started across, a sniper opened up. Yarrow was last in the file and when he made his dash for safety, his helmet fell off in dead center of the open space. Nothing was of less interest to him than the helmet at that moment and he was ready to go on, when he found that newly located friends can be converted by rigid military training into enemies—even mortal enemies. Shellhamer ordered him to go back and get the helmet. "I hated him," said Yarrow afterward, but the colonel stood there until the war correspondent dashed out to retrieve his steel chapeau. The German sniper was evidently so flabbergasted by Yarrow's foolhardiness that he forgot to shoot.

When Yarrow wrote his account, he led off with, "I left my face prints in Normandy. . . ."

Bill Walton wound up in an arboreal setting. "I landed in a pear tree—a rather good shock absorber," Bill wrote three days later, "but the trouble was I didn't filter on through to the ground. Instead, I dangled three feet above the ground unable to swing far enough to touch anything. My 'chute harness slipped up around my neck in a stranglehold covering the knife in my breast pocket. I was helpless, a perfect target for snipers, and I could hear some not far away. In a hoarse, frightened voice I kept whispering the password, hoping some-one would hear and help. From a nearby hedge, I heard voices. I hung still for a moment, breathless. Then I heard some more clearly. Never had a Middle Western accent sounded better. Quietly, Sergeant Auge, a fellow I knew, crept out of the hedge, tugged at the branches, and with his pigsticker cut my suspension cords. I fell like an overripe pear."

The sergeant was with two other paratroopers, and it was an hour and a half later before five more joined them. They met Brig. Gen. James M. Gavin, assistant division commander of the Eighty-second, and he was efficiently putting out his small force in a perimeter de-fense. The position was not only tough but untenable and their only escape route was through three quarters of a mile of swamp to a rail-way track. At 7:30 A.M. they all plunged chest-deep into the muddy water, followed by machine-gun fire, and most of them made the cross-ing safely. The rest died or drowned on the way, and the Germans must have been mystified by Walton, who carried his waterproofed typewriter above his head like a crown jewel. It was seventy-two hours later, only five of which had been snatched in fitful sleep, before Walton could sit down in a full-flowered apple orchard and write his story. "It would have been wonderful," he stated, "if you could ignore the shelling, the dirt, and the fatigue." *Time*'s editors used two columns for Walton's story for which he had suffered an unarmed anxiety such as few men will ever know. At that, he was more fortunate than others who were treed that night. Many had their throats cut, or their bellies sliced open, by German bayonets.

Lt. Col. Edward "Cannonball" Krause of the Third Battalion of the 505th, had charged into the center of Ste Mère Église, which was asleep. With his eager troops, he rousted the local Germans from their beds, the town and its roadway were secured, and safely into the battalion's books went a notation for having liberated the first French town in World War II.

The night was pitch black, and attacks and counterattacks were still going on. It was a couple of hours before the landing craft would hit the Normandy beaches. The Negro drivers of the truck company stirred slightly in their sleep, but did not completely awaken despite the slight rocking motion and a distant thunder of guns.

Captain Herman Wall, CO of the 165th Signal Photo Company, and his military cameramen went ashore with the first assault waves of infantrymen. Wall was carrying his camera. A fearfully loud explosion rocked him, and nearby, Peter Paris, a soldier correspondent of *Yank* magazine, was killed instantly—the first press beach fatality.[2] Wall's leg tingled strangely, and he looked down. He was standing on only one—the other having been shot off cleanly. Dropping to the ground, he managed a tourniquet, then passed out, still clutching his camera and its precious film. For nearly an hour, he lay on the beach under 88 fire before he recovered consciousness. He was hauled out to a British destroyer, refusing in his semi-delirium to give up the camera until he was assured that it and its film would be taken straight to the Southampton courier for the run to London. Then he let the surgeon amputate. His pictures, among the first from the beaches, will live forever, and a few days later, the *Stars and Stripes* paid tribute to his

---

[2] Paris, a sergeant from New York, and Corporal Joe Cunningham, of Brooklyn, were the two *Yank* magazine staffers who attended the Chilton-Foliat parachute school for training. Paris cracked his head the first jump, while Cunningham was injured on his third; neither qualified. Paris had been greatly relieved afterwards to be slated for the "safer" beach landing.

exploit. "A young Signal Corps officer . . . exemplifies the courage that has been shown by our troops. . . . His leg had been amputated and re-amputated. As a shattered arm was mended, and the Army surgeon prepared to give him another transfusion, he kept asking that his camera and film be brought to him [but] . . . he had accomplished his mission."

Early on June 6, Lieutenants Fuller and Brightman, with correspondents Grandin and Austin, found themselves just off the French coast opposite that sheer cliff face which bore the great misnomer of all code names, Easy Red Beach. During the voyage, Grandin and Austin had clacked away at their typewriters, and Grandin had also put together about thirty minutes of recording about the British marshaling yards and about the scenes and noises aboard, the forbidding shore ahead in the half light, the bombardment, and the anti-aircraft display while the air drop was going on. Brightman and Austin were the first to try for an actual assault, going aboard one of the Rhino ferries about 4 A.M. Grandin and Fuller were to follow in the next load, bringing the jeep and recording equipment. An LCT had crashed into the bow of their own craft, however, and the ramp stuck, trapping them for several hours. Other correspondents elsewhere in the flotilla were having better luck getting in, but Easy Red was not coming quickly under control.[3] The VII Corps correspondents were hitting various parts of Utah with elements of the Fourth Infantry Division, which was pouring along the causeways over the inundations back of the beaches.

The airborne divisions were rapidly securing inland areas when Fessenden awakened Wilder on their LCT. There was a stifling stillness over the craft, which was packed with a tank destroyer unit.

"Where are we?" asked Wilder, as if he had been dozing in a duck blind. "Are we sneakin' up on 'em?"

"We're back in England," Fessenden told him. "The LCT caught fire in the middle of the Channel, so the skipper brought us back out of the landing lineup."

Both of the lieutenants were glum about their prospects, and it was

[3] The *Chicago Tribune's* grounding of Jack Thompson, denying him a third airborne trip, was abrupt. The message said: "JUMP NO MORE. MCCORMICK." This made it possible for him to get space with the assault wave on the First Infantry Division's sixteenth regiment at Easy Red, the bloodiest part of bloody Omaha beach, H-hour plus sixty minutes. He kept wishing he had gone with the paratroopers.

D plus two before they were to make it in. When they got their radio set in, it didn't work. Hard luck also dogged Fuller and Grandin. They trundled their jeep off toward the beach, with everything lashed tightly to it, just as a new belt of fire swept from German guns. The jeep nosed over a few feet from shore and went into a chuckhole, completely out of sight. When the jeep went, so did all the recording equipment, generator, bedrolls, extra paper, pencils, everything.

Grandin and Fuller, doused to the skin and wearing gas-impregnated clothing, did not even look back, they ran straight ahead to the foot of the cliff. Panting and straining, they climbed the forbidding natural wall which had made the landing so costly. Just as they reached the top, a German artillery barrage began pasting the vicinity. They pitched themselves into the first protective hole in the ground. In keeping with their luck so far, it was no ordinary one. It was a slit trench which the Germans had been using as an open latrine and both of them fell headlong and face down. Shellbursts made it unwise to seek a change of environment.

For a full half hour, Fuller and Grandin shared the security of the latrine and grew more grateful for its shield with each passing minute. When the shelling was finally counter-batteried and the rocking earth settled back, the two of them crawled out, shed their impregnated gas-resistant outer garb and, lucky for once, much of their smell with it.

Not more than a hundred yards away, they found other correspondents huddled in a hole with Brightman. He was cursing like a record with a broken wall. "We've had nothing but trouble here," said Sam. "Portable radio won't work. We lost the antenna. We've strung some wire on this fence and are trying that now." The operator pounded the key, pressed the earphones, listened in vain. He removed the headset after a few more tries and passed his hand wearily over his eyes. "No good," he said. "Can't even raise static."

"Damn!" said Brightman. All the while, the correspondents pattered away at their keyboards and their stories, with accompanying carbons, were being turned out in stacks. This was D-Day and the world was waiting.

Nothing seemed to have worked as planned. The Navy's courier boat, when Fuller searched the beach, was nowhere to be found. Brightman decided to try the *Augusta,* and grabbed up a handful of carbons which he hoped to be able to move between the military traffic running off General Bradley's ship. Fuller took up another set and tramped back to the beach with Grandin. They planned to promote a Navy ride back across the Channel. O'Reilly and Thompson both urged them on, even though their first quest was unsuccessful, and an additional load of copy and negatives was given to them. The rules about staying in France once landed were very strict, but Fuller believed the only out was a hand-carry. Since Grandin's apparatus for recording was at the bottom of the sea, Fuller decided to take Grandin with him to a point where he could talk his impressions into an open mike. On the beach they encountered cold and wet Richard Stokes of the *St. Louis Post Dispatch* and Tom Treanor of the *Los Angeles Times*. Both were Coast Guard correspondents, neither of whom was supposed to have come onto the beach. Stokes was ready to go with anybody, but Treanor had gone over and back once, was again in France, and was going to stay there. Fuller left Treanor, and with Stokes and Grandin and a big pouch of copy, the trio stepped onto a boatload of wounded which shoved off for England.

About this time, the Negro convoy drivers were yelled suddenly awake, and all hell yawned as the water splashed about them in bomb attack. The ramp went down and a running MP came up to the lead truck.

"Give me your tag and get going," he ordered.

"Boss, I ain't got no tag," said the first driver.

"You can't get off here without a tag," the MP snapped.

"That's fine," said the boy, his eyes on the littered, unfriendly beach ahead. "I don't want off heah."

The MP waved them on, and the dangers of going to sleep at the wheel were never more graphically demonstrated than for this surprised truck company that first Normandy day. There was a rumpus about it later, and about Tom Treanor, too. Both had messed up the regulations and the rules.

The parent unit in England claimed that some commander had deliberately "stolen" the truck unit to bolster its own transport deficiencies. Meantime, Tom Treanor, who himself was there "illegally," got the story of the "illegal" truck company—one of the few humorous developments in what had been a weary, costly, valorous day.

"When this Army makes a mistake," one of the Negro drivers told Treanor, "it do make a big one, that's for sure."

Back in Portsmouth, the second wave of correspondents was making its feelings known in profane terms as it was held at Cranberry

House up the Winchester Road. The newsmen were demanding to be lifted across the Channel, professing not to need anything in the way of services, food or transport. Just to get there. All along the south coast, we had been watching the ports for the first Normandy stories ever since Colonel R. Ernest Dupuy, acting SHAEF Public Relations Officer, had told a hundred war correspondents in London at 9:31 A.M. on June 6, "This is it." A major named MacArthur was the communications liaison with the Twenty-first Army Group on press matters. A little more than twelve hours after Colonel Dupuy had put out the first SHAEF communiqué, MacArthur came rushing over to the headquarters tent where Redding and I were waiting. "We finally have a story in," he said, "one from Normandy. It came in at Dover."

"Dover?"

"Yeah," he said, "and funny thing, too, it came by pigeon, and it's for Reuters. Signed by a man named Reuben." [4]

It didn't strike us that this was awfully unusual. After all, that was the way Paul Julius Reuter started his news service.

---

[4] This was not Reuben's only "first." When he worked his way back to the beach with his main story, he asked one of the LCT skippers to get him out to Maj. Gen. J. Lawton Collins' command ship. From Reuben, Collins had the first reports of the 101st Airborne Division drop and learned that its commander, Maj. Gen. Maxwell D. Taylor, was alive. Reuben dictated his report to Collins' stenographer for an hour, after which the general asked if he had had any sleep. Reuben shook his head wearily, whereupon Collins said, "Give him a batch of ham and eggs, and let him have my bunk."

... TAKE 7 ────────────────

Bradley Moves In

As Fuller landed in England and promoted a jeep for the wild ride to deliver Grandin to Broadcasting House in London, the south coast came to life and the teletypes clicked furiously with queries from London bureaus and networks: "Reuter's wants any news Marshall Yarrow who went by glider." "CBS hears unconfirmed Larry LeSueur dead on beach." "Life asks tracer rumor Bob Capa shot near Carentan." "AP believes Roger Greene hurt. Inform pls." "Larry Rue unheard from Jack Thompson. Wants check."

Editors were worrying out the story of the beaches and their manpower engaged in picking it up. Lucky when they had drawn pole positions in the race to the invasion site, they now gnawed their nails for fear the story had engulfed their men.

Time had just edged over in to D plus four when Fuller deposited Grandin and dropped his pouch of beach-produced copy at the Ministry of Information in London where the censors went to work on it. At 3 A.M., Grandin went on the mike and was piped through to the U. S. He had enough material to provide talk for several days, so decided on consultation with New York not to go back himself. Hal Peters, another Blue Network correspondent, would replace him, returning with Fuller.

Fuller got ready to turn around fast. He rounded up a portable radio set and gathered PX supplies and toiletries to replace what had been lost when the jeep sank. Just as he was leaving London with Hal Peters, W. W. "Bill" Chaplin of NBC hopped aboard to relieve John

McVane, who had broken his leg shortly after arrival in Normandy.

Fuller was to be the hard-luck man the entire first week. Back in Normandy on D plus five, he found the correspondents had promoted bedding and clothing, making all his PX purchases in that line unnecessary. His colleague, Lieutenant Jack Hanssen, had come in on D plus four with a four-vehicle convoy including a BBC recording unit, the commercial Press Wireless radio link, and an Army transmitter which had power enough to convey voice to London, where it could be spliced into the already existing trans-Atlantic routes to New York. With the call-letters, JESQ—Jig Easy Sugar Queen—and mothered by Lieutenant Jim Rugg, the transmitter was the hope of the radio commentator. All this made the small replacement set Fuller had brought with him look puny. Only the candy and cigarettes he brought along were smile-producers.

Colonel David Page, his First Army chief, did not smile, however. Fuller had violated the strict rule about going off the beach and back to England, had encouraged and actually assisted war correspondents to go with him. Page threatened poor Fuller with court-martial, even though his last instructions were that failure to get copy out would be the most inexcusable fault. Nothing came of this, because the correspondents were about to go to General Bradley and tell him the whole story. They were ready, they said, to assure the commander that it had been only the resourcefulness of Fuller and his physical scramble back to London that had helped get the story of the beaches to the world.

At Cranberry House where the "second wave" was holed up, one of the most vociferous in appealing for lift across the Channel was James McGlincy of UP. Yet a combination of circumstances provided him with one of the earliest stories from the beach, and it was well played by all UP clients on D plus one. Bert Brandt, the Acme photographer, brought back his own pictures to England and was interviewed by his Scripps-Howard colleague, McGlincy.

It was a neat corporate one-two and got McGlincy a better story than would have been the case on the other side.

Phil Bucknell of *Stars and Stripes* brought his story of the parachute drop near Ste Mère Église out the hard way, by making the crossing with casualties—as one of them, in fact—and his terrifier ran in the London edition on June 14.

By the end of the first week, the flow of copy had been established, though in a somewhat rickety manner, and the courier boat was running with sufficient regularity. There were seven jeeps and three three-quarter-ton trucks with drivers available to the First Army Press Camp, which occupied an old château near Colombières. Looking every minute more like a pigsty, it had been the residence of the German Gestapo chieftain of the district, who had whip hand over the Russian labor force, and his room upstairs had a grim note on the door warning anyone who opened it that a gun was aimed at it and was set to blast the intruder. The French woman who had taken care of the place during his regime stayed on, but she could not keep up with her new tenants who managed the premises like a looted railroad car. When rations were brought in, usually the ten-in-one variety, they were dropped in the middle of the floor and everyone clawed through them to get the tidbits he fancied most. This meant there was an ever-growing litter of hard wafer cakes, toilet paper and empty cans. Also the correspondents foraged among the Normandy farms, and butter having been a rare commodity in England, they proceeded to buy butter and bring it to the château. Not trusting their bunkmates, they stored this new-found treasure in their bedrolls at night. In the morning they would find themselves in greasy pools which added a new rancid quality to an already overripe atmosphere. Everyone had dysentery as a legacy from this.

The aggravation of limited manpower, which dated from the 1943 planning, now came home to roost. Lieutenant Charlie Rhodes went to Colonel Page with the suggestion that he be allowed to round up some French men and women to help the meager mess force and make up for the housekeeping deficiencies of the correspondents, who were drowning their sensibilities nightly by gulping down Calvados. This strange, almost flammable liquid was made from juicing the bitter apples of Normandy and turning the cider into a sort of microbe housing project. Page approved, and some inroads on the Augean stable began to be made right away. Utensils were washed and the place swept out, but as long as the correspondents stayed there, it was never home sweet home.

On June 12 the "magic carpet" war-correspondent tactic blossomed and a fist fight was narrowly averted between Clark Lee of INS and Henry Gorrell of UP. The "magic carpet" is a wink at the truth of a dateline, saying in effect that the writer has been somewhere he hasn't been. On this occasion, with the invasion seven days old, Maj. Gen.

Maxwell D. Taylor's 101st Airborne Division encircled Carentan and his paratroopers opened the main road between Omaha and Utah beaches, linking both and making a beachhead forty-two miles wide.

Lieutenant Roy Wilder was on hand when Clark Lee, a big, gutty guy, came back with a rush from the Carentan fighting, having accompanied the troopers into the town. Just as he was preparing to go to his typewriter to write an eyewitness account, he was told that Henry Gorrell had already filed an exhaustive piece on it. Lee spied Gorrell, clean, shaven and unfatigued, and expressed his doubts that Gorrell had been in Carentan. Gorrell had gotten his story by interviewing the wounded as they were being evacuated, an "eyewitnesser" of sorts, once removed. Lee doubled his fists, but was persuaded not to commit mayhem.

By the evening of that same day, there was a total of sixteen Allied divisions in France. The original 176,000 men and 20,000 vehicles allocated to the assault phase June 6–7 had been increased to 326,000 men and 54,000 vehicles, while 104,000 tons of stores had been landed to back them up. The Eighty-second and Ninth divisions were jamming straight across Cotentin. In fact, Maj. Gen. J. Lawton Collins' VII Corps was the only one which could now move because of General Bradley's decision to let the V and XIX Corps protect the build-up. With the British tied up around Caen, movement, which always makes a better story than stalemate, drew the correspondents over into Cotentin. General Collins was delighted with this turn of events, and when he came upon Acme photographer Andy Lopez and AP lenser Harry Harris, he asked who they were. They told him.

"Do you know what sector you're in?" asked the general, buoyantly.

"Sure," said Harris, "First Army."

"First Army, hell," said the general, darkening. "This is the Seventh Corps!" Pride in unit grows with success in the field, and VII Corps was having it all at the moment.

During the day, D plus six, the heavy truck which Lieutenant Jack Hanssen had rolled over the Normandy sands was in place, bigger news to the newspapermen than anything since the invasion. The Diesel engine kicked over on D plus seven and Press Wireless was ready to move copy. Albert McGeagh, with his crew of seven, had no idea of bridging the Atlantic with the set, because it was powered with only 400 watts. PREWI's call letters had been carefully picked— SWIF (somewhere in France)—and to the amazement of the technical handlers and the fervent hallelujahs of the typewriter fraternity, it was found to be coming in crisp and clear at the receiver located at Baldwin, Long Island, N. Y. Press Wireless thus made it possible to have a story ground out in France, go through censorship, and be in the hands of an editor in New York in twenty minutes. Hank Gorrell filed the first story to be transmitted.

In a trailer haven at Montgomery's Twenty-first Army Group, I was the American member of his communiqué staff, which included a former Oxford don, Major Christopher D'Ollier Gowan, and a peacetime Canadian lawyer, Major A. Smith-MacDonald.[1] Twice daily we put together a terse document which was the official record of the commander's battle day. We also listed items which could be discussed "on the record" and some warnings about items which were not passable by the censor. It was there that I learned that casualties and a man's color can turn highly political. Hitherto, the problems from my viewpoint had been limited to defending American terms from the British, who, from Monty on down, said they included slang which could not be understood in the British Empire.[2] It did no good for me to countercharge that Monty's oft-used briefing term that he was going to "hit them for six," a cricket equivalent of a home run, would bewilder America.

From the very first planning, it was emphasized that casualties in Normandy were never to be a communiqué item. This subject was to be the exclusive province of Number 10 Downing Street in London and the White House in the U. S. Casualties had been a rankling subject with General Bradley, brought to a peak in early spring, 1944, when one columnist contended the Normandy losses would run as high as 90 per cent. A statement like this, when a soldier is taking stock, can have a severe effect on morale, quite naturally, and it was one of the reasons Bradley had encouraged high-ranking visits before D-Day to reassure the men.

[1] The First Canadian Army's PRO was Colonel Richard "Dick" Malone, who was with Monty's P&PW detachment at Southwick before going into Normandy. An experienced newspaperman, he is now the editor of the *Winnipeg Free Press.*

[2] It was well known that Monty used the BBC nine-o'clock news as an alarm-clock in reverse, always tuning it in just before retiring. This brought many accusations from time to time in press camps later that he cued his major releases to be sure to hit BBC's top news show. Whether this was true or not, Brigadier Neville was always conscious of 9 P.M. and how the doings of the day were handled.

Two things happened on June 16. The Army transmitter was finally in, and could move voice signal to London for passage on to New York, and General Bradley chose to talk about the great *Verbot*—casualties. In a meeting with the correspondents, he told them there had been 15,883 U. S. casualties, of whom 3,283 were dead.[3] The Americans, he said, had taken 8,300 prisoners in the same period. The Chief Press Censor of First Army was Major Robert M. Hughes of Greer, South Carolina, and a veteran of a lot of D-Days by this time, including the ones in North Africa, Salerno, and Anzio, as well as Normandy. None was more respected or better liked by the war correspondents. He operated about as close to the bone of security as a man could, even though he had never been around the press before. A rangy, tall and normally slow-moving fellow, he was really fast about passing this story. He knew exactly what he was doing, and he did it deliberately. Press Wireless was busily beaming copy to the U. S., and voice could now be transmitted on Jig Easy Sugar Queen. The story went out, and Bradley, who had always claimed Normandy would be a sharp battle, no more, no less, was vindicated in his judgment.

Montgomery's chief press censor, Lt. Col. Pat Saunders, who had an office in the same trailer with me, was livid, and there was pandemonium in his circles, with recommendations of severe treatment for the First Army censor. Although Bradley never gave his opinion, of course, correspondents were inclined to think it more proper that the man who had the actual responsibility for the soldiery give an accounting rather than statesmen. The debate roared up and down London, but SHAEF's censors did not become too excited.

Color came into the picture when Lt. Col. Herb Bregstein, the photographic officer with ETOUSA back in London, got on the phone to me with an urgent request for the First Army photo officer, Lt. Charles Rhodes.

"We've got to have some pictures quick of Negroes in Normandy," he said. Rhodes quickly came up with some clear ones of Negro troops unloading beach shipping. When these were sent up to London, Bregstein was back on the phone in great agitation. "These are exactly what I *don't* want," he said. "No labor stuff, please, I want fightin' stuff." His tone changed as if he were cupping his hands for secrecy at

[3] There were 55,000 seaborne troops involved in D-Day, of whom 4,649 were casualties, about one-third dead, the rest wounded and missing.

the mouthpiece. "The White House is on the War Department's neck on this one, so let's have it fast."

When Rhodes was again on the line, he said he would have to go hunting again, that he had been roving the front, but had seen nothing to meet this specification. He called back later and said he had studied the build-up chart at First Army and found that a Field Artillery Group was coming in, consisting of three battalions, two of which were manned by Negro troops. Arrangements were then made for two Negro correspondents to come over on a special trip, Rudolph Dunbar of the Associated Negro Press and Ollie Stewart of the Afro-American newspapers. They were to visit the Field Artillery Group in a support position for a jump-off near La Haye du Puits, and it was immediately obvious to Rhodes, their custodial officer and guide, that they were after no war story. The white colonel who commanded the group received them graciously and talked freely to them about his unit. Their questions sought to justify claims in the Negro press that the Negro was held back because of his race. The colonel never angered, never evaded. Finally, he broke it off by telling them he was a soldier commanding a unit which had no special niches based on color and that he had been with the outfit since it was formed in the U. S. "I have never talked race," he said, "and I do not intend to now when we are about to go into a fight. No matter who falls here he will bleed red, and it will be American blood." He turned and left them, and they left Normandy.

The waist of Cotentin was completely girdled by now, and the Ninth, Fourth and Seventy-ninth Infantry Divisions turned north toward Cherbourg. Before D-Day, Ernie Pyle was being syndicated by Scripps-Howard to nearly 300 newspapers with a combined circulation of 11,500,000 and by the time the battle moved close to Cherbourg he had passed the 300 mark. Homer Thomas, a junk dealer back in his home town of Dana, Indiana, described as well as anyone the secret of Ernie's success: "He comes as near writin' like a man talkin' as anybody I've ever read." While such fame as Ernie's is rewarding, it was dangerous, too. During a shelling in the last stages of the Cherbourg resistance, the stuff was dropping too closely and the newshawks decided to run for better cover. Everybody made it to the new point but Ernie, and his mates began to worry. Eventually, he showed up. "Some guys jumped out of their tank back there," he said somewhat shamefacedly. "They recognized me from my pictures. I had to stop and talk a little." To the little guy from Dana, Indiana, even though shellfire terrified him, it was no excuse not to be neighborly.

The remnants of five German divisions had stumbled back on Cherbourg, one of Hitler's "hold at all costs" points. The correspondents swung in close behind the troops, and when at last the fight was on for the town Lieutenant Jack Hanssen, with W. W. Chaplin of NBC and Larry LeSueur of CBS, made one of those wild runs down the last incline into Cherbourg to get past the city-limits sign which would qualify them for use of the dateline "IN CHERBOURG." "At the time," said Hanssen, "a minute was so interminable, it made you feel like an old resident to have been there that long."

With the pressures becoming too great, General Karl Wilhelm von Schlieben walked out of the Cherbourg garrison to give up, but he would not order his men to stop fighting, which was a baffler for General Collins. Meantime, Lieutenant Rhodes was having trouble with General Collins' intelligence officer in trying to get both correspondent and Signal Corps photographers in position to photograph the capitulation. For every *"Nein!"* of von Schlieben to complete surrender demands, the intelligence officer had a "No" for Charlie's entreaties. When the intelligence officer was momentarily off guard, Charlie slipped his leash and went directly to General Collins, telling him of his plight and how this was a historic moment which should not go by unrecorded. "Lieutenant," said General Collins, firmly, "you have a point." And the cameramen surged in.

The Psychological Warfare brethren were busy outside Cherbourg raining persuasion on von Schlieben's men. Taking advantage of the rapidly dwindling food supply, the surrender leaflets had a last line which said, ". . . and don't forget your mess kit!"

On June 26, twenty days after the landing, Cherbourg fell. General Bradley had once said it would take "ten days if we're lucky, thirty days if we are not." By any standards, it was not bad. JESQ was moved up to the Hotel Atlantique and, having been out of action only five and a half hours for the transfer of location, was now in handy position for the correspondents. JESQ stayed four days, until the crossroads town of St. Lô began to beckon in the south, drawing it and the correspondents away from Cherbourg, the dead city and the dead story.

In the press camp, there was a prophetic incident when UP's James McGlincy, armed with a souvenir German pistol and fortified with

Calvados, came into the sleeping tent one night, waving the gun and looking for "the enemy." Rightly assuming the gun to be loaded, his "friends" promptly rolled out of their sacks and disappeared to safer territory until one of their number disarmed him. It was a laughable incident, but a finger pointing to the future. It was probably occasioned by anti-aircraft shooting down a German pilot, who parachuted in to find about a thousand correspondents, soldiers, officers, French people and neighborhood dogs around the spot where he was falling. When he hit the ground, he found himself surrounded by a curious welcoming committee. As he was hustled off, Lieutenant Hanssen paraphrased a previous Churchillism. "Never in history," he said, "were so few captured by so many."

Back in England, the question of command of the ground forces was coming to a fine international boil, and Montgomery was being run by his fellow nationalists for that office. This put the Twenty-first Army Group P&PW office in a front seat, and, as I was to find, a warm front seat. It was July when a meeting was held in our trailer one day in which the statement was made that the Third U. S. Army correspondents and press camp were going to be held indefinitely in England, and would not be allowed to go to the Continent, although it was known that Third Army's headquarters was on the way in.

"Are you sure?" I asked.

"Sure," said Saunders.

My feeling was that check should be made with either Colonel F. V. Fitzgerald at First U. S. Army Group in London, or Colonel Dupuy, at SHAEF, so a call was put in to Fitzgerald after the meeting. He was told of the statement. "There must be some mistake," he said, "They're moving to the south of England now." When I hung up the phone, it did not occur to me that anything was out of line, but a deathly stillness fell over Gowan and MacDonald. Then they left the trailer, reappearing almost immediately with Saunders. The air turned a bright blue as he called me insubordinate for challenging a position taken by the Twenty-first Army Group. He said I would get a stiff rebuke, adding firmly: *"Monty* is now and will continue to be the ground commander in Normandy, and *he* will say when forces or press or anything else will move."

There was no alternative but to call Colonel Fitzgerald again. "I've outlived my usefulness here," I told him.

"Pile in your jeep and come to London," he said. "We're about to move anyway, and you should be back here."

My Eighty-third communiqué chore for Twenty-first Army Group was my last, and "Shep" and I checked out.

Lt. Col. Kent Hunter, fresh from Washington on assignment as public relations officer for General Patton, gathered his staff at Brockheath, about twenty miles from Southampton. It included that steady old hand, Major Bill Drake, witty and amusing Captain Ernie Deane, the ex-horse trainer Capt. Percy "Jack" Widmer, and Lieutenants Don Witte and Jim Campbell.[4]

Two days later, in spite of the assertions of Lt. Col. Pat Saunders, they landed in France and went into their camp near Nehou where they were to spend three weeks.

In the strategy to keep the German Fifteenth Army tied up in the Pas de Calais area, a dummy Army Group had been assembled in London and given a skeleton staff. Lt. Gen. Leslie J. McNair was brought on from the U. S. as if to command it. The long-time chief of the Army Ground Forces, he was no friend of the Army public-relations officer nor did he ever see any reason for his existence. He had insisted that no spaces be allocated in the division structure for this kind of military utilization, and it was because of him that all division commanders had to resort to the dodge of having special assistants or men on detached service up from regiments who did this work. He could not have failed to know that he was thus being end-runned, but he did not change the manning tables. And yet he had once asked me why the press didn't "pay more attention to the poor, old, foot-slogging infantryman."

As General McNair came on from the U. S., word was received that

4. On July 5 their first correspondents joined them, including Ed Ball, AP, Jack Belden, Time & Life; John Brockhurst, newsreel pool; A Schrod, Time & Life artist; H.J. Broderick, photo pool; Norman Clark, London News Chronicle; F.J. Cooper, BBC; Kenneth Crawford, Newsweek; Bob Cromie, Chicago Tribune; E.A. Currivan, N.Y.Times; E.H. Dodd, AP artist; Joe Driscoll, N.Y. Herald-Tribune; Robin Duff, BBC; Pierre Gosset, Agence France Presse; S.S. Gotlieb, photo pool; Tom Grandin, NBC Blue Network; Donald Grant, LOOK; Phillip Grune, London Evening Standard; Tome Hoge, Stars&Stripes; Pierre J. Huss, INS; Saul Levitt, YANK; Robert Littrell, Reader's Digest; R.A. Loveland, Cleveland Plain-Dealer; Paul Manning, McNaught Syndicate; S.J. Maynes, Reuters; B.J. McQuaid, Chicago Daily News; John Mecklin, Chicago Sun; Bob Miller, UP; Ralph Morse, LIFE & photo pool; Tom Priestley, newsreel pool; W.J. Prince, London Times; William Reusswig, King Features; Cornelius J. Ryan, London Daily Telegraph; Bill Shadell, CBS; Duke Shoop, Kansas City Star; R.L. Stokes, St. Louis Post-Dispatch; Tom Treanor, Los Angeles Times; J.H. Wellard, Chicago Times; P. Whitney, San Francisco Chronicle; R.T. Wingert, Stars&Stripes cartoonist; W.H. Wolf, Newspaper Enterprise Assn.; Ira Wolfert, North American Newspaper Alliance; Ernest Hemingway, Colliers, and D.E. MacKenzie, New York Daily News.

the campaign Ernie Pyle had carried on for months had finally borne fruit in two ways. One was that all soldiers would be allowed to wear stripes on their sleeves for overseas service, and the other was that combat infantrymen would get ten dollars a month extra pay. Congress did him the honor of nicknaming it the "Ernie Pyle Bill."

The Twenty-ninth Infantry Division was fighting doggedly toward the stepping-off point for First Army's planned operation COBRA, the attack on the St. Lô web of roadways. In a sudden action, unheralded by either artillery or small-arms fire, Major Thomas Howie, formerly an instructor at Staunton Military Academy and up from Abbeville, South Carolina, sent his Third Battalion of the 116th Infantry Regiment knifing into Martinville. The combination of bayonet and ground fog surprised the Germans and carried the battalion far enough to link up with the other regimental elements by 6 A.M. on July 17. The Second Battalion, now on Howie's flank, was already under orders to push on toward St. Lô, but it was evident that the unit was not sufficiently strong, so Howie's enterprising Third was given the task. He called in his company commanders to his CP to give them the attack order. Howie, much admired by officers and men alike, concluded this short meeting with the statement: "See you in St. Lô!" Almost at once, German mortar fire came crashing in on the CP, and Howie was killed. His executive officer, Captain William H. Puntenney, took charge, but the attack did not get off. This was the beginning of one of the war's most moving stories, a rumor of it catching up with Hal Boyle of AP, who then followed it to its end.

Maj. Gen. Charles H. Gerhardt, the Twenty-ninth's commander, called for Brig. Gen. Norman D. "Dutch" Cota, of Bryn Mawr, Pennsylvania, to set up Task Force C (C for Cota) on the evening of the day Howie was killed. Its mission was the capture of St. Lô. Lieutenant Charles Rhodes had two jeeploads of correspondents headed for St. Lô. His party included Bruce Grant, *Chicago Times;* Hal Denny, *New York Times;* Andy Lopez, Acme Newspictures; Clark Lee, INS; and H. R. Knickerbocker, *Chicago Sun.* Cota briefed them under a tree, and answered all their questions in detail. He was a popular figure with the press.

Cota's task force was to make its thrust in midafternoon of July 18 after other elements of the Twenty-ninth had gone over the rim of the dish of ground in which St. Lô nestled. Leading the march was a flail tank, equipped in front with a revolving metal drum to which chains were attached to detonate any mines in the road. To get into St. Lô, it was necessary to follow a road which ran over some high ground, then dipped sharply downhill, taking a hairpin turn to lose altitude.

The engineers and the flail tank moved slowly, trying to get the way completely clear so vehicles could make a smart run for it. It was late in the day when Cota's courier came up on a motorcycle and told Rhodes if the correspondents wanted to come on that "the way was clear." And what a liar he was!

The jeeps peeled out of the column, charged downhill, changed direction and went past the St. Lô distillery, then up a small incline. The ever-fearsome 88's began to explode, and German machine gunners who had traversed carefully and coolly now let go at them. The jeeps went off the road, and the correspondents spilled out. Grant dived for what had been a machine-gun emplacement and Lopez right after him. They found themselves in the hole with a companion, the late German gunner, who was dead. Both Grant and Lopez presented ostrich-like pictures, their buttocks up as they were draped over the gun barrel, their heads down in the hole.

While the Germans were having their fun, they gave away their own positions in going for unremunerative targets, and the press thus became beneficial to the rest of the drive because well-directed tank and artillery fire showered in on the Germans and silenced them. Once more getting into the jeeps, the correspondents went on into the heart of the town. Cota, with his arm shot through and in a bandage, was directing the battle as if totally unscratched. Andy Lopez bounded out of the jeep and began shooting pictures as fast as he could. There was still great doubt that the American forces then in St. Lô could remain since so many Germans still held out on the high ground. This made it very precarious for the correspondents. After hurried consultation with Cota, they all bolted back up the hill. But Cota's task force stayed in St. Lô, even though German gun positions surrounding them made it a rough residence.

Boyle picked up new clues of his story on Major Howie, whose casual remark, "See you in St. Lô," had crystallized a determination among his battalion to see the prophecy come true. General Gerhardt ordered that Major Howie's body would go in. As the armor of the 747th Tank Battalion, part of Cota's task force, swept into St. Lô early on the nineteenth, an ambulance was in the column bearing the lifeless body of Major Howie. Even in death, he moved with the men who revered him. The strange procession, like a medieval pageant, finally halted in front of a church, one wall of which had been reduced to a pile of rubble. As the crescendo of shot and shell produced concussion and casualties about them, the men tenderly removed the body of Major Howie from the ambulance, carried him on their shoulders into the church, and placed him high on the debris before the battered altar. There Major Howie made good his prediction in part. He could not "see" the others, but he was on view when they came into St. Lô.[5]

After dinner on the twentieth of July, General Bradley went to Colombières to talk to the correspondents about COBRA, a combination of carpet bombing from the air and a surge of several divisions through St. Lô. He did not tell them that his old FUSAG headquarters was being left behind in Bryanston Square and that it was beginning to appear in France redesignated as Twelfth Army Group as a part of the deception campaign in which General McNair figured.

Five days later heavy bombers made the ears hum and the carpet was laid as tons of explosives rained on the crossroads town and its environs. So great was the concussion that wind whipped soldiers' uniforms a mile away, and when some of the Germans came out of it, their heads were pulled back as if under a checkrein and they were gasping for breath. American soldiers caught in the "shorts," or by them, were in like condition, or paralyzed in such a way that they could only lie on the ground and groan.

Lt. Rhodes was again grouped with war correspondents who were to go through St. Lô in the wake of the Second Armored Division, by arrangement with the Second's public-relations officer, Captain Harry Volk, of Cleveland, Ohio. As the bombs fell, some of them not far away, Bede Irvin, an AP photographer from Des Moines, Iowa, waited too long. Just as he finished a yell of warning, a fragment caught him. Bede, dead before he hit the ground, became a statistic—the eighteenth correspondent casualty of the war.

When the bombing was over, a Thirtieth Infantry Division rifleman came along with a helmet swinging on his arm. It had three stars on it. "Fella wearin' it," explained the soldier, "was killed down there with one of them shorts." He gave it to Charlie, who turned it upside down and looked at the name on the band. Printed there was "Leslie J.

[5] Nobody could know it then, but when St. Lô rebuilt its church after the war, the parishioners felt its premises would be incomplete without a bronze relief plaque to Major Howie, who came all the way from Abbeville, S.C., making some of the pilgrimage in death and providing a part of the inspiration for their liberation.

McNair." "He may never have cared for the likes of me," said Charlie softly, "but maybe he won't mind if I bring in his helmet." [6]

Costly as St. Lô was, it took a while for even the top commanders to realize how catastrophic for future German hopes in France it had been. Over in London, Wes Gallagher broke his AP story that General Bradley was now being elevated from his First Army job to that of an Army Group commander, co-equal with Monty in the charted command, but much more powerful in actual strength. That strength was now pouring in all directions through the hole in the German front. Part of it was roaring off toward Paris, and another element swung down, sharp right, around the sentry-like spire of Mont St. Michel, into Brittany.

The British press erupted. Monty had been "demoted," his celebrated and deserved war record "tarnished," and the editorial fun threatened the nest of Allied solidarity which General Eisenhower had guarded so zealously. General Bradley did not feel it his place to explain that this was a planned development from the beginning, but never forgave Monty for not silencing his adherents at home.

General Bradley was somewhat apprehensive about Lt. Gen. George S. Patton, too, who was chafing at the bit. Patton had been briefed by Bradley on the St. Lô breakout, because he would have to come into it shortly afterward for the exploitation phase. Suddenly, Bradley learned that the Third Army press had been briefed also, and he jumped Patton over the phone about it. Patton insisted he had only told his staff, that his public-relations officer, Lt. Col. Kent Hunter, must have leaked it. "I'll can him," Patton told General Bradley, "just as soon as I can get another guy." My sympathies went out to Kent Hunter. Who could tell what would happen next with a general who would even help run a mimeograph machine if it could make a point for him?

Third Army's correspondents were rudely introduced to the war, even as Fuller and Grandin had been in Normandy. After their run through the bottleneck at Avranches, their tents were pitched for the night along a hedgerow adjacent to a sunken road. Their latrine was dug for them approximately seventy-five yards away, but the

---

[6] It occurred to nobody, least of all Charlie Rhodes, that the public-relations officer frowned on by McNair not only took his helmet, but was helping to get and bring out one more story of the "poor, old, foot-slogging infantryman" in one of his finest fights.

naturally lazy scribes used the roadside ditch. About 2 A.M., a combination of Field Marshal Von Kluge's artillery and a Luftwaffe plane zeroed in on an ammunition dump a mile away and the night was rocked with a tremendous explosion. The correspondents, tearing from their tents, hit the roadside ditch!

The next day Lee McCardell of the *Baltimore Sun* asked Major Bill Drake for transportation back to England. He based his request on having seen a Navy two-and-a-half striper, who was a part of the Third Army press censorship detachment, spading a deep personal foxhole. "When I see the Navy digging holes in the ground," said McCardell, "all is lost!"

By this time, I had been given the job of covering the General Bradley trailer, nucleus of the nervous system of American forces in France. This meant I had on call Captain Jack M. Warner, a still cameraman, son of the Warner Brothers executive producer, and Lt. Benny Wetzler, a former Hollywood movie cameraman who had been with Frank Buck in the *Bring 'em Back Alive* days. General Bradley's aides, Majors Chet Hansen and Lew Bridge, kept me posted on important pending arrivals which would provide bulletins for the press and shots for the newsreel and photo pool.

On August 7, the day of a visit from Prime Minister Winston Churchill, we walked up the pathway toward the Command Post, and noticed that a major general was lounging against the hood of a jeep a few yards from the aides' lean-to. It was only ten minutes before Churchill was to arrive, and it always seemed to me that a small portion of that time revealed more of Bradley the man and leader than was ever displayed otherwise in so short a period. Bradley came to the door of the trailer, looked out, spoke to us pleasantly enough, then his eyes fell on the lounging general. A cold flicker crossed his countenance.

"Chet," he said sharply to Major Hansen, "get me General Eisenhower on the phone."

Chet picked up the receiver. "Shellburst," he said, waited a moment. "General Bradley is calling General Eisenhower."

When the Supreme Commander was on, General Bradley came right to the point. "Ike," he said, "this is Brad. I'm calling about that general I sent you the papers on. I want him out of here—now!" There was a moment's silence on Bradley's end. "I want him sent home, and never put in a command position again." There was a longer silence this time, then Bradley came in ruthlessly, "No, Ike. I want him sent home, busted back to a colonel, and to have nothing whatever to do with training. He has shown that he can't lead men, and if he can't lead 'em, he can't train 'em." He hung up with an agreement that the general would be moved immediately.

In less than half a minute, he reappeared in the door, and the man who had been so firm on the phone now had great compassion in his face. In his hand he held a letter, which he gave to me. "Read it very carefully," he said.

It was a penciled note, on cheap ruled paper, and its salutation said: "Lt. Gen. Omar N. Bradley, Commanding Officer, Company G, 26th Infantry Regiment." It went on in the clumsy scrawl of a woman whose whole life had crashed in with the receipt of a "The War Department regrets" telegram. She poured out to the commander of the U. S. invasion forces the story of her only son. Her husband had died ten years before. This son had been with the First Infantry Division in Africa, Sicily, and had hit Omaha Beach in the first elements ashore. Lots of other boys, she said, "have been in the Army longer than mine," but had never left the States.

"After all my boy went through, he's dead now," she wrote, "and I can't sleep very good at night. I keep wondering—wondering if he's buried good. Could you perhaps tell me?" And then she went on to apologize for bothering him when he was "so busy and all." It was the kind of written word which clutched the throat, and he watched for its effect. When I finished, he tapped the letter with his finger.

"As soon as you can," he said, "I want you to take a photographer back to Omaha Beach, and find this boy's grave. Take a picture of it and bring it to me so I can send this lady a letter and the picture. It's a poor replacement for all she has lost, but it may make her rest easier."

In total time out of Bradley's day, and with the head of the British Empire coming up the row of poplars which lined the drive, he had taken five minutes to fire and demote a major general who could not lead the men entrusted to him, and had taken steps to ease the sorrow of a now childless widow he would probably never see.

That day we got some very good pictures of Winston Churchill, but the ones which really counted were those taken by a Signal Corps corporal late in the afternoon. With the help of the graves registration unit, we found the cemetery cross with the dog tag so new on it that it was still untarnished. Three French youngsters with their arms loaded with flowers were nearby, so we asked them to come over and put some of them on this mound of earth. As they did it, we took the picture. True, it was one of those pictures which was never published, even though it came clear and sharp out of the developer that night. This picture had more than the composition and clarity they teach in the photography schools. This one, with General Bradley's accompanying letter, had that abstract quality—peace of mind.

. . . TAKE 8 ——————————————

The Penetration of Paris

Concern about the way the invasion story was being handled in the press showed itself in high places after the breakout of the First Army at St. Lô and the free-wheeling, headlong pursuit of German units began. There were twenty-one U. S. divisions in France at this time, placing a strain on First Army and leading to a shift of strength into Patton's Third Army, which was treating the world to the strange spectacle of literally tearing itself apart and accomplishing its mission while so doing. Divisions of the VIII Corps swung around into Brittany and went off slam-bang in the direction of the coastal ports of Brest, Lorient and St. Nazaire to the south and west, while the rest of that highly mobile force plunged off to the east and north toward Paris.

Failure of the British-Canadian wing of the Allied command to snap the lock on Field Marshal von Kluge's counterattacking Germans at Falaise led to press comparisons at the expense of British valor. Editorials were highly critical of the British inability to close the gap and destroy the enemy. Winston Churchill abhorred this trend especially, and asked Monty for an accounting. He also asked for some information about future plans for British arms, in case he had to stand up before his public with a defense. But the situation was moving fast, and changing fast.

Lt. Gen. Lewis H. Brereton, the Ninth Air Force commander, was still smarting from the bombing "shorts" at St. Lô which had killed many Americans, and he with Maj. Gen. Elwood R. "Pete" Quesada, the flamboyant forty-year-old airman who bossed IX Tactical Air Command in support of First Army, swung into the press spotlight in a series of incidents. The Air Forces, the tactical Ninth and the strategic Eighth, had had the war to themselves for months, providing the only action communiqués prior to D-Day. Tons of bombs had been rained on the Ruhr, Hamm, Schweinfurt, Regensburg, Bremen, Berlin and other German areas. Locomotives had been strafed and blown up, bridges blasted, and there was a daily score of victories and losses in the air-to-air conflicts. But the minute the GI began to close with the Germans the focus of interest had swung sharply to ground level, the hedgerows and the foxholes, where battle was intensely personal.

General Brereton's headquarters appeared not to understand, or to be willing to accept, this change as a logical development of this new phase of the war. They were considerably jolted when the 14,600 sorties flown by the Ninth Air Force and the RAF on D-Day attracted less press interest for its bombing and strafing than for its carrier elements which delivered the paratroopers. Each of the services had a quota of spaces for war correspondents, and this ominous Ninth Air Force attitude became noticeable to four men it had taken to France— Lee McCardell, *Baltimore Sun;* Stanley Frank, *New York Post;* Gordon Gammack, *Des Moines Register-Tribune;* and an artist named John Groth, *Parade.*

Gammack had sought Air Force accreditation when he came to the United Kingdom from Italy, where Major Jay Vessels had been a fabulous and favorite Public Relations Officer with the Thirteenth Air Support Command. Gammack talked to Ninth Air Force PRO Colonel Robert Parham and his assistant, Major George Kirksey, a one-time UP sportswriter. He explained that he could not devote all his time to writing about Air Force activities, because his paper expected him to cover Iowa boys, no matter where or in what activity he found them. At the time the four correspondents were taken to Normandy on D plus eighteen he was led to believe that this was all right. Most of their coverage was filed through Press Wireless at First Army, or on First Army teleprinter circuits to London, but their housing and care devolved upon Advance Headquarters, Ninth Air Force. They were dependent on Ninth Air Force Advance for their transportation, too.

The Ninth Air Force public-relations establishment, dating from the London days, had been an odd one. In March, 1944, it had received, on its request, five officers—Ben Wright, Tom Yutzy, Arnold Leo, Haynes Thompson and Bill Pratt. It also had a workhorse in Lt. Col. Chet Shore. The Ninth's public relations at headquarters was somewhat of a closed corporation, pivoting on Colonel Bob Parham and Major George Kirksey, the latter, among other things, busy at the typewriter over a story of General Brereton's transient career. Parham assigned Major Don Dresdon as the public-relations officer for Quesada, who disliked the craft generally. With Dresdon, Haynes Thompson was slated to handle Air Force D-Day requirements, while Wright, with two other men, was sent to Middle Wallop in England with a tactical reconnaissance group because most of the operational information would come back there first in the developed pictures of photo flights.

Three correspondents came to visit this group on the eve of D-Day —Duke Shoop, *Kansas City Star;* Gordon Gammack; and Lee Carson, INS. Lee Carson, a charmer of the first order, wangled herself into a flight by batting her eyelashes at the group commander and got one of the good D-Day aerial stories. It was played heavily because of early lack of communications to get the ground or surface story out. Gammack was not particularly happy about this sojourn with the Ninth, since the pilots at that base flew only photo ships.

Dresdon and Thompson arrived early in Normandy, according to plan, and Wright came with the tactical reconnaissance outfit when it moved over to Voilly on July 10, some ten miles from Ninth's press camp at Grand Campe. Wright made a nightly trip by jeep to Grand Campe to post the daily operational story which was being relayed to London.

As America printed less and less of the Air Force story, while the ground-gaining infantryman took up more columns of space, Parham and his men became somewhat truculent, and were evidently showing pressure from the Ninth Air Force staff.

From high places came charges that the correspondents were neglecting one of the big stories of the war—the co-operation of fighter-bombers with the fast-moving tank columns. The correspondents were somewhat taken aback, since they had not only been aware of the story, but also had written it copiously. Finally, Gammack was told flatly that he was "skating on thin ice." It was made clear to Gammack,

Groth, Frank and McCardell that, to be sponsored by the Ninth Air Force, it was no longer enough to use a general date line "At an Air Base in Normandy." There was even an attempt to fix the percentage of copy which must be about the Air Force.

At the time of the aerial carpet-bombing of St. Lô, both Parham and Kirksey came to the Continent to watch the show, and it was while waiting for the first wave of the aircraft to appear that Major Wright was told by them that "the dissatisfaction of the correspondents" with Dresdon and Thompson was so great they were being taken back to London. Wright was delegated to take over. Subsequent events made Wright believe that the wheels were already turning to have the correspondents' accreditations withdrawn by Ninth. Before they were granted transportation each day the correspondents were already being asked what kind of a story they were going on. If the story had an Air Force angle, a jeep was available; if not, no jeep. Wright's appointment late in July was followed ten days later by a red-line message to him which said that the four correspondents were to be returned to England.

Maj. Gen. Ralph Royce, commanding Ninth Air Force Advance in France, posted much bigger news than this, which was that Brereton was going off the top of Ninth to Allied Airborne Army and that he was being replaced by suave and handsome Lt. Gen. Hoyt S. Vandenberg. Wright called in the correspondents, read them the red-line message and, with an eye on the recent leadership change of the Ninth, proposed that they take some Ninth Air Force jeeps and get going to other press camps, since Paris was about to fall. McCardell took the offer, ran for a jeep and, with the driver, headed east. Gammack came to see me at Twelfth Army Group, and Wright arrived with Frank to file a story about the same time. Word of the banishment leaked out, and the cause was taken up strongly by Fred Graham of the *New York Times* and Jack Tait of the *New York Herald Tribune*. Even as Gammack was talking to me of some way to beat the rap, a feedback from the U. S. of the Graham-Tait story was sudden and violent because of the high readership of their papers in Washington. Their theme, much like that of Stanley Frank of the *Post,* had been that the Ninth Air Force was publicity-mad. Across the Channel in London, a SHAEF Public Relations Division spokesman promptly declared that "if public-relations personnel are guilty of ballyhooing and trying to dictate to correspondents, there will be some changes." There were.

Colonel Robert Parham, who had faithfully carried out the edicts of the Ninth Air Force staff during the Brereton regime, was relieved and replaced by Colonel William P. Nuckols, until then Air Force spokesman in the SHAEF Public Relations Division. He was the elder statesman of Air Force public relations even then, having had the longest consistent time in the career field. Meantime, within a few days of the closure on Paris, when Lt. Gen. Vandenberg came to the headquarters near Laval, Wright was called in to explain a petition Vandenberg had received from the correspondents' corps protesting the recent ban. The petition said Wright "was clean" and he recommended that Vandenberg see the press, particularly Graham and Tait, along with the four upon whom the ban had been placed. As a result, one of Vandenberg's first acts as commander of the Ninth was to apologize to the press, call off the order for banishment to Britain, and tell the correspondents they could "go anywhere and cover anything you damn please." For this opener, and his continued interest, Vandenberg went through the rest of the war with a reputation as a public-relations-minded commander, a view subscribed to in full by the correspondents' corps.

While the Ninth Air Force was having its troubles, General Bradley, after watching the festive spirits of some of his own high-ranking men, threw a censor clamp on his generals. He ruled that all quotes of general officers in the Twelfth Army Group would have to be seen by him personally before any copy could be passed for publication, thereby making himself the highest ranking military censor of all time. He had an aversion to "talking generals," but no one believed his order would last long. It was felt that the number of stories he would have to read would be so great that, with the press of other duties, he would wear down. But he did not wear down, no matter how long his day might be otherwise, and he was often seen reading the various pieces during late hours in his trailer after he had finished his nightly game of "catch" with his aide, Major Lewis Bridge. He had his own brand of protection, too, and when he sensed the boys were really testing him, he slowed the pace of his reading. This became known around the press camps, and correspondents began to see to it that they used no quotes by generals. There was one general who did not figure in all this. The censors all had an unsigned memorandum which said that General Bradley was the final arbiter on quotations of generals "except in the case of General Patton, whose remarks, thoughts, opinions and most casual statements shall be stricken from all copy without further reference."

The beacon up ahead was Paris, and Twelfth Army Group was contemplating it from a location outside Laval. Redding sat in his trailer and worked on plans for the entry of the press into the French capital. The major considerations were communications and roofs over the heads of the entourage. The fever was running close to the top of the thermometer with the heady prospect of liberating that city of four million, which meant to so many, so many things. War correspondents, censors and public-relations staff were slated for the Scribe Hotel, about halfway between the famous landmarks of the Madeleine church and the Café de la Paix. Kalisch was making notes on the dispositions of Signal Corps photographers to insure that the freed capital would be lensed from every angle. He marked recognizable backdrops of Paris which must be posted for sure—the Invalides, the Eiffel Tower, the Arc de Triomphe, the Place de la Concorde, the Champs-Élysées, Notre Dame. Around these places, action, emotion, picture opportunities were sure to swirl.

Communications were apt to be as impossible as during the early hours of D-Day, so Redding sent me to Colonel Nuckols and Brig. Gen. Richard Nugent, deputy chief of staff for Operations of Ninth Air Force, to arrange, if possible, for a Thunderbolt on a base near Paris to make courier flights to London. This was to augment a Hurricane, which the RAF was to fly each evening from Bayeux. Bayeux was a long way from Paris and valuable hours could be saved if there were a closer takeoff point. They co-operatively marked off a unit scheduled to go into Chartres, and teletyped the commander to be prepared to scratch one aircraft from all operations for this mission.

A somber note swept over the correspondents' group when word came that Bill Stringer, the genial American who worked for Reuters, had been killed in German crossfire as he was jumping it a little, trying to get to Paris through Versailles ahead of everyone. The press had attended only a few days before the funeral of Tom Treanor, of the *Los Angeles Times,* after his jeep had been crushed by a fast-moving tank near Le Mans. These losses had the effect of painting the stakes for all the war correspondents, should they let too much valor swamp discretion.

On August 21, Third Army, goaded by Patton, had scampered over the Seine on both sides of Paris.[1] General Bradley was not at all sure the Germans were going to declare Paris an "open city." He believed the contrary, that they would try a fight for it since it was a supply cache, and the hub of a communications network.

A group of the newspapermen came to General Bradley and asked him to do everything possible to save the city from artillery destruction. He assured them that "not a cobblestone in its streets" would be harmed. One of the reporters wanted to know which division would be assigned to take the city, and the general ducked that one by saying he thought the correspondents were in sufficient numbers to do it themselves. He was actually hoping he could by-pass the city, with its hungry, its problems, and the slow-up it would inevitably cause. The "task force" of public-relations facilities, correspondents, censors, communications, and administrative accessories were jammed in the direction of Rambouillet, a few miles south and west of Paris on the N–10 highway.

The first marker of the "task force" trail was Corporal Gene Ford, a Second Armored Division PRO photographer, who was trying to hook on even though his division was not very close. He was standing ruefully at the roadside, holding a half-filled bottle of cognac and leaning against a destroyed German tank. "I've just met a war correspondent," he said. "A real big one—Ernest Hemingway." According to Ford, a long way from his native Los Angeles and its bewitching types of hospitality, he and Hemingway had come upon the tank at about the same time. As they looked cautiously down into it, they saw not only two dead Germans inside it, but also between the driver's legs three full bottles of cognac. Ford and his companion reached simultaneously, and Hemingway came up expertly with two of the bottles. Back outside the tank, the suggestion was made that they have a drink. Ford opened his bottle, and both of them belted it strongly, whereupon Hemingway, with his two flagons intact, hopped in his jeep announcing he had to get on to Rambouillet. "You might say," said Ford, "I have just put on a party."

Reports of the Free French uprising in Paris, and details of the

[1] As the Seventh Armored swept along the outskirts of Paris, one tank crew was surprised to be hallooed in English by a striking French girl in a pair of patched American levis. Tomboyishly leaning over a fence, Danielle Darrieux, the film star, was wearing what she had left of her prewar American "wardrobe."

street fighting, were being brought back to Rambouillet in driblets by regular French couriers. Hemingway, after arriving as just one of many noncombatant word merchants, started to gain luster in a military sense. He looked like an officer to the French informants, who began the day by addressing him as "Capitaine," progressed to "le Colonel" after a time, and finally wound up with "Mon Général." Hemingway, not at all feazed by this recognition of his commanding mien, issued orders whenever the situation seemed to call for them. The French couriers were paying no attention to General Leclerc—who was only the leader of the liberating force.

General Bradley, who shortly before had been so hopeful about not having to send a force into Paris, could no longer hold out. As both a grand gesture and an expedient, he decided to send the Second French Armored Division of Major General Jacques Leclerc straight into Paris via the Porte d'Orléans. On August 24, at 10 P.M., one of the Second French Armored's captains hauled up in front of the Hôtel de Ville in Paris with a detachment of light tanks and some accompanying infantry and the liberation of Paris was on. The French Armored division took great proprietary interest in this entry, partly because these Frenchmen had not been home since the fall of France in 1940 and craved the liberation with the fierce appetite of the starving. The "task force" spent the night in Longjumeau, bogged in tightly by the French main column. When morning came, Kalisch wanted to get in with his cameramen. Redding saw a real difficulty coming up, in that everybody would soon bolt on his own and find his way, come what may, into the center of Paris. He feared exposing the precious communications facilities to unknown risks so left them outside Paris with the censors, instructing all that they would have to send dispatches back out for filing.

A French captain loomed as yet another impediment and made a roadblock of himself near the Porte d'Orléans, stopping the correspondents edging up to the gate of Paris. He said firmly that "only the French would enter Paris." Kalisch protested that "Eisenhower's instructions" were that everyone should enter. Ernie Pyle, to whom news had just come that his daily column was in 310 newspapers, and that Western Newspaper Union, which serviced ten thousand weeklies, had signed with his editor, Lee Miller, for an additional once-weekly piece, was hot to try for an end run. He had an audience of more than 16,000,000 waiting to hear from him. "I can't see the liberation of

Paris," he grumped, "from five miles out." The captain, seeing the fury of the press mounting, began to take water. He said he would let the public-relations people go. Kalisch balked and said they were all official. "Official" was the magic word. If they were "official" they could pass, so the dam was broken.

Charles Wertenbaker and Bob Capa, of *Life* and *Time,* told their driver, Private Hubert Stickland, of Norfolk, Virginia, to swing in behind a passing armored car. It turned out to be an excellent choice, since it was General Leclerc's own. In this grandstand seat, they passed through the Porte d'Orléans at 9:40 A.M., August 25, and claimed afterward to have been first in a Paris *arrondissement.* The column was breaking into many splinters, though, and it would be hard to tell whose entry was first. Larry LeSueur charged off to the heart of this city he knew so well. He was pulled at, kissed and fussed over by dozens of mademoiselles, estimating a hundred happy kisses for each 100 meters of progress. The emotional and joyous mood of all French men and women along the ways moved hard-boiled men to tears, and they too felt the ecstasy of release.

Bill Hearst, heir apparent of the publishing mogul, and his jeep-mate, Fred Mackenzie, of the *Buffalo Evening News,* had hardly gotten well started into Paris when some French soldiery evicted them, and they had to come back in again with the Leclerc column.

Bill Walton, *Time's* Normandy paratrooper, had a much more pleasurable entry into Paris than he had had into France. He was lost in the best possible way and found himself detoured into exuberant Montmartre. One of the district belles clambered on the hood of his jeep which was inching its way through the throngs. The girl started off a thousand-volt cancan, with skirt held appropriately high and without regard to her lack of lingerie. As she approached that furious finale when the cancan dancer reaches hand to instep and stretches one leg out and overhead while spinning round and round on the other foot before that crashing fall into a split, Walton's driver, wide-eyed, became concerned. "If she tips your way," he said, "there goes your helmet."

When General Bradley had selected the Second French Armored Division to make the run into Paris, his chief of staff, Maj. Gen. Leven C. Allen, made one prophetic statement. "They may go into Paris from the south," he said, "but they'll be hard to get out on the north." How right he was! Tank drivers coming to a remembered intersection would cut out of their column and make a beeline, either for home or for the home of an old girl friend. The mademoiselles climbed up on the tanks and went down through the turrets. Many a tank either went amok or ground to a stop at the curb.

The liberation radio station in Paris, Radio Nationale de France, tempted several correspondents who liked the idea of getting a story fast and were not concerned with Redding's edict about clearing with the censors at the Porte d'Orléans. James McGlincy of UP prevailed upon the management of Radio Nationale to let him broadcast to the world, and incidentally United Press, his story of the liberation. McGlincy read his piece hopefully into the microphone—hopefully in the sense that he did not know whether the UP monitor was tuned to the frequency. His gamble paid off, however, and it was picked up. Larry LeSueur, with lipstick all over his face and his war correspondent uniform shredded of buttons and cloth for souvenirs, was second up to the mike and delivered his reactions for CBS. After them came Paul Manning of Mutual, Seaghan John Maynes of Reuters and Robin Duff and Howard Marshall, both of BBC. This wink at military censorship brought an immediate and hot-tempered reaction from Redding who had by this time arrived at the Scribe Hotel where the coups by the three British and three American correspondents were the talk and envy of other reporters. All six were suspended for thirty days, which meant they could not file during that time.

The reaction was hardly what Redding expected, because the six now had a perfect excuse not to do any work, and had thirty days and nights to live it up in Paris, a city so generously inclined at the moment that even the 1,000-franc rate for a night's wrestle plus breakfast had been rescinded. If the six had been admired for their enterprise, they were now envied as their colleagues tumbled to the magnitude of the wages of sin. Redding's answer to this was to ban them from the Continent for the period of their suspension.

There was another violation of the rules on which an order had been out for two weeks. Lee Carson, INS, had "jumped ship" on a Normandy press visit, and the SHAEF Public Relations Division wanted her "apprehended and returned to London." She showed up in the lobby of the Scribe, where Major Frank Mayborn of Temple, Texas, was just checking in from London as the first SHAEF PRD representative.

When Lee was handed over to the major, he changed swiftly from the Angel of Wrath to the Southern gentleman at the sight of the attractive and elusive reporter. "How nice to see you. It's good to see that you got here safely." And that ended that summary punishment for infraction of rules!

That very morning the manager of the Scribe had said good-by to the last of his German "guests" and he was now busy getting used to English. The girls in the streets were having the same trouble, and had not yet learned that the right answer was "Yes." Invariably they came back with a smiling, *"Ja wohl, ja wohl."*

There was an air-raid warning one of the first two nights in Paris, and A. J. Leibling, of the *New Yorker,* rushed to warn a comrade who was chambered with a doxy in one of those rooms with multimirrored walls and ceilings. The friend had been modest and doused the lights. When Leibling came dashing in, he snapped on the light switch, whereupon, he said, he was confronted with the sight of a thousand nakednesses of which his friend's "were uppermost."

Charles Collingwood of CBS, with Bill Walton, had decided that the Montmartre was the place to regroup before going forward. In fact, they couldn't have been less interested in going forward and wound up the first phase of their penetration into Paris in the Royal Fromentin Hotel. The Royal Fromentin fairly rocked with welcome the rest of the day and night. When Walton awoke in the morning, it was to waves of cheering. Opening an eye at a time, he saw an unbelievable vision, a figure clad from head to foot in a red silk dressing gown waving and bowing in the grand manner. He arose, stumbled closer, and it was Collingwood, acknowledging the applause of a newly acquired "fan club" in the street below, a wild assembly of street-walkers and other Montmartre habitués. Collingwood addressed the girls in the street for more than an hour.

Redding had instructed Kalisch to get back out to Porte d'Orléans and stay out there with the communications, which were to be brought in later because street fighting was still active. Kalisch, however, delivered the convoy safely on August 26, and Lieutenant Jim Rugg set up the military radio link, JESQ, in the Tuileries gardens, ready for business.

The big story on everyone's mind that day was the entry into Paris of General Charles de Gaulle, symbol of the resistance, the tall leader of government-in-exile and the big question mark in France's political future. Kalisch, with his remarkable nose for news, felt that de Gaulle would come under the gun somewhere along the route when he made the grand entry, and he busily made plans to have a Signal Corps camera at every likely point. He felt it would have to be a place of high drama, not just anywhere along the way, because drama would appeal to a French assassin or a German propagandist. He chose three main points and placed his bets on them: the Arc de Triomphe, the Hôtel de Ville, and the Cathedral of Notre Dame. Of these, he favored the Arc de Triomphe, because if de Gaulle were to fall there, his entry and his long resistance would be rendered hollow indeed. But if Kalisch was wrong as to the place, he was not wrong as to certainty of an incident.

BBC's Robert Reid was set up with a recorder at Notre Dame. De Gaulle, carrying destiny on his shoulders, was met at the entrance by Dominican Father Raymond-Leopold Bruckberger, chaplain-general of the French resistance who had fired a machine-pistol himself in the Paris liberation.

As they entered, Reid began his word picture. "The general is being presented to the people," he said, caught in the moving spectacle. "He is being received. . ." A splattering of shots rang out, and piercing screams found their way into Reid's recording.

"They have opened fire . . ." he said, quite unnecessarily, but words often fail a man when he doesn't know what's going to happen next, and whether it will be to him. There were sounds of disconnection as people trampled over the wire from his microphone. The connection was renewed, and Reid went on with his story. De Gaulle, as if he had not heard, marched on up toward the waiting Cardinal Souhard and Monsignor Beaussart. *Te Deum* was being played on the same organ through whose pipes the shots had been fired.

Kalisch, omnipresent with his Signal Corps photographers, stood behind a pillar and noted with satisfaction that the cameras were catching every step of de Gaulle's walk into the hearts of the French people. If there had been doubt about his acceptance before that moment, he had now swept Paris off its feet—and his fearless demonstration won them to a man, for the time being anyway.

General de Gaulle had appointed his friend, General Pierre Koenig, military governor of Paris, and when Kalisch came in from Notre Dame, he found that Redding had had to clamp down on release of the pictures. The military governor did not want the world to know that de Gaulle's re-entry into Paris had been opposed in any way.

Kalisch brought all his persuasion to bear, and, after a two-hour delay, the pictures were okayed for transmission. Kalisch bolted with his precious negatives, and grabbed Captain Ernest Deane, who was about to go out on the town. "Tonight you're going to be a hero," said Kalisch. "We're going to get a liaison plane at Longjumeau and you're flying to Bayeux to catch the Hurricane courier to London. Put these films on it—they're hot!" Ernie, whose mind was made up about how to spend the evening, did not find this a very charming idea but got into the jeep with Kalisch and sped to Longjumeau. When they arrived, a Twelfth Army Group liaison plane was coming to a stop. They flagged the pilot who said he was supposed to pick up press stuff for the London courier at Bayeux.

"Unless I take off right now," he stated, "I can't make the connection. The Hurricane can't cross the Channel after 8 P.M." Instructions were to fire on any aircraft after that time. Kalisch told him to get going—Ernie climbed in with his candy-striped press bag full of film and the plane took off for Bayeux.

Ten minutes later, a wild-eyed press courier dashed out in the field. "Where's my plane?" he bellowed. Kalisch, who had been watching the speck disappear in the distance, pointed to it. "Who told him to take off?" the courier asked. "Wait until Redding hears of this." Kalisch departed in the darkness without comment.

The arrangements at Chartres airfield for the Thunderbolt never did materialize, which probably made the commander happy. He had been leap-frogged forward by the time Paris was liberated, and there was no one on the field to fly the first pouch to be taken there.

When the fall of Paris had appeared imminent, Third Army's press camp had moved into Pithiviers, forty-four miles south of the city, and its Mackay Radio moved approximately 60,000 of the first words of the liberation copy which came down hand-carried by Lieutenant Jack Hanssen. On the twenty-sixth, the speed of written dispatches improved when the first allied aircraft, a short-run L-5, landed in the heart of Paris to carry pouches out to Third Army's Mackay punchers.

The loyalty of old employees in Paris touched the big-league newspapermen who checked in at their former bureaus. Managing Editor Eric Hawkins, who had put out the last edition of the Paris *Herald Tribune* before the coming of the Germans in 1940, went with John O'Reilly to the plant, just off the Champs-Élysées. They found Renée Brasier, a business office worker, cleaning the place, and some of the linotype operators who had been with the paper since 1924 were there to greet them.

At 2 Rue des Italiens, Henry Gorrell, Richard D. McMillan, and Ernie Pyle found that all the United Press mahogany desks had been pirated by someone, but one of the office hands had hidden all the battered typewriters in his home. It was here that McMillan and Reynolds Packard had worked for Ralph Heinzen, the fabulous bureau chief whose penetration into French politics has never been matched since.[2]

The *New York Times* office at 37 Rue Caumartin, in the district where some of the most beautiful girls in the world plied the oldest trade with a new eagerness, was visited by Hal Denny, Fred Graham and Gene Currivan. They found their office equipment scattered throughout the building, but their former employees had it all spotted. They had hoarded other things throughout the occupation and they were ready to restore the place immediately, and get back to work.

At 21 Rue de la Paix, Helen Kirkpatrick was touched by silent reminders of the past. All the last 1940 editions of the *Chicago Daily News* were piled by the door as they had been delivered by the postman after the staff had fled. The maid had reported twice each week to clean the office—even though she had been unpaid all that time.

---

[2] Heinzen's contacts with Pierre Laval were so good that he was especially helpful as a tipster to Fleet Admiral William D. Leahy during his tenure as U. S. representative to the Vichy government.

The Nervy Exploit of Sam Magill

When Maj. Gen. Leven C. Allen predicted that the French Second Armored Division would go in on one side of Paris, but have a hard time getting out on the other, he could have enlarged his prophecy to include the press. The war left Paris behind, but the war correspondents hadn't the heart to do likewise. The Scribe Hotel, from the very first day, became a fanciful place, its lobby filled with aimless human tides, everyone afraid to leave it for fear of missing something, everyone afraid also that anything he could find there would fail to measure up under the eyes of his editor or program director. Being born among us was the journalist mendicant, who would pluck at the sleeves of soldiers on leave in Paris to get stories.

If the war correspondents were disinclined to chase off after the Armies now going full-tilt through old, hallowed battlefields such as the Marne, Soissons, Château-Thierry, nothing was deader for them than the Brittany peninsula. Yet hundreds of men in three American divisions—the Eighth, Twenty-ninth and Second—were at Brest alone, where scar-faced, sinister Lt. Gen. Herman Bernhard Ramcke, the veteran paratroop leader of the battle of Crete, was denying the Biscay ports of Brest, Lorient and St. Nazaire to Allied use. He had more than 45,000 garrison troops and remnants of five divisions. Maj. Gen. Troy Middleton, commanding the VIII Corps, had already been in contact with Ramcke by radio, the latter seeking rules on the exchange of wounded. After this, he sought audience with General Middleton, coming out of Brest under a flag of truce. A forbidding enough figure when alone, he was formidable indeed when he stood beside Middleton's command trailer. His feet were planted firmly, wide apart, and two Doberman pinschers were at leash from each of his hands. Middleton was short with him, said there was nothing for them to talk about except the terms of Ramcke's surrender, adding that it would be wise for him to give up soon. Middleton assured him American pressure would be increased. Ramcke departed and took his Dobermans, nervously licking their chops, with him.

Colonel F. V. Fitzgerald, General Bradley's P&PW chief and one-time secretary to a governor of Nevada, had sent me to determine a likely capitulation time for Brest. His hope was to interest some of the war correspondents who had taken up sentry duty in the Scribe. Middleton's impression was that Ramcke was a stubborn fanatic, who would see the campaign through to the bitterest end. Optimistically, he guessed at the fourth to the sixth of September, but he warned this could be in error by as much as ten days. When Shep and I spun back to Versailles, where Twelfth Army Group was located, we were not the only ones with news. Colonel Fitzgerald accepted ours, then told us that we were being transferred to a new "trouble-shooting" assignment.

"The Ninth Army is just coming on the Continent," he said. "It's back at Périers—fresh from the U. S. and San Antonio, Texas. They have no experience in the field, and particularly with what it will take to handle war correspondents. You'll have to organize that from scratch for them." Shades of Grosvenor Square, almost a year ago! But this time there was experience to draw upon, and the flaws of the first, troubled paper planning in London had shown themselves.

General Bradley described Ninth Army as "green but ambitious." Led by lanky, tall and completely bald Lt. Gen. William H. Simpson, described later by Frank Coniff of INS as having "the finest head of skin in the Army," the Ninth Headquarters staff at first looked like an aggregation of National Guardsmen on their annual summer encampment.

The Périers stop was to be short, and after the round of introductions and talks with key people, I sat on a folding cot, typewriter on my knees, and wrote out the memorandum giving birth to a Ninth Army press camp. To it was attached a summary table of equipment and manpower needed, including signals and general communications, motor pool and messing facility. When this was shown to the staff officers they looked at me incredulously. A mobile radio link capable of transmitting voice to London, a press teletype circuit to the main switch at Twelfth Army Group, half a hundred vehicles, dozens of men of peculiar talents, an establishment large enough to take care of fifty war correspondents—it was unbelievable! "When we were in San Antonio," one colonel said, "I never saw two newspapermen in a week, and only then if *we* called 'em up."

Word came that the Ninth Army was going to put feet under itself by taking over the Brittany segment of Third Army, the VIII Corps and its five divisions. The fact that Ninth was actually being spring-boarded into operations gave urgency to my requests, so I took a copy of my proposal to General Simpson's aide, Major Johnny Horn, of Greenwich, Conn. "Show it to General [Brig. Gen. James E.] Moore," he said. "He has a grasp of these things. If he okays it, that'll stop the rest of the staff debating over it."

The quickness with which General Moore pondered the recommendations, and the questions he asked, which were both penetrating and reasonable, gave me great respect for him from the beginning.

"You've had the background in it. If you say so, I'll take your recommendations," said he. Not only did he take them, he had each of the requisition forms signed by General Simpson himself! No supply dump would ever argue with that signature, and the personnel section stirred itself to get the men and talents specified.

On the third of September, as capitulation around Brest seemed more remote than ever, the Eighty-third Infantry Division, commanded by Maj. Gen. Robert C. Macon, of California, Maryland, was stretched 185 miles along the Loire from the Bay of Biscay to a point east of Orléans. Its job was to guard the north bank of that slow-moving stream and provide a flank protection to the wild-running Third Army. The thinness of this line had perturbed Maj. Gen. Manton S. Eddy, whose XII Corps was open on that side of Patton's thrust.

"Doesn't that flank worry you?" Eddy asked Patton one day as they were scanning the map.

"Not me," said Patton blithely. "It just depends on how nervous *you* are by nature."

With the German Armies now clearing out of France very rapidly and falling back on the prepared positions in the Siegfried Line, Hitler had sent a direct order to *Generalmajor* Erich Elster to round up all German forces in the south of France, from Bordeaux to Marseilles, and bring them back in column to Germany. Even though Lt. Gen. Alexander M. Patch, with his Seventh Army, was rolling up from the Riviera, on Hitler's map it looked easy for Elster to skin between Patton and Patch through the Belfort Gap. None of this was known to Colonel E. B. Crabill, of Palm Beach Shores, Florida, whose 329th Infantry Regiment of the Eighty-third had surveillance from seventy miles west of Blois to the vicinity of Orléans. He summoned his Intelligence and Reconnaissance Platoon leader, First Lieutenant Samuel W. Magill, of Ashtabula, Ohio. Magill's area extended from Blois to Orléans, about forty-five miles along the eastern edge. His unit had been beefed up by a platoon of quadruple .50-caliber-mounted half-tracks, a platoon of 105-mm. howitzers, and a hundred Frenchmen of the FFI. In using the latter, it was necessary to teach them scouting and patrolling and reporting.

The colonel was disturbed for an unusual reason. "Sam," he said, "what's happened to all those Germans who were shooting at us from the other side of the river?" Sam indicated his own worries about it, too. Both of them knew they had orders not to cross the Loire, but between Magill and Crabill there was an understanding. The colonel did not tell Sam to violate any orders, he just told him he wanted him to know what was going on. He had never been in the habit of spelling out method for Sam.

Magill went back to his I&R platoon and talked over his problem with his driver, Corporal Christopher Vane of Baltimore, Maryland. Leaving the major portion of his unit in charge of Sergeant Herbert E. Berner of St. Louis, he told his Belgian interpreter, Felix van de Walle and his radio operator, Robert A. Alvey of San Diego, California, to get aboard. At Mer-sur-Loire, Magill crossed in a rowboat to Muides, a small village where the French were so happy to see the American they built him a raft to bring the jeep and his crew over as well. Contact was established almost at once with a member of the Free French, who said the Germans had all withdrawn farther to the south. He had heard a rumor that there was a German element of unknown strength willing to surrender to the Americans, but not to the French. Magill sent a message back to Berner telling him of his plan to move deeper into German-held territory and instructing Berner to get other members of the twenty-four-man platoon across the river and placed at intervals to insure a radio relay.

Magill found his forward movement suddenly restricted when his small patrol ran into the flank guard of the Eleventh Panzer Division, a tough tank battalion. Thousands of German troops, in columns and in every kind of conveyance, were filtering past it on all sides. Alvey cranked up his radio and fed back dozens of messages to the 329th, giving locations, march objectives, strength and state of equipment. One of these radio messages brought an air strike which destroyed two thirds of a ten-mile-long German column on the Route Nationale east of Chateauroux. The Magill patrol took frequent cover, once spending five hours in the woods. Eventually the main body of the Germans, behind the formidable Eleventh Panzer, flowed by.

With the XIX TAC, commanded by Brig. Gen. O. P. Weyland, strafing a column miles further to the south, Magill now thought seriously of the possibilities of prisoners from whom he could get the more detailed information which Colonel Crabill wanted. With his mind on Germans who might surrender, Magill ran up a white flag of truce and Vane drove the jeep ahead toward Issoudun. There was occasional, desultory fire from the roadsides, as much from surprised French as from the disorganized Germans.

The bridge leading into Issoudun was alive with German guards, who held their guns on the approaching jeep, but let it come up to the bridge. Van de Walle, in German, asked to talk to the commander, and they settled back to await some major or, at most, lieutenant colonel. "Look," said Van de Walle suddenly, "that officer coming up on the other side of the bridge. See the red stripes on his pants leg. That's a major general." Hastily Magill got out of the jeep with Van de Walle and they moved forward to meet the German, who asked what they wanted and how they came to be there.

Sam's mouth was dry, but through the Belgian, he said: "I came here to see you because your cause is hopeless. I know you're trying to get back to Germany, but thousands of troops are in your way now waiting for you to come in range. I thought if I came to talk to you, you would see that you could surrender with honor—and save the lives of your men who will otherwise die unnecessarily." Because of the shambles he had noted in his 100-mile penetration, Sam was of the opinion that the General's strength at most, would be around two battalions.

The German consulted a moment with his staff. "How much strength do you represent?" he asked.

Sam was thinking only of his platoon, rather than the division. "I've got my platoon. . . ."

The German turned apoplectic. "What?" he spluttered. "Surrender twenty thousand men to a platoon? *Phantastisch!*"

When Van de Walle translated twenty thousand he choked a little and Magill almost fell off the Issoudun bridge. In carrying out Colonel Crabill's simple order to find out what had happened to the Germans, he had stumbled right into the main column. Stunned as he was, Magill, who had once thought he wanted to be a minister, turned his seriously honest face to the German general, and repeated that it was not the platoon which was important, but the inevitable clash of arms which awaited the column up ahead. General Elster quieted somewhat. The lieutenant was not so wrong, after all. The column had been sniped at constantly by the Free French and the Communist FTPF (Force Tireur Partisan Français), while the planes of XIX TAC came out of the sky at all daylight hours to harass him. His losses had already been great. A surrender, he said, might be negotiated if certain terms could be met—terms which would insure surrender with honor.

"What are the terms?" asked Magill.

"A show of force," said Elster.

"How big?"

The German studied a moment, looked at his tired but determined men. "If you can confront me with two battalions," he decided, "it could be a surrender with honor." He might as well have asked Magill for the moon, but Sam told him he would be back the next day with word from the division commander.

Night was fast falling, and on the way back, Sam changed drivers to give Vane a rest. Big, burly Ralph Anderson of Lancaster, Ohio, took the wheel and pointed it toward Beaugency. The road was blocked from time to time by logs which had been thrown across it by snipers. The rules demanded that headlights be blacked out, but as long as Magill was way out of the rule book already, he told Anderson to turn on the lights for quick flashes to see if the road was clear, then run for it to the next turn. By using this harrowing method, they avoided roadblocks. By the time Sam got back across the Loire and reported to Colonel Crabill in his bed, it was past midnight. Crabill thought enough of the proposal to get into his clothes and drive to Château Renault, where General Macon was awakened and informed.

Macon shook his head. "We're stretched paper-thin now," he said. "We've got 185 miles covered by a bare 16,000 troops as it is. I don't know where I'd get two battalions. Besides, we might get over the river and get caught in the wringer and lose a lot of men." Sam talked earnestly of his belief that the German wanted to give up, not fight, and he pointed out that if the German column came on, it was eventually sure to clash with some elements of the Eighty-third in a fire fight anyway. Macon still said no, but did send the news forward to Ninth Army headquarters in Mi Forêt, six kilometers from Rennes itself. Crabill and Magill walked away from the General's quarters unhappily, but Crabill was not through backing up his lieutenant. "You go back down to the General at Issoudun," he said, "and talk to him some more. Let me know if you have any ideas of anything else I can do."

Still with no sleep and, worse yet, with no solution, Magill again put the Loire behind him. His brain was numb and he dozed in his seat, while Anderson watched him out of the corner of his eye and pulled him back each time he began to slump precariously to the outside of the jeep. Van de Walle was better off, having caught some snatches while Magill had been with Crabill and Macon. Suddenly an idea struck Anderson. "Remember when we were talking to Elster," he said to Sam, "and he brought up the damage by American planes?" Dull as his senses were at that moment, Magill immediately woke up. Maybe Elster would accept a show of force in the air! Magill had never asked for air support before, since his mission was to find out things, but wherever possible to avoid getting entangled in a scrap. The lonely party in the jeep took on considerably more elation than they were entitled to and, by the time they met with Elster on the Issoudun bridge again, they were eager.

Meantime, the field telephone on my tent pole rang. It was Capt. Tom Roberts, PRO of the Eighty-third, to give me a brief rundown. The Ninth Army's reaction to the news of a possible 20,000-prisoner bag was contrary to expectations. Brest and the other ports looked like an elusive prize, and Ninth Army, characterized by General Bradley as "green and ambitious" was now showing its ambition. They wanted those 20,000 prisoners. My tipster didn't have to spell out the chance Lieutenant Sam Magill had to dwarf the famous Sergeant York exploit of World War I when he picked up 132 Germans single-handed. By the phone circuits available, it was finally possible to get Twelfth

Army Group at Versailles and Lt. Col. Bert Kalisch came on. By yelling as loudly as we could, I described for him the situation below the Loire and the possibilities for story and pictures. Asking him to send any interested war correspondents first to Beaugency for a check-in with Colonel Crabill, I told him of my plan to leave on September 8 and the hope that I could join Magill among the Germans to get a running account of his adventure to fill in the later arriving press.

The Ashtabula lieutenant, at the time I was phoning, was again talking to General Elster. "My general has asked me if you will accept a show of force in the air," he said. Elster was mystified. "I will radio to my division," explained Sam, "asking them to send a group of planes. They will be instructed to look for a flare we will place on this crossroads. After they come over, they are to return and look for a cloth panel on the ground. If I put out a white one, it means you are satisfied and will negotiate. If I put out a red one, they are to wait twenty minutes, then strafe and bomb your column." The General was not convinced that Magill was not running a colossal bluff, and that went double for Magill. But Magill had that honest face. General Elster agreed and Alvey cranked up the radio. Back over the relay went the message to Colonel Crabill. The time for the show of force was set for 2 P.M., September 8. In a few moments, a return message came through from Crabill: "Have made request through Ninth Army. Am also going myself to XIX TAC to get everything I can."

Magill set up shop in the small lobby of the Hotel d'Angleterre in Romorantin. It was a soldier's dream come true. The FFI gave them six German PW's to do the cooking, washing and other chores. It was as if they were installed for good.

At 1:30 on the afternoon of the eighth, Magill and the Germans reported to the Issoudun bridge, and the flares were installed at the intersection letting their smoky trails go upward on the still day. As the two o'clock deadline neared, Magill and the Germans looked speculatively up at the sky. The deadline came and went. It was 2:15 and the Germans began to mutter. Then, 2:30 and the sky was still blank overhead. Magill told Van de Walle to request patience, but the Germans were fast running out of it. What's more, they felt they had been bluffed—and almost successfully. Then, at 2:47 P.M., sixteen Thunderbolt fighter-bombers came over in formation. Sam had no way of knowing whether they were the ones, but he had to chance it.

"Van," he said, "ask him, quick! Which'll it be, white or red panel?"
Van de Walle put the question.

Elster looked at the planes, making a graceful bank, so pretty yet
so lethal and ominous. "Make it white," he said, and the panel was
immediately spread in the field. The planes had come so low, some of
the German soldiers hit the dirt. Now they looked on in wonder and
relief as the sixteen Thunderbolts returned, waggled their wings, then
flew off to the north to do battle elsewhere.

This was the crucial time for Magill. Had *he* now been bluffed?
Had he sent his only chance of salvation flying off, and would General
Elster now refuse to negotiate? But General Elster kept his bargain.
"Will you send an officer with full power to discuss terms?" he asked
tiredly. "I will send one of mine to act as liaison with you." Sam
agreed, took on a non-communicative German colonel in the already
crowded jeep, and headed back to Romorantin with the tidings. When
the word came through to Beaugency, Crabill designated Lt. Col.
Jules French, of Merrifield, Virginia, as exchange representative with
the Germans, while Macon himself went down to talk with Elster.

"I could hardly stir up any interest in Paris for this story," Kalisch
said, "and I don't know if anyone is coming. I told 'em any tip from
you was good enough for me, but it's tough to buck the Folies Ber-
gères these days."

We crossed the Loire on separate ferries late on the eighth and
Kalisch, to make plans for his photographers, went straight to Romorantin to join Magill. Shep and I went by easy stages down Magill's
primitive trap line of communications—a radio link here in a house,
there in a corner of an inn, and over there in an attic. Gathering
background materials on each man, I had a story on them all.[1]

---

[1] The members of the platoon south of the Loire included: Sgt. Edward
Hatcher, of Beckley, W. Va.; Corporal Lemuel Sistler, Batavia, Ill.; Albert
Biro, Cleveland, Ohio; Robert F. Glasgow, Wheeling, W. Va.; Michael J.
Marino, Willoughby, Ohio; Edward J. Monk, Lawrence, Mass.; Michael J.
Demeter, Cleveland, Ohio; Donald E. Wilkinson, Wellsville, Ohio; William
Reeves, Cincinnati, Ohio; Sgt. Robert W. Roller, Clover, Va.; Corporal David
Alcala, La Verne, Calif.; William Longmire, Elizabethtown, Tenn.; Corporal
Arnold Goodson, Wolf Creek, Tenn.; James H. Reilly, Thomaston, Conn.;
James E. Townsend, Petoskey, Mich.; Robert H. Housenecht, Muncy Valley,
Pa.; Arnold J. Marcum, Marlinton, W. Va.; Robert J. Burns, Watertown, Mass.;
Stanley Pope, Caledonia, Minn.; Sgt. William L. Adams, Baltimore, Md.;
Corporal Morris Weisburd, New York City, N. Y.; John W. Baird, Jr., Embar-
rass, Wisc.; and Sgt. John North, Bryan, Ohio.

Immediately upon our arrival at the Hôtel d'Angleterre, new logistics obstacles began to appear because it had become clear that the final act of taking the 20,000 troops was not going to come off quickly. We informed Twelfth Army Group that the surrender was on, but at least ten days away. Three correspondents, however, were on the way: Collie Small, UP; Charles Haacker, Acme Newspictures; and Fred MacKenzie, *Buffalo Evening News.* They were charging by jeep down the Paris-Orléans road, and Collie had come away so fast he was still wearing his pajamas under his clothes. Highly upset to find they were so early, they nevertheless came down to Romorantin. Shortly afterward, Hal Boyle, AP, and Ivan H. "Cy" Peterman, *Philadelphia Inquirer,* arrived.

Kalisch's negotiations with Lt. Col. French and *Generalmajor* Elster were going along famously, it being Kalisch's plot to be sure every phase of this spectacular achievement would be on film record. To start the movie, he needed a day with his cameramen in the German assembly areas, and a guarantee that General Elster would not at the last minute demand the film. General Elster agreed to talk it out. Driven to the headquarters by Private First Class James B. "Sandy" Sandeen, Kalisch was presented to Elster, who found that Kalisch's mother had come from Württemberg, birthplace also of both Field Marshal Erwin Rommel and Elster himself. After a chat, as always, Kalisch was in, this time because of his German-born mother. So friendly was their relationship that Kalisch suggested a public surrender, like that of Cornwallis. Certainly it would be with honor, but this could only be proved if he had pictures to show, and outdoor pictures at that. Kalisch needed this condition badly, because he had no lights for indoor shooting. "Agreed," said General Elster, after fifteen minutes of Kalisch's oratory, "I will make a public surrender, but it must be with an honor platoon and a proper military ceremony."

Kalisch promised to deliver his end, and suggested that the token of capitulation be a Luger rather than a sword which would look as out of place as cameras would have at the time of Cornwallis. This arrangement was approved by General Macon, who told Kalisch he could select the spot and time of the surrender.

Kalisch inspected the area from Orléans to Blois. He first thought of the main square in Orléans at the foot of the statue of Joan of Arc. Pictorially it was perfect, politically it was dynamite. The French authorities convinced him that massing 20,000 armed Germans in a town full of armed Maquis might result in riot and massacre. Reluctantly Kalisch looked elsewhere and found another suitable spot—Beaugency. Two roads converged on the blasted bridge. At the junction stood a house which provided a perfect camera platform and press gallery. He spoke to the proprietor, M. Hertschap, and got him to clear the second floor. Carefully, Kalisch figured out the best time for shooting film and set the surrender hour at 3 P.M. Some of the staff wanted to change the time—but when General Macon agreed, the cameramen heaved a sigh of relief.

General Charles de Gaulle was extremely interested in the details of this surrender and asked for strong assurances that the weapons of the 20,000 Germans be placed under U. S. Army guard. De Gaulle already saw France's up-coming troubles with the lawless FTPF Communists who were raiding and pillaging the countryside and would submit to no orders. De Gaulle knew what might happen if the weapons of 20,000 men fell into Communist hands. He could order the FFI one day to give up their arms, and they would, but he was equally sure the FTPF would not.

This posed Magill and his platoon with another problem, and the problems were serious enough already. There was the need to provide hay and feed for a thousand horses in the German column, fuel for 2,000 commandeered vehicles, and bread for twenty thousand troops. The big risk, however, was that the Germans, having refused to surrender to the French, were being allowed to carry their arms, loaded, all the way to the Loire.

A secondary concern was the Château Valancey, home of the Duc de Talleyrand, grandnephew of Napoleon's foreign minister. A British agent got in touch with Lieutenant Magill and said it was absolutely necessary that all German columns be diverted from the Château, the reason being that, under the Château, 480 of the most priceless of the Louvre art treasures, including the Winged Victory and the enigmatic Mona Lisa, had been hidden for safekeeping. Immediately, a part of Sam's platoon had to spot hundreds of mines across the Château road in order to make it noticeably impassable and divert any stray detachments.

As we were first looking over the Château grounds with one of the household staff, it was early in the morning. We were all startled when a sparkling-eyed, black-haired girl in her late teens appeared suddenly at one of the spacious second-floor windows sans a stitch of clothing.

She held her arms wide in a gesture of welcome and greeting. *"Ooo, la-la,"* she said blowing a kiss, *"les Américains!"* We all waved, then she seemed to sense for the first time her state of nakedness, crossed her hand over her breasts, and pulled back from the window. We saw her no more. "Who was that?" somebody wanted to know. The guide explained that she was a protégée of the duke's. A little later we met the duke, who was seventy-three.

The war correspondents were busily writing day-to-day developments of the Magill-Elster saga, but did not know that all their copy was being held up by the censor. The ruling was that not one line of the story would hit print until the last PW walked into the Beaugency cage. Although this news disturbed our Romorantin contingent, they were somewhat sobered to realize how delicate our situation really was, seventy-five-miles deep in German territory. Who really had who south of the Loire was something nobody knew for sure. The Germans were armed, the French were hostile, the custodial force was small, and some of the correspondents trying to join us were being nipped by Germans over whom General Elster seemed not to have control.

On September 12, the extreme fluidity of the situation was illustrated when a trio of correspondents departed the Third Army press camp to cover the surrender. In the jeep were six-foot-six and skinny Wright Bryan, *Atlanta Journal,* who had weathered two aerial D-Day runs with both paratrooper and glider-tug planes; Ed Beattie, UP; and John Mecklin, *Chicago Sun.* They were tooling down the road near General Pershing's old World War I headquarters town of Chaumont and found themselves less than a hundred yards from a German roadblock before they recognized it as such. All three of them were captured, and Wright was wounded in the shinbone. He was carted off to a German hospital. Beattie was a major coup, the Germans thought. He had been based in Berlin before the war and was well known to the crowd around Dr. Josef Goebbels.

John Mecklin, who had fallen young and whole into the hands of the Germans, was waved off and sent back to the Third Army press camp, which got him a lot of needling. He was compared with the fish too short to cook which is thrown back in the lake, but his worst blow came from the traitorous conduct of his colleagues. When Mecklin returned to the Third Army press camp, he was loquacious about his experience. The rest of the correspondents fed him on

brandy, questioned him closely, and at intervals, left the tent where
he was holding forth to file their stories. Mecklin got around to sending his own version a day later and got a blast from the *Chicago Sun,*
which reminded him next time to file first, then talk, since he had been
scooped on his own adventure by every paper in the states.

News flashed into Atlanta, Georgia, contained the statement that
Wright had been "wounded in the fleshy part of the leg." An *Atlanta
Journal* cohort, Sam Dull, called Mrs. Bryan in an attempt to be
reassuring. "I wouldn't worry yet, Ellen," he said, "because we both
know there ain't no fleshy part of Wright Bryan. They must have
captured somebody else."

Kalisch had sent a message to his old roommate, Lt. Col. George
Stevens, the celebrated Hollywood producer-director, asking him for
a sound-on-film crew to be emplaced at the Beaugency bridge. George
dispatched a unit bossed by Captain Joseph Biroc, whose professional
Hollywood lensing had never presented anything to equal this genuine
article, and backed him up by Lieutenant Bill Montague, late of Columbia Pictures in Hollywood, and First Lt. Joseph Zinni of Philadelphia, photo unit head with the Eighty-third. Midway in the march-
up of the Germans, two more correspondents joined us, Robert Barr,
BBC, and Alton W. Smalley, *St. Paul Dispatch-Pioneer,* nailing down
a Minnesota angle. Smalley found it in Stanley L. Pope, one of
Magill's platoon, and Pope had a good story in that, while he was
completely courageous in the face of desperate odds, he had a horror
of the day when he would actually be in a spot where he would have
to kill. This package capture had uncommon appeal to Pope. By
stretching his circulation field somewhat, Smalley included John W.
Baird, Jr., who came from the town of Embarrass, Wisconsin.

The German columns, three of them, moved up toward the desti-
nations of Orléans, Beaugency and Blois. They included Wehrmacht
(Army), Kriegsmarine (Navy), and Luftwaffe (Air Force) troops,
with the Navy admiral making the trek in a horse and buggy of
ancient vintage. Magill's platoon had broken camp and parts of it
were riding at the head of each column.

Colonel Crabill was still anxious about these armed columns and
wanted nothing to excite them. Hal Boyle and Cy Peterman had
almost been in an incident when they planted their jeep at an intersection where the column made its turn for the last miles. Peterman
was standing in the jeep, taking pictures.

A German lieutenant worked himself into a lather. "Look pretty," he said to his men. "Look nice for the American photographer. Let him show the Americans what real German soldiers look like." Then he lashed himself with his riding crop and was getting a little frothy at the mouth. "Get the hell down from there with that camera," said Boyle to Peterman, "and let's get out of here. First thing you know, you'll be shooting pictures, and he'll start shooting pistols."

At this point Major Charles Madary of Baltimore, Maryland, Army manager of the Scribe, arrived from Paris with a coeducational group of correspondents, including Geoffrey Parsons, *New York Herald Tribune;* David Anderson, *New York Times;* Erika Mann, *Liberty;* Lady Margaret Stewart, Australian Consolidated Press; Betty Knox, *London Evening Standard;* and Lee Miller, *Vogue.*

Crabill did not want this new batch of sightseer correspondents to go across the river until the next day, so we made arrangements for them in an Orléans hotel and prepared to sweat out the next day, the seventeenth, when Generals Elster and Macon would perform the last rites.

The Paris correspondents were briefed the next morning on the complete plans, then Crabill authorized me to take them over. "Tell them to be careful," he said. "We haven't got the Germans in the cage yet, and their guns are loaded." One of the feminine war correspondents was Erika Mann, daughter of the famous Thomas Mann, who had suffered persecution and endured exile because of Hitler. As we came upon the leading elements of the column and passed alongside it down the road, Erika was emotionally moved, began to talk incoherently, then uttered profanity in the German tongue, and finally as the command car slowed, she got out. When I could get the jeep stopped and get back to her, she was less than a yard from the marching Germans, her hands on her hips, her tongue stuck out, rendering a juicy Bronx cheer right in their faces. That was the end of the ride, because she was bundled up and the retinue went back to the Beaugency bridge to await the rest of the affair. By then, no Germans would be armed, and it would be a lot safer for her to stick out her tongue.

At 3 P.M. *Generalmajor* Eric Elster came up to the bridge in his battered Citroën, got out, surveyed the scene: the battery of motion picture cameras, the microphone, and General Macon backed by division, corps, Air Force and Ninth Army staff representatives. He probably did not notice some hasty scurrying at the left of the receiving group, where I hustled Lieutenant Sam Magill into position with the staff. He had been sitting on the fence, because nobody had seen fit to include him. As Magill came up, one of the Ninth Army colonels, fresh from the States, and seeing his first German soldier, looked about with some disgust, wondering at the discipline of the Eighty-third Infantry Division for having "gate-crashing" lieutenants at a time like this.

Lt. Col. Jules French placed himself on General Elster's left. "Shall we go, Herr General?" he asked, quietly.

Elster, pulling down on his tunic and straightening his cap, managed a smile. *"Ja, mein Oberst,"* he said, and they moved out.

The whir of the cameras was like a hive of bees, and *New York Times*man David Anderson wrote that this must have been "the best covered surrender of this, or any war." What no one knew then was that the story was being smothered by a trio of airborne divisions—the American Eighty-second, and 101st and the British First—being dropped in the Netherlands at Nijmegen, Eindhoven, and Arnhem.[2] The censor pulled the stop off both events at the same time, and relegated Magill's tremendous exploit to second-string position. But Paramount News made a special out of the movie film, labeling it unreservedly, "The Strangest Story of the War," and afterward, in the November 11, 1944, *Saturday Evening Post,* Collie Small, UP, wrote of the event and described the setting:

"News of the war south of the Loire drifted into the bar at the Scribe Hotel in Paris where correspondents gather nightly to plot new ways of poisoning the censors, who also drink at the Scribe bar, but from different stools—like big-league umpires and ballplayers. The inevitable happened almost immediately. Army public-relations officers, who never tire of devising new ways to torture weary correspondents, announced prematurely that 20,000 Germans were surrendering

[2] For months, Walter Cronkite, UP, and Bill Boni, AP, had been earmarked as post-Netherlands liberation bureau chiefs in Amsterdam for their respective agencies. Neither expected in his wildest dreams that they would become journalistic "firsts" by going to their jobs in gliders. Cronkite, with William Wade, INS; Gladwin Hill, AP; Homer Bigart, *New York Herald Tribune;* Bob Post, *New York Times* (who was lost in action); and Andy Rooney, *Stars and Stripes,* had been original members of the close coterie, "the Writing Sixtyninth," or air correspondents who covered the first B–17 raids on Berlin. When Cronkite and Boni set forth with the 101st and Eighty-second Airborne Divisions on September 17, 1944, it was the thirteenth airborne mission for which Cronkite had been briefed—all the others having been scrubbed.

the following morning. Three hours later, they frantically announced it was all a mistake, and for everyone to stay as far away as possible, because the Germans might not surrender after all. Unfortunately, three of us left between announcements. . . ." "Unfortunately," Collie Small wrote, but this exploit of Sam Magill got Small a contract with the *Saturday Evening Post,* and tripled his salary, among other things.

Sam Magill, who crossed the English Channel a lieutenant, went home a lieutenant at war's end. This was partly because Colonel Crabill said he felt Sam's platoon "was more valuable to the security of the regiment than another battalion of infantry would have been, and I never considered him replaceable in that job." Once, much later, he was offered a captaincy if he would leave the platoon, but he refused, saying he would see the "boys" through to the end of the war, which he did. The nervy exploit of Magill, who violated orders, penetrated into German-held territory a hundred miles, and brought off the first big PW bag for the Ninth Army, finally was put on orders for the Legion of Merit eleven months after the incident. The war was over, and he was about to go home with the Ninety-ninth Infantry Division. They didn't give him the ribbon in the Scribe bar, or even in a ceremony. He had to go to a Ninety-ninth Division supply room and draw it.

Birth of Ninth Army Press Camp

One might say that Sam Magill had earned a trip to Paris. Anyhow, he got it, because Colonel Crabill told him to take off a few days. While he was in Paris, Mary Welch did a ghost-written by-line piece on him for *Life* magazine. Lee Carson wrote of his exploit for INS and Virginia Irwin, *St. Louis Post Dispatch,* drew him out for a feature.

As this was going on, the last act in the drama of Brest was being played. Across the bay from Brest on the Crozon peninsula, Ramcke, with nearly a thousand men, was still holding out. The Pont de l'Espagnol, a rather large triangle of land, extended toward Brest across the estuary and the entire area was fortified with a heavy, twenty-foot-high masonry wall of large granite blocks. Originally French naval fortifications, these had been improved by the Germans with pillbox approaches.

Maj. Gen. D. A. Stroh's Eighth Infantry Division, with its Twenty-first and Twenty-eighth regiments in the lead, had the Crozon assault. The Thirteenth Infantry took on the Pont de l'Espagnol reduction, an ominous and forbidding chore since eight hundred yards of clear, fire-swept ground led to the wall and it had to be a frontal attack. To Lt. Col. Earl Lerette's Third Battalion went the assignment to storm the wall. Lerette was a cheerful and inspiring leader and he needed those characteristics for this one. Colonel Robert Allen Griffin, the Thirteenth's Commander, was immensely gratified when General Stroh backed up his regiment with fifteen battalions of field artillery and two squadrons of fighter-bombers. The Third Battalion literally walked inside the barrage, and only one of the pillboxes sassed back until destroyed by flamethrowers. Almost immediately, word came that General Ramcke was ready to talk terms with an officer of high rank. Colonel Griffin sped over and on the way was intercepted by Brig. Gen. Charles D. W. Canham, who said he would take the surrender.

General Ramcke's aide, a German captain, beribboned, freshly pressed, was not satisfied with Canham's rank, and said he would have to speak to Ramcke. He went back through the huge steel doors and returned after a few minutes to say that Ramcke "preferred to surrender to a Corps Commander." Canham retorted that Ramcke would surrender to him, and at once. The German haughtily asked him to display his credentials. Back of General Canham was a tank destroyer with its guns pointed directly at the steel doors, and the approach was bristling with American soldiers. "These," said Canham, "are my credentials."

The German then took Canham and Griffin through the maze of cement and steel into an office where Ramcke, in a paratrooper camouflage jacket, was sitting at his desk. He had a bottle of champagne brought up and drank to the health of his captors as arrangements were made for the safe removal of himself, his staff, and more than 800 men in the stronghold with him. Canham and Griffin enjoyed the drink very much [1] since it signified the end of a long, bitter campaign. The Thirteenth Infantry had had only forty casualties, unbelievable when measured against the fortifications.

Crozon was ablaze with bonfires that night, with champagne corks popping all over the peninsula. But Paris continued to hold the war correspondents, and there was only one newspaperman present at this celebration. He was General Ben Lear's ex-public-relations chief during 1941 maneuvers, my old boss, now busy seeing that his men were enjoying themselves. Colonel R. A. Griffin, the Thirteenth's CO, in civilian life the publisher of the *Monterey* (California) *Peninsula-Herald,* was the only member of the press on Crozon that day.

On the nineteenth of September the Brittany ports were finally in

---

[1] Drinking with German high-ranking captives later aroused press criticism, especially when the 101st Airborne Division took Field Marshal Hermann Goering and photographs of Brig. Gen. Gerald "Jerry" Higgins and his staff interrogating the Luftwaffe chief showed glasses on the table.

Allied hands. As the troops poked around among the smoking, silent piles of rubble, a personnel action memorandum was being circulated simultaneously in the headquarters of VIII Corps, the Second, the Eighth and the Twenty-ninth Infantry Divisions.

At VIII Corps, it caught up with Captain James A. Griffith, of Grove City, Pennsylvania, a one-time foundryman, and Captain William Moody, a former insurance man from Goldsboro, North Carolina. At the Eighth, the dragnet produced a group of lieutenants—Thom Patterson, the son of a Haskell, Texas, banker; Erle Richardson, an insurance salesman from Marion, Alabama; John H. Pecor, a General Electric toolmaker of Youngstown, Ohio; and John F. Kennedy, a bank bookkeeper from Cohoes, New York. The Second Infantry Division had reached out for other lieutenants, including George K. Williams, a restaurant operator from Pomona, California, and Harry Correa, an electric-appliance salesman from Baltimore, Maryland. Williams had had the dreadful experience of diving into his foxhole in Normandy, then having an 88 dud fall in the hole with him. He was somewhat upset for several days after that, and sometimes had nightmares about it.

Lt. Col. John Hightower, who had the First Battalion of the Second's Twenty-third Infantry Regiment, sent for First Lieutenant William Brown, an ex-floorwalker at Macy's in New York. He was the only original officer left in B Company. "I have a request here for a lieutenant with a college education," he told Brown. "An honor assignment to Ninth Army headquarters." Brown looked at him tiredly. He had arrived in France on D plus six as a forlorn replacement and had just completed 105 unbroken days and nights in the line. Everyone he had known in his unit had first gone in, and then gone out, either as the principal in a burial party or back to a field hospital. He could not yet believe in Brest's stillness. "You've ducked every bullet so far," Hightower was saying, "and there aren't many like you left. I'm sending you back to fill this request." Brown shook hands with him, said good-by, and saluted. He started out to join the small collection of battle-hardened men bound for something described as the P&PW detachment. These officers, and the enlisted men who would be joining them, were to become the Ninth Army press camp, to make an establishment which would be talked about by war correspondents forever.

In the fact-sheet which we prepared for the correspondents who came to the press camp, the preamble stated with some pride: "These men came to the Ninth Army press camp as a reward for long hours, hard fighting, and a job well done in the line. Each of them was told when he left his old organization that this assignment had been earned by him, and the job itself is entirely and unbelievably new to him. Most of them arrived in Normandy no later than D plus one, and fought an average of 85 days in the line from Omaha Beach to Brest. About 75% of the officers have been decorated for gallantry in action, and all the men can tell plenty of life in a foxhole."

Their P&PW destination caused consternation among them all, however. PW had a much more generally known connotation than Psychological Warfare, and the men deduced they were headed for something like Police and Prisoners of War. None of them wanted that.

They arrived in trucks around midnight, one night late in September. Lieutenant Williams was in the lead vehicle. "Where do we bed 'em down?" he asked, and a place under the trees was indicated. The men piled out, and in a few minutes were curled up in their muddy blankets on the ground.

"Sorry there are no tents up for you," one of the Ninth Army soldiers said apologetically.

"It's okay," said Sergeant Erwin Ehler, of Wharton, Texas. "Nobody's shootin' at us, and that makes everythin' real nice."

In no time, they were all asleep, the first time they had stretched out on the ground outside a hole for weeks. Some of them stirred violently as the night wore on. Others ground their teeth in the tenseness of nervous systems which had not yet unwound and might never do so. One of the number had an upset stomach, which on any sudden sound would cause him to retch violently.

The next morning, they all lined up, and the study of past records gave us leads for assignment. Technical Sergeant Leroy G. Ehrman, of Perryville, Pennsylvania, had all the measurements and experience for the top kick and Technical Sergeant Walter W. Carroll, of Goldthwaite, Texas, was the obvious choice to run the motor pool. "Ask me to do anything but put my shoulder to the wheel," he said. The whole of his right shoulder had been mangled by a direct hit, and it was largely reconstructed of silver plate.

The nearest we could get to cuisine capability was Lieutenant Williams, and he was teamed with Sergeant Lawrence W. Gudger, of Cary, Kentucky, the mess sergeant. The gastronomic outlook was

neither too good nor too bad. The rest of our first arrivals [2] were
parceled off into driver, mess, motor-pool and administrative chores.
Our first move was a run for the equipment dumps along Utah and
Omaha Beaches, where we would draw to the limit of the requisitions
signed by General Simpson.

The ride to the beach was uneventful, as all our manpower was
loaded in two big trucks and the trip was made in the daytime. We
moved from pick-up point to pick-up point down the beach, working
our way eventually to the last dump about twelve miles east of battered Isigny. It was here that we were to get all the jeeps with their
attached trailers, thirty of them, each to be individually receipted. We
had some borrowed drivers as well as some drivers who were doing
it for the first time. By the time we had accomplished all the paper
work and established ownership for jeeps, trailers, and trucks, with
all the supplies aboard, the sun had set.

Darkness enveloped the beach quickly then. First the sun turned
the water red and went down as if drowning in its own blood. Everything became as black as a Disney drawing board across which the
animator upsets an ink bottle. Rules of the road were that all driving
be done with cat's-eye headlights. The pace had to be steady, and
since our route took us through several French villages and towns,
everyone had to stay closed up. The cavalcade started well, and we
did all right through Isigny, the first traffic center, but as we were
progressing along a Carentan canal the column suddenly broke in the
middle. There was first an excited yip, a great splash, then a chorus
of jeep horns raucously sounding from the rear of the convoy which
had stopped cold. As I edged my portion of the procession off the road
away from the canal, it was narrowly missed by a cumbersome and

---

[2] The list included Ellis J. Latham, Manchester, Ala.; Floyd F. Kennedy,
Elwood City, Pa.; George M. Chapke, Chicago, Ill.; Marion F. Streeter, Rich-
mond, Cal.; Charles C. Jindra, Kingfisher, Okla.; James L. Gregory, Auburn,
Wash.; Theodore H. Purdy, Mays Landings, N. J.; Alva D. Owens, Indiahoma,
Okla.; James L. Ott, Thomasville, Ala.; Percy W. Stahl, Bowling Green, Ky.;
Harold E. Fry, Mt. Vernon, Ohio; James T. Adams, Truman, Ark.; Eugene T.
LeFaver, Nashway, N. Y.; Robert R. Moore, Cherry Lake, Fla.; Salvatore Gril-
lone, Philadelphia, Pa.; Daniel P. Galanty, Newark, N. J.; George L. Russe,
Brooklyn, N. Y.; Inez Martinez, Elsa, Tex.; J. L. Morris, DeBerry, Tex.; Willard
M. Smith, Norwood, Mo.; Herbert L. Frank, Houston, Tex.; David Tannen-
baum, Cleveland, Ohio; Anthony L. Bosco, Brooklyn, Ohio; Alvin J. Lyons,
Baltimore, Md.; Edward M. Nelson, Hendersonville, N. C.; Robert E. Selm,
Cincinnati, Ohio; Andrew B. Holmes, Watumpka, Ala., and Lester R. Moore,
Madison, Wisc. More were to join later, but these were the first.

powerful tank retriever, commanding the respect of its size and letting the rest of the road traffic look after itself.

Running back to the break in the convoy, some of the men fished Private James Adams, of Truman, Arkansas, out of the water. He had given ground, shying away from the retriever, but the quarters were so close that a swipe from the rear end of the heavy vehicle caught Adams' trailer, jackknifed it, and he shot off into the canal as if from a catapult. The night was pitch-black and by the strangest of luck, Adams had escaped with only a soaking. Partly with the cold of the night, his teeth were chattering. How he missed being pinned under no one could guess. The rest of the jeeps were pulled to a road-way shoulder out of town, where we waited for two hours until we could find a wrecker. The wrecking crew gave us a receipt for the quarter-ton, and at almost midnight, now with twenty-nine jeeps and trailers, we headed out for the Mi Forêt near Rennes. At 4 A.M. we pulled the tired string into our motor-pool area. The men rolled up in their blankets at the side of the convoy and soon were sound asleep.

Ninth Army had divided itself by many miles in our absence, the forward section having been shoved into a small sector of the Ardennes, with the headquarters itself in Arlon, Belgium. The press camp stayed with the rear echelon for the time being and we used the time for some "dry runs" which included setting up tents and familiarizing the men with the odd requirements of a press camp. It was all very different from the simple, every-man-for-himself life in a foxhole, and demanded a change in point of view for each soldier now part of a service unit which had the mission of looking after others.

The press camp was far from complete in that it did not yet have its mobile military radio transmitter, with JEEP as its call letters, which would be the voice link to London. The Press Wireless transmitter would not join us until we were ready to go into business. These two facilities alone would add about a dozen men and half that many vehicles and trailers. Teletype punchers had not joined us yet either, although we were assured by Colonel Joseph Miller, Ninth Army signal officer, that we would have our own tie-line to the Twelfth Army Group switch as soon as we reached the neighborhood of the forward echelon. The press censorship detachment, earmarked for us by Colonel Richard Marrick, SHAEF's chief press censor, was slated to include between eight and ten officers and enlisted men, under one of the most reasonable and diplomatic blue-pencilers, Captain Edward

C. Lavelle.[3] There was no need for this detachment to hook on, however, until the Ninth Army's destination was firm.

The pot began to bubble one night when a Ninth Army colonel called from Arlon telling me that the unit should load up and move out the next morning at six. As we were about to do this, the Deputy Chief of Staff, who was boss of the rear section, rescinded the command which, it turned out, had been from a colonel with too firm a clutch on his cognac. He even forgot the next morning that he had ordered the movement. The next night he took his usual stand by the jug and called to ask where we were. He was adamant that we be on the road the next day. This time his order coincided with the plan of the rear section, so the cavalcade was formed and the leap-frog forward got under way.

Although General Bradley had been publicly acknowledged, finally, as co-equal with Monty in command and was now reporting directly to SHAEF, as Monty did, he was apprehensive about the future. He had thirty-one American divisions under his Twelfth Army Group, while Monty's entire weight in Twenty-first Army Group consisted of fifteen British Empire and Canadian divisions. It was on October 18 that Bradley attended a strategy conference in Brussels and came away with the feeling that, sooner or later, Monty would be wangling himself an American Army. Bradley did not feel secure from Monty's tendency to poach, and he appeared particularly sensitive about the First Army, his old command of such tried and true capability, which was rubbing shoulders so chummily on the British right flank near Venlo in the Netherlands.

As we were beginning our skip from the Mi Forêt to Arlon, General Bradley was giving instructions for Ninth Army to disengage in the Ardennes and roll north into Maastricht, there to take over XIX Corps which had pushed its nose through the upper reaches of the Siegfried Line. He also planned to put a second Corps, the XIII, in that narrow twenty-mile long sector. Nineteenth Corps, just then

[3] The Ninth Army press camp's censors included Captain Edward C. Lavelle, the chief, West Hartford, Conn.; Captain James A. Robbins, deputy, of Springfield, Ill.; Lieutenants Albert Kilarjian, Belle Harbor, Long Island, N. Y.; Jay B. Stringer, Itasca, Ill.; Richard Caplin, Haverhill, Mass.; Dudley V. I. Darling, Pleasantville, N. Y.; Herbert Theune, East Stroudsburg, Pa.; and Samuel R. Floyd, Lake City, S. C.; Sergeant McCormick W. Kennedy, Silver Spring, Md.; and Corporal Jacob P. Wachtel, New York, N. Y.

switching from the command of Maj. Gen. Charles H. Corlett to Maj. Gen. Raymond S. McLain, had three divisions, the Second Armored, the Thirtieth and Eighty-third. Thirteenth Corps was under Maj. Gen. Alvan C. Gillem, Jr., and contained the Eighty-fourth and 102nd. If Monty was going to get an American Army, General Bradley was determined it would be his greenest one.

All unaware of these developments, I outran the convoy into Paris and spent the time there not too profitably, asking if Ninth Army could get any correspondents interested in a war. Paris had been made into such a shambles by the determined press stand that Brig. Gen. Frank A. Allen, Jr., an ex-First Armored Division combat commander, had been marched in to take the broom to the situation. He was made chief of the SHAEF public-relations division. If Faid Pass had been a sad spectacle, so was the lobby of the Scribe Hotel. There were 500-odd men and women based in the rumpled hostelry. The lobby milled with humanity, day and night, like a refugee collecting point. Work and play were common to the same room at the same time. Allen took old soldier's steps at once and ordered the place policed up, and spruced up. In league with Captain Harry Butcher, General Eisenhower's aide, he got the place running in less irregular fashion. The censors, public-relations officers and communications men were assigned to offices. The mess began to run right. One of the best and most cheering developments was the increase of Press Wireless sending power by its boss, Stanley Grammar. Yet, the war was miles off on the borders of, and in some places, inside Germany. Bed and board at the front was not too gay a thought. Numbers of spaces went begging at all armies, while in Paris, the censors were pawing over an average of more than 3,000,000 words a week, as well as checking 35,000 still pictures, and 100,000 feet of movie film every seven days. No group was more vilified than the censors, yet *Time* magazine, which assigned Sherry Mangan as a correspondent to cover the correspondents and appropriately based him in Paris, said, "The wonder is not that an occasional piece of copy gets stuck in censorship, but that so much gets through as quickly as it does." [4]

[4] One of the hardest censor stops to understand about this time was on the 442nd Infantry Regiment, the famous Nisei unit from Hawaii with the motto "Go for broke!" Having been in the Southern France invasion with Seventh Army, it was intensely interesting to one of the most attractive war correspondents, Lyn Crost, *Honolulu Star-Bulletin*. She tried to break the story of its return from France to Italy, but was shushed out of it. But no amount of

Actually, the briefings at any Army along the front by that time were more war-flavored, as well as closer to the fighting and the men who fought, than the briefings at SHAEF. There was much pulling and hauling between the correspondents at the front and those in Paris, the former contending that if they stayed with the battle line, they were entitled to the stories there. Resentment was heaped on the policy of putting over-all censor stops from front to rear areas so that correspondents at SHAEF briefings in Paris could expand on the very things which the genuine war correspondent had endured danger and discomfort to get.

General Patton had injected a fillip, too. A far cry from General Pershing of World War I, who was ever reluctant to release identities of fighting units, Patton demanded and eventually got the right to release the numbers of divisions when an attack was launched. He felt that more advantage accrued in morale when a unit knew that it was identified with a battle than could be gained by denying knowledge to the enemy of the strength being used against him. In the Patton program a story labeled "AT THE GERMAN BORDER" or "INSIDE GERMANY" was a lot better for the soldier, when he read of his action, than a "PARIS" dateline. A "Supreme headquarters spokesman" relaying the battle report secondhand was much paler, too.

The laggards in Paris were daily being treated with more and more scorn by the up-front correspondents, who were also merciless with their own stay-at-homes. It was common to play tricks on this kind of correspondent. Third Army, for instance, had one British journalist who was known for never leaving the press camp; he depended for his news on what he heard others talking about. Cornelius Ryan, *London Daily Telegraph,* and John Prince of the staid *Times* caught him tuning in one day after Patton had taken Nancy, so they spun a yarn about having been in Nancy that day during a strong German counterattack which had retaken the city for the Germans, adding that German *Fräuleins* were driving some of the tanks. The eavesdropper dashed to his typewriter, filed a fast eight hundred words, and two hours later had a service message back from his paper congratulating him and asking for eight hundred words more. By this time, Major Bill Drake heard of the gag and was greatly concerned about international repercussions if this was an American prank on

secrecy about the 442nd, and its 100th Battalion, would have been possible without a universal face-lift, since its membership was exclusively Oriental.

the British correspondent. He was relieved to find that not only was it a British joke all around, but that Mackay Radio had held up the first story and faked the congratulations. The erring correspondent finally tumbled. He did not show up for breakfast the next morning, but came down about eleven with his baggage packed and asked for transport back to England.

While I was in Paris, General Eisenhower was making one of his periodic appearances before the press. Larry Rue, *Chicago Tribune,* asked him, now that the armies of his widespread command had advanced to their present locations, what he considered his mission to be. There was no hesitation on the part of the Supreme Commander, who declared it to be the same as it had always been—to meet and destroy the German Army west of the Rhine. He was two months ahead of the abortive offensive of Field Marshal Gerd von Rundstedt, which was to cuff us about while giving that opportunity.

The best I could get from the SHAEF public-relations division before taking off from Paris was that they would let it be known that fifty war-correspondent spaces were open at Ninth Army. With that, we sped up the road and caught the convoy of Ninth Army (rear), with its press camp contingent, near Verdun. The convoy spent the night just north of Longwy. Things were happening fast then, with General Bradley's desire to put Ninth Army hastily on the left flank of the First, just north of Aachen. We pushed on through Bastogne, Marche, Liége, and on into Maastricht. Momentarily, the Ninth Army, with its rear echelon closer to the front than its forward headquarters, was all in a real war zone at last, and the Ninth Army press camp— the one everyone would always remember—was ready for business. The first of our correspondents walked in while we were unloading into and taking over the Hôtel du Lévrier et l'Aigle Noir. He was Franklin Banker, AP, who had been poking around XIX Corps troops and among the ruins of Aachen, the first major German city to fall to the Americans.

Maastricht Roster

Maastricht has been a European crossroads for centuries. When the Romans were rippling out in all directions, they came to the Maas and crossed it, hence the name: *Maas* for the river, *tricht* for the crossing. Thereafter, Maastricht had a history all its own.

Its solid and somber surface conceals hundreds of miles of subterranean caverns at varying depths, great, dark, meandering labyrinths, which have been enlarged and changed in direction for centuries to provide the town's building materials. Some of the openings from these winding tunnels in the rock are in Germany, others in the Netherlands, still others in Belgium, and through the war these quarried passages were important links and hiding places of the underground. Through them many British and American pilots who were shot down escaped toward the Channel coast. Only a few Dutch men and women knew how to negotiate the passages quickly and surely from Germany straight on into Belgium. There were "wait stations," where pilots and fugitives could rest until the other, or Belgian, end of the network was lined up to take them through.

The townspeople of Maastricht, "that tear on the nose of the Netherlands," had used one small segment of these quarries as an air-raid shelter capable of housing 70,000 people easily. The Queen Wilhelmina art collection, including Rembrandt's "The Night Watch," was stored away in them with full co-operation from the Germans, who never realized that running right alongside the air-raid shelter and the art sanctuary was a path to freedom for allied airmen. On some of these walls, with ancient scratches going back to the Romans, can be seen the newer markings, where men whiled away their time by chiseling modern inscriptions. One of them: "Izzy Bernstein, Brooklyn, passed this way, 1943, on way back to Brooklyn." This escape route was not nearly as interesting as the *maison-de-tolérance* or bawdy-house relay across France and Belgium, but there was greater safety in the quarry trail.

As only a few knew the way through these pitch-black arteries, so only a few could really tell what forces moved beneath the surface of the average Netherlander. In the first orgy of release from their oppressors, the citizens of Maastricht had turned violently from their quiet ways. One of the first to feel the passions of these normally steady people was one of the town's more notorious collaborating women. Veterans of the underground laid rough hands upon her. Her head was shaved, and she was paraded through the streets in a flat-bed cart. Those who hazed her insisted that she raise her skirts above her waist before the jeering crowds. Such were the tempers of the citizens who lined the ways that they saw nothing repugnant about the chorus shouting derisively at the pathetic creature: "Oh, look! Now we see what only the Germans have seen for four years."

The Dutch innkeeper, Mynheer van Egerschot, of the Hôtel du Lévrier et l'Aigle Noir (the Greyhound and the Black Eagle), watched this demonstration with misgivings. He had known mutterings against himself throughout the occupation, but he had not paid too much attention. The plain truth was that he had had no control over the "guest" list in his hotel since the morning of May 10, 1940. On that date, Hitler's legions were in the Town Hall square of Maastricht in strength. Less than four hours after the Netherlands border was crossed, jack-booted German soldiers came to the Hôtel du Lévrier and posted themselves at its door. From then on, it was an officers' billet.

Mynheer van Egerschot was an independent Dutchman and he did not like this kind of hotel operation, but he was realistic enough to know that an innkeeper with from fifty to a hundred beds can hardly hold up an armed and arrogant flood tide. He opened his doors, registered his "guests," and had them on his premises for fifty-one long months. During that period, his Dutch neighbors could walk down the Boschstraat and right past his dining-room windows. Though food was short for them, and their wives were forever trying to find new ways to make tulip bulbs edible and appetizing—they tried them fried, boiled, roasted, and broiled, but no way was ever found to make them tasty—they could see Mynheer van Egerschot bowing in that stiff way of his as he ushered German officers to tables and seated them. They could also see them being copiously served with steaming food. With German officers in his hotel rooms and his kitchen supplies guaranteed by their presence, Mynheer van Egerschot was far better off for comforts than any of his old neighbors. With resignation, he went about running the place almost by habit. Naturally, the towns-people were unable to see where resignation terminated and co-opera-tion began. Particularly strong suspicion was leveled at his son, Willem, who was carefully being prepared to follow in his father's footsteps. Willem had attended the best hotel schools in Germany and Switzerland, and already knew the business well. Since Willem was young, he affected gaiety in the presence of the hotel's German residents.

Willem married during the occupation, and his choice had been the belle of Maastricht, Yvonne Ramakers, the daughter of the owner of the town's leading garage. Yvonne, convent-educated, was completely at home in four languages—French, German and English, in addition to her native Dutch. She was inclined to tell her husband, more than listen, in all respects save one. She stayed away from the hotel, but she listened with great eagerness to her husband's after-hours stories of and about the "guests." She asked detailed questions about what the tenants did, what they said, what their jobs appeared to be, and her ears always perked up a little extra for casual disclosures about increases in traffic through the district. With these bits and pieces of information, she made regular bicycle trips to the homes of friends, relaying what she had heard in as great detail as she could recall it, and she was pleased to find that some of it had a way of being valuable in the planning of the Dutch underground.

When I brought the military portion of the Ninth Army press camp into Maastricht in October, 1944, it was one of those rainy, unpleasant nights which visit themselves regularly on the Low Countries in winter. Even though we thought only of getting in somewhere warm and dry, we were also entering the ominous situation now rising to the Nether-lands surface. The Hôtel du Lévrier, marked off for us by Captain Winship Wrigley, of Atlanta, Georgia, of the quartering party, an-swered all of our immediate requirements, so we pulled much of our equipment into the long hotel entranceway and crawled away to bed. Mynheer van Egerschot was as powerless to say "no" to the Americans as he had been with the Germans.

After our night's rest we began to unload. As the trucks were lightened, the drizzle still kept the streets awash. Our instructions were that the stay was probably to be protracted, so everything was taken off the trucks. Part of it was stowed in the hotel court under tarpaulins and the rest installed inside in fixed positions for long use. The small dining room was turned into a communal mess hall. The private dining hall was converted into a combination press-and-briefing room, with a huge map of Western Europe covering its entire forward wall. On this map Captain Bill Moody and Lieutenant Harry Correa were to keep a record of the daily situation as well as of the division locations all the way from the Channel to the Alps. Field tables were placed in rows across the room, facing the map. On the floor above the lobby, a large room was set aside for the press censor detachment of Captain Ed Lavelle. This gave the censors a quiet place to read, badly needed in a press camp where conversations are always carried on somewhere between loudly and at full shout.

Before long, the log jam in Paris began to break and war correspondents started to join us. My office had been set up deliberately in a corner of the lobby lounge, just to the left inside the door, and a field phone to the Ninth Army switchboard sat on my desk. Less than twenty feet away in one direction was the teletype, while—almost from the first day—ten feet in the other direction a constant and violent poker game was under way. There are some creative jobs at which a man can be said to be working when he's only looking out the window, and in an Army press camp it is good business to have a day-and-night correspondents' poker game running in the public-relations office. This was not so mad as it seemed in the beginning, and was actually a mutually protective device. In such close quarters, only the legitimate propositions were ever broached. It would have taken a brave and foolish war correspondent to attempt any chicanery or to try for special favors, when the slightest tendency to lower one's voice alerted the volcanic poker table and blanketed it with instant silence as competition became watchful and wary. Thus, all my arrangements with any correspondent could be heard by everyone else. No side deals, or charges of side deals, were possible.

One day when the correspondents were out doing the soggy front in hope of a story, we decided to swap desks in my corner of the room. As we dragged and horsed the furniture around, three men in civilian clothes presented themselves to me in the lobby.

"We are black-market police," said the spokesman. "We would make search this hotel."

"For what reason?"

"The van Egerschots have been German-friendly."

"What do you mean by that? In what way?"

"All during the occupation, they had Germans in this hotel." The other two nodded in corroboration.

"That doesn't prove much. They've got Americans in the hotel now. We didn't ask them if we could come in. I suppose the Germans didn't either."

"It is not the same," said the Dutchman firmly. A Dutchman is a hard man to shake loose.

"All right, we have no objection to your search, but we will have a man with you at all times. You are to take nothing off the premises without permission. When we came in here, the U. S. Army became liable for all the property and for any property damage. You will report anything you find, and if you need anything for evidence, we will have to list it as having passed to the Dutch police. Is that understood?"

The Dutchman nodded stiffly.

By now, all of us were skeptical. Nobody could have gone through France and Belgium without knowing that a great many of the very finest looting expeditions started under pretext of a legal search. The Dutchmen displayed their identity cards, but official-looking documents had become easy to manufacture in every country under the German occupation. One of our sergeants was detailed with them, and they went up the stairs to the third floor, intending to start at the top and work down. No one gave a thought then to the fact that Willem van Egerschot was up there making a room check with one of Lieutenant Thom Patterson's billeting clerks.

The furniture moving began again. As all hands were put to the task getting a heavy desk out of the lobby, we proceeded with jerky movements toward the lounge. There was a piercing scream overhead. Partly from something instinctive when I heard a crash above me near the stair well, I shrank back from what appeared to be a flash of flying rags. The chandelier smashed against the wall, and a falling body brushed my right shoulder and fell with a sickening crunch for a head-and-shoulders landing on the tile floor. The body was Willem van Egerschot.

The Dutch police had cornered him on the third floor, and when they started menacingly toward him, manacles in hand, he bolted in fright. Somehow in that narrow hallway, he darted past the trio and hurdled the guard rail at the head of the stairs to leap across to the first landing. His jump was not good enough, and he hit the chain of the chandelier, bounced off the stair railing, and tumbled head over heels to the ground floor. Miraculously, he was not dead. The stairwell bumps must have broken his speed of descent. He was dazed, but not unconscious. The policemen came thundering down the steps, taking them three at a time, loudly crowing in both Dutch and English that the escape try proved him "guilty." Old Mynheer was by his son's side almost instantly, sobbing, clasping and unclasping his hands as tears rolled down his cheeks. "Oh, my son, my son," he wailed in English. "He have suicided himself . . . he have suicided himself."

Soon a shrieking ambulance siren focused the attention of the whole neighborhood on the Hôtel du Lévrier. The news went from stoop to stoop as Willem was taken on a stretcher from the hotel, and hurried off to the hospital. His father, denied a seat in the ambulance, came back into the hotel and paced up and down. He would cry out, clap his hands to his forehead, look for solace to the ceiling. "He's playing it like Sydney Greenstreet," said Lieutenant John Pecor, who had seen so many people die by then he could not be unduly disturbed. The name "Sydney" stuck with Mynheer van Egerschot.

The soldiers went back to their work, and the Dutch policemen, pleased with their success and reading into it complete vindication, now turned their attention to the cellar. "We have reason to believe," said the spokesman, "that Mynheer van Egerschot has a radio somewhere under this hotel which he uses to keep in touch with his friends, the Germans." It sounded fantastic, but off to the cellar they went. Mynheer van Egerschot spat after them in apoplectic rage, started pacing again, then grabbed his felt hat and clapped it on his head. Having decided to walk to the hospital, he was going to gamble on chances of being admitted.

There were sounds of tapping, hammering and chiseling from time to time below the lobby, but we were all busy above getting set for the evening meal and briefing. The presence of the police even slipped our minds and we only thought of them again when Mynheer van Egerschot came wearily back from the hospital. Griff and I were reminded to check up on the search party. Using a flashlight, we went gingerly down the steep stairs. The light first picked up the coal bin, then went over to the opposite far wall, where it revealed three of the drunkest Dutchmen since the liberation. They had not found their radio station or any link with the "German friends," but they had chipped their way through an echoing wall. It turned out to be the hotel wine bin, whereupon they fell to toasting their lucky day. The tops had been knocked off many bottles of choicest vintage, and after the contents were drunk, the bottles had been tossed in the general direction of the open hearth of the hotel's furnace. The floor was littered with broken glass from the near-misses and the debris of chipped stone, while the atmosphere of the cellar was heavy with a permeating odor—so heavy, in fact, it appeared almost to be dew point.

One by one, we struggled upstairs with them, each of them having difficulty even hitting the steps. None among us could untangle their mumbling, not that it would have made much difference since it was unmistakably Dutch. Griff was disgusted. "This is the first time I ever heard of a policeman hunting for a radio station in a wine bottle," he said. We steered them into the street, and hung them against the walls of the building. Slowly, they began to go hand over hand from window sill to window ledge in the direction of the police station. Although they had violated the instructions against removing anything from the premises without permission, we felt the police inspector would probably leave us alone, and this was worth it. They never came back.

The losers on this day were the Ninth Army war correspondents, who had been wading the mud at the front fruitlessly in search of story material, only to come home and find that a first-class melodrama had been played less than ten feet from the briefing room, and twenty feet from their poker table. These developments, the stuff of thrillers and movies, intrigued our correspondents. With the front mired down and the weather usually foul, many of them felt encouraged to sit it out in the hotel lobby, waiting to see what new intrigue would creep out of the woodwork and present them with a feature.

The XIX Corps, the Ninth's initial sole possession, had been inherited from the First Army, and was headquartered in Heerlen, forty kilometers from Maastricht. That city, surrounded by the mighty slag piles of the Netherlands coal mines, had been taken long before, but a combination of circumstances had not only caused XIX Corps to halt, but to stay. The rains were on, and the long run from the beaches had enervated the forces as well as depleted supplies. Artillery ammunition was rationed. Gasoline was in meager supply, and a tussle was on to see who would use it, Patton or Monty. The greatest hazard, however, was the watery obstacle of the interlocked rivers and reservoirs ahead, all tied to the controlled flash-flood capability of the 180-foot Schwammenauel dam at the headquarters of the Roer River. This brooding mass of water, which could be sluiced across the front at any time as long as the Germans held the dam, could raise the river level in a wall twenty-five feet high and expand the stream's wid'a from fifty yards to a mile and a half. The taking of the Roer dam and its associated reservoirs was imperative before anyone could go anywhere, and they were in the First Army's sector, near Duren. Always a Ninth Army concern because of the impact the dams could have on its operations, the Roer dams tended to dominate most Ninth briefings.

Captain Lavelle had more twinges about the Roer dams than about almost any other problem. Long before First Army, the Ninth Army had a feel for their importance. It was Lavelle who told First Army's chief censor, Captain Eugene Nute, about them. While General Simpson had never underrated them, neither did he go as explosively high on them as First Army. When Nute went into the subject at First Army, a sudden panic engulfed the front and lashed back to Twelfth Army Group which issued an immediate directive: *Stop all mention of the Roer River dams. Repeat stop all mention.*

This precipitated a weird situation one day when Lewis Gannett, of the *New York Herald Tribune,* came to Lavelle. "You mean," said Lew, "I can't say one word about them in a story?" Lavelle repeated the directive, fresh before him. "Here's a Baedeker published before 1939 and it tells all about the Roer River dams. All I want to send is exactly what's here." Some day, reasoned Gannett, the dams would be news, and he wanted his office to have the information handy.

Censorship had come a long way in war since "Cy" Peterman's June 6 story about the raindrops on the Plexiglas of his Marauder which had seemed to say "D-Day, D-Day." Cy was proud of it and had used it in his lead, but it was killed—because it gave weather information. Lavelle thought it would be complete lunacy to stop a quote from a prewar Baedeker, so he passed it and sat around in a cold sweat for a week. Nothing happened from the military point of view, because there were sound heads at SHAEF. But the blacklash came at Lewis Gannett from his news editor who was stunned to read at cable rates a 1939 guidebook description of the Roer dams. We began getting service messages asking that Gannett be sent home, implying that he must have had a mental relapse and was again reviewing back numbers of books!

The slim pickings for anything like top news made the poker game take on a semblance of perpetual motion. Kibitzers sometimes were three deep behind players, and threats of mayhem sounded through the night. Wes Gallagher, the AP's major-domo of the Western Front, not only ran the affairs of his agency from the Channel to the Swiss Alps, he was the local Doc Holliday who sat humped at the green cloth and surveyed the competition like a glowering panther in a tree. Tense moments developed often, leading only to shooting off at the mouth, since none of the participants carried pistols to protect their honor, or lack of it. None of these frays with words were as conclusive as they might have been with weapons, but all of the correspondents were experts at colorful oral barrage. Marcel Wallenstein of the *Kansas City Star* preferred *chemin de fer,* but he played poker since it was in season. If the UP was represented in the game by either Ned Roberts or Jim McGlincy, or if Frank Coniff of INS had a hand, it gave Gallagher a chance to take out some of his competitive drive in hours of fun. If joined by John Mecklin, who was inclined to paper the house with IOU's, the table was sometimes as explosive as a carpet bombing.

In order to encourage the game to break up, and to get players and kibitzers out of the hotel and up front, Griff suggested a maneuver. "Let's get a reputation for a bum noon meal," he said, "and they'll hit the road." After that, Lieutenant George Williams and Sergeant Gudger conspired with the Dutch chef to do a poor job on the luncheon menu and to put the food out half done, or completely cold. As an added encouragement to the correspondents to get out, it was the known policy to feed forward headquarters troops well at noon. Sometimes the writers found good features out there even though the actual battle lines were stagnant. Through this wrench of the gastronomic tract, the lobby quieted and the poker conclave melted away in the daylight hours. Our main goal was being achieved as the diary of the war got written and trickled through to home editions.

There was all the difference in the world between the nearby First Army press camp, in Spa's Hotel Portugal in Belgium, and the Ninth Army. First Army never got over its days in the dirt in Normandy, and its dig-in manner of living. No Army on the continent could shake from First the honor of having been the broad back and the strong shoulder of the drive, nor could it ever be taken from the First Army press camp that it contained the veterans of the most battles. But big and bold as First Army was, and mobile as Third Army had proved itself, the war correspondents began to gravitate to Ninth on a big hunch. As the armies came closer to the Rhine, it was obvious that a gigantic wheeling motion and shift to the north and east would be dictated. This made Ninth Army the best bet in the early winter of 1944 to be the one which would skirt north of the Ruhr, Germany's industrial heart, and point straight at Berlin.

Top writers, photographers and radio commentators attached themselves early, and were prepared to entrench with the Ninth Army for the duration. Even though the Ninth was an unknown combat quantity, the correspondents thought it a winner and placed their stakes accordingly. Proximity to the British Twenty-first Army Group on the left, plus a British awareness of Monty's incessant campaign for a bigger role in the allied operation, influenced a large interest in Ninth Army from the British Empire correspondents. If only adjacent to British arms, the Ninth was worth watching, and should Monty take it over one day, it could then be included in that favorite British headline, "Monty's Men." Thus, Ninth Army press camp was heavily international.

Britain's major newspapers were strongly represented. Noel Monks, who had begun his war corresponding in Abyssinia, was not only a first-ranker among all the military writers present, but stood that way with his paper, the *Daily Mail*. He had done much to emblazon the magnificent record of the RAF in the Battle of Britain. Jimmy Holborn fed the *Times* and roomed with Michael Moynihan of the *News-Chronicle,* who later changed off with Ronnie Walker. David Walker, one of the best informed on continental affairs in peace or war, had unusual competition on his own paper, the tabloid *Daily Mirror,* in the form of a pen-and-ink concoction, a cartoon-strip girl called Jane, an absolute must for British readers. Hardly a day passed that she didn't manage to get almost all her clothes completely off. The one day she did coincided with a British advance of eight miles! Whether this was an example of that fallacious philosophic premise, *post hoc ergo propter hoc,* there was no denying Jane was powerful stuff for a mere writer like Dave Walker to compete with, but he tried manfully and with some success.

The British provincial chain of the publishing giant, Lord Kemsley, started us off with E. W. Kingdom, and then replaced him with a journalistic jumbo, Larry Fairhall. The *Daily Express* had Laurence Wilkinson, who had hitherto covered the war from what most of the "pros" referred to as a "comfort station," the neutral capital of Portugal, Lisbon. The Laborite daily, the *Herald,* split its chores among Stanley Bishop, Wing Commander Charles Bray and beauteous Iris Carpenter, a stunning blonde operating from quarters given her in the various field hospitals. Peter Lawless spent part of his time with First Army, part with us, and was the *Daily Telegraph's* man. That well of deep thought and sound information, the *Observer,* gave us Eric Wigham.

The pet of the press camp was Alfred M. Lee of the midlands *Huddersfield Examiner.* His home town was near the dreary moors of the Brontë sisters and his circulation on a clear day was about as far as a young man could see, but he chose the Ninth Army press layout to ride with to the end of the war. There wasn't a British boy in the American Ninth, nor any Huddersfield angle to write about, but stay he did. Lee had made a gold strike as he came through Brussels before he joined Ninth Army, in that he located a German map depot which housed the charts of Hitler's ill-fated "Operation Sea Lion"—the invasion of England which never came off. Included was a Huddersfield set, disclosing the very plans for destruction of and taking of his provincial city. Four of them, beautifully prepared to the scale of one inch to 10,000, even included his own house, not, he was pleased to see, an objective of first importance. The maps, with Lee the discoverer, went home for a time to go on exhibition, startling his good neighbors and bringing home to them the nature of total war.

He may have preferred a British sector, but he never said so, probably because British nationals used to pressure to keep the provincials out of press camps. When provincials sought equal representation, this brought the numbers up to a size British commanders did not like to cope with. Nine different times, from Maastricht to the Elbe, it was necessary for me to defend and "show cause" for Al Lee to keep him from being sent back to England. But Alfred M. Lee, though British, represented a policy dear to me and supported constantly by me. Once the agencies, networks, magazines and big newspapers were cared for, we tried always to fill our quota with regional, sectional, or territorial correspondents. They were the greatest morale producers carried by the military forces, because where others must cover the "big picture" or the general story, these men could bring out the human detail, citing names, home towns, parents, street addresses. Their stories, published, broadcast, heard and read in the home areas, meant more to enlivening a soldier's attitude than any other thing save a letter from home. Many a dull day has been brightened by mail which contains not only assurances that all is well at home, but also a clipping from a favorite family newspaper, or word that some broadcaster has used an interview or account in the man's own words of an action at the front. Literally hundreds of times, such letters would say, "Ever since the story was published, all your old friends have been calling to say they saw it, too, and Nancy said it made her cry just to hear them talk about you. . ." or ". . . and after the radio used it on the broadcast, a man from the station came out to the house and gave us a record of what you said. Now, when we play that record again it's like having you here with us." These things speak to a man of a life he wants to believe in, but which has come to seem to him as improbable and remote as a dream.

The principle Al Lee represented was worth every rebuttal we successfully entered for him. The Ninth Army was exceedingly fortunate in this respect with its American regional representatives, who worked endlessly on the home-town boy. The venerable twosome of Louis Azrael, *Baltimore News-Post,* and Holbrook Bradley, *Baltimore Sun,* literally lived with the Twenty-ninth Infantry Division, now on the Ninth Army front, formerly with First and Third. A Maryland national guard organization, the Twenty-ninth had taken casualties which reduced its numbers of local boys, but it managed to have a lot of them through to war's end. Led by ex-West Point quarterback, scrappy Maj. Gen. Charles Gerhardt, the Twenty-ninth had a long pull from the first minutes of Omaha Beach and the record of its fights was not nearly so well or appealingly written by the Army's historical services as it was by the daily outpourings of these two men reporting to Maryland's two greatest newspapers. If Maryland remembers it had a Twenty-ninth Infantry Division in World War II, a lot of that memory was enriched by Azrael and Bradley.

Gordon Gammack, the hard-bitten Iowan of the *Des Moines Register-Tribune,* was jeepmated with Vic Jones, *Boston Globe,* who saw to it that the Ninth Army's New England elements got their full credits. Gammack was zeroed in pursuit of the Iowa boy and in this he was extremely effective. There was a steady, good-natured competition between Gammack and Jones, and Gammack had prevailed on his driver, Private Ralph Curtis, of Davenport, Iowa, to paint a large, red "IOWA" sign on the windshield. Jones complained that this was unfair. "Gammack just sits in that jeep like a sultan," Jones told me. "Some GI spots that sign, and yells to ask him where in Iowa he's from. Gammack says, 'You from Iowa?' The kid says he sure as hell is ... maybe it's Ottumwa, or Cedar Rapids, or Sioux City, but all Gammack has to do then is step out and interview him." Jones said he had to walk all over the place like a peanut vendor asking, "Is there anybody here from New England?"

Try as we might, we could never get Massachusetts, or New England, painted on the jeep so it was readable. The letters had to be too small. Once we tried an abbreviation, putting "MASS." on the opposite side of "IOWA." The results shook us. Jones and Gammack were steaming along next day, watching for somebody to come up for their bait, Gammack with his "IOWA" hook out and Jones with his "MASS." Riding not far behind the battle lines, they came suddenly upon a unit resting in an assembly area, just before pushing off into the attack. A GI, seeing the "MASS." sign, ran out and, in some agitation, flagged the jeep down. "Father," he said, laying his hand on Jones's arm, "I want to confess." After that unnerving experience, Vic cleaned his side of the windshield, and left the billing to Gammack.

From the *St. Paul Dispatch-Pioneer* came Alton W. Smalley and he paired off in a jeep with Gordon Grant of the *Tampa Tribune.* They had a Mexican jeep driver, undoubtedly a manly guy, but who answered to the name of Inez Martinez and came from Elsa, Texas. The trio was a closed corporation, and Martinez made their jeep colorful by shredding inner tubes to give it flared hub caps. It was always washed, highly polished, and had a certain carnival atmosphere in all the surrounding drabness. Very few men from Minnesota or Florida ever stuck their heads up in Ninth Army territory without becoming a story for home consumption at the hands of these three wild men. Martinez was as shy as Smalley and Grant were voluble, except when mud splashed his jeep, or snow forced him to chains, or the jeep coughed to indicate the motor pool was giving it cursory handling. Then he swore in Spanish, and saints took cover. No one knew much about him. He was uncommunicative even with his correspondent teammates, except to indicate he understood their wildest suggestions, which he took off to perform unflinchingly. The Red Cross passed me a communication one day that Martinez' father back in Texas was greatly concerned because he had not heard from his son in six months. The usual procedure was to call in the man and tell him to take pen in hand. When Martinez brought Smalley and Grant in that night, Griff sent him to me. I told him about the message. He held his head down, giggling a little as he always did.

"Hee's keeding," he said.

"Do you mean you have written your father?"

"No, I no write," said Martinez. "He no can read eet. Ever'body know thees."

"But somebody could read it to him if he had a letter from you."

"No," said Martinez with finality, but patiently. "Nobody could read eet. I no can write. My pop—he know thees, too."

So he went back to polish his vehicle, and I sent off a letter to the Red Cross in Texas telling them to convey to the elder Martinez that his son was in fine health and ran one of the best jeeps in Ninth Army.

Jack Shelley, of radio WHO in Des Moines, did on radio what the individual newspapers did in print, and he was constantly reproducing for home consumption the voices of Iowans thousands of miles from home. He had a following of almost everyone in the state. One-armed Jack Bell, *Miami Herald,* and Jess Krueger, *Chicago Herald American,* added to this category of local interest, and as far as I was concerned there was always room for one more, two more, or as many more of the same kind as were willing to join us. They were the fine basis on which morale was built, did their jobs in a businesslike way, and were never any trouble.

On the third floor of the Hôtel du Lévrier we had lined one room with drapes and turned it into a studio from which our radio correspondents could be piped to the nearby Press Wireless link to the U. S. As regulars Howard K. Smith, CBS, and Robert Massell, Blue Network, were the American teams. BBC was alternately represented by Stanley Maxted and Stuart MacPherson, a pair of Canadians who stood well with all their colleagues. Smith had only recently been sprung from long internment with his wife in Switzerland. With our studio arrangement, it was possible for a radio correspondent to write his story on the first floor, be censored on the second, and broadcast from the third—everything complete inside the building, like a YMCA. Our military radio station, however, with JEEP as its call letters, was set up out of town.

The news agencies were bellwethered, but not led, by Wes Gallagher, who not only covered Ninth Army for AP but called the turn on dispositions of all other AP men. His editorial conferences over the field phone in my "office" were constant, choleric and color-ful, and woe betide the AP man who shared his jeep with any rival. "Get 'em the hell out of that jeep," he used to order top-of-voice. "They're no buddies of yours—they're just trying to be on top of AP's best story all the time." Hal Boyle, by now almost as much a part of First Army as its general, Courtney Hodges, was a floater on occasion, and had license to make AP "three deep" in war corre-spondents anywhere he went. News agencies normally had only two spots at any Army. Our regular second AP man was Kenneth Dixon, who had replaced Franklin Banker. Hal Boyle described himself as a "poor man's Ernie Pyle" because he wrote in the same personal way about soldiers, and Dixon stayed completely corporate in his defer-ence to a peer by calling himself a "poor man's Hal Boyle." Gallagher stayed with Ninth Army all the way—it was going to Berlin, wasn't it? —but after Dixon, there was another AP change, Bob Eunson.

Roberts and McGlincy were UP's two until Roberts was replaced by Clint Conger. INS took only one of its available spaces, giving it to Frank Coniff, formerly of the *New York Journal-American*. At the crucial winter battle period, Boyd Lewis was a UP workhorse and popular guy all around. Agence France-Presse secured its Ninth Army coverage from Pierre Fréderix, and occasionally Louis Deroche, Georgia University educated. Our down-under agency, Australian Consolidated Press, was responsibly handled by Godfrey "Jeff" Blunden. S. J. P. Lissagorsky traveled the Ninth Army sector for the Agence Belge. Rudolph Dunbar, whose range in music ran from piano to the more complicated roles of guest conductor of a Paris symphony, came with us several times as war correspondent for Associated Negro Press. Flora Sokolow represented the Combined Polish Press. By far the most intriguing member of our group was a uniformed Russian correspondent from Tass, D. Kraminov, with a Red Army lieutenant colonel named Andrei Piliugin as aide. The aide took more notes than Kraminov, the writer. They never filed over any of our communications facilities and their material, if there was any, was never censored.

Richard Rowland was Ninth Army's Reuter's writer, and he was followed by another long-timer for the same agency, Willie Steen. In between was Harold Mayes who took off on leave to London once, leaving me instructions to take his office messages and file appropriate answers. There are really two languages, English and American. Reuter's Chief War Correspondent Sidney Mason was horrified almost immediately by American corruptions of the English language and tumbled to the deception. Mayes was sacked, treating me to my first ghost-writing lesson that the word habits of an individual are the key to this anonymous profession.

The individual big newspapers in the U. S. gathered us an unusual array. Fred Graham, a former police reporter of the *New York Times;* Lewis Gannett, book critic who went off to war to encounter grosser adventures than those offered by the fiction which went across his desk at the *Herald Tribune;* Hugh Schuck, of the tabloid *Daily News;* and Max Lerner, *PM,* representing the more than slightly left-of-center viewpoint, were on our roster. When Lewis Gannett came, he was fresh from the poker-playing in France where the franc was cheap, pegged at fifty to the dollar. He loved his poker, so joined up with the cutthroats. Fortunately he won, and only then did he realize that the Dutch gulden with which he had so carelessly backed his judgment was rated three and three quarters to the buck and that he had come into a small fortune.

Ronald Steed, a man of Falstaffian appearance, was with the *Christian Science Monitor.* The *Chicago Tribune* started with William Strand, who moved away in favor of Hank Wales, veteran from World War I. The *Chicago Sun*'s John Mecklin left Third to come to Ninth.

The photographers were normal for photographers, leveling off somewhere between the hectic and hysterical. Henry Griffin, noisy, persistent and pugnacious, cocked his lens often and everywhere for the AP. He had been at the White House for years before coming to Europe. "I couldn't think of a new angle for Roosevelt's cigarette holder," he said. Fred Ramage, a conniving Cockney but a favorite flimflammer when pictures were to be taken, was with Keystone-International, the British photo agency, and *Life* magazine was in good position with a nervy New Zealander, George Silk, who would go into a gun muzzle to get a clear negative. Two from the newsreel pool, but specifically representing Universal and MGM's *News of the Day* respectively, were Frenchmen, Raymond Majat and Gaston Madru.

The never-ending puzzle was Nemo Canberra-Lucas, who wrote for the Portuguese language daily in Rio de Janeiro, *Anoite*. His stories of the war were flowery enough to bower a hedge and somewhat travelogue-y in nature; he seemed to use the war as a background for a world tour. "Aye spik seben langwidge," he once told me, "Angleez da bast." This startled us all, and made us wonder how he managed, but he turned out 700-to-2,000-word *opera,* all in Portuguese, which were tough propositions to process. First, he had to translate them into his "bast Angleez" for the censor, who hopefully put a clearance stamp on them. Then the copy went to the teletype puncher, who would invariably scream, since his transmission had to be letter for letter, a painful chore. Nemo could never quite understand the Geneva convention, which ruled that war correspondents were noncombatants. Taken to watch a fire fight one day in the 104th Infantry Division by the PRO, Lieutenant Mort Kaufman of New York City, he was left alone for a moment and he took that opportunity to borrow a rifle and enter into the shooting like a Chinese celebrating his New Year. Mort had to disarm him and explain that correspondents were restricted to pencils rather than pistols, typewriters rather than tommy guns. Nemo had simpler ideas of war. He thought everyone on "this side" had a right to put holes in anybody on "that side."

Language problems always cause difficulties, but Nemo compounded his by completely misunderstanding the simplest things said to him in passing. He roomed with two men least likely to be irritated, Hugh Schuck and Al Lee, but they blew up one morning at the wash basins. Nemo had been first and was drying off when Hugh came up to lather his face for a shave.

"Good morning," said Hugh.

Nemo's eyes widened. He grabbed Hugh by both his arms and took on an appearance of great consternation.

"Who you say get shot?" Nemo asked.

That was all. Hugh, his face half lathered, and Al Lee, still in his undershirt, appeared before my desk. "He's got to go," said peaceable

Hugh. "I can't go through life trying to explain basic English to that punchy Portuguese."

Three days later, a single room opened up. Normally, the singles were fought for, with many arguments about length of time in the press camp, real and imagined priorities and rights, and so on, but in Nemo's case, everyone backed off to let him have it.

Breakthrough and Turmoil

Negro truck drivers, when first entering Maastricht, were taken aback by the Dutch children who pointed and shouted at them in English. "There's Black Peter," they said. Small children ran to their mothers' skirts, but the older ones stood their ground defiantly.

The press camp of the Ninth Army soon learned about Black Peter, too. In the Netherlands, December 6 is St. Nicholas' Day, which corresponds in some ways to our Christmas, while Christmas itself is observed there only as a church holiday. St. Nicholas was actually a Turk, the Bishop of Myra in the province of Antalya. He became the patron saint of children, sailors and pawnbrokers, obviously a man who saw a little good in everyone, and the stories of his benevolence were brought to the world at large by seafaring men. Hence, the St. Nicholas of the Netherlands does not come fat and jolly with reindeer from the North Pole, but cadaverous, in conical hat and flowing robes, up from Spain by boat. And he has an indefatigable assistant, a dwarf-like busybody who sneaks up on all Netherlands children when they are unaware and particularly when they are doing something they shouldn't. He makes notes of their misdoings, and when St. Nicholas' Day comes and St. Nick is about to hand over a present, then up pops Black Peter and tells what he knows. The good saint then has to ask for certain promises of better behavior before he can give the present. This naturally reviled helper of St. Nicholas does most of his skulking around, legend has it, by coming down the chimneys and watching from back of the blaze in the fireplace. This gets him all covered with soot and begrimed with smoke, which is why he is called "Black Peter."

The Hôtel du Lévrier was housing less than 150 people, but by the last week in November the words and pictures produced by the men under its roof reached out to approximately 278,000,000 people daily on all six continents. The actual operation to back them up involved first a complex, twenty-four-hour grind of communications. Our own military radio voice circuit, JEEP, a truck unit with its own power trailer, could hook into BBC receivers in London and there record the programs from the Netherlands. The teletype rolled out reams of words, which went by land line through Twelfth Army Group's switchboard at Verdun, then on to London or Paris. The commercial Press Wireless transmitter was rigged about three blocks down the Boschstraat from the hotel, with its long V-shaped antenna held skyward over a small pond by three 100-foot poles. Using the water to bounce the signal, it came in clearly at the receiving station at Baldwin, Long Island, N.Y. The motor pool, with fifty-four vehicles ranging from jeeps to trucks, fought hard to keep in full operation. No matter what the rough daily travel demands were, the mechanics, working in the cold and messy weather, kept the record spotless and no correspondent was ever marooned for lack of transport. Correspondents had to sign up for jeeps the night before and in signing give a destination so anyone else going that way could pile on.

The exercise of administrative watchfulness over the comings and goings of the correspondents was no small task. Each army had its own press group, and there was a big tendency to regard assignment to a given army as establishing exclusive rights. Any interlopers invariably meant trouble, and attempts were made to beat them off. The Army PRO had to check with each of the divisional PRO's daily to keep track of developments which had story makings. An occasional floating newspaperman, or radio reporter, would come along with only a few days to spend, and ask me to "line up about ten men from northern Ohio in a tank outfit," or "get me eight men from Iowa who have won the Purple Heart," or even "find me four men from Brooklyn who are in foxholes along the front." The correspondent could then sit down at the poker table, or go off to look at the town. We would poll the divisions, who would go through their card files, locate the men in battalions or regiments, and report a time when they could all be available at the division headquarters. Full particulars were then

put on a memo for the correspondent, who had only to make good on
the appointment. Only once did we ever draw the line on this helpful
practice, and it was when a short-wave programmer asked to have
"twenty Spanish-speaking soldiers" selected for a show to be beamed
south of the border. "I really only need one," he said, "but I'd like to
audition twenty to get the right one." The front was hardly set up for
a talent hunt, nor was it any place to tell nineteen fighting men that
they "wouldn't do." He needed one, he got one.

One of the most delicate aspects was the maintenance of imper-
ceptible control over this mass of volatile temperament. Walking on
eggs was simple by comparison. War correspondents bore the simu-
lated rank of captain, in case they were captured, a status established
by the Geneva convention. As long as they were safely with our own
forces, however, they assumed the rank of Field Marshal, in most
cases, and recognized no conventions.

Their regular military mess bill was $5.25 a week for food, and
their lodgings were free. In addition, the Ninth Army press camp
asked a $4.75 fee each seven days, making the total a round $10.
The extra charge was agreed to by all the participating correspondents, and the resulting fund was administered by Lieutenant Thom
Patterson. For want of a better name, he called it the "Widows and
Orphans Protective Fund." It could be used to buy extra food, to pay
civilian help, or for entertainment. Every device was used to make
the camp a place of respite after the mud and cold of the front, so
the first use of the fund was for the hiring of a six-piece Dutch string
orchestra and a blond girl singer. It gave the place quite a lift every
night when the dining-room door swung open to a Strauss waltz or a
current popular song. The singer was a cutie, and she managed to
have enough low-cut gowns to make a change every night in the
week—one could tell what day of the week it was by the order in
which she wore them. The orchestra was more interested in the food
they got each night than in money, and the throat with which the
singer crooned always yearned for that nightly square meal. It was
obvious from the start that the glances trained on the girl by some of
the gathering were too intent. Lieutenant George Williams, aware of
the high voltage sex had put upon the place, set a sign on the piano
which warned: "Anyone caught fraternizing with the singer will have
his head shaved." The next morning three correspondents came down
to breakfast with their hair cropped. Bragging!

My pleas to Redding for permanent assignment of Lieutenant George Fuller and Lieutenant Lyman C. "Andy" Anderson, a newspaperman himself before he came into the Army, from the Twelfth Army Group talent pool to the Ninth Army press camp were granted, and we started a "home-town news service." Not only did we service the war correspondents, but with Fuller in the radio production slot, and Anderson on press, coupled with Lieutenant Bill Brown who herded the Signal Corps photographers into picture assignments, we began to turn out supplemental radio program material, stories and photos for direct mail to radio stations and newspapers not represented by their own staffers. Three times each week, Fuller did a JEEP feature for inclusion in the BBC "forces program" which was broadcast back to the front and tuned in by the troops. It corresponded on radio to *Stars and Stripes,* the soldier newspaper. All the rest of Fuller's time was spent making interview recordings which were sent to individual radio stations in America. The sounds of gunfire on Fuller's recordings were real. With Private Andrew Holmes, of Wetumpka, Alabama, his combination jeep driver and power generator operator, Fuller would install his recorder in a ground depression or behind a hill, then crawl out to some forward position with a long microphone wire stringing out behind him. Cowering in a hole with some infantryman, he would make the recording. He would then crawl back, Holmes would rerun to be sure they had it, and they would pack up and be off to a new location. There were regular calls to Fuller, too, to do the Ninth Army segment for NBC's "Army Hour," which was on every Sunday afternoon during the war.

Lieutenant Anderson, in combination with Brown, monitored the press side of our home-town service. Each of the divisions and special units with Ninth Army had makeshift, but active, public-relations sections. From November, 1944, to May, 1945, we put out an average of 15,000 stories, photos, and wire-recorded interviews each month to cities and towns in the U. S.[1] These might vary from a post

---

[1] General Eisenhower was always concerned about the lack of "personal touch" in war coverage. He once wrote Generals Bradley and Devers: "Much of the publicity with respect to the achievement of U. S. ground units in this theater has been impersonal and generalized in character. Many opportunities have been lost to publicize forcefully the extraordinary achievements of . . . units in specified situations. . . . These matters may not seem weighty to you when you are engaged in operational problems of the greatest magnitude . . . but . . . a personalized presentation of achievements of units of this great force

card, announcing that a soldier had been decorated or promoted, to a full-scale 500-word feature giving in detail some battle action involving a man or men from a single area. The pictures were sometimes of the fighting, but mostly singles or groups keyed to some common activity. Recordings could be one-minute statements by a soldier identifying himself by name and home town and telling his story, or full fifteen-minute segments using several soldiers from the same town. This was the kind of thing General Eisenhower was to pay tribute to when he said: "I know of no thing which so improves the morale of the soldier as to see his unit, or his own name in print— just once." [2]

In full swing now, the Ninth Army press camp was just picking its collective teeth after Thanksgiving Dinner, when a Dutch girl, Mary Bury, who had been helping us as an interpreter, came to me about a problem which was worrying her. "Maastricht," she said, "has several orphanages. Most of the youngsters cannot remember a family, or good food, or a happy St. Nicholas' Day." She said St. Nicholas' Day in the Netherlands came on December 6, and that it had the gift-giving and feast aspects of the American Christmas. She wondered if the military and war correspondents of the Ninth Army press camp would like to put on a party. Since the Ninth Army front was quiet after the push to the banks of the Roer earlier in November, everybody jumped at the chance to do something which would be a change and have something to do with kids.

"How many are there between the ages of—say, three to twelve?" Mary estimated sixty, or maybe sixty-five. "Could they be brought to this hotel?" That would be easy. "Would they be wearing wooden shoes?" Never forget pictures, or picture possibilities, with photographers around. *Klampen?* Oh, yes, some of them had nothing else. "We'll put on a party they'll never forget," Mary was promised.

Griff and the staff were called in and asked for ideas, and the unholy atmosphere of the press camp began to warm with a new inner light when we broke the news to the correspondents. Everyone gave up his candy ration. A kitty bucket was placed by the piano. The blonde sang, "Oh, give me something to remember you by," and for once the response from her audience was spiritual. The

would result in a greater appreciation at home and this, in turn, would have a beneficial result on the morale of every organization."

[2] Remark made before a conference at SHAPE, Paris, September 6, 1951.

bucket was full of guilders in no time. Lieutenant Williams found a Dutchman who believed he could make ice cream from powdered milk if we could give him some sugar and other ingredients. "Von't be best ice cream," he said, "but dey never had any yet, so it vill be best dey ever had." When the kindly Dutch baker across the street from the hotel heard what was up, he offered to make something special if we could provide him with supplies. Rations were chopped without protest.

There was a sharp jog in our St. Nicholas' Day plans the first of December. A Dutchman, in morning coat and high hat, with the manners of a plenipotentiary, came to call.

"You do a bad thing about the orphans," he said.

"A bad thing?"

"You have only Catholic orphans. There are others, the Protestant ones of the Dutch Reformed Church. They are in greater need."

Apologetically, he was reassured that this was an unintentional oversight. We had assumed that all had been included in our invitation. We told him, by all means, to have the sixteen Protestant orphans present. A crisis had come and gone.

Another immediately came to the doorstep. Mary Bury reported that there was strong feeling that the orphans should be screened. Some of them had had parents who were collaborationists with the Germans. We were shaken a little by this one. The lot of an orphan was not hard enough in the vengeful climate left over from the occupation, it seemed. "The press camp is putting on the party," I told her, "and we're entitled to make up the invitation list. We want *all* the kids between three and twelve. They have one thing in common— they have all endured a loss, and that's enough to qualify them to come here." Her face broke into a happy smile, and that crisis was over.

When St. Nicholas' Day came, the Americans were at a loss about what to do next and surrendered themselves completely to the technical advice of Mary Bury and her Dutch friends, who took the money and did the shopping, being instructed only to spend it all.

They found the Dutchman to act as St. Nicholas and fitted him out in the customary flowing robe and towering conical hat. He had a breast-length *black* beard, too. Griff was dismayed when he saw the Dutch version of St. Nicholas. "There wouldn't be a kid in Grove

City who'd speak to me," he said, "if I tried to pass off a guy who looked like that as Santy Claus."

The girls also produced a Black Peter, who was a veteran in the role. As he progressed with his make-up, we all fell to disliking him. Griff and George Williams pulled the dining tables into a C-shaped circle, with places for eighty-five to be seated, all with their backs to the walls, and with the center, where a throne was built for St. Nicholas, in full view of everyone. The correspondents were to be stationed around the walls so they could help with the "guests," and they were looking forward to it. Every eight feet down the table length was a big wooden shoe, and in it a tall candle burned. At every plate was an array of candy, which had looked so plain when it came in the PX issue, but now began to take on the extra glow of childhood dreams. In the kitchen were three tubs of a snowy-white version of ice cream, pale but sweet, and on the stove were great pots of steaming hot chocolate, something none of the orphans had ever tasted.

Promptly at three o'clock in the afternoon, almost as if the children had waited in the street, a great clatter of wooden shoes taking short steps on small feet announced the coming of the orphans. They responded to gentle steering and the dining room, the linen, the well-set tables widened all their eyes. The line was stalled somewhat as they wanted to stand and look. A dull old mess hall to us was a stick-candy world to them. Eventually all were seated.

The first element of the parade of edibles was cake, then ice cream, and hot chocolate. The candy was put away in pockets for later. The food was gulped down, faces got gooey, and there were calls for copious refills of the hot chocolate. When every stomach had lost its wrinkles, the electric lights were doused and only the candles in the wooden shoes provided their gleam. A warming expectancy fell over the dining room, and the adults were curious since most of them had never seen this spectacle before.

With the stately tread of a church processional, in walked St. Nicholas. The eighty-five pairs of small eyes in the room were brighter than the candles, and anticipation was thick enough to make it difficult to breathe. St. Nicholas took his throne and started to talk in the hush about how everyone should be good, and how important this would be if they were to grow into the Dutch men and women their country would need. Then he opened a huge book he carried into which we had put the names of all the orphans. This was the time for which everyone was waiting. There was a scurry of feet over the tile in the outer lobby, and St. Nicholas raised his eyes from the book to determine the nature of the intrusion. A childish gasp was heard in the room. Black Peter came running in, and stood impudently at St. Nicholas' left. The kids all eyed him nervously, as if Lucifer himself had charged the sanctuary. St. Nicholas seemed neither to favor the presence of Black Peter, nor to be displeased. His eyes went back to the book and he called a name.

It belonged to a six-year-old, who made the long walk from his chair to the lighted semicircle about the throne. His face had been scrubbed almost down to the true skin, and his cheeks were shining red. His hair had been combed with water, but by now had gotten away from its slick and was tousled. There was some telltale chocolate around his mouth, and he had the winning smile of a cherub. St. Nicholas addressed him in Dutch and asked him if he had been a good boy, to which he bobbed his head with great conviction. There was a derisive noise from Black Peter, and a fearful shadow crossed the little boy's face. One could almost feel him searching his memory for any wrongdoing of which he might have been guilty.

"That time last August," teased Black Peter in his sinister way, "did you really wash your hands and feet before you went to bed like the Sister said?"

The six-year-old stood his ground and said he had.

"All right, all right," said Black Peter, with a casual wave of his hand. "I just wanted you to know I was watching."

A sigh of relief went over the whole dining room, as St. Nicholas gave the boy his present, after which he ran all the way back to his chair. St. Nicholas returned to the book, called another name, and the process was repeated. One by one, the presents were distributed, and a new parade was formed. Too much excitement, and too much hot chocolate started taking toll, and a youthful exodus to the toilets began. Hugh Schuck drew one little girl who spent more time there than she did at the table, but he was her willing chaperone. She got a great kick out of hanging possessively to his hand, and so did Hugh.

Frank Coniff wrote a story about the party which he filed through the censors. "The only military secret you'll find in that," he said, "is that soldiers are suckers for kids and dogs." He could have added war correspondents, too.

It was 5:30 when the party broke up, and the recessional march took our small guests out the door. The noise of the wooden shoes receded in the distance as their wearers, loaded down with presents and candy, headed for home with a new impression of the world in which they lived. There was only one dissenting note, which is normal for all children's outings—many of them were sick on the way home. The powdered-milk ice cream had been too rich for their small stomachs.

As the tables were being shifted back into place for the evening meal, I returned to my desk and started to sit down when my knees bumped against something which moved. An eight-year-old girl was crouching there, one of the Dutch Reformed Church orphans, who looked at me with big round eyes trying to determine whether the smile she saw was the prelude to some scolding.

"I stay behind," she said, still holding the hand extended to her to help her out of her hiding place. "I wanted to say thank you."

"How is it you speak English so well?"

"I learn it in school," she said proudly. We talked on, and she did have a very good grasp of the language for one so young. The school, she said, was just up the street, and she passed by the hotel every day.

"Won't they be looking for you at home?"

"I think so," she said, fleeing toward the door, then back to me. "Will you walk home with me?"

Who could resist a charmer like this one? We went out of the hotel together, and the streets were completely dark now with the blackout on, so I could only trust in her guidance. She was sure of herself, however, and though she hung tightly to my hand, from the sound of her wooden shoes she was dancing along happily. Her chatter was continuous, too. The orphanage, a cold-looking warehouse type of building, was only two blocks from the hotel on the same street. As we came up, there was a flash of light in the door. With a shawl over her head the director was coming out.

"Lei," she said in relief, "where have you been?" Then she saw me. "I hope she was no trouble."

"Not at all. It was my fault. I was showing her over the hotel, and you were gone before we had gotten back. I brought her home."

Lei looked up, her eyes shining in the reflected light from the crack in the door. Turning to go, I paused. "When I take a girl home like this, I expect to be kissed good night." And I'm sure I got the one that was saved for the Prince in that fairyland for which she yearned.

The poker game was gathering when I got back to my desk, but it wasn't so profane that night. There was too much of the echo of happy childhood still hanging over the place.

Every day after that, the orphans from down the street came to the window, tapped on it to attract attention, then waved and went on to school. Sometimes we would meet at the door and talk, and occasionally we'd walk home with them.

There was disquiet in the air, which nobody could quite pin down. On December 7, after the St. Nicholas party, we had to take the entire press camp out to Castle Remberg, over the border in Germany, headquarters of Maj. Gen. Robert W. Hasbrouck's Seventh Armored Division, to attend a briefing for the projected attack of the Seventh Armored against a German salient near Geilenkirchen. If wiped out, this salient would reduce the line by half and leave no thorns in the Ninth Army front. General Hasbrouck thought the attack would go around December 11, and his PRO Captain Nils Jacobson invited all the correspondents back to cover it.

Previously, in mid-November, the Sixth SS Panzer Army of the Germans had shown ostentatiously near Cologne, and the Fifth SS Panzer Army was slightly north of them. Von Rundstedt appeared ready to hit any American forces unwise enough to try bounding over the Roer. Moreover, von Rundstedt had shown himself extremely sensitive and hostile to any thrusts against the Roer dams in the First Army section. First Army's intelligence summary, when December was a third gone, fixed the forty-five miles between the Schwammenauel dam and north into Monty's sector as the most likely to be lively during the early winter, but all things indicated a German defensive. Even though we had been briefed on the Seventh Armored's line-straightening action, there was no further call from Jacobson. The Seventh Armored did not attack on December 11.

As winter locked in some of the roads in the wild Ardennes to the south, press camp denizens in the Hotel Portugal in Spa were complaining about First Army's apathy in not allowing them to jump forward to the attack areas surrounding the Schwammenauel dams. The correspondents would come in each night half frozen from long trips to and from the front, and Major Casey Dempsey was under heavy criticism to move up, though First Army's deputy chief of staff rendered a firm negative on this.

On December 15, Lieutenant Charles Rhodes was sent up by

Major Dempsey to the 106th Infantry Division to brief the PRO on the way the press operated in the First Army sector, and to find out what facilities the 106th had. The division was completely green, and Rhodes found communications to the lower units in bad shape. He went back to Spa expecting to come in again later when they were more settled.

Major Reavis O'Neal, an Air Force PRO, had been visiting the front-line press camps and started out early on the morning of December 16 for Paris, where he was based. As he entered the wooded Ardennes, not far from Bastogne, what with the snow and the on-rushing Christmas season, he decided he wanted a Christmas tree to take to Paris with him. He heard a great deal of ominous rumbling, the sound of tanks, but it was the season of peace on earth and he whittled away with his pocketknife at the stringy tree until he finally cut it down. Throwing it in the back of his jeep, he went on to Paris.

At 5 A.M., earlier that day, five extremely sharp attacks were launched by the Germans into the Ardennes. They surged over the Twenty-eighth and 106th Infantry Divisions, engulfing them. Major O'Neal drove up to the Scribe Hotel in Paris that afternoon and, more to check where he had been than anything else, went to the big map in the briefing room. A violent rash of red arrows of penetrations into Belgium caught his eye, and he went up for a close look. One of them went straight over the area in which he had left the stump of his Christmas tree.

The press camp of the First Army whose members had been demanding a forward movement was now suddenly in a highly dangerous position. Interrogations gave the goal of the drive as Antwerp, and it was known that Colonel Otto Skorzeny had sent American-uniformed and English-speaking paratroopers into rear areas. All that was standing between First Army headquarters in Spa and the Germans was a palace guard of a few clerks, and a minute military-police force. The First Army correspondents now were climbing aboard their jeeps and asking the quickest way west to Dunkirk. The ponderous First Army headquarters, engaged in its first retrograde movement in World War II, was falling back initially to Chaudfontaine, not far from Liége. The press camp left the Hotel Portugal, expecting to billet itself in the casino in Chaudfontaine.

We had undertaken an immediate survey of facilities for bedding, housing, feeding, and otherwise absorbing the First Army correspondents, should they swing north and need help. Our briefings indicated a possibility that the German advance was reaching for Liége in a northwesterly direction. Almost as soon as we started the survey, Lieutenant Rhodes was on the phone asking whether there was a building in Maastricht if the whole press camp decided to come there. This was our first indication of the load we might have.

Divisions were siphoned off the Ninth Army front until only the 102nd and Twenty-ninth were left, backed up with layers of artillery in depth. Both the Second and Seventh Armored Divisions thundered southward to help first with the blunting, the holding, and then the counterattack. The roar of armor treads shook downtown Maastricht. As a precautionary measure, we instructed all our crews to have everything operational, but to pack all but the working essentials in case we had to uproot and move fast.

The Ninth Army press camp censors braced themselves for a dilemma of their own. There were wild reports that Captain Eugene Nute, the First's censor, had laid aside his blue pencil and taken off with a Garand rifle leading a squad. Captain Lavelle had about 28,000 words of First Army front copy land on his desk on the nineteenth, and lacking the normal security guidance, he adopted "common sense" as the best rule. Lavelle decided that he and Nute had to get together quickly or the handling of stories originating in the same sector would make less and less sense, so he loaded up in a jeep on the twenty-second and headed for Chaudfontaine. With Jack Shelley, of WHO, in Des Moines, Iowa, he drove south. When they got to the press installation—the Chaudfontaine casino—two trucks were burning furiously before the entrance, what was left of three Belgian civilians was scattered about the area, and near the portico of the hotel a limp bundle of green and muddy clothing turned out to be the dead body of Jack Frankish, UP. Colonel Andrew, the First's P&PW chief who had replaced Colonel Page, was killed in the same blasts. When Lavelle found Nute and his contingent, Nute had a roll of bandages in his hand, and nearly everyone had glass cuts about the face.

The First Army correspondents headed en masse for Maastricht where there was a full battery of operating communications. As they poured in on us, we accepted all filing, irrespective of source, and pumped it to the U.S. and England in the order received. The Ninth Army's press camp had become a refugee center, and the corre-

spondent population alone went up to eighty-nine. Corridors, hall-
ways, lounge and lobby were a litter of bedrolls. Neil Sullivan had
his head bandaged and was shaky with memories of another close call
in the Italian campaigns. Jim Cassidy, of WLW, Cincinnati, couldn't
get the memory of Jack Frankish out of his mind. "Cy" Peterman
felt it would be another Kasserine Pass, but he filed that night without his customary battle with the censors. There was too much else
to think about. Wes Gallagher came in with a report about our hosts
of a few nights before, the Seventh Armored. "They disappeared into
that hole in the line," he said, "nobody knows where or how they
came out." The Germans knew where they were, however, because
their determined defense of St. Vith held that von Rundstedt element
several critical days.

Sheer hysteria characterized many of the first press offerings from
the Bulge and Captain Lavelle told his staff to be generous with the
blue pencil. Lavelle, who always considered himself best off of any
front-line censor in that he was included prominently in every briefing
given General Simpson on operations present and pending, had as
good a picture of the Bulge as any high-ranking commander. His
guidance and his areas of wariness were therefore of the highest level.
It is extremely hard for a censor to win a popularity contest,[3] and the
Ninth Army press camp was fortunate to have Lavelle, who never had
a voice raised against him or his censor group either from the military
staff or the press. At the height of the Bulge, when both Ninth and
First Armies were depending on him, the handle was 214,055 words a
week.

When the Ardennes erupted, Monty had been busily concentrating
for the ultimate battle of the Rhineland and naturally he called a halt
on that. "I was forced to consider the possible effects of the enemy's
thrust upon the dispositions of the Twenty-first Army Group," he
said, "for . . . we were starting the process of transferring the bulk of
our weight to the extreme northern flank. I therefore ordered the concentration for the Rhineland battle to stop and had plans prepared
for switching British divisions from the Geilenkirchen sector to the
west of the Meuse in case of any threat to our northern flank." He

---

[3] Wes Gallagher cabled AP, New York: "WHAT COULD HAVE BEEN UNHOLY
MESS WAS SAVED BY GOOD SENSE OF FRONT LINE FIELD PRESS CENSORS. . . ." One
of the better Christmas presents for Captain Lavelle was Gallagher's appearance to read congratulations from Kent Cooper, AP's general manager.

also ordered British 30 Corps to the vicinity of Louvain-St. Trond in Belgium. This was a tactical maneuver, but it became one of military and political journalism's great focal points in the days ahead and provided fretful paragraphs in postwar memoirs [4] as well as ammunition for argument wherever soldiers and armchair strategists gather. The differences between Field Marshal Montgomery and General Bradley now broke out with partisan violence equaled only by the clash in Belgium. On the nineteenth of December, General Eisenhower decided to shift command of all elements north of the Bulge to Monty, letting Bradley retain those south of the German gouge in the lines. This meant Bradley had only Patton's Third Army, while Monty picked up the American First and Ninth, more than doubling his strength. Bradley's attempt to put the Ninth in reaching distance of Monty as a pawn had reckoned without von Rundstedt.

General Bradley, he later wrote, heard that the newsmen in Paris were nervous about developments, when they had reports of Skorzeny's paratroopers loose in the rear areas. (Even he made that fine distinction of Paris "newsmen," rather than call them "war correspondents.") He did offer to open a press camp in or near Luxembourg, where his headquarters was located, so they could come forward, see better and worry less, but this would have meant they would have to advance 240 miles to be anywhere near the front.

Hal Boyle [5] walked into the jitteriness which prevailed from the Skorzeny paratrooper foray when he came home one night to find the door locked to the house where he, Bill Heinz, *New York Sun,* and Neil Sullivan, Pathé News, were in residence. Heinz and Sullivan had gone to bed early, and were asleep when Boyle went out in the snow,

[4] In the early 1950's, when General Bradley was visiting SHAPE near Paris, he was standing beside the front entrance when Montgomery drove up. SHAPE's chief information officer thought the reunion of the two would make a good picture. Monty bounded over and his greeting was warm, as was Bradley's. There was evidence, however, that Monty had carefully read Bradley's memoirs, *A Soldier's Story,* and had missed none of its emotional criticism of him. At the end of their conversation, Monty waved cheerily and said in parting, "Now, Omar, take care of yourself. Don't stay up too late at night—writing."

[5] During the behind-lines scare caused by Skorzeny's Nazi fanatics, Lew Gannett and Lou Azrael had their Negro jeep driver stopped by a wary MP at a crossroads. The MP asked, "What's the capital of Texas?" and "Who plays football in South Bend?" Their driver couldn't answer, but he said, "Come off givin' me a hard time, boy. You know I ain't one of them gnat's eyes!" The MP waved them on.

cupped his hands, and called into the crisp night: "Heinz! *Hey, Heinz.*" There was no sign from indoors, and Boyle was about to yell again, when suddenly he clapped terrified hands over his mouth, fell to all fours in the snow, and looked warily about him. With German saboteurs roving the countryside, only a fool would be yelling a name like Heinz in the night. Satisfied he was not going to be picked off, he rose again: *"Hey, Sullivan."* Sullivan let him in. "It's great to have a roommate named Sullivan," Boyle said, "on a night like this."

The whole section north of the Bulge was nervous, but not frightened.

On the twenty-fourth, Brigadier A. G. Neville, Monty's P&PW chieftain, came to Maastricht, talked with the Ninth Army's mystified G-2 section, which could not quite understand what it was he wanted. He had lunch in our press camp, met Nute in the lobby and enjoined him to "be sure and send us guidance," and then went back to Brussels. Since all this was inconclusive, Lavelle and Nute took off for Brussels, too, going by First Army, now in Tongres. When they sped into the Belgian capital, it occurred to someone it was Christmas eve. The Montgomery censors, snugly billeted in Brussels, were in the midst of a party. Since there was nothing which could be ironed out that night, Lavelle and Nute, frozen to the marrow, partook of the warming fluids.

On Christmas Day, before and during lunch, the basic Bulge censorship agreement was made. For First Army, Nute would put together the "Pass" guidance, and forward it to Twenty-first Army Group with a thirty-six-hour embargo on action and place names. This would be communicated laterally to Ninth Army. Date lines could use cities, villages and towns as indicated, but armies and units were to be blanketed until further notice. On the afternoon of that bleak Belgian Christmas, Lavelle and Nute headed back to their separate press camps. Lieutenant Rhodes had returned to the Hotel Portugal in Spa, and ran it as First Army's forward press camp. Peter Lawless of the *Daily Telegraph* had never relinquished his room in the inn at any time during the battle, even though a German column passed a few kilometers south of the city. The old tourist resort which had been Kaiser Wilhelm's imperial headquarters in World War I, and from which he had fled through Maastricht to his exile in Doorn, in the Netherlands, was untouched.

On the night of January 2, the Ninth Army press corps and some of its censors attended the tired-voiced briefing of Lt. Gen. Courtney Hodges, the First Army commander, which was given in his war room in Tongres, Belgium. Nute took Lavelle into a corner and outlined to him the censor guidance, which included an embargo on announcing the attack in the Ardennes salient, aimed to restore the original line as of December 16. Nute outlined the divisions which would be named as participating in the attack. Eyewitness stories, including the precious place-date lines, would be permissible after the passing of thirty-six hours.

When the correspondents came back to Maastricht, they were in considerable heat. First, they criticized the attack plan which was to throw its main weight on the tip of the horn which had gored First Army. This was attributed to Monty's characteristic caution. Wes Gallagher was particularly incensed that the attack had not been moved over somewhere on the deep shoulder of the Bulge east of Liége. He felt this would have a chance of snaring Rundstedt forces and he thought Patton would like nothing better than to come up from the south through Bastogne to help Hodges close the trap.

Noel Monks had his dander up about the long thirty-six-hour embargo on the release. He looked at Lavelle, then at me and made a prophecy. "I'll bet anybody ten gulden," he said, "that BBC will have it first again. They always beat us and they'll do it again with all this time on their hands."

The censors' honor was at stake, so Lavelle took the bet. "They didn't beat you on the Roer River attack by the Ninth Army," he said, "and they won't on this one."

"They'll have it on the nine o'clock news tomorrow night," said Monks.

The correspondents went off the next day to watch the attack, bundled to the eyes as the weather was bitterly cold. Lavelle sat back to let his in-basket pile up against the embargo time deadline, and all was quiet. The teletype suddenly sprung to life. "APPROVAL GIVEN FOR YOU TO RELEASE FORMATIONS AT YOUR DISCRETION PROVIDED YOU ARE SATISFIED THEY HAVE BEEN IDENTIFIED IN BATTLE. SHOULD THERE BE ANY SPECIAL CIRCUMSTANCES WHEN FORMATIONS SHOULD NOT BE RELEASED YOU WILL BE NOTIFIED IN ADVANCE."

This made it sure that First Army would be credited with the attack the following day. The teletype again: "AS FROM TODAY SHAEF HAVE AGREED TO CANCELLATION OF 36-HOUR TIMELAG ON NEWS IN

AREA OF GERMAN COUNTEROFFENSIVE AND ARMIES WILL RELEASE
NEWS THEIR SECTORS AS HITHERTO."

Lavelle got Nute on the field phone, and when they started to talk
about their common dilemma, another message was handed Lavelle:
"REFERENCE PPW 138 OR 2 JAN AUTHORITY FOR DELEGATION RE-
LEASE OF UNITS HEREBY CANCELED AND NO REPEAT NO DIVISIONS TO
BE RELEASED WITHOUT ARMY GROUP APPROVAL."

"What are you going to do?" asked Lavelle.

"I'll call you back," said Nute.

An hour later, the teletype awakened. "STOP ALL MENTION OF FIRST
ARMY ATTACK UNTIL 1730 REPEAT 1730 HOURS TOMORROW THURS-
DAY 4 JANUARY. THIS EMBARGO ON ANNOUNCING THE ATTACK WILL
HOLD DESPITE LIFTING OF SHAEF NEWS EMBARGO. GUIDANCE WILL
FOLLOW." Nute's instructions now were clear, and so were Lavelle's.
When Lavelle went down to the lounge in the press camp that night,
Noel Monks handed him ten gulden. "BBC didn't have it on the nine
o'clock news," he said. "I owe you."

Lavelle spent some time generating confidence among them that
the long delay would hold and went back to his office. Ken Dixon of
AP followed him up, his forebodings not canceled out as easily as
Monks'. Dixon, still muttering disbelief, left when the phone rang. It
was Twelfth Army Group relaying yet another instruction. "The
following statement released tomorrow at 1100. . . . In the Ardennes
salient, we counterattacked yesterday morning in the Grandmenil
area. Good progress is being made against stiff opposition. Gains were
made to the south of the Rochefort where some commanding ground
and a village have been taken against strong resistance. Active patrolling by Allied forces and by the enemy continues in Holland."

Lavelle asked Twelfth Army Group if this constituted an overriding
guidance from SHAEF. He was told that this was SHAEF's statement, then that BBC had already announced it at one o'clock that
same afternoon, just eight hours *ahead* of the news show Monks had
bet on. Then, before midnight, when the press camp was mostly
asleep, the telephone rang long and hard for Lavelle. SHAEF had
announced the drive at 11 P.M., a few minutes before. A BBC correspondent at Third Army was said to have broken the news of the
attack during the "talk up" period before his regularly and properly
censored piece. Even with the damage done, First Army demanded a

hold on eyewitness stories, and Lavelle went to bed without waking up the correspondents—preferring to talk to them at the morning briefing.

The room was filled with a sleepy but interested crowd. Gallagher, the hell-roaring Hibernian, was humped over his typewriter. Monks was sitting forward, his hands flat on his knees looking searchingly at the map. Jack Fleischer, UP, was serious and intent. Frank Coniff looked like the sophomore the coach talks to during half time. When Captain Bill Moody finished the briefing, he said, "Does the censuh have anythin'?"

Lavelle walked up front. "You can save yourself the trouble of filing any flashes before going out today," he said. "The first Army counterattack was announced by SHAEF at eleven o'clock last night." He then handed a ten-gulden note over Al Lee's head to Noel Monks. "BBC," he explained, "had it, inadvertently, at one o'clock yesterday." Lavelle then read them SHAEF's announcement for 11 A.M. that day.

"I love that part about active patrolling in Holland," said Boyd Lewis.

Throughout the room, SHAEF was given a blistering. Dixon filed a careful story. Lewis and William Steen of Reuter's followed suit, Steen chewing on his mustache as the censors looked it over. And Coniff brought his in like a hard-charging lineman, with his characteristic crack, "Let's go, big red team." Lewis went back to his typewriter and soon turned in a piece which set the tone: "Indignation expressed by correspondents on the Western Front over censorship restrictions imposed upon front-line reporters covering American counteroffensive. Some correspondents resented what they said was a deliberate effort top censorship authorities subordinate actual front news upplay SHAEF release. . . ." Lavelle went to Lewis, always a reasonable, responsible man, and talked to him about changing the tone even though this was not a military security matter. Lewis agreed, and it was finally transmitted: "Part of the indignation generated by guidance given field press censors. . . . It wasn't until five today that correspondents permitted to give initial modest advance but by that time anyone who'd followed earlier guidance had done damage. Correspondents believe such distortion unfair to doughfeet who slugging their way through Ardennes. . . ."

The Correspondents' Committee of First Army lashed out at the SHAEF vacillations on releases, which said in part: "The whole situation is one which recurs every time an attack is launched here by First Army, or elsewhere for that matter. Elaborate timelags, security embargos and official statements are set up in advance for each offensive primarily to assure that security will not be violated, but equally important to assure that our correspondents get the break on first release of news. . . . Prior to the present First Army attack . . . we felt that a timelag of 36 hours would be satisfactory for both security and coordination. . . . The correspondents knowing of this embargo all went off to the front to live for awhile and get their stories, planning to return to the press camp in time to meet the embargo and file. . . . Then it happened . . . a statement to the effect that 'the allied forces counterattacked in the Grandmenil area against strong enemy opposition' which would be included in the SHAEF communiqué . . . 14 hours after the attack started and hours before the original embargo would expire. We protested, but there was no change. We also learned that BBC had broadcast a 'report that First Army had launched a counterattack on the northern salient of the salient bulge' at 1300 hours on the day of the attack, 3 January. . . ."

But SHAEF lived unhappily, too, and the answer was within the correspondent fraternity itself. BBC's Cyril Ray, prior to broadcasting his properly censored copy, used his "talk up" period on Third Army's radio to state that "the First Army launched an attack on the Northern flank of the German salient today." He made the unauthorized disclosure at 1 P.M., January 3, and BBC went along with it through subsequent broadcasts—all of which were presumably monitored carefully by the Germans. Cyril Ray was disaccredited, one more instance which found certain war correspondents more equipped with zeal to outwit security for a "beat" than with concern for changes in enemy deployment which their news might cause and which might increase the casualty list.

On January 6, all the press camps in Twenty-first Army Group, which now included First and Ninth, were told to post a notice that Field Marshal Montgomery would meet the correspondents the next day in Zonhoven. The weather was still cold, and the roads in sloppy shape, so Lieutenant Williams was instructed to accompany the press party with a trailer carrying hot doughnuts and three full urns of steaming coffee.

Monty was in good form in the frigid hall. He did two unusual things for him, however, speaking graciously to a woman correspondent, and inviting the assembled press to light up their cigarettes. It was well known that he cared little for women journalists, and to smoke in one of his staff meetings was unknown. But he had points to make this day. In setting the stage, he started with December 16: "Von Rundstedt obtained tactical surprise. He drove a deep wedge into the center of the First U. S. Army and split the American forces in two. The situation looked as though it might become awkward; the Germans had broken right through a weak spot and headed for the Meuse. As soon as I saw what was happening, I took certain steps myself to ensure that if the Germans got to the Meuse, they would certainly not get over that river. And I carried out certain movements so as to provide balanced dispositions to meet the threatened danger. These were, at the time, merely precautions, that is, I was thinking ahead. Then the situation began to deteriorate. But the whole Allied team rallied to meet the danger; national considerations were thrown overboard; General Eisenhower placed me in command of the whole northern front." Monty did not state that the command switch had been made after most of the U. S. divisions of First and Ninth Armies were engaged or taking positions to form a crust over the breakthrough, that the moves he made of British divisions had little to do with blunting and halting the enemy penetration. The inferences were there that the Americans needed a guardian.

The ensuing brawl was so raw that the Prime Minister rose later on in the House of Commons to make some assertions designed to set the records straight and heal the wounds. This was thirty-two days after the Germans had opened their abortive attack, having been driven back after exhaustive matériel losses and 120,000 casualties. Churchill said he had "seen it suggested that the terrific battle which has been proceeding since December 16 on the American front is an Anglo-American affair. In fact, however, the United States troops have done almost all the fighting, and have suffered almost all the losses."

It was perhaps best summed up, however, as the press came pouring out of the doorways, cold and stiff, after the long Montgomery conference in Zonhoven. Lieutenant Williams was doling out the coffee and rolls to warm them, and he put the picture in perspective succinctly. "Monty had about as much to do with winning the Battle of the Bulge," said George, "as he did with providing this coffee." [6]

The succession of eighteen- and twenty-hour days while the front was being established, coupled with some exposure, toppled me with a bad attack of the flu. Trying to work through the dizziness compounded it, and for two days and nights I was down in bed, removed from the turmoil and babble of the Hôtel du Lévrier. When my eyes finally opened just before eight o'clock one morning, Lei was sitting beside my bed, her schoolbooks on the floor by her chair. "I come to see you every day," she said. "They let me pray you get well." To one who had had only weighty worries up to this point, it was touching to be worried about.

[6] The American press filings after Monty's conference were very warm and nationalistic as well as annoyed by his contentions. One of the men, Hugh Schuck, of the *New York Daily News,* cabled: "... TO BORROW EXPRESSION OF AMERICAN GENERAL TONY MCAULIFFE AT BASTOGNE, 'NUTS TO YOU, MONTY.' "

. . . TAKE 13 ——————————————

Signs of Spring

Willem van Egerschot was released from the hospital and police surveillance as the New Year began and, with his wife, moved into the hotel to help with its administration. The burden had been becoming more and more of a weight on old Mynheer, or "Sydney" as everyone now unfailingly called him, and his wife was ill much of the time. The shock of the near-death of their only son had given the elder van Egerschots a somber outlook. They were embittered, too, by how quickly their neighbors had assumed them guilty.

It was necessary for me to have an investigation run immediately and quietly by the Ninth Army Counter-Intelligence Corps detachment, and a thorough look was given to the Dutch police records to determine if Willem was a genuine political case, or dangerous in any way. The suddenness with which the Dutch police had dropped him and concurred in his hospital release seemed to indicate that, at worst, he may have been unwise. The report came back "negative" and the police statement, as relayed to me, was that they had "no further interest at this time." This was interpreted by the CIC as a face-saving gesture. CIC took the further position that he was unlikely to figure in police matters again on any count, real or fancied, left over from the period of the occupation. The younger van Egerschots then fitted themselves gradually into the press camp routine, offering their multi-lingual facility to help in the Dutch, French and English conversations which were commonplace in our daily international business.

The press camp was short two of its long-time residents as the

181

result of two jeep actions. One of them occurred near Liége, during the Battle of the Bulge when the roads were iciest. The driver of Hank Wales' jeep drove broadside into a ten-ton trailer at a dark crossroads. Hank braced with his feet rather than his hands, and on impact rose high in the air like an acrobat propelled from a teeterboard. His ground collision gave him a mouthful of teeth in the wrong places, and such a severe jolting that hospitalization was required. Lewis Gannett came to a similar bad end trying to dodge a stream of heavy traffic going in the opposite direction. He too was slammed hard in the face. His helmet crashed through the windshield and when he came around he was in a ditch spitting teeth and minus glasses. The score was seven (real) teeth, and two dentures (store), and one tooth through his lower lip. By good fortune, his hospitalization route took him to Major George Friedman, a face-lifter in civilian life. He took thirteen stitches to restore Gannett when the infirmary's other medic had decided one would do it. Gannett was grateful for this, since he healed with no scar, probably the only book reviewer who has been worked on by a face-lifter.

An aura of Hollywood hovered over the Hôtel du Lévrier, partly because it was lively and full of kindred spirits of the creative and entertaining arts. Lt. Col. George Stevens, who ran SHAEF's first-string motion-picture camera crews along the front, made the Maastricht hotel his home most of the time and did some of his super-vision from there. From his outfit, he had assigned to us on a perma-nent basis Captain John Holly Morse, as unit boss, and a veteran first cameraman of many a Hollywood film, Captain Jack McEdward. Morse was the husband of the doll-voiced singer, Wee Bonnie Baker. My first meeting with Stevens and some of his men had been almost a year before in a small London pub and club, the hangout for an odd lot of humanity. One of the regulars was a British girl who ran an unusual "business" she called Services, Unlimited. For a fee in proportion to the difficulty, wildness, or rudeness of the request, she could fix anything. Furnished apartment on short notice for long stay? Black-market filet mignons for a party of twenty? Hard-to-get theater tickets? Hotel room outfitted with companion of the opposite sex? Name it, and she'd arrange it. She herself was personable, charming, unavailable.

One of the many stories of the place involved an American who, besides being a regular habitué of the offbeat swillery, was outstanding even in that family of freaks. He was a collector and wearer of odd glass eyes. He had an array of them—one with the white of the eye clear, one with it bloodshot to match the good eye when it was veiny and red from excesses of the night before, and one which was crossed like old Ben Turpin so that it looked squarely into the side of his nose. But the night to remember this American and talk about him forever came when two Englishmen were standing next to him quietly discussing the severe inroads the Yanks were making on the London liquor supply. At first paying no attention, the American finally caught the drift of their conversation. He had had enough to be incensed, but he chose not to launch a tirade. He decided instead to invoke his own kind of protest. With his back to them, he carefully inserted a new glass eye and, at the right juncture, whirled on them and glowered, not saying a word. Both the Englishmen were so startled that they abandoned their mugs of ale and fled. The American turned back to his drink very pleased with himself, at which point the sturdy bartender was rudely shaken as for the first time he noticed the man's eyes. One of them contained, in lieu of pupil, a full-color reproduction of a defiantly waving American flag!

In association with the British director, Carol Reed, Stevens and his teams were shooting, among other things, portions of the SHAEF official story in documentary form which was eventually to become a full-length feature called *The True Glory*. Reed, accompanied by Sergeant Guy Trosper, his scenarist, was in and out of the Ninth Army press camp, too, as it provided a good vantage position from which to view the Allied combined effort. The U. S. Ninth Army and the British Second Army flanks were only a few miles up the road near Sittard.

"Who is this Reed?" Lieutenant Patterson asked Captain Morse one day.

"Oh," said Holly, well acquainted with the role of being married to a famous face, "he's Diana Wynyard's husband."

"The hell you say!" said Patterson with new respect.

Marlene Dietrich joined us in the press camp on several occasions when she was making her USO appearances for the troops along the Ninth Army front. Part of it may have been that it was good publicity business for her, and part of it social, but one of her primary interests was extremely personal. She spread the word among all the newsmen, knowing they would always be close to the leading combat troops, asking them to do something for her. She, too, had fallen under the spell of the Ninth Army's chances of being in line to make the final run into Berlin. "Please," she asked each correspondent, "if you get to Berlin, ask for Frau von Loesch. She's my mother. No matter where you find her, get a message to me." She gave each of the writers the last known address she had for her mother, whom she had not seen since the thirties. She also had heard rumors that the parents of her husband, Rudolph Seiber, were somewhere in the old Sudetenland border region of Czechoslovakia. These members of her family were always on her mind, even though she clowned gaily and daily on all manner of improvised stages. The highlight of her soldier show was an incongruity which only the well-established glamour of a Dietrich could survive—she played a saw in true hillbilly style.

The press was fascinated when she once confessed that she wore genuine, khaki-colored, long-john underwear. When the boys laughingly expressed their doubts, she obligingly and in an unembarrassed way posed backstage for the photographers in her personal woollies. This set her up as a very regular guy, and nobody ever quarreled with any of her other claims about life along the front. If Marlene said it, it must be so. Gordon Gammack, upon hearing her tell of the times she had to change in freezing makeshift dressing rooms, gave her his prize possession, his portable Coleman stove. "Oh, thank you so much," said the husky-voiced Marlene, "for this, I shall never forget you. It will warm my heart—and more, too, probably." Then she advanced on the hard-boiled Iowan and kissed him in a way which gave him a passing vision of the Casbah.

In the German border towns Marlene was a phenomenon. German children born after she was banned from German cinema screens would run after her and ask if she was not Marlene Dietrich. Blanked out she may have been by Hitler's henchmen, but her pictures were cherished. A remarkable woman, and an extremely intelligent companion, she told the correspondents of a recent trip to America and to Hollywood between USO tours. They wanted to know if things had changed much at home. "I can only tell you about Hollywood," she said. "I went into this restaurant. At one table was Louella Parsons. In a front booth was the same producer I had seen there a year ago promising to make the same star out of a different girl with the same ambition."

One night in nearby Aachen, another Hollywood delegation was on its way to the press camp. That first major German city (165,000 population) to fall to the American forces was a shambles, and a lonely MP had to stop all vehicles going in and out to determine whether they had business there. All drivers and passengers had to show their passes. A lumbering command car came up to the checkpoint in the dark, and he asked for identity cards. Turning his cat's-eye flashlight on the first one, he cried out in unbelief. "Frank McHugh! Not Frank McHugh from Toluca Lake, California?"

"The same," said McHugh, until now nodding drowsily under his helmet. "Why?"

"I live just down Navajo Street from you," said the excited MP, "just a block away."

"No kiddin'," said Frank, equally surprised to come upon a genuine neighbor in this desolate town. The old-time Hollywood comedian got out of the car to talk a bit.

"I sure am glad to see you," the MP kept repeating. "Real glad. I couldn't feel happier about anything, unless," and he put a knuckle in McHugh's ribs, "unless that girl who lived next door to you had shown up instead—you know, Mary Brian."

"Oh," said McHugh, putting on his familiar comic sternness, "so it's not me you're glad to see? It's Mary Brian you want!" Sure, the MP said, he'd like very much to lay eyes on the movie queen. "Okay," said Frank with the air of Aladdin about to rub his lamp. He turned toward the command car. "Hey, Mary, there's a guy out here wants to see you." Sure enough, Mary Brian, of 4204 Navajo Street, got out of the car, too. The MP threw his helmet on the ground, yipped, and wound his arms around Mary as if she were a mirage that would fade unless he held her tight. The Navajo Street reunion in Aachen might have been going yet, had it not been for a third member of the USO show, June Clyde,[1] a movie star also, who reminded them that they were due at the press camp a few miles up the road.

Brian Aherne came to Maastricht in *The Barretts of Wimpole Street,* and there were several other less stellar attractions, all of which, on nights off, came into the press camp to offer some technicolor relief from the drabness of words on paper.

Otherwise American-style entertainment was exceptionally sparse,

[1] June Clyde was married to Major Thornton Freeland, another of Lt. Col. George Stevens' camera chieftains, who was based off and on in the Ninth Army press camp. June's family reunion took place there.

confined to a single, well-worn record which went with the ancient-vintage phonograph in the lounge near the poker table. The disc was the late Bunny Berigan's "I Can't Get Started With You." It was a special favorite of Frank Coniff's and he played it over and over until the rest of the room would first beg and eventually threaten him if he did not desist.

The Ninth Army press camp became a true crossroads for correspondents of all nations, partly because of its established reputation for an international population.

Monty retained the correspondents of the Twenty-first Army Group in Brussels at the svelte Canterbury Hotel and, when they wanted to do the front, they only came up for trips with conducting officers. This did not keep them from emulating the Paris crowd; in fact they even went it one better. After a good evening meal in a restaurant, served by a tuxedoed waiter, they would go into the streets for a stroll and were only a few steps away from the district wherein some of the most attractive girls do the most earnest solicitation in the world. After a spot of this heady fare, they would return to their rooms, put a piece of paper in the typewriter and begin: "ON THE WESTERN FRONT . . ."

While General Bradley disliked the too-tight allegiance the press seemed to get for the Army to which it was attached, the several attempts of Redding to have correspondents take up quarters at Twelfth Army Group fizzled because it was too far from action on the one hand, and the over-all picture was not as complete as the one which could be found at SHAEF.

Ninth Army's open-gate policy tended to break down other boundaries, and from Luxembourg to the English Channel at least, the press movements became freer.

On February 7, when the Nijmegen sector blazed with an attack by the First Canadian Army, it was the beginning of strenuous events which wiped the west bank of the Rhine clean of German forces. The Ninth Army's long preoccupation with the Roer River dams met with heartening developments three days later when the V Corps of the First Army captured the buttress, though the departing Germans blew the works and spilled tons of muddy, vicious, swirling water down the Roer where Ninth Army waited on the banks across from Julich. Ninth had its greatest strength to date, three armored and seven infantry divisions. General Simpson came to the press camp highly optimistic and briefed the corps on Operation Grenade, the plan for vaulting the Roer at long last. Lt. Col. George Stevens pulled his sound-on-film crew, with Captain Joe Biroc in charge, into the press camp and, for the first time in the war, a full briefing by an Army commander was put on film outlining exactly how the play of divisions and special units was to go. It was actually a remarkable pictorial document in providing a measuring device later between concept and result, though Operation Grenade was doomed to further waiting because the flood from the blasted dams was complemented by thawing snows of the previous heavy winter.

Valentine's Day was approaching, and with that strange logic which is natural to an Army, a decision was made at Twelfth Army Group to isolate two officers, Lt. Col. Joseph W. Smith of Beckley, West Virginia, and Lieutenant Ross Hazeltine of Indianapolis, Indiana, and give them the task of running a campaign against fraternization with the German girls. A thankless job, besides being impossible. They were up against the liberal view credited to General Patton that "fornication without conversation is not fraternization." The Third Army had been cutting quite a swath through Germany with wordless wooing. Lt. Col. Smith and Lieutenant Hazeltine had to dream up such slogans as "Be wise, don't fraternize," and "VDMT" (spelled out, Venereal Disease Means Trouble).

As we came up to Valentine's Day, with love [2] taking such a beating along the front, Ninth Army's press camp thought it about time to re-establish the venerable saint and some of his laundered symbols. Our old-fashioned method of honoring the subject was to

---

[2] It had not been a winter entirely without true love, since John Wilhelm of the *Chicago Sun* married Margaret Maslin, a Red Cross doughnut dispenser from Port Chester, N.Y., in a special Ninth Army press camp spectacular. It was a PRO field day, with Major Casey Dempsey, First Army's press handler, as best man; Major George Daum, of Denver, Colo., the Chaplain and PRO of the 102nd Infantry Division, tying the knot; and myself, the Ninth Army PRO, giving the bride away. We had to get the moon-eyed Wilhelm married to get him back on his feed and, more importantly, back to covering the war. He took all the whoop-te-do pretty well until he was being spliced "for law" (civil) before the ceremony "for church." This was done by Mynheer M. van Kessenich, the Maastricht burgomeister, who lectured him about getting an early start on a family. "I have ten children already," said the burgomeister, "and the stork is at my wife's apron again." *Life* magazine's William Vandivert and George Silk shot the whole wedding affair in detail, including some twenty-five military men and war correspondents kissing the bride, a picture story which *Life* eventually ran.

stage a St. Valentine's Day dance, and we prevailed upon a group of the Dutch girls to join in the fun.

On the wall across the lounge from my desk for weeks there had been a pen-and-ink sketch accomplished by Gordon Grant of the *Tampa Tribune*. It was of a voluptuous girl, clad in transparent raincoat, carrying an umbrella, wearing galoshes. Her figure showed through in remarkable bloom and clarity. Gordon had lettered across this picture: WAR CORRESPONDENTS LEAVING FOR PARIS WILL PLEASE REMEMBER TO WEAR THEIR RUBBERS. This picture had been up so long that no one thought anything about it until the Dutch girls began to arrive and collect in the lounge. It was about nine o'clock and Robert Massell of the Blue Network had just gone up to the third-floor studio to do his nightly stateside splice into the network news. The girls first became interested, then clustered around our masterpiece. One of them came into the lobby, took me by the arm, and led me to it, asking for an explanation. "What means it?" she asked. Assuring her it was nothing except a caricaturist's dream of an ideal situation in a rainstorm, I backed away and quickly made a plot with Griff and Lieutenant Williams to get the picture off the wall. While I moved to the main electric switch, Griff took up his position in the doorway of the lounge. When the lever was pulled he was to grab the picture from its moorings and dash out of sight with it into the second kitchen.

On signal, the switch was pulled, and there were a couple of small screams from the girls. They did not notice Griff among them, then scurrying away with the picture. The lights came up, the picture was gone, and no one was troubled further. No one, that is, but Bob Massell. He came running down the stairs, his head in his hands. "What the hell happened?" he moaned. "I had such a pretty script tonight. I was reading it, just about to hit the punch line, when every goddam light in the joint went out! I had to stutter all the way to the end. I don't know yet how I finished." Contritely, we explained and, still muttering, Massell climbed back up the stairs to wait for the recheck which was bound to come when the broadcast was concluded in America. Sure enough, one of the girls at Blue Network was anxiously calling him when he put on the earphones. "This is Blue calling Bob Massell," she said excitedly. "Was it a bombing or something? Were you hurt? You sounded frightened. Tell me what happened."

"Hello, New York," said Bob when the circuit switched to him. "Honey, you'll never know."

With spring and its all-out campaigns not far away, the public-relations officers of all the Armies were called into Paris a few days later to talk about the spaces now available in which they could accommodate war correspondents.

Boyd Lewis, one of the Ninth Army's old hands, was now the UP top kick in Paris on SHAEF matters, and he introduced me to Ann Stringer in the lobby of the Scribe. She was a UP coworker, a beautiful girl with long, shoulder-length hair and butter-melting eyes. "I'm sending her up to Ninth Army," said Boyd, "and I want you to look out for her. She's leaving today." After she had departed, he explained: "You remember Bill Stringer, with Reuter's, who was killed near Versailles last August? That's his widow. I'm worried about her, because she insists she wants to finish what Bill started. I really think she wants to get killed, too." SHAEF was still trying to enforce its rule that women correspondents were to "go no further forward than women's services go," by which SHAEF meant field hospitals with their nurse detachments. Liberal interpretation was always given this edict by Lee Carson, Iris Carpenter, Rhona Churchill and Martha Gellhorn among others, and for them this meant as far forward as surgical teams would be called and often included battalion headquarters. Nobody in his right mind wanted to get any closer than that.

The morning we were heading back, the Roer jumpoff by both First and Ninth Armies was well under way. Ninth was going through long-viewed, but until now unattainable, battered and blasted Julich.[3] In the Scribe lobby on the way to my jeep, a copy of the *Herald*

---

[3] General Simpson had a sure feel for public relations and what the correspondents wanted. When Colonel William P. Nuckols, the Ninth Air Force PRO, organized an airlifted expedition of war-correspondent aviation specialists to tour the front lines and get a "commanders' report" on the quality of tactical air support, they were to be briefed by Generals Bradley, Patton, Hodges and Simpson. Simpson thought there would be a lot of repetition in what he would have to say, so he had me select a sergeant who had been in the lead during the taking of Julich. "Bring him in mud, beard and all," he said, "and don't clean him up." After his opening remarks, in which he said he thought they had had enough from generals, Simpson introduced the sturdy but bedraggled sergeant to give his version of what tactical aviation meant to men like him. The sergeant, who had sneaked, crawled, and run forward behind skip-bombing and strafing, was the hit of the tour for the correspondents and made the most effective presentation in behalf of tactical air power.

Tribune Paris edition caught my eye on the hotel desk. It had a prominent headline over a story which began with the date line: "WITH THE FIRST TROOPS IN JULICH—(UP). . . ." It was "By Ann Stringer." Look out for her, indeed!

Fred Ramage that very day had the experience of being shelled and of diving into a cave to escape. His sudden charge into the dark recesses alarmed the previous resident of that haven—a German Wehrmacht officer, complete with Luger pistol—who, much to Ramage's relief, chose immediately to surrender. "Thought I'd never live to take another picture," he said later, "let alone a PW." Hugh Schuck spent twenty minutes in a hole by the Julich *sportspalast* the same day, while mortars were tearing it to pieces. It was a long twenty minutes, but he covered his terror with his philosophic turn of mind. "There was a guy in the same hole from Brooklyn," he said, "so I got a good story out of it—which is what I was there for."

The press camp was well populated for this first sign of spring and the resumption of offensives, and when Ann had arrived she was billeted in the home of a substantial Dutch burgher who lived two doors down the Boschstraat. The Dutchman had been one of those who had brought the Dutch Reformed orphans to our St. Nicholas party, and he had responded during the Battle of the Bulge by offering to take in a few of the overflow correspondents from First Army if it became necessary. Ann's arrival was the first time we had sought to take advantage of his offer. While no one in the press camp had enthused over any of the other feminine war correspondents, Ann's presence was greeted warmly. Charming, gracious, and with an air of innocence, she was the type of woman to whose defense men spring automatically, and she brought on a surge of gallantry among her male competitors which was totally unlike them.

As I made my way back from Paris, the date line on Ann Stringer's story was causing a teletype message to precede me. It was a reiteration of SHAEF instructions, which were to be brought to Ann's attention in the form of an ultimatum, reminding her that her stay with Ninth Army would promptly be cut short if she did not abide by the rule that she go "no further forward than women's services go." This did not qualify her to pick up date lines such as "WITH THE FIRST TROOPS IN JULICH." The message was lying there on top of accumulated papers when I got back to my desk late that afternoon. Across the lobby in the press room, I could see Ann typing away thoughtfully, rounding up the events of the day for her file to UP in New York. A half dozen of the regulars were also working, and Lieutenant Correa was taking up copy as they finished, assigning each bit a priority number, then passing it on up to the censors. Ann's UP colleague, James McGlincy, was at the desk next to her equally engrossed in his copy.

I held back until Ann finished and handed in her story, not wanting to destroy any train of thought or get in the way of her chances to be first in filing. My own wish had always been to pay no attention to sex officially in dealings with correspondents. If women or men chose the profession and moved into areas of danger, it seemed to me it should be of no military concern. The double standard seemed entirely out of place, but SHAEF made the rules and one of them was in my hands for enforcement. Ann, after turning away from Lieutenant Correa, saw me for the first time and smiled. Still in possession of my copy of that morning's *Herald Tribune,* with her story outlined in red pencil, I handed it to her. She was delighted with it, her first genuine combat story in the ETO. She showed it to McGlincy and he, too, was pleased. But the mood changed abruptly when I read them my SHAEF message, since McGlincy, as the senior UP hand at Ninth Army, was included by implication. Ann burst into tears. As one man the rest of the press turned to find out what had caused her sudden change. Every glance made me that much more of a villain. The normal revulsion of any war correspondent for a military attempt at enforcing a rule rose like a tidal wave as Ann dashed out and ran to the ladies' room on the first floor. McGlincy let his Irish hackles rise, and began to berate me.

"You saw the message," he was told. "I didn't make it up. If UP chooses to represent itself here with a woman, it knows the hazard. I can look the other way if you use a date line to protect me, but when 'WITH THE NINTH ARMY IN GERMANY' is not good enough, and you have to use a pinpoint like 'WITH THE FIRST TROOPS IN JULICH,' there is no way I can duck SHAEF putting the finger on me for enforcement." McGlincy said I had been mean and rude to Ann, that my action was uncalled for. As far as I was concerned that closed the incident. It was only another of the many outbursts against authority.

That night, Griff and I had been in bed for about an hour when McGlincy popped into our room, turned on the lights, and shook me awake. "That Dutchman has her locked in," he said. "I want to get her out of there."

"Locked in where?"

"He's got her locked in his house. I brought her home tonight from the club. She had been crying after you abused her, so I took her over there. When we came home, the Dutchman let her in, but pushed me back out in the street and slammed the door in my face."

The clock on the night stand was right at midnight.

"After all, that's a private house," I reminded him. "This Dutchman probably has some ideas of propriety. He possibly thinks it's a little late to be letting you in."

"Propriety hell," said McGlincy, now pacing the floor, and he vowed he was going to get Ann out of that house. "I'll give her my room," he said. "I'll sleep in the lobby." He stormed out of the door, slamming it behind him and leaving all the lights on. Griff turned them out, and we both went back to sleep thinking it only one more of those nights. "Women," said Griff, as he spanked his pillow, and punched it under his head.

In the morning I came downstairs and went to my desk where my usual fare was a pot of hot chocolate in preference to another batch of powdered eggs. Right at the foot of the steps, McGlincy was asleep in his bedroll. He looked very strange, and on closer inspection was found to have one strip of adhesive bandage going from ear to ear and another from his forehead to the back of his neck, giving him the appearance of a hairy hot-cross bun. It was hard to tell whether the furious red at the edges of the cloth was blood or some medicinal daub. A quarter hour went by and Lieutenant Pecor came into the lobby on the way to the dining room. He was shy a batch of front teeth. Next came Barney McQuaid, *Chicago Daily News,* one of whose hands was wrapped tightly about the knuckles. Ann came to breakfast, too, and her eyes were swollen from crying. From all appearances, it was the starter of a great day, or the aftermath of an explosive night.

Explanations came rather quickly from all sides, but they started with none of the press corps principals. The Dutchman from the house next door came in and buttonholed Sydney. There was a furious flurry and an accusatory waving of a finger under Sydney's nose. He beckoned for me to join him. "My friend," he said, "is very upset." His friend corroborated this by walking angrily in a small circle about the lobby. "There have been a shooting," said Sydney.

Our callers now increased as two U. S. Army military policemen walked in. It was not yet 9 A.M., and the place was jumping with lawful authority and righteous indignation. The Dutch neighbor had asked the Maastricht police to inform the American military and have them come to the hotel.

"And who has done this shooting?" The Dutchman walked stiff-legged to the sleeping McGlincy and pointed. He then crooked his finger in invitation for us all to accompany him. Sydney got his hat and the MP's tagged along with us to the street from which the morning fog had not yet lifted. The Dutchman paused dramatically before his door and put his finger on a hole in it. He then plunged his hand in his pocket and came up with a flattened leaden pellet. Swinging open the door and leading us into the vestibule, he indicated a line around the wall, up to the ceiling, and down to the floor, undoubtedly a tracing of the course of a bullet.

"The man who brought the woman home last night," Sydney explained, "he wanted to come in, but my friend does not think it right. He shut the door. The lady, he says, understands. She says good night and goes to bed. The man pounds on the door, but my friend pays no attention. He goes to bed." There was more discussion to indicate that McGlincy had eventually gone away, which matched up with his presence in my room. The Dutchman went on and with gestures showed that McGlincy reappeared at the door to resume his pounding. "My friend," said Sydney, "he says the man comes back. My friend gets up, comes to the door to tell him to go or he will send for the police. Then he closes the door—and there is a shot, through the door and the bullet goes around this room." The military police corroborated this, saying it matched with events as told to them by the Dutch police. Ann had left the home of the Dutchman, probably to his vast relief and in the hope of keeping peace. As McGlincy was getting his bedroll out of his bedroom so she could have it for the night, a further altercation, for no discernible reason, developed in the hotel corridor. Ann took the occasion to lock the door, separating herself from the hallway carnage, and eventually the various contestants went off to bed.

Ninth Army had McGlincy's shooting affray to account for, since it had been launched against the premises of and in close proximity

to a Dutch national. Pecor's teeth, McClincy's bottle-whipped noggin,
and McQuaid's bruised knuckles were all family incidents of which
there was no need to take official notice, but the Dutchman was in
no mood to accept other than summary retribution. A Ninth Army
order called for McGlincy's act to be brought to the attention of
SHAEF in Paris and of Virgil Pinkley, European general manager
for UP, as the first action. McGlincy never saw his nocturnal shooting
as an international breach of conduct. He felt only that Ninth Army
was using a convenient excuse to cause him personal trouble. He was
withdrawn to Paris, and another ripple in the press camp calm,
which had been forecast months before when he had come gun-
waving into the tents in Normandy, was now past.

Ann Stringer never moved across the rear areas without causing
something of a sensation. Not long after the shooting scrape, she
was riding in a jeep with Frank Coniff and Hank Wales, her long
hair flowing out behind. Wales was the local Duncan Hines and had
the cooking delights of all the division commanders' chefs on file,
so he was steering them to the best feed bag in the vicinity when they
drove past a battalion of GI's. There was a long, dragged-out whistle.

"You'd think," said Hank in his gravel voice to Coniff, "that
them guys never saw a jeep before."

On March 6 Ninth Army had a visit from Winston Churchill.
Long before Hitler had exploded into Poland, Churchill had been
telling his countrymen that the Austrian corporal was a mad dog not
fit to be loose in the international thoroughfares. Consequently
Churchill had not been in, or welcome in, Germany since the thirties.
So there was great propaganda to have the architect of disaster for
the German Reich appear on its soil, and the man of the celebrated
derby hat and well-chewed cigar savored the possibilities.

He was first to call on General Simpson, there to be joined by
Field Marshal Montgomery, under whose Twenty-first Army Group
the Ninth Army still remained. Churchill was to be accompanied by
Field Marshal Sir Alan Brooke. The Prime Minister desired to pay
a call at Julich on the Roer before which the Allied forces had stood
so long, and he particularly wanted to stop for a while among the
well-photographed and well-publicized and so-called invincible dragon's teeth of the Siegfried Line—those tank traps which had long since
been by-passed. The entourage was to proceed on a well-marked
route, with the V.I.P. party covered by General Simpson's armed

jeeps fore and aft. Behind this group, at a respectful distance so too much attention would not be attracted to the forward party, it was my task to bring on the press and photographers as it would be a top story for them.

Julich provided them with one poignant photo, an excellent one to add to the many secured by Fred Ramage of Keystone-International. The contrast between Churchill and Montgomery showed itself when a festive board, inside the ruined Julich citadel, was laid with alcoholic beverages befitting the celebration. Churchill approached the table with some alacrity, while Monty seated himself at the entrance of the citadel and looked the other way as arms were upraised in toasts. To some viewers the picture of Monty had the look of Carry Nation.

The dragon's-teeth site was on the road from Maastricht to Aachen, barely inside the German border. General Simpson's aide, Major John Harden, of Kingstree, South Carolina, called me over when the motorcade halted beside it. "The general wants you to collect all the cameras, both professional and personal. Put them in a place out of reach of the correspondents for a short while, but assure them they will get them back immediately and that there will be plenty of opportunity to take pictures later. Give me the signal when you have all the cameras," he said. Taking a camera from a professional photographer in the presence of anything which might make news is like asking any other man to hold still while his teeth are knocked out. There was a rumble of dissension when the request was made, then a roar of protest, but the V.I.P. party waited patiently and made no move toward the dragon's teeth. With much reluctance, the cameras were surrendered and were parked across the roadway. "All the cameras have been collected."

With that, Churchill, Montgomery, Brooke and Simpson walked into the dragon's teeth, each carefully picking one of the pyramidal cement protrusions which had been so emblematic of Hitler's impregnable defenses. The correspondents watched in increasing fascination, as did all the rest of us, who had no idea what was in prospect. Almost on a count of three, the four men opened their flies and proceeded to wet the Siegfried Line, using man's oldest and most debasing affront to bespeak their contempt.

If the correspondents had grumbled and squawked before they knew what was going on, Fred Ramage and Henry Griffin now almost choked with frustration. The writers only guffawed, but the cameramen suffered mortally to be denied this collector's item. After the V.I.P.'s rebuttoned and rezipped, the recovery of the cameras was permitted and the normal pictures of the foursome were taken for publication. Behind every one of these, however, was photographer disappointment at not having the one that got away.

By thus stepping in the way of history and grounding the cameras, I had left another niche unchallenged to General Patton. He actually enjoyed it when some soldier photographers gathered around him as he made good on an early campaign promise—giving Hitler his own version of a comeuppance by standing defiant and spraddle-legged while he peed in the Rhine.

Taking Goebbels' Place

Bitter things were being written and far more caustic things were being said privately about inferiority of American equipment, not only in the press, but also in communications of field commanders. The supply line had been under the critical gun, too. As early as Africa and Sicily, regimental commanders had been dismayed to see the faith of the American soldier in his weapons shaken or destroyed. In Sicily, Colonel James M. Gavin heard wounded paratrooper 2.36 bazooka-men crying out not so much from their painful wounds, as from frustration with weapons they had been given. "I held my fire until that tank was almost on top of me to be sure," sobbed one of them to Gavin, "but when I blasted him, it bounced right off. Then he got me." [1] Many a commander like Gavin made solemn promises to himself about the high priority he would give to ordnance improvements if he ever found himself in a position to do so. Complaints from the battlefield were often answered to the effect that, if "the equipment was properly used," it would do the job. But proving-ground tests were no comfort to the soldier who found himself faced by the extremely accurate 88-snouted German tanks.

The Battle of the Bulge had highlighted the shortcomings of the

[1] "The incidents did occur several times," wrote Colonel Gavin to me. "We counterattacked that night and the following morning went out to collect our dead and wounded. We picked up at least a half dozen with pieces of bazookas ground into them by tank tracks. I am sure worse things have happened but I sure don't want to be around when it happens that way again."

supply line, much of it laid to the door of Lt. Gen. John C. Lee's
Services of Supply headquarters for having lodged itself in Paris,
where officers and men could easily allow their minds to wander to
more pleasant things than munitions delivery at the spearheads.

As Ninth Army's Operation Grenade billowed out across the
Roer River on February 23, a letter from the Pentagon arrived
on my desk, disclosing the concern of the War Department Ordnance
over barbed criticisms being directed at it. The most recent and
bitter complaints were that American armor was inferior to the
German. Even though German factories were under constant bombing, and their labor force was operating with a minimum of sleep,
there were reports that 200 modern tanks were going each week to
their fighting units. During the pre-Bulge refitting, eight of Hitler's
fifteen Panzer divisions on the Western Front had switched completely to the Panther and Tiger tanks. In America the finger pointed
rudely at Ordnance drawing boards and test centers as the weak spots.

Coming through public-relations channels, the Pentagon communications asked if encouragement could be given to story material,
using quotes of tank crews, making the point that American armor
was indeed equal to, and in some conditions, superior to that of
the enemy. This was an occasion for front-line laughter of the
mirthless order. It happened that a tanker sergeant was dining that
night at the press camp, visiting one of his old friends among our
drivers. When he read the letter, he grunted and then expounded
on the lighter-weight armor of the U. S. Army, which his outfit compared to a well-advertised cigarette lighter: "We call 'em Ronsons,"
he said. "They light up the first shot."

Nevertheless, more for the certainty of explosive reaction than in
the hope of getting stories, the Pentagon request was included
in our weekly circular letter to all division and special unit PRO's.
Nothing much came of it, although General Patton did make a Third
Army statement pointing up the difference in American and German
armor, the former going for speed, the latter for weight. It would
have been only one more mailroom incident, except that Frank Coniff,
INS, and Seymour Freidin, *New York Herald Tribune,* were shown
a copy of the newsletter by First Lieutenant Elmer Blasco, PRO of
the Twenty-ninth Infantry Division. Both of them blew a gasket
to think that the Pentagon was seeking public-relations putty to calk
the gaping ordnance seams. Captain Lavelle came to me with their

copy, although he had already passed it. "There's nothing of a security nature in either of these stories," he said, "but they will probably rebound on you. I thought you should see them." Both treatments were vitriolic, as Freidin and Coniff were both high on the armor inferiority subject anyway. There was no desire on my part, certainly, to interfere. But what could have been an explosive climax to the tales of ammunition and fuel shortages, and other criticisms, died aborning. As the cables of Coniff and Freidin were being punched, almost assured of prominent place in the news the following day, on that same March 6, Patton turned Maj. Gen. Hugh Gaffey loose with his Fourth Armored Division on a run up the south side of the Moselle River toward Coblenz and the Rhine. In forty-eight hours, this fast-moving armor-plated contingent plunged almost forty miles into the German rear areas. Ground-gaining mileage always makes better headlines in war than some of the more pedestrian, but equally vital, facts of life. The best spot Coniff's blast commanded was a wrap-around of grocery ads, while the Fourth Armored's scramble got a major display on the front pages.[2]

On our right First Army was going hard for Cologne, whose famous cathedral spires loomed ahead as the First plunged over the Erft River and onto the Cologne plain. The cathedral city was in for a bad time now, similar to the fate which had overtaken Aachen the previous autumn.

Ninth Army was arm and arm with the British near Venlo, and elbowed its way over to the Rhine. The Second Armored Division sent its spinning treads along the west bank, drawing a string around the German forces, which eventually totaled a bag of 53,000 for the Montgomery forces. Everything foretold by General Simpson in

---

[2] It came up in a SHAEF press conference, too, and General Eisenhower explained: "Some very broad statements have been made that seventy-five per cent of the equipment used by the allies is definitely inferior to the equipment used by the Germans ... that is silly. But it's perfectly true that when the Tiger and Panther tanks appeared upon the battlefield there came against us a tank that in a tank-to-tank duel was capable of knocking ours out, particularly at extreme ranges. Also, there is one other item of equipment in which they have comparatively held the edge—their bazookas are more penetrating. Once you break through and are not meeting the other fellow's tank, I think every tank commander would rather have the Sherman.... The tank sergeant and the tank lieutenant when he talks about the quality of tanks, he means 'When I meet the fellow in a village street.' In that circumstance we would be idle to say that the Sherman can meet the Panther or Tiger on equal terms...."

his briefing to the press was now coming off, and on schedule. Although it was the first significant picture of Ninth Army's capability, it had much to do with Eisenhower's later assertion: "If Simpson ever made a mistake as an Army commander, it never came to my attention. . . . Alert, intelligent, and professionally capable, he was the type of leader American soldiers deserve."

The date line all war correspondents were seeking, whether they were Ninth or First, was Cologne. Ninth's men mixed freely with First's en route to Cologne, even though it was a First Army objective. Again it was the old struggle to get inside the city limits to make the date line valid. Frank Coniff, edging from door to door down a roadway, spotted a soldier up ahead taking refuge in a gutter as bursts of German fire pinned him there. Coniff, torn between wanting the soldier's name and address to tie into his Cologne battle story and not wanting to risk his own neck unduly, conducted one of the most disjointed of interviews. As he moved up, the Germans brought mortars to bear. Each time Coniff bolted from his doorway, he would hear the dull pop of the booster charge which meant another missile was on the way. Counting the time, he would run back to his doorway and flatten himself until the explosion. It took him five trips, a word at a time, because the soldier himself was in no mood to stick his head up for an interview with a madman anyway. A half hour later, Coniff, still without his Cologne date line, crept back to the haven in which he had left his jeep with its driver, Marion Sparks. "Get anything?" Sparks asked. "I found a soldier out there named George Sullivan, of San Antonio, Texas, and if there is anybody in or near Cologne who is scared worse than I was—it's Sullivan, and I don't blame him."

Ken Dixon found a soldier behind a tree intently studying the terrain, trying to decide whether to dash ahead. "Hi," said Dixon, in hopeful pursuit of a paragraph. "What are you doin' here?"

The soldier glanced at him, then in a real neighborly Tennessee hills vernacular gave Dixon a definition of the simplicity of war he never forgot. "Why, suh," he said, "there ain't really nothin' to do up heah 'cept shoot folks."

The attack on Cologne had in its wake a whole welter of correspondents trying to make good on an "In Cologne" origin for their stories, and the military forces were treated to the strange sight of this motley collection of grown men sprinting into the Cologne city limits a few feet, spinning on their heels, and running back. Once they had regained their jeeps, they told the drivers to pour on the coal, high-tailing it to the press camps. On seeing these wild flights in the opposite direction to the advancing columns, several American commanders were reminded of the admonition Confederate General Nathan Bedford Forrest had made to his couriers. "When going to the rear," he said, "always walk. I'll shoot any man I see running to the rear." But Forrest knew nothing about date lines, or how exaggerated their importance was to become. However, the number of correspondents was so infinitesimal in relation to the vast masses of matériel, equipment and manpower going forward that, at worst, they caused only a minor ripple with their headlong rearward scramble.

We were still in Maastricht, on direct order of Colonel Joseph Miller, the Ninth Army signal officer, who did not want Press Wireless and Lieutenant Louis Muhlbauer's JEEP mobile military transmitter cluttering the communications of Ninth's three corps—the XII, of Maj. Gen. Alvan C. Gillem, Jr.; the XVI, of Maj. Gen. J. B. Anderson; and the veteran XIX, of Maj. Gen. Raymond S. McLain— which were now all over the Roer and in the Rhineland. "You're miles behind the front," moaned Larry Fairhall, the Kemsley Newspapers correspondent, thinking of the long tiring jeep hauls, and he waved his hand peremptorily when reminded that he depended on the Ninth Army's land-line teletype circuits which could not yet be put across the Roer.

Hugh Schuck had another of his weird adventures as the German front crumbled. He drove into a small village in the gathering darkness and asked an officer standing in the square where the nearest American headquarters was. The officer, a German major in the medical corps, started speaking in German and Schuck started running. "Night never fell slower," said Hugh. Once when chasing after Generals Eisenhower and Simpson, Hugh's jeep was strafed in one of the first appearances of German jets. Hugh's characteristic good humor stayed with him. "Gave me a headache," he reported, "trying to get all my 180 pounds up into my helmet." [3]

[3] Hollywood screen writer Sammy Fuller, a sergeant in the 16th Infantry Regiment of the 1st Division, fought with his unit into the streets of Bonn until darkness fell, when he and his men took refuge in a house. In the next morning light, he found he had slept with his neck against a piano leg. As he sat up rubbing it, he noticed a sign on it. The place was obviously a museum or shrine. "Hey," he said, shaking a Tennessee sergeant named Johnson who was

There was a full-scale boundary row, reminiscent of the cattle ranchers' trouble with the nesters in the Old West, involving the photographers of the Ninth and First Armies. It really dated from the Battle of the Bulge when most of the divisions of the Ninth had gone down to help First re-establish its fractured front and Harold Siegman of Acme Newspictures challenged the right of Fred Ramage of British Keystone International to be there.

At 3 P.M., on March 6, as both Maj. Gen. Terry Allen's 104th Infantry Division and Maj. Gen. Maurice Rose's Third Armored Division were moving street by street into ruined Cologne, in the direction of the Rhine banks and the landmark of the twin-spired Cathedral, the progress slowed. Elements being followed by Harold Siegman were pessimistic about getting to the cathedral that night. Without the cathedral for his identity point, Siegman had no picture, so he went back to First Army press camp.

Meanwhile, Lieutenant Charles Rhodes and three Signal Corps photographers were coming along in the rear of C Company of the Thirty-sixth Armored Infantry Regiment, which was being urged on by its commander, First Lieutenant Robert J. Cook of Wellsville, N. Y. C Company had a handful of tanks ahead of it. Along with this Cook "task force" was Fred Ramage, his camera at the ready. Two hours of hard fighting later, with the light fading fast in the drizzling afternoon, the German resistance suddenly broke around the cathedral. The tanks clanked into the Platz before the miraculously spared edifice and one stopped right in front of it. The cameramen ran ahead to shoot off a pack of negatives apiece and get out. As if in deference to the mighty religious shadow in which they had halted, the tanks cut their motors and peace fell over the scene. Carefully, the turret of the tank just in front of the cathedral was opened slightly as if to test for snipers. Ramage, Rhodes, and the Signal Corpsmen made their lens settings, preparing to catch the first soldier coming out of his armored hole to survey the spectacle of battle success, a picture which, without caption, could indicate the end of a fighting day. The soldier lifted himself up through the turret, and stepped out on top of the tank to look about. He took off his helmet and ran his forearm sleeve across his face to remove some of the grime. The photographers were about to click their shutters, when

snoring next to him, "know where we are? Sure as hell, this is Beethoven's house!" "Don't know him," said Johnson, sleepily. "What outfit's he in?"

a lone German 88-gunner who had bided his time provided them with one of the most horrible, dramatic pictures of the war.

The cameramen were actually sighting when the German gun barked. The cameras snapped, partly because of the compulsive start given them by the renewal of fire, and the leg of the soldier, severed just above the knee, was seen to go flying in the air. There was one long scream of shock and pain from the soldier as he somersaulted over into the mud of the street. All other tank turrets closed at once, and the battle was resumed. In the street, the legless American soldier was bounding around on one knee and the leg stump. His screams could be heard above the firing. The photographers kept their cameras working, as one of Lieutenant Cook's medics crawled to the soldier and applied a tourniquet. The wounded man still called in agony while litter bearers snaked forward to him. As the German shots became spasmodic, so was the soldier reduced to gasps and his movements to mere muscular jerks. With the German gun silenced, the litter bearers carried the dying soldier away.

The cameramen ducked into the cathedral, took several pictures of the interior, came out, and ran to their jeeps. They had two date lines, "Before Cologne Cathedral," and "In Cologne Cathedral." When Lieutenant Rhodes and the Signal Corps cameramen later told Harold Siegman that he had left too early and that the armored thrust had actually gotten to the cathedral, he was naturally disappointed. But he turned livid when he found that Ramage, a British picture poacher and from the Ninth Army, had the only agency pictures of the final act of Cologne's capture. He went roaring to Major Dempsey to demand that boundaries between the Armies be re-erected to protect sectors for accredited correspondents, and Dempsey called me saying he believed we had better do it if we wanted any peace of mind. I agreed, although it didn't seem possible that this would worry us much in the future, since Montgomery was going to have Ninth Army for the Rhine crossing north of the Ruhr while the First would stay south of that industrial area.

That same day, the Ninth Armored Division's Combat Command B under Brig. Gen. William M. Hoge ordered a task force led by Lt. Col. Leonard W. Engeman to make all haste north of the Ahr. As it approached a small village called Remagen, First Lieutenant John Grimball, of Columbia, South Carolina, with Company A of the Fourteenth Tank Battalion was sent plunging after the fleeing

Germans who were still using the Ludendorff bridge. Along Grimball's route an old German was working in his garden and one of the American soldiers thought he might be a *Volksturmer* or an informer, staying behind and using his age as protection. He laid three quick shots in the direction of the old man, who hit the dirt. But the bridge was uppermost in Grimball's mind and he urged his outfit forward fast. Although Lt. Gen. Walter Bedell Smith, Eisenhower's chief of staff, later picked the Remagen exploitation as part of one of the six great Eisenhower decisions of the war, an item of considerable importance to that development was Lieutenant Grimball's concentration on the bridge, at the risk of by-passing the old man.[4] Grimball's fast-moving action was not only of great military, but also of far greater political, impact, for as the bridge was reached and Lieutenant Karl Timmermann of West Point, Nebraska, took his infantrymen over the span, the old man got up and removed himself to safety. Nearly seventy years old, he still had a great future. His name was Konrad Adenauer.

The Ninth Armored jammed over the bridge before the German demolition team could blow it, startling the allied camp with its prospects at a moment when all emphasis was being given to Monty's plan for a full-scale crossing assault in the area of Wesel.

The requirement to get our press camp up to the front now had us in a scramble for suitable housing. Ninth Army had ridden out the winter in a good installation in Maastricht, but Larry Fairhall's squawk about "miles behind the front" was true, and the chorus was taken up now by Wes Gallagher, Noel Monks, Frank Coniff and most of the others. Ninth Army's main headquarters was to be München-Gladbach, but there was going to be trouble finding a built-up area there which would hold all its vast staff and support troops. For the press camp, this meant a hunt for something which would take a family of about 165 people, military and civilian and

---

[4] A German civilian had reported to General Hoge that the bridge was set with demolitions and scheduled to be blown at 4 P.M. With forty-five minutes to spare, Colonel Engeman, at Hoge's urging, checked on the progress of the task force by messaging Lieutenant Grimball: "Get to the bridge as rapidly as possible." The South Carolina lieutenant reported back on his radio with a quiet drawl: "Suh, I am already theah." With only ten minutes to spare, Timmermann's infantry raced to the other side of the bridge. Later to die, Timmermann, with Grimball and thirteen other officers and men, was awarded the Distinguished Service Cross for this feat.

of both sexes. In the bludgeoned Rhineland our spot would probably be some distance from the headquarters.

As a preliminary the radio correspondents were permitted to jump forward to a beat-up castle in Eschweiler in the XIX Corps sector. Lieutenant Muhlbauer and his JEEP radio, as well as Lieutenant George Fuller, went along. Muhlbauer opened his wave length, calling BBC, which answered immediately. This made his trio—Howard K. Smith, CBS; Robert Massell, Blue Network; and Stanley Maxted, BBC—very happy for the time being.

Wes Gallagher and Noel Monks reported that they had talked to a regimental commander of the Twenty-ninth Infantry Division, who had Schloss Rheydt as his headquarters just south of München-Gladbach. There was some possibility that the Twenty-ninth would be getting out, and they believed it would be ideal for the new press camp. Even though all the war correspondents blandly said they had no needs for themselves other than communications, a place to eat and transportation, no one who had ever dealt with the press could take such protestations at face value. They are a comfort-loving lot, and since the Ninth Army had provided clean sheets twice weekly in Maastricht, an orchestra in the dining room and various other fillips, none but the unwise would want suddenly to wean them of this creamy diet.

Considering it best to make as many of the arrangements as possible before the actual move, the Ninth Army press camp elected to do what none had done before—namely, hire a professional hotel keeper and staff as well as additional civilian help. Our estimate was that our progress through Germany would probably be from one stark ruin to another, with limited facilities for light, water, sanitation and accommodations generally. We gave ourselves forty-eight hours to set up each forward location, and the civilian staff had the responsibility of making the selected site look and run like a hotel while we were in residence. We had been fortunate in Maastricht. Now we found that Willem van Egerschot wanted to get away from the town until memories dimmed and his troubles were forgotten. He and his wife represented an experience factor hard to find, and some of the Dutch help in the hotel also indicated their willingness to join the cavalcade. The proposal was put to the correspondents, along with evidence of lack of foresight in other armies. Each correspondent would now be billed for $15 a week, of which $9.75 would go into the "Widows' & Orphans' Protective Fund" to defray the costs of civilian help. The suggestion was accepted by the correspondents, and Ninth Army gave approval to the inclusion of "Allied nationals" in the press camp.

Griff, Willem van Egerschot and I set forth on a reconnaissance tour and looked at three spots before we checked the Gallagher-Monks tip, Schloss Rheydt. It was the most promising. An ancient castle dating from about 1275 A.D., a combination museum and showplace in years gone by, it had taken on tourist flavor in the thirties when it was given to a home-town boy who had gone far, Dr. Josef Goebbels. It was overpoweringly German in its architecture and moated all around, with a single entry by drawbridge. Driving into the foreyard through an arch over the planked span, we found a large inn-like enclosure. The castle was easily adequate for our military strength, and the yard made an ideal motor park. The moat, of only scenic interest to some, took on added meaning for us, offering a way of running one leg of the Press Wireless antenna across it to gain bounce and a clearer signal to the U. S. The Schloss itself looked like a great L-shaped stone heap.

The regimental commander was unhappy to hear that his eviction was so close, but took the news with the profane philosophical attitude of all lower units. The Schloss was actually no bargain, even though to the infantry colonel it was a seat suitable for a Sultan. The lighting was on limited power from München-Gladbach, but we remembered the store of Coleman lamps we had picked up on Omaha Beach the September before and had never used. Water had barely pressure enough to reach the sinks on the first floor, which meant it would be necessary to install a tank and keep it at perpetual boil. For proximity to the news, it was good. With Ninth Army going into München-Gladbach, the briefing officer, Major A. Kenly Thorne, of Parkersburg, West Virginia, had only a short ride to get to our press gatherings.

John Betwinek, chief of Press Wireless, followed up our preliminary survey to check the location in a communications sense. Colonel Joe Miller was asked to tell us how soon we could be picked up on the teletype circuit. Betwinek pronounced the Schloss ideal for his unit, and Miller said he could make the teletype tie in three days. Setting March 12 for our move forward, this gave us two days. The Twenty-ninth's regiment had lived in the Schloss with the usual GI abandon, and the place was a mess. The van Egerschots were given a truck and driver and told to approach the nearest slave labor camp, where a polyglot collection of hungry humanity was now aimlessly free, being unable to penetrate the battle lines to go home. Our hope was that some would elect to go through Germany with us, being paid for the work they did. Before we left Maastricht, the Netherlands government had assigned nine uniformed Dutch Army guards to us as a security force, and we had ten Dutch civilians on the staff. When the van Egerschots returned, there was a truckload of Russians, Poles, Czechs and Slovaks, and our civilian population was swollen to twenty-seven, all delighted with the prospects of regular food and eager to work. The interior of the Schloss began shortly to shine, and the floors to show through the caking of mud and dirt. An old Russian saw the pile of logs in the back yard and began cutting it into fireplace lengths for the big fires which would burn perpetually on the first and second floors.

The crust of the front along the Rhine was quiet, but in the rear all was a tremendous commotion as Montgomery assembled twenty-six divisions and some strong special units, brought up Navy landing craft, and enshrouded the area in smoke to deny its observation by the Germans. As a result of Remagen, his Rhine crossing had lost some of its news punch, but he was going to have it for size, that was sure. The buildup pause made our move timely, and the correspondents accepted the three-day break while Press Wireless was being brought up to the Schloss. The teletype was left in Maastricht, with Lieutenant Patterson in charge of the punchers until Prewi was again active, whereupon the Schloss teletype would cut in and the last vestiges of Ninth Army's press camp could clear out of Maastricht.

M-Day (for moving, that is) found the war correspondents rolling into the Schloss at noon, grudgingly delighted to be so much closer to their work, and particularly intrigued to be based now in the country estate of Dr. Josef Goebbels, a free press operating from the home of the man who had put a clamp on so much of the world's print for so long. While the cleaning was going on, we had thoughtfully made a showpiece out of the Goebbels master bed, putting it out in the main corridor with a sign on the headboard which read: DR. JOSEF GOEBBELS SLEPT HERE—AND DID OTHER THINGS, TOO! Goebbels' prowess with the ladies had been widely heralded. This was underlined when we found a motion-picture directory in German, which listed, with pictures, all the actors and actresses in the industry in 1944. Alongside some of the photos of the comely cinema queens were penned X-marks, or double X's, and private phone numbers.

When Gallagher, AP cameraman Henry Griffin, Gordon Gammack and Vic Jones took cots in what had been the Goebbels master bedroom, they naturally thumbed through the directory. Knowing how Goebbels' propaganda office monitored the German movie industry, and could say the word which could put anyone in, or have her thrown out of a film career, Gammack put in words what the others were all thinking: "I wonder," he said, "how many of those girls got in this book by getting in that bed?"

Even the most elementary privacy had now been forsaken, and each correspondent had to get used to living barracks style, at least six and sometimes nine to a single room. We had provided only folding cots without mattresses, and the guests threw their bedrolls on these. Comfort depended entirely on the individual's personal equipment. The dining hall was on the grand scale, with a high ceiling and outfitted with a series of long tables at which stood high-backed chairs. The fireplace at the entrance end of the dining hall was fully ten feet across, head high, and into it were cast seven-foot logs. A roaring fire was necessary to take the chill off the damp stone hall. We even brought the orchestra on from Maastricht for the first week, so the break was not too pronounced.

The attitude and manners of the press camp changed now that we were in Germany. Most of the French correspondents seemed to consider their SHAEF accreditation a license for looting. The CID was beginning to turn up at all press camps asking questions, particularly about individuals who were art fanciers and who were known to be running penknives around canvases found on castle walls, taking them out of the frames and shoving them off to Brussels, Paris, and Switzerland for quick sales.

The first meal, dinner, was well cooked and well served, and the fireplace cast dancing shadows on the walls. After dining, we had to assemble the civilian staff, and particularly the new slave-labor portion, and talk to them through the interpreting van Egerschots about that special breed, the war correspondent. Throughout their feverish cleaning, our help had assumed they were preparing for the coming of some "gentry." Now, after seeing the muddy, unshaven arrivals and noting how quickly the place was littered, the charwomen and the maids were recalculating. But no matter how clearly it was explained, or how high the mark set for sanitation, our new-found civilian staff was never again as inclined to make the Schloss shine as they had been that first day.

Up to this point in World War II, ever since the campaign had begun with Normandy, nothing but the changes of division commanders equaled the turnover of public-relations officers, though the latter did not go down as battle losses. The highest-ranking one was, of course, Colonel Robert Parham, who augured in trying to hold the line for the Ninth Air Force staff. Major James T. Quirk of Philadelphia went off the PRO job at First Army early in August, 1944. Lt. Col. Kent Hunter was being threatened by Patton before Third Army started to roll in Normandy, and eventually got the sack later in 1944. Nearly all these "firings" started with the correspondents, who flared up over real or fancied grievances and set out to "get" somebody. The always vulnerable scapegoat on any Army staff was the public-relations officer, who was felt by the correspondents to be representing his personal views rather than carrying out the instructions of the staff with which he worked. If he carried out instructions to the letter, rather than tempering them with common sense, he could easily find himself boxed with either press or staff, or both. A known hazard of military public relations is that the PRO can make recommendations, but must abide by the orders of his superiors. It is also known to all but the naïve that, when the chips are down, his superiors may not be in position to back him. He is there to be sacrificed if the going gets rough. However, there was nothing too disgraceful about being pulled off a public-relations job. Major Quirk, in fact, was given several public-relations lives and made good on all the others. It was he who replaced Hunter and he stood quite high with the Third Army press corps. The test of the public-relations officer was his ability to weather the "protest meeting." None of them had lived a full life until he knew what it was like to be the butt of one. When he went into one, he went alone; and he went down, or survived, alone. The first of them for me occurred in the second-floor sitting room of the Schloss the night before General Simpson was scheduled to appear in our briefing room to explain the Ninth Army's role in the Montgomery Rhine crossing. It was less than three weeks after Larry Fairhall's complaint that Maastricht was "miles behind the front," at which time the Hôtel du Lévrier had

buzzed with press accusations that Ninth Army had "gotten too comfortable," that it was "reluctant to move into the field," that, of all
its elements, the press camp was "the most entrenched and reluctant
of all."

At the same time that this anvil chorus from the press corps was
being pounded out, the Ninth Army's signals office was adamant in its
insistence that the press camp stay out of the Rhineland. Press Wireless was ready to move any time the Army would permit it to do so,
but the British seldom used it because it banged straight through to
New York. They preferred and used the free teletype service, so any
change of location which did not involve a guaranteed teletype was
unthinkable to the British. The signals office had found it impossible
to re-establish quickly the cable severed by the retreating Germans.
The press camp, once restrictions were called off and the line in, had
moved promptly. The correspondents, airily dismissing creature comforts, had been led by Hank Wales, who said they would "all be glad
to live in tents."

The protest meeting brought about thirty of the correspondents
together in the big lounge and sitting room, and Noel Monks was their
spokesman. With twenty-six divisions, four brigades, commandos,
naval units and paratroopers in the last stages of getting ready to cross
the Rhine, the correspondents' complaints were that personal services
had dropped off since Maastricht! The things they missed were the
things we had had to leave behind in the Hôtel du Lévrier, integral parts
of a first-class hotel, but hardly suitable for our present nomadic life
of the road. Everett Walker, managing editor of the *New York Herald
Tribune* who was on a visit at the front, came to me when it was
over, laid his hand on my arm. "Not for all the money in the world,"
he whispered, "would I have your job."

A rather tense silence fell over the room when the correspondents
were asked to recheck their memories as to exactly how long ago it was
that they had disavowed the very personal comforts for which they
were now bellyaching. Vic Jones of the *Boston Globe* was fumbling
with the dial on a radio in the far corner and suddenly struck the
Stuttgart wavelength just as Dr. Josef Goebbels was introduced from
Berlin to address and exhort the German people to greater resistance.
"Come on over," he called to his colleagues. "Let's listen to our
landlord." The tension snapped with a round of laughter, and the
Ninth Army press camp's first protest meeting was over.

... TAKE 15

A Piece of Germany

As the patchwork pieces for the Rhine crossing were being moved into place, there was evidence of great concern at Twenty-first Army Group headquarters that maximum credit be given to Monty for bossing the river jump. Ninth Army was once more to go into action with Montgomery at the reins, one of a trio of armies, the others being the British Second and the Canadian First. With the water barrier breached near Wesel, Monty's forces would have immediate and wide-open access to all of Germany north of the Ruhr. Remagen had been heralded by the press to such an extent that it dented any chances of Monty getting the play the British command appeared hopeful for. On the profit side, however, it did draw away important German forces which would otherwise have been held in the Wesel area. Disappointing though Remagen was to the Twenty-first Army Group staff, their Rhine crossing was still being prepared for in unhurried fashion. Stacks of ordnance, reservoirs of manpower, smoke-screening accouterments, and Monty's determined clinging to the need for airborne assault all took time. His plans called for 1,300 medium and heavy guns to support the British XXX and Canadian XII Corps, while the American XVI Corps was to have 600 field pieces. Nearly 60,000 British and American pioneer and engineer troops, with tons of bridging equipment, were to be involved.

General Simpson came to Schloss Rheydt and gave his usual advance briefing to the war correspondents on an important operation. His report went into details of the Ninth Army's portion of the attack, with some discussion of the relationship of Ninth to the Twenty-first Army Group master format. He explained that his sixteen-division Army, now at its greatest strength, would put the XVI Corps in the assault, first thrusting the Thirtieth and Seventy-ninth Infantry Divisions over, using Navy landing craft. The Ninth would then skirt the northern side of the Ruhr so that the industrial heart of Germany would be sealed off and the southern flank of Monty's other two armies would be protected. The latter would then be free to bolt for the Baltic. There were implications in this of a greater story, but it occurred to none of the press. The plan reflected farsighted British policy to deny Denmark to any Russian advance. For the correspondents, looking at the well-studied map with its new arrows, the attack lines stirred one great anticipation. The Ninth Army's direction was almost a straight line to Berlin.

When General Simpson finished his formal outline and asked if there were any questions, the first one was voiced by Wes Gallagher and reflected some of the feeling about Monty's command. "How soon will the Ninth Army be released for publication in this operation?"

"I don't know," said General Simpson frankly. "I think Field Marshal Montgomery will announce us in due time."

There was a rustle among the American correspondents, a supporting whisper from some of the British Empire writers, while the London contingent remained uncomfortably quiet. It was indicated that Twenty-first Army Group was about to retrieve some prestige. Captain Lavelle had already been told that Twenty-first Army Group could only be called "an Allied force." No American leadership was to be indicated at the outset, and none of the participating units would be identified until the word came from Lt. Col. Pat Saunders, Monty's censor chief.

General Simpson, with his usual clarity, responded to a query by Noel Monks with a description of the role of the British Sixth and U. S. Seventeenth Airborne Divisions—a total of 14,000 excellent fighting men who were to land between the Rhine and Münster to pave the way for the amphibious movement of Second British Army. This brought to mind the absence of BBC's Stanley Maxted, who had taken off a few days before on a special mission. A veteran of the beleaguered First British Airborne Divisional drop at Arnhem, it was guessed that he was going again. General Simpson further explained that, although the first Ninth Army elements would move by assault boats and landing craft, the XVI Corps's main strength was scheduled to use ponton bridges and thereafter to echelon division-by-division across the rear areas of those who had preceded them in order to wall in the Ruhr. He emphasized that the strategy of SHAEF pointed toward the destruction of the steel sinews of war in this vital area. Meanwhile, the hardened XIX Corps, which had come all the way from a D plus six entry into Normandy and was spearheaded by its well-tried iron-clad colossus, the Second Armored Division, was to head east and keep going. Somewhere around Paderborn, he thought, it would link up with First Army elements.

No amount of emphasis given by General Simpson to the Ruhr could take the war correspondents' eyes off the XIX Corps and its apparent Berlin compass-setting. Their gamble on the unknown Ninth Army now appeared to be paying off. General Simpson did not hazard any guesses as to length and duration of advance because he was under orders to confine himself to the phase lines drawn by Twenty-first Army Group. It seemed to all, however, that a successful crossing of the Rhine would put the Ninth Army in an exceptional position, particularly if the Rhine defense was weak. Nobody asked the point-blank question as to whether, if the Germans did slump quickly east of the Rhine, the Ninth Army would be rolling so fast it would be disinclined to observe Monty's phase lines. As a final word, General Simpson said the Rhine crossing was to start late on March 23. He wrapped up his maps and drove away, leaving the correspondents to decide where they now wanted to place themselves for the assault.

Our press population had picked up a little and some changes were made. John MacCormac, *New York Times,* who was yearning for a return to his beloved Vienna, had replaced Richard J. Johnston, much to the latter's unhappiness since he had wanted to see the Rhine operation through. Howard K. Smith was notified that Eric Sevareid, a network old-timer, would have priority on the Rhine crossing story for CBS, although Howard was the Ninth Army regular. Smith's gamble, wintering with the Ninth to hold a place, was not turning out so well as the others.

Lieutenant George Fuller, who was busy with Ninth Army's radio coverage, had been doing almost as well as the professionals on the BBC's "Combat Diary." Before the Roer crossing, which he had used as an exercise for the bigger Rhine adventure, he had gone to a

105-mm. gun battery just prior to H-hour. He had recorded the actual orders given in the preattack briefing, then followed through by picking them up as they were phoned to the guns. Making a quick sprint to the gun-sites, he was installed in time to count out the seconds to H-hour and follow with descriptions of the attack barrage. Packing up quickly, Fuller and his driver-generator operator, Andy Holmes, had raced back to the JEEP transmitter to re-run the recording for the censor. When it was passed, he piped it to London. BBC, in a superb editing job, incorporated this into a thirty-minute program, and a very good one. Now Fuller began to frame his approach to the Rhine crossing.

There were much more cumbersome censorship restrictions on the Rhine than on the Roer. Captain Lavelle, with knowledge that the drive would be launched at about 9 P.M. on March 23, received orders to hold any announcement until 4 P.M. the next day. But nearly twenty-four hours before the troops of the Fifty-first (British) Division, in four battalions, were to step off for the Rhine venture, Patton injected his own jibe at Monty's ponderous preparations by urging the U. S. Fifth Infantry Division across the Rhine and into the village of Oppenheim.[1] This meant that elements of two armies, both American, had preceded Monty over the river. In both cases, the Americans had gone over by opportunistic speed or stealth, while Monty's arrangements were tremendous and ostentatious.

Early on March 23, the Ninth Army correspondents went out to join forward units, the Thirtieth and Seventy-ninth Infantry Divisions. Some of them elected to take positions in the landing craft. They were unhurried, since the censorship stop on all copy held until 4 P.M. the next day. The stop at this time of day, incidentally, almost insured a clean gift for the British "national" newspapers, the bulk of which were morning editions, and provided a comfortable handling margin for major treatment in U. S. afternoon papers—in both cases playing into the hands of maximum readership. The extreme care of the arrangements, plus the hard-fisted clamp on designating the American Ninth Army as such, made it certain that Monty would get full credit.

[1] Captain Charles W. Sanford, of Thomaston, Connecticut, American censorship representative at Twenty-first Army Group from D-Day to the end of the war, said: "Major Gowan would not even put on the map the fact that Patton had crossed the Rhine before Monty's attack until at least twelve hours afterward."

All this also gave BBC ample time to get together a fine, well-edited documentary for its widely listened-to nine o'clock news.

As Fuller took off with Andy Holmes, Colonel Joseph Miller's office gave us the heartening information that BBC had been granted a special extra wavelength by Twenty-first Army Group, which would be used by a transmitter at Eindhoven. Thought only to be cued to the historic importance of the offensive, and naturally assumed to be only an avenue by which more traffic could be squeezed off the continent through the British terminal, it made Fuller surer than ever that all he had to do was deliver a program and BBC would be ready for it.

It was quite dark when Fuller and Holmes worked their way to a church steeple less than a mile from the banks of the Rhine in the Thirtieth Infantry Division sector. They ran into their first obstacle when a bearded sergeant barred them at the church door. "This is the only observation post for miles," he told Fuller, "and it's so jammed with artillerymen now, there ain't room to step. You and that noisy rig of yours could screw us up proper. It'll be soon enough to catch hell when we open up." Fuller pleaded and cajoled, and said he would put the generator and the operator so far back there would be no way of hooking it up with the steeple. He said he would box the whole recorder so no lights, not even the tiniest, would show. He said he only wanted to stay a few minutes after the fight started. The sergeant had his own problems, all of them so personal he couldn't care less about whether anybody at a radio could hear the opening salvos of the Rhine campaign. After extracting some elaborate promises from Fuller, he let him proceed.

Fuller and Holmes added more than 150 feet of cable to their already extended cord, so George could get all the way to the top of the steeple. The tall steeple, pock-marked with shellfire, had somehow survived all the shots aimed at it. On this occasion, it resembled nothing so much as an anthill. Fuller clambered up to the very top, and there waited for the bombardment to begin. With a grandstand accommodation, the seconds ticked off as he awaited H-hour. Andy Holmes was ready to kick over the generator and start the recording. George counted to himself: "Five, four, three, two, one. . . ." The front blazed along the Rhine, and spurts of fire blossomed above it. Phosphorus shells lighted the water, and landing boats could be seen slipping into the river as the barrage patterns appeared to engulf and destroy everything in the German defensive zone. In the throbbing church steeple, which shook often from hits, there were crisp trans-mittals of orders by phones for range changes, elevations, traverses.

All this, the profanity, the frustration of inability of the gun positions to hear, the yips of elation, the curses for failure to com-prehend, was fed for a quarter of an hour into Fuller's revolving wire. To get much of it, he merely went step by step, and slowly, down the ladder, keeping his microphone open as he passed from one tier to the next. He joined Holmes and had him cut the generator. He had loads of time now, and waited to get some sounds of the overhead passage, come daylight, of the airborne armada.

Back in England, the British Sixth Airborne loaded up in the early hours of March 24. Doon Campbell, of Reuter's, was delighted to find that he was assigned to a glider which had a jeep aboard. Trans-portation would be a difficult item to come by on the other end. He was not so happy when he found it loaded to the top with hand grenades. He asked searching questions about what might happen to a jeep loaded with grenades if it suffered from a hit. The answer was not reassuring.

BBC made up a team, with Richard Dimbleby in the tug ship pulling a glider in which Stanley Maxted was the passenger. Maxted had a trailer in which a transmitting station had been packed and he was sure he would make broadcasting history by letting people hear the battle going on around him. BBC had laid out $160,000 for the apparatus riding with Maxted. Dimbleby had a ringside seat to watch his colleague being cut loose, then would get back to England to give an air picture of developments below. Among others, Robert Vermillion, UP, and Geoffrey Bocca, *London Daily Express,* were with the Sixth British Airborne, too. Bocca, a youngster, was soft-spoken and very eager to help any of his associates. Vermillion had already jumped with the airborne in Southern France and had allowed his typewriter to be dropped in one of the bundles of ammunition. He was surprised when he actually ran it down. As he was scheduled to jump again, and Bocca was going in a glider, he prevailed on the youth to take the machine with him.

The American Seventeenth Airborne Division was coming from bases in France, commanded by that parachuting pioneer and one-time West Point gymnast, Maj. Gen. William "Bud" Miley. With the Seventeenth were Robert Capa, *Life,* making good at last on that "champagne contract," and the Allied Airborne Army's chief photographer, Lt. Col. Albert McCleery. CBS' Richard Hotellet was scheduled to view the whole show from a hovering B-17.

The two great aerial fleets converged over Brussels, took new bearings, and headed for the Rhine. Around 10 A.M., March 24, the daylight drop began with the arrival of the paratroopers who spilled out in a clear sky. Vermillion, Capa [2] and McCleery took their silken way down. Much to his surprise and relief, Campbell landed safely and immediately put as much distance between himself and the nest of grenades as he could. The tug plane with Dimbleby aboard towed Maxted to the point of cutting loose and all went well in the first stages, then Dimbleby thought he saw the glider hit by an explosion of some kind and lost sight of it. Maxted's glider had indeed been hit and crashed into an orchard in flames. Maxted received a broken rib and was hit over the eye with a shell splinter. "The worst casualty," Maxted told the medic who worked on him, "was the transmitter. It burned up in about a minute and a half—around 40,000 pounds' worth of equipment belonging to BBC went up in smoke." BBC took both disappointment and loss rather understandingly and with magnanimity, considering that when Maxted got out of the hospital later in London and went to his BBC mail box, he found that the accounting department was urgently asking him to settle a one shilling sixpence phone bill to Birmingham which had been "in arrears for some time."

When Robert Vermillion wrestled out of his harness, he looked around for Bocca and the glider. He met a British officer who reported to him that Bocca's glider had been smashed and was under heavy fire. Bocca, he said, had certainly been killed [3] and it was improbable that the typewriter could be found. Vermillion was dependent on his pencil for the story.

[2] Capa lay pinned down in an open field, unable to get out of his parachute as blistering fire swept the area. Capa began cursing in his native Hungarian, which caught the attention of a paratrooper nearby who was also shrinking into the dirt. "Hey, bud," he said, "them Jewish prayers ain't gonna do you no good here."

[3] In 1947, when Vermillion was sitting on the night desk of UP in New York, he had a phone call. A British voice sparkled over the phone: "I say, old boy, I'm awfully sorry about what happened but I do want to explain about the typewriter. This is Jeff Bocca." Bocca was shot five times on landing, was captured, escaped, was recaptured. One of his wounds was suffered at the drop zone when he was crawling to retrieve the Vermillion typewriter. "I did try," said Bocca, "but really, Bob, it simply was full of holes."

If the airborne drop was a bust for Maxted, it was also a fizzle for Fuller across the river. The planes did not pass close enough to provide engine noises for his recorder. After a few trials, he gave up and before noon he was back at Schloss Rheydt to get his recording passed by the censors and ready to roll when the 4 P.M. stop was pulled off.

At General Bradley's headquarters, when the staff gathered that morning for the regular briefing, the general was in high good humor over Patton's morning phone call. Patton had told Bradley how the Fifth Infantry Division had gone over the Rhine the day before. There was solace in this for Bradley, who was still chafing from reflections cast on him in the Bulge and the fact that Ninth Army was riding again under Monty's banner—albeit anonymously. The briefing audience itself got a lift out of the report of Lt. Col. Richard R. Stillman, of Paris, Kentucky, Third Army's liaison officer. He did not mention Monty by name. "Without benefit of aerial bombing, ground smoke, artillery preparation or airborne assistance, the Third Army at 2200 hours [10 P.M.], Thursday evening, March 22, crossed the Rhine River," he said.

Throughout the late hours of the morning of March 24, the Ninth Army's war correspondents streamed in, muddy, red-eyed and tired, home again to Schloss Rheydt. Their tenseness was showing from the ordeal of the river operation. Many of them had gone in with the early fire fight. Their tenseness was matched by mine. Early that morning one of the communications operators had come to me with a startling announcement. "The teletype has gone dead," he said. There was no power, he explained, and he couldn't raise anyone.

When I got on the field telephone to headquarters, I learned that all communication by land line to the rear from Ninth Army was gone! The radio link still worked, but it was in the open, so all conversations on it were severely restricted. The cause of the trouble was a mystery. "Maybe it's sabotage," said the harried signal officer on duty. "They could lay hands on the line almost anywhere since we've come into Germany. We have a crew out running the cable now, making a check." I put a hush on all the operators. We still had time to 4 P.M., and something might come through. Griff and I could only shudder to think of the flap it would cause if the word got out— considering that the British correspondents were the constant teletype users and that this was a supreme British story.

Around noon Richard Hotellet arrived in the press camp carrying a heap of billowing parachute silk. He had had to bail out when his plane became one of the fifty-five lost in the airborne effort, and he had fallen on our side of the Rhine—uninjured. Griff had had the kitchen prepare that rare thing for us—a good noonday meal. The correspondents, with time to unwind and write in leisurely fashion against the four o'clock release time, dawdled over their early lunch, thinking how nice it would be to write on a full stomach and with plenty of time to compose their thoughts. Lieutenant Patterson pulled me away from the table just as I started chewing my first bite. Captain Sam Brightman was calling from Twelfth Army Group. "We've been trying to raise you by teletype," said Sam. "We couldn't do it, so I'm having to tell you this by phone. SHAEF has overruled Twenty-first Army Group's embargo of four o'clock, and the Rhine crossing is released as of noon today."

The complications were now fantastic. The teletype was out. Not one of the correspondents who had the eyewitness accounts had yet written his story. The release of the Rhine operation, according to my watch, would be made in Paris in exactly three minutes! Aside from the fact that once again the Paris correspondents would knock the edge off front-line stories, they would have a beat on filings from the battle area of half an hour or more.

My announcement in the dining room caused a great spewing of coffee. Chairs were shoved back and upset with crashes. The correspondents, making wild chewing motions at the food in their mouths, gulped and ran to their typewriters. Their curses of disgust ricocheted off the walls, but they were soon concentrating furiously on their work to the exclusion of their professional pain. We watched in a cold sweat as fifteen minutes went by. The first British correspondent finished and filed with the censor. With some relief we noted that it was Noel Monks, with a morning paper, where some delay did not matter. His story was clocked in and Lavelle picked it up to read it. At this juncture, the teletype operator, his face streaked with grease and perspiration, tugged at my sleeve. Out in the corridor, he whispered, "The line's back in. We're ready to roll." The timing could hardly have been better, and the place became heady with exhilaration. "Yuh know what knocked us out?" the excited puncher went on. "It was one of them dumb bastards with a bulldozer fixing the road. He sunk the blade too deep at the shoulder, and caught the Ninth Army cable with 100 lines in it. Cut it right in two. They've got fifteen of the lines spliced now and one of 'em is ours."

Lieutenant Fuller had found himself in the most strategic position of all the correspondents. His own radio recording had been reviewed by the censor in its entirety, passed, and he was ready to transmit. Most of the other radio correspondents were going to settle for eye-witness accounts and did not have the background noises which were on Fuller's documentary. Fuller had Lieutenant Muhlbauer crank up the JEEP transmitter at Schloss Rheydt quickly. "This is Muhlbauer, Jig Easy Easy Peter," he droned into the mike. "Calling BBC in London."

"This is BBC," came crackling back. Fuller took the mike. "I have everything," he said, "everything in preparation for the crossing, color, gunfire, the bombardments. Can I send now?"

There was a short silence. "Wait," said BBC. Fuller and Muhlbauer eased back, and Andy Holmes took his hand off the key. All of them thought it only a temporary hold, while BBC was lining up some circuits. Ten minutes went by.

"This is Fuller in Germany calling BBC," he said into the mike again. "I'm ready to send. Can you take me now?"

"Wait," said BBC.

This went on for five hours, and once during that time Fuller and Muhlbauer heard another call to BBC on their wavelength. It was a BBC correspondent, and a British voice. The answer was different for him. "We'll take you," said BBC.

Fuller tried again after this. "Wait," said BBC. Only then did it dawn on Fuller that there was no room for an American accent that day on BBC. Dimbleby was back with the air story. Chester Wilmot was filling in from the ground forces. That night, all the way from the Rhine back to the air bases, BBC depended on its own.

In the press camp that night, they called it "Operation Freezeout." SHAEF's ruling to move the release time forward became the subject of a protest meeting called by Wes Gallagher. Fuller wrote an account of his experience with BBC, which was sent to the Ninth Army staff for action to Twenty-first Army Group and SHAEF. The intention of the British to monopolize the story in every possible way was further underscored when Second British Army turned loose the place names and divisions in the Rhine crossing at the same time SHAEF's announcement was made. This promptness was unheard of on the part of British Second. Not only was it unprecedented, but their release contained the numbers of divisions which had not yet crossed the Rhine and were not yet in contact with the enemy.

"To the war correspondents," Lavelle wrote in a letter that night, "this all looked like a frantic bid for publicity."

There was no answer from SHAEF to the protest, and the Fuller report came back from Ninth Army with a notation by one of the lesser officers: "Let's not get in any official arguments at this time."

"How far does a guy lean over backward," said Fuller, "before he's lying down on the job?"

The Prime Minister, Winston Churchill, was at Monty's head-quarters as the Rhine reports came in the first day. Late in the afternoon when the press was still bitter about SHAEF's action, word was passed to me that General Eisenhower proposed to meet Churchill on the Rhine in the Ninth Army sector the next day. He had no objection to the press coming along. When I made the announcement, Hank Wales said he'd like to go and, such was the temper of the occasion, he grew violently angry when the word was passed to others. He wanted it all to himself. Although Hank was not happy when he embarked on the expedition the next day, it turned into a better story than he figured on. General Eisenhower was suddenly called away, and Churchill put the bite on Monty to cross over the Rhine in a landing craft. Monty interposed no objection, and Wales crossed with them—an eyewitness to another Churchillian achievement. There was something ironic about the *Chicago Tribune* having its correspondent fight to keep this resounding British exploit as an exclusive.

The prospect of moving again was before us, and once more the greatest worry was the lack of guarantees on land-line communications. Nearly all wanted to get going anyway. As divisions of the XVI Corps were getting into place along the northern side of the Ruhr, and the XIX Corps, according to plan, was slicing along behind XVI with the Second Armored Division in the lead, the distance back to Schloss Rheydt was again raising the familiar plaint, "miles behind the front." We had to get on the other side of the Rhine as soon as communications would stand up.

Service messages came to several correspondents to be on the look-out for special ways the 1945 Easter season services were being observed at the front. The hunt for such a seasonal feature was about to begin when a chaplain, Captain Joseph Shubow, of Boston, Massachusetts, a rabbi with the Signal Corps battalion which had laid the trans-Rhine cable, knocked on my office door. "I have heard many times about your place here," he said, "and I was sent back by the Jewish boys in the battalion to ask if there is any way we could have the use of your main dining hall for two hours one afternoon." He explained that there were eighty-seven Jewish soldiers in the unit and they would like to hold the Passover rites in the castle home of the great Jew-baiter of all time, Dr. Josef Goebbels. It was the intention of the men, he said, to furnish the appropriate food and all they would need was the use of the dining hall and some tableware. After a hurried consultation with the correspondents, who jumped at the opportunity, the chaplain was assured of the two hours between 3 and 5 P.M. on the day of the Passover. Profuse in his thanks, the rabbi got in his jeep and drove away to spread the word among his flock. In the meantime, we went to work on assembly of the combat record of the battalion, its decorations, and prepared the statistics in a handout available to all correspondents. Griff was worried about using Goebbels' dishes, because it meant such a quick wash job in the midst of preparation for the regular evening meal, but he saw no other way.

On the day of the Passover, the rabbi appeared just before lunch. He was loaded down with the paraphernalia of his clerical office, and with him were four soldiers carrying tinned salmon, sardines and other canned fish for the ceremonies. The Signal Corpsmen were left to themselves. At 3 P.M., the place quieted down and the doors of the great dining hall closed. The room where Dr. Goebbels had thrown some of his greatest parties in the heyday of the Nazi regime was now devoted to the rites of a people whose extermination he had vowed. Promptly at five the doors swung open and there was a big flurry of combat boots over the stone floors as the religious meeting broke up. The chaplain came to say thanks. "All the men will remember this day for the rest of their lives," the rabbi said, "and no matter where I celebrate the Feast of the Passover in the future, this scene will live with me forever."

The press was already busy writing stories of the occasion. The atmosphere was happy all around as the rabbi's jeep rattled over the drawbridge. That is, it was happy except in the case of Captain Griffith. The chaplain and his eighty-seven charges had barely cleared the area when Griff, in a thundering temper, charged into the office.

"Goddammit," he shouted. "You can't trust anybody anymore. But this was for the correspondents, so they'll pay for the story they got tonight."

"What are you babbling about?"

"Those guys," said Griff, leveling his accusing finger in the direction the Hebraic soldiery had taken. "You know what they did? Every damned one of 'em stole a Goebbels plate for a souvenir. We ain't got enough left to set the table." [4] So everyone ate from his mess kit on the night of the Feast of the Passover.

The mounting pressure to get the press camp across the Rhine, and the Passover observance provided the pun of the day. "Since we have had the Passover celebration around here," said Al Lee, "let's pass over that Rhine bridge with the press camp." Griff and I, after being told to aim in the general direction of the Wesel-Berlin cable and not get too far off it, set out on survey. The Ninth Army had its eye on a series of residences and apartment buildings in the outskirts of Haltern, but we held to the cable proximity and settled on a small village called Gartrop Buhl, built around Castle Gartrop. Once again we had a watery moat over which the Press Wireless antenna could be strung. Although the teletype machines could not actually hook onto the cable from the castle, they had a solid connection a mile off. Our location was in what appeared to be a safe V-position between expanding, holding, and exploiting actions, eight miles from the front along the Ruhr, fifteen miles from action on the North and forty miles back of the Second Armored which was mowing a narrow swath through Germany's crumbling resistance. With their usual singleness of purpose—the chase for the Berlin date line—the war correspondents began to grumble almost as we were ready to move in because our location was so far from the Second Armored. The fact that Field Marshal Model's fractured Army Group, a total of more than 300,000 troops still inclined to fight, had been crushed into the Ruhr only ten miles away, interested the correspondents not at all. Berlin, and Berlin only, had their eye. The pressures on me were from four directions: the correspondents tailing after Second Armored, the XVI and XIII Corps commanders whose fighting troops were being ignored, and the Ninth Army staff, especially signals, who wanted

[4] On the tenth anniversary of this event, Rabbi Shubow commemorated it with a special service in his Boston Synagogue. But on this occasion, I understand, no souvenirs were taken.

the press camp to stay in range. Castle Gartrop was a partial answer
to three of these, but left the war correspondents in a rampageous
frame of mind.

The castle was the hunting lodge type, with a huge wild boar
stuffed and hanging by the leg on a chain from the high ceiling in
the main entrance hall. The walls were covered with row after row,
from floor to ceiling, of tiny stag skulls with protruding horns, souvenirs of decades of family hunting. "Never have to worry about a
place to hang your hat in here," said Bob Vermillion. "Just throw it
in the air and it'll catch somewhere." The van Egerschots arrived
right behind us with the civilian crew to give the castle a liberal
application of the scrub brush and a good dousing with DDT. Word
went back for the movement of communications to start—Press Wireless first. As a partial, if not complete, service to correspondents
running up ahead, we made arrangements with XIX Corps for an
artillery liaison plane to carry in a pouch of press copy each day and
drop it in the castle yard. Before the end of March, the Ninth Army
press camp was over the Rhine, and in operation. None of the other
armies could say as much.

Ninth Army was continually being joined by new correspondents,
and it became necessary to get some more spaces for military staff
and civilian workers. With an interpreter I went into the village with
the intention of levying some housing. The first place, a sturdy stone
structure, was open and its owners, or previous residents, had fled.
So had the occupants of the next one. One more house would answer
our current needs, but this third one had a door which was locked
and evidently it was being lived in. After we pounded on the door for
some time, it suddenly swung open to reveal a twenty-year-old blonde,
about equal parts of fair beauty and haughty arrogance. The interpreter addressed her in German, explaining our need of one more roof.

"*Nein,*" said the attractive girl, holding her ground defiantly.

"What's this '*Nein*' business?"

"She says Americans were here before during the fighting," the
interpreter explained. "She says they gave her a paper—a clearance—
it protects her against having anybody take the house again."

"Let's see the paper."

The girl, round and firm, and eloquent of hip as she flounced up
the stairs, came back almost immediately with a folded sheet of
white paper which she gave me. Some of her arrogance faded and

an anxious look came over her face as she watched me open and read it. What was written on the paper might well give her some worries in the future.

Stifling an urge to laugh, I handed it back to her as solemnly as I could and told her that we would look elsewhere. A wave of relief swept over the girl's face. It was probable that she had had misgivings about the paper, and it was obvious she knew nothing of the English language. Now the paper seemed to have done everything the American who gave it to her had said it would.

"The paper," asked the interpreter as we went on down the street, "what did it say?"

"Nothing much, but she's earned the right to have us pass her by." The paper bore a message printed in ink, evidently by an American who had enjoyed himself and who had a sense of humor as well as generosity of spirit. "To whom it may concern," he had written. "You are now looking at the best piece in Germany."

. . . TAKE 16 ──────────────

Berlin Next?

When we moved into Castle Gartrop, it was still within German artillery range and two observation flights came over low to take a look. Almost immediately, eight rounds of artillery fire gouged up a pasture 400 yards off, but that was all. Our Press Wireless station, after being the only radio link with New York north of the Bulge during that dismal December offensive, was now the first press commercial link east of the Rhine.

North of the Ruhr, the American strength was stretching out. The Second Armored Division of the Ninth Army and the Third Armored Division of the First Army on the south were rolling irresistibly forward in one of the greatest encircling movements in American military history toward a juncture at the small German town of Lippstadt. If the Ninth Army correspondents were wailing about being jeeped over miles of crushed roadways, the crew with First Army was equally noisy. When Captain Harvey Hudson of Olney, Illinois, who had replaced Captain Nils Jacobson as PRO for the Seventh Armored Division, tried to get some correspondents up to his unit, which was involved in First's advance, it was unavailing because they felt they "could not get up to the division and back in a day."

To get our Press Wireless unit over the Rhine was no mean achievement, because of the requirement for three 80- to 100-foot poles on which to rig the antenna. When we called for Press Wireless to hurdle the Rhine, Prewi Manager John Betwinek wanted to pull the poles he had and bring them along. But he quailed at the thought

226

of coming up to one of the Rhine ponton bridges and facing the MP's who were trying to keep the way open. None of them would be enthused about having those long pine poles in the middle of bridge traffic. It was at times like this that we all used to think fondly of the fanfare with which a 250-watt radio station is set up in America. Invariably there is plenty of time, and a stylish launching clambake with a mayor to make a speech, a preacher to invoke a heavenly blessing and a sales manager ready to drum up business. Our communications never had any luxury of time, nor was there any excitement in the communities where we set up. Strictly speaking, no more than a hundred people ever had an interest in our Press Wireless station at any one time, but the interest of those hundred people was vital. Their attitude was never, "Will it work? Will it be open for business on time?" but always, "It better work and it better be on time."

Before the close-out in Schloss Rheydt, all correspondents were warned that Prewi would move copy up to midnight prior to the day of the jump. That day was not set until postholes were dug east of the Rhine, and poles long enough for the task were cut, set, tamped and rigged with a pulley rope to which the antenna could be quickly raised. For the twenty-four-hour moving period the correspondents would have only teletype, which was working a mile from Castle Gartrop and was fed by an hourly jeep courier. Promptly at midnight, Prewi said good-by to Baldwin, Long Island, New York, and its equipment was covered and strapped tight for transit. This interval provided us with our greatest worry, because any fast-breaking news event during the muted hours or any accident to the equipment on the road would invite a peculiar brand of crackling hell around all our heads. Just as the sun was coming up on another day the Prewi trucks lumbered into the courtyard of Castle Gartrop and moved into position. The motors had hardly died when the crew spilled out red-eyed from the all-night ride, unrolled the antenna wires, and strung them to the poles. Less than ten hours after Prewi had gone off the air at Rheydt, with the Rhine behind and the press camp eighty-five miles forward, Betwinek, mike in hand, was ready to try for re-establishing connection with New York.

There was considerable insecurity about Prewi taking to the air at Castle Gartrop, just as there had been about the Prewi set at First Army during the Battle of the Bulge, which had been ordered out of the headquarters town of Tongres to Huy, twenty miles away. German artillery was much closer to Castle Gartrop in the Ruhr pocket than it had been in Tongres, and there was no way of knowing how many by-passed enemy remnants there might be to the north. The possibility was always there that the minute Betwinek signaled for full power and the broadcast started, the sizzling atmosphere would make Castle Gartrop a good zeroing point for German marksmen.

The switch was thrown. "This is John Betwinek in Germany *across* the Rhine calling Prewi in New York," he said. This was a historic moment for his crew. First, Third and Seventh Army press radios were all still west of the Rhine. But that's all there was to our opening ceremony. No mayor, no local celebrity, and the only chaplain was one from the Thirtieth Infantry Division warning us not to store supplies in the chapel because it would violate the Geneva convention. ". . . Betwinek in Germany *across* the Rhine calling Prewi in New York," he repeated.

New York answered, loud and clear, and we were in business. "Your signal is very good," said New York, "better even than the last location."

Even with the tie to New York re-established, we had no phone to Ninth Army headquarters in München-Gladbach, nearly eighty miles away. This meant the censor had to make that round trip every day to get his guidance before he could pass copy from the war correspondents. Also, to post our information-room map, Captain Bill Moody or Sergeant Ed Nelson of Hendersonville, North Carolina, his assistant, had to make a similar run. With full knowledge of the thin edge of fortune which had permitted us to get an eighty-mile lead and reduce the jeep ride for war correspondents by 160 miles a day, the whole staff was in a mood to count itself lucky, but the chorus of discontent was in full voice. "You're still miles behind the front," moaned Larry Fairhall.

Betwinek came in with a service message he had been asked by Noel Monks to send via New York to London to Stanley Horniblow, editor of the *Daily Mail*. "SIX YEARS OF WAR," it said, "AND COMMUNICATIONS ARE NOW WORSE THAN THEY WERE IN THE FIRST YEAR!" The Prewi contingent was naturally incensed at this kind of reward for its all-night creep over blacked-out roads trying to protect delicate equipment, and its resumption of operation in less than ten hours.

The teletype circuit, which had appeared solid, was starting to act up because of difficulties in repairing the German cable. "You'll never be able to run this place without squawks," opined Wes Gallagher. "You might as well get used to it."

To make everyone feel at home, another protest meeting was called. The theme was a little more serious this time, and demands were made that we uproot again immediately to follow in the wake of the XIX Corps. "We're already eighty miles ahead of headquarters and having a tough time getting censor guidance and keeping the situation map up to date. We've already outrun the teletype and we're having a hard time keeping it working."

"Who the hell cares about the teletype?" asked Hank Wales. "Prewi's all we need." There was a loud rebuttal from the British correspondents.

"The day the majority of both nationalities agrees to settle for Press Wireless exclusively," I promised them, "is the day we'll pick up and go as far forward as we can get. We can arrange for a courier flight to take care of the censor and the map." The meeting broke up with loud grumbles, the Americans nipping at the British and vice versa, and all of them sharpening a claw now and then on the press camp.

As Ninth Army began to deposit itself in Haltern, the signals section announced it could now take the teletype as far forward as Gütersloh, seventy miles east. The correspondents, by this time, had elected to live with the XIX Corps, so Lieutenant Fuller took the JEEP transmitter and its operator, Lieutenant Muhlbauer, there while Captain Lyman Anderson went to take charge of the Ninth Army "forward press camp." Maj. Gen. Raymond S. McLain, the corps commander, was acting as a benevolent host. The XVI Corps, still fighting a tough battle for the Ruhr, was getting practically no attention, while the divisions scamp ring east, with their supply lines protected by the XVI Corps, were running into small opposition. When stories brought back by air were filed from Hamelin, with due reference to the legendary Pied Piper who lured the children after his tuneful playing, the parallel was not lost on the press camp sitting alongside the Ruhr's 300,000 armed and fighting Germans. But no amount of talk about the importance of snapping shut and destroying the Ruhr, taking with it Germany's war-making capacity, ever dented any war correspondent's consciousness. The Berlin date line was all that mattered. Captain Anderson reported that the nightly protest gatherings included the proposal that all the civilian staff be jettisoned to make the installation "more mobile" since they were prepared to "live off the land." This was characteristic. They asked for operation by magic wand, rather than good sense, but they were always in dead earnest.

The showdown came in a small village called Isselhorst, between Gütersloh and Bielefeld, and the correspondents used it only three nights, two of them for protest meetings that this site was far short of assistance to them.

As patiently as possible, it was again explained that the teletype was the sole retarding factor. Everything they demanded could be done if it could be left behind. David Walker, *London Daily Mirror,* one of the most level-headed of the correspondents, broke the ice and he was followed by Noel Monks. "I believe we have been asking for the impossible too long," said Walker. "Much as I would like to have the teletype service to London, I vote that we take Press Wireless as our sole communications outlet and get on the road." Al Lee, from the *Huddersfield Examiner,* and one whom the increased costs would really hurt, chimed in favorably, whereupon there was little the rest of the British could do but go along. At last it had become plain to them all. Late that night Griff and I put on paper our plan to have Ninth Army carry forward to us each day's censor guidance and map postings. We also made our arrangements to hit the road on the morning of April 12, uprooting the Press Wireless and taking it along, the teletype staying in Isselhorst.

Sometimes tragedy pays a dividend. None of us could know when our odd caravan began wheeling down the road that our small problems would be solved by a situation which shook the world. Already eighty miles ahead of Ninth Army headquarters, we were leaving it still further behind. We had no known destination, and we had no knowledge of conditions ahead. We were heading for the Elbe River, generally south of Magdeburg, where battle was about to be joined. Pulling off the road near Wolfenbüttel to spend the night, it was hardly comforting to think Press Wireless had been off the air nearly eighteen hours. Without unpacking, we spent a fitful night of worry and wonder. On the road early, I had to halt my lead jeep as the convoy approached Osterwieck. A column of tanks was stalled, the commander saying the town was full of looting Poles and Russians and he didn't want to get mixed up in it. As we edged cautiously forward along the row of tanks, one of the turrets suddenly crashed open and a sergeant with his headset still on shouted back down the column:

"The Old Man's dead!"

"Eisenhower?" He was the "Old Man" to the ETO military forces.

"Naw, not him," said the sergeant. "Roosevelt. I heard it on my radio. Died just like that, they said." He snapped his fingers.

Everything now became secondary along the fighting sectors as word was passed in that strange way that outstrips the best of contrived communications. F. D. R. was no more. After the early shock of realization that it was really true, in the way of all soldiers who translate everything in terms of what it means to them personally, we took stock of its effect on the press-camp situation. In the midst of our wildest and longest move of the whole war, with the communications system out, and no known location up ahead unless Captain Anderson was nailing something down, the death of the President provided the respite needed. It meant at least a twenty-four-hour reprieve, because nothing filed from the European armies that day or the next was likely to get any attention. All the space would be allocated to our late commander-in-chief. On down the road we sped.

Still well ahead of us, the Second Armored was putting out feelers for establishment of a bridgehead over the Elbe, the last water barrier before Berlin. Frank Coniff was talking to Hank Griffin, the AP photographer, both of them watching the Germans' systematic pasting of the ponton bridge. "It has to be a helluva picture to get published now," said Coniff, "but I've got an idea. Why don't you get a big sign painted—*Franklin D. Roosevelt Memorial Bridge?* As soon as they get this ponton in solid, you can set the sign up, shoot the picture, and it'll go anywhere." Griffin sprang into action and found a suitable board on which the legend was painted. With it, he cowered all day near the site, but the bridge never stayed in long enough for him to get his picture. Eventually it went out permanently, and the Second Armored bridgehead consisting of a reinforced battalion was wiped out, too. Hitler sent three divisions out of the Berlin sector to turn back the Second Armored's thrust over the Elbe, the first time in more than thirty months of fighting that the "Hell on Wheels" outfit had to go in reverse.

Farther south, the Eighty-third Infantry Division's bridgehead,[1] with the 329th Infantry Regiment of Colonel E. B. Crabill, and the I&R platoon of Lieutenant Samuel W. Magill, was holding and being deepened toward the town of Zerbst. When Crabill was asked by the press, who thought he represented their best chance to get rolling for Berlin, how much opposition there was ahead of him, he grinned amiably. "I don't know much about what's in front of us, but I hear we by-passed the remnants of five divisions—maybe as many as 23,000 troops—back there when we came along the Harz mountains."

Our convoy was intercepted at a crossroads near Oschersleben by Captain Anderson at 11 A.M. Much to our relief, he had staked out the estate of Dr. Oscar Rabbethge at Klein Wanzleben for our new home and it was even now being vacated by the headquarters of Second Armored. It was the pivot of the large-scale sugar-beet interests of the Rabbethge family, who had had the use of some 4,000 slave laborers, and at one time, it was claimed, they had provided nearly thirty-seven per cent of the world's beet seed. Both of the Rabbethge brothers had lived, worked and studied in Colorado and Western Nebraska, where they had traded knowledge of processing and growing the beets with the large sugar companies before the war. They lived imposingly and well, we were glad to note, since our population in the press camp, already large, was growing fast as we moved closer to Berlin.

Press Wireless' crew went into action immediately, barely stalling their vehicles in the courtyard, then going back down the road about ten miles where they had spotted the last growth of tall trees. By nightfall they were back with three seventy-footers, the best they could find, and the holes were dug and ready. There was a high hill back of the estate, and they took advantage of this elevation. We had come 180 miles over a winding route, the guns of the Second Armored were rumbling six miles north of us, and the Elbe was only ten miles east. The period of grace was running out, and correspondents were moving in with Roosevelt reaction stories picked up from the soldiers along the front. They wanted to file as quickly as Prewi could take them.

Griff had the courtyard in an uproar, with the vehicles being un-

---

[1] The Eighty-third Infantry Division called its span "The Truman Bridge," and it stayed in until the territory was given up to the Russians after the war in compliance with the Yalta agreement.

loaded and the housing being parceled out. It was warm now, the sun coming down brightly on central Germany at this time of year, and the soldiers were put into pyramidal tents on the spacious lawn. The Rabbethge house was a mine of supplies, including dishes, linen, pots, pans, silver, a huge working kitchen, a laundry room and a furnace with hot-water capacity sufficient for the needs of the whole camp. The travels of the press camp had seasoned everyone, and we were operational in short order. Prewi dragged its poles into position and was ready to go on the air.

At 5:30 P.M., April 13, bacon was sizzling in the kitchen from the cases of ten-in-one rations we had brought along and a phone was working over a line left us by Second Armored. We were more than 100 miles ahead of Ninth Army headquarters. Betwinek announced he was ready to try New York. It was Castle Gartrop over again. We were within easy artillery range from two directions, and we were in what had been a very hard-hitting headquarters site until that morning. Would Prewi's signal provide an aiming point? Betwinek shrugged, opened the mike and called New York. The answer came back clear, and reported the signal good again. We had another first —first on the banks of the Elbe. While we were awaiting a chance to remind the correspondents how easy it had been to get the press camp forward once they had dropped the land lines and teletype, Vic Jones, *Boston Globe,* came in. "Hey," he said seriously, "don't you think you're *too* close up? The G-2 of Second Armored just told us that the PW interrogations report the Germans are trying to mount an airborne drop this side of the Elbe tonight." Three days ago, the verdict was too far back; now, too close up.

Griff made a quick inventory of our weapons, just in case. Our possessions ran more to typewriters than firearms, but we had one fifty-caliber machine gun, plus the normal issue of carbines as well as souvenir German Luger and P-38 pistols. Lieutenant Williams placed the machine gun on the slope where it had a maximum field of fire and the soldiers were posted on a perimeter well out from the camp proper. The nine Dutch Army guards were assigned to their posts and given instructions to be unusually alert that night. Griff made an early round of the outposts and went to bed in the small quarters we shared with Captain Moody. By the time I returned from the Dutch sentry posts, it was pitch dark. With the whole area blacked out, I had to feel my way along the walls of the building until my door was found. The dark seemed more menacing with every step. Feeling for the door, I finally found the knob, and opened it softly, not wanting to awaken the others. There was a slight rustle from one of the beds.

"Say something in English damned quick," said Griff. A blinding flashlight beam hit me in the eyes.

"Hold it!" I yelled.

"A couple of seconds more," said Griff tensely, indicating Moody who was also holding a gun in his hand, "and we'd have let you have it. When you come this way again, don't come sneaky like. Come makin' a big noise."

He made a check of the outposts toward morning, and I went around them again as the sun was coming up. To the relief of all, no airborne attack came.

General Eisenhower had decided, although it was not known to anyone but his commanders and his closest staff, that the Elbe-Mulde river line was a natural obstacle at which it would be ideal for the Allied forces to meet the Russians. His decision had been made long before, when it appeared quite unlikely that the Americans and the British could get to this water barrier ahead of the Russians. Considering how truculent the Russians became about such things, it must actually have been a meaningless line to them because they accepted it even though it was nearly seventy-five miles deep into their own Yalta-agreed occupation zone for the postwar period. Military estimates were placing at around 100,000 the number of casualties it would cost to take Berlin. The British press had hints that Churchill wanted an all-out drive on the German capital from the west, and that he was irked with Ninth Army's withdrawal from Montgomery's Twenty-first Army Group. Few knew yet the Elbe-Mulde was the hold line.

There was a great clamor for a briefing from General Simpson, who was coming up to be an overnight guest of General McLain at XIX Corps in Wanzleben, about six miles from the press camp. I met him there, and led him by jeep to the Rabbethge estate. When his aide, Major John Harden, joined me in the jeep and Generals Simpson and McLain fell in behind us, Harden seemed inordinately glum when I asked him how long it would be before we shoved on from the Elbe. "Nothing like that today," he said, gazing across the fields.

"What then?"

"I hope you're comfortable where you are," he said. "You'll probably be there a long time."

Only the night before, Redding had called from Twelfth Army Group to say he was sending some extra communication equipment to the Ninth Army press camp. This was to cross the Elbe with us and eventually become the permanent Berlin press transmission terminal. Lt. Col. George Stevens had pulled in his sound-on-film camera crew under command of Major Joe Biroc, and they were with us, ready. The correspondents had been urgently requesting General Simpson, so when word had come that he would be there, it seemed a good time for me to post them on all that was known about facilities. The press room was jammed to the rear door, our press corps numbering seventy-six at the time. After outlining the meaning of the extra communications, I told them we would be able to go into operation on the other side of the Elbe before Prewi was pulled up here, which meant there would be no break in service.

"You say Redding is sending us the radio facilities?" asked cynical Wes Gallagher, sitting in the front row.

"He's the one who called me."

"Well, if he gives us anything extra, it'll be the first time," rasped Gallagher. "I'll go further and say if he does it, I'll kiss your arse right in the middle of the Wilhelmstrasse."

Rhona Churchill, the lone woman correspondent in the room, cleared her throat right behind him. Gallagher reddened slightly, but not much. The room roared at his discomfiture. But the mood that night before General Simpson's arrival was one of confidence that the drive for Berlin would be the next action, and at an early date, even though the Russians were massing a million men not far east of the German capital. And now General Simpson's car, carrying him to deliver the word, was coming up the tree-lined drive.

General Simpson went straight to the press room, and his aide promptly pinned up the briefing charts. The first map showed the Ninth Army position as of the date, and nobody thought this unusual, although all were anxious to see what was underneath.

"Gentlemen," he said, "before I talk about any plans for the future, I think we should take a little time to recapitulate and show what we have really done since we crossed the Rhine." The correspondents settled back, as he recounted the staggering figures of men, machines, mileage, bridging, ration tonnage, and the vast miscellany of war which it had taken to shove the Ninth from the Rhine to the Elbe. He consulted his notes frequently and talked for nearly an hour. He then turned to the situation as of that day, indicating somewhat fondly the 329th Infantry's bridgehead anchored on Zerbst, as if it were a fading dream, this only portion of the Ninth Army over the river. He made no move to change the map, and licked his lips as he looked out over the expectant faces. "I have just had a telephone call from General Bradley, my boss, and General Eisenhower," he said, "and they have given me the new mission for the Ninth Army. I am ordered to hold on the line of the Elbe River and wait for the Russians."

There was an audible groan all over the room, and the correspondents hardly heard the General thank them for having been with the Ninth Army through its final battles. He had talked to them in an operational press conference for the last time. To the press corps, this was a staggering disappointment. General Simpson went to his car, waved good-by, and headed off toward his new offices in Brunswick. "Imagine," cried Noel Monks, "Roosevelt not two weeks in his grave and Stalin double-crossing his memory already."

"God damn politics," said the normally calm Robert Massell, of the Blue Network.

Almost to a man, the British war correspondents filed messages to their editors asking for a week's leave at home. The censors passed the requests, but no explanations. This threw London's Fleet Street into a dither, and the messages, firm and clear, came back immediately. "Extremely morbid thought," said one. Others said succinctly, "Are you crazy, old boy?" and, "Under no circumstances desert post now." This turned the correspondents off the military and onto their own editors. They entered rebuttal requests for leave in London, or Paris, but these only netted more refusals.

On April 18 another pall fell across the press camps, and men sorted over their memories of the scruffy little correspondent who had been well known to them all. Around on the other side of the world, Corporal Landon Seidler on Ie Jima, a small way station in the Pacific, fashioned a wooden casket and on top of it nailed the famous dog tags of one he and all other GI's had considered a friend. On a wooden plaque over the grave, Seidler carved the words: "At this spot, the 77th Infantry Division lost a buddy, Ernie Pyle, 18 April 1945." Ernie's long search for the one with his "name on it" came to an end in his forty-fifth year, straight and final from a Japanese machine gun. At least, I had never had to use the obituary he wrote for me.

News of the halt to further advance seeped down to the front, where correspondents had gone to talk to division commanders. Some of the commanders estimated the number of casualties it might have cost to take Berlin in the thousands, but correspondents felt denied even so. The soldiers, who had the best chance of being casualties, began a jubilant relaxation when the persistence of the rumor made them believe this one to be true. Berlin was just another pile of rubble to them. Even Prewi's crew sighed with relief. The stall at the Elbe meant no more pole hunts, crash setups, holes to dig, and wild night rides with cat's-eye headlights over miserable roads.

The last focus of story attention was on the meeting with the Russians. The whole front was alive with radio pleas beamed eastward asking advancing Russian units to locate themselves. With Lt. Col. Kalisch, up from Twelfth Army Group, I thought Lieutenant Sam Magill's I&R platoon was in an excellent position to have this stroke of luck. By now, Magill's platoon had amassed more than 500 patrols inside enemy lines, twelve of his men had been awarded Purple Hearts, and only Christopher Vane, of Baltimore, Maryland, who had been killed while on leave, had been lost. More than 24,000 Germans had surrendered to these twenty-four men. We talked to Colonel Crabill about keeping the platoon out deep in the point of the bridgehead, hoping that it would be first to grab the Soviet hand. Kalisch even prevailed upon Lt. Col. George Stevens, who had allowed Biroc to return to First Army, to bring the sound-on-film camera crew back. Kalisch had such a reputation for luck, Stevens placed his money on Bert again. "What makes you think Ninth Army will meet them?" asked Biroc, who was dead tired when he arrived. "I have been twelve places and 500 miles along this front in the last week, and everybody thinks he's going to be the one. I think the Russians have all gone back home myself."

On the twenty-fourth of April, some Russian division commanders began to warn their troops that they were about to meet the Americans somewhere along the Elbe and a Soviet detachment that day ceased fire when an American flag was waved. After the Russians showed themselves and rushed forward, it turned out to be a diehard German SS unit waving the flag and the Russians were mowed down. That

same day, Second Lieutenant William D. Robertson, of West Los
Angeles, California, with a patrol consisting of Corporal James J.
McDonnel, of Peabody, Massachusetts; PFC Frank P. Huff, of Washington, Virginia; and PFC Paul Staub, of New York City, set out
for Torgau to check the area for refugees and PW's reported to be
in the vicinity. Robertson picked up an American Navy lieutenant who
spoke Russian and about thirty other allied PW's as he went along.
On April 25, the patrol had worked its way to a riverside castle, and
the wreckage of a blown bridge was showing directly ahead. Red
Army Private Itsylvacho noticed some soldiers on the opposite bank
and called them to the attention of his commander. Robertson had
been told by the Germans that the Russians were on the other side.
First he waved a white flag, but that was surrender stuff, and he
didn't think it appropriate. Moreover, the flag did stop small-arms and
artillery fire. Robertson and his men broke into a shop, and found
some water colors. On his white flag, he painted a blue field in the
upper left-hand corner and a series of red stripes. It was a sorry-
looking replica of the Betsy Ross design, but Robertson felt that
distance would be in its favor. No sooner was the banner finished than
it was waved energetically and Robertson began advancing gingerly
over the bridge girders. Private Itsylvacho started from the other side.
They met in the middle of the swirling water and, each hanging on
to a girder, reached out to shake hands. Even though they couldn't
converse they understood greetings which signified linkage of Marshal
Ivan Konev's Army Group and General Bradley's Twelfth.[2]

[2] At first the plan was to have Maj. Gen. Emil Reinhardt, of Atlanta,
Georgia, the Sixty-ninth's Commander, meet Marshal Konev in a formal ceremony, but Robertson put a great deal more punch into the occasion with his
youthful exuberance. Robertson told me he intended to go back to California
and become a doctor. He received his medical degree from the University of
California in Berkeley in 1951, interned at Army's Letterman General hospital,
did another year in the Army, studied neuro-surgery while taking a residency at
a London hospital. He is currently practicing medicine in Hawthorne, California, where he is married to the former Nancy Quamstrom, a one-time U.C.L.A.
"Sweetheart." Lee Carson, on April 27, 1945, wrote a story which pointed out
that although Robertson was publicized throughout the world as the man who
made the preliminary juncture, Lieutenant Albert Kotzebue, of Houston,
Texas, was actually the first American soldier to greet a Russian unit. Major
Frederick Craig, of Friendship, Tennessee, confirmed to her that Kotzebue at
the head of a jeep patrol of twenty-eight men contacted the 175th Russian
infantry regiment and horse-mounted Cossacks commanded by Colonel Gar-
dieve, a mile and a half west of the Elbe at Zannewitz at 1:30 P.M. on April 25.
Robertson's patrol made its contact at 4 P.M. that day.

Robertson was from the Sixty-ninth Infantry Division, and correspondents swarmed in to get the details of this episode. Lee Carson, of International News Service, interviewed everybody. "I was so overjoyed to meet the American," Private Itsylvacho told her, "and so glad, and so astounded that I didn't know what to·do—whether to just take a ride with him in a jeep, drink vodka, or fight Germans."

The Russian major told her that the Americans had given them a good welcome, a warm reception. "We've always said that when the Russian Army meets the American Army, it will be a great holiday for the whole world—except the Germans."

Among those on hand was a representative of SHAEF's public-relations division, Lieutenant Leo Perlman, a fledgling lawyer from Brooklyn, who hastened back to Paris where he was normally based and immediately became the lion of the hour among his French friends. One fine French family convened a party of twenty and gave a dinner for him. Everyone was plying him with questions as they were eating, and the host wanted to know which American division had made the contact. Leo's French, with the Brooklyn accent, was careless. It had not occurred to him that "sixty-nine" is a familiar *maison de tolérance* term in France. To be proper he would have given the numerical designation of *"Soixante-neuvième,"* or Sixty-ninth, but he slipped. *"Soixante-neuf,"* he said, giving the equivalent of the figure 69. There was a clatter of silver around the table, and the host, first taken aback, then leaned forward in animated admiration. *"Quelle organisation!"* he said. "You mean ze Américain armee have ze division complete of men wiz zis preferance?"

After the historic meeting of forces at the Elbe, there were only the ragged edges of war-correspondent nose-thumbing at the military. Taking a driver from the Twenty-sixth Infantry Division, Virginia Irwin, *St. Louis Post Dispatch,* and Andrew Tully, *Boston Traveller,* made a run for Berlin. They were suspended on their return. Seymour Freidin, *New York Herald Tribune,* and Freddie Ramage, the Keystone International photographer, went across the Elbe for some entertainment by the Russian commander. In the midst of it, the commander suddenly clapped his hands and produced a trembling, voluptuous German girl in her late teens as a present to Ramage. Freddie thanked his host, and said he was not interested. The girl ran to Ramage, went down on her knees, and kissed his hand before fleeing the room. Freidin climaxed this soiree by going into Berlin. While he was returning to the inevitable suspension which awaited all correspondents who violated the "hold line" to that extreme, he came through the German prison camp town of Luckenwalde about halfway between Berlin and the bridgehead. This was a press bonanza—this Luckenwalde!

By accident, Freidin encountered Lieutenant Amon Carter, Jr., son of the venerable Texas publisher of the *Fort Worth Star-Telegram,* a PW since the day Rommel's Afrika Korps overran his battalion of the U. S. First Armored Division at Faid Pass in February, 1943. At about the same time, UP correspondent Bob Vermillion made his own kind of jeep rescue of Ed Beattie, a brother UP-hand who had been captured Sept. 12, 1944. Vermillion and Beattie returned from Luckenwalde by way of Lieutenant Samuel Magill's outposted platoon at Zerbst. Freidin stayed the night with Lieutenant Carter, and brought out with him a cable message which Amon, Jr., wanted sent to his father at the *Fort Worth Star-Telegram.* By the coincidence of an earlier invitation from General Eisenhower, through Secretary of War Stimson, Carter, Sr., was at that very moment visiting in the Ninth Army area with sixteen other leading newspaper executives who had been asked to come to Europe especially to view the "horror camps." One point in this tour included a visit to the Eighty-third Infantry Division at Calbe for a luncheon and a look at the 329th bridgehead.

Lieutenant Carter, knowing nothing of this, of course, and being the designated Red Cross parcel-handler of the PW camp, chose to wait with the other prisoners and not come in with Freidin, but he did want his father to know he was safe. The camp was expecting liberation momentarily. Throughout the war, war correspondents had been receiving queries about various soldiers for whom they were to be on the lookout, and one of these was Lieutenant Carter. So, when Frank Coniff heard of Carter's whereabouts, he charged out of the bridgehead and found his quarry in downtown Luckenwalde foraging for food. Where Freidin had failed, Coniff talked Carter into accompanying him to the Elbe where he would be better able to make a plea for a convoy to pick up the other allied PW's.

Lieutenant Carter agreed to go along, and Coniff took him in. They stopped at the headquarters of Lt. Col. Granville A. Sharpe of Burlington, North Carolina, for lunch, then roared on into Calbe, arriving just as the Eighty-third Infantry Division luncheon for the publishers was breaking up. Lieutenant Carter stepped out of the jeep and confronted his father, saying quietly, "Well, here I am, Dad." The elder

Carter, choked and silent, embraced his son and held him tightly, patting the back of his head. Lieutenant Carter made an immediate and eloquent plea for the convoy to get his comrades, and was assured that a convoy of a hundred trucks was already being formed up. It would be led by his recent host, twenty-four-year-old Lt. Col. Sharpe. The festiveness of the finale along the front caught up Hank Wales, when he went to get some background on Sharpe. The youthful colonel explained he had come straight out of college ROTC into the Army. Hank, burying the twinkle of his eye as he thought of the long, bloody trek of the Eighty-third from Normandy to the Elbe, looked Sharpe up and down with pseudo-scornfulness. "Humph," he said, "never worked a day in your life, eh?"

... TAKE 17 ————————————————

The Last Battle of the Press

Even before the Battle of the Bulge, Lt. Col. Jack Redding had come up from Verdun to Maastricht to talk about plans for the entry into Berlin. It was then assumed that the Russians would get there first and that the Allied press party would have to arrive airborne with me as a likely custodian. This was the first time I heard of the "Berlin list" of war correspondents, which was being selected in a series of press-military table poundings which passed for conferences in Paris. The "Berlin list" finally contained some fifty-nine names and its first two priority groups—a total of twenty-three names—included all the radio networks and wire services, as well as pool correspondents for still photographs and motion pictures. At most of these conferences the military were represented by Lt. Col. Thor Smith as well as Redding, and these two had more than 300 different press organizations to deal with. Smith held the line for SHAEF Public Relations Division, while Redding was Twelfth Army Group's iron man. By all manner of testing the "Berlin list" of fifty-nine assured complete world coverage of the capitulation of the German capital, should it ever come off. The "Berlin list" was never used for the purpose intended, but the day came when it was drawn on in haste. The war's greatest press spectacle, and debacle, was hastening toward us.

Late on May 4 two rain-drenched Germans, Admiral Hans Georg von Friedeburg, the German naval commander, and Colonel Fritz Poleck of the Ober Kommando Wehrmacht, arrived outside Field Marshal Montgomery's command trailer on Luneberg Heath. Monty had waited a long time for this, so he did not hurry. With a fine sense of theater, he finally presented himself in the doorway and said curtly, "What do you want?" His tone was one he saved for a batman late with his tea.

What the Germans told him prompted a phone call to General Eisenhower. It was exactly 7 P.M. on May 4. The Germans, Monty, said, had been authorized by Grand Admiral Karl Doenitz, now heading the last vestiges of government, to surrender. Hitler had been dead five days.

As soon as Allied headquarters in Reims had the word, Captain Harry Butcher, General Eisenhower's aide, notified Brig. Gen. Frank "Honk" Allen, chief of SHAEF's public-relations division back in Paris. It was not yet known, of course, if coverage of the surrender would be possible, but somebody remembered the "Berlin list," just in case. While the list was being checked, General Allen immediately sent two of his lieutenant colonels to Reims, one British and one American and both experienced journalists—S. R. Pawley, who had been news editor of the *London Daily Telegraph,* and Burrows Matthews, former editor of the *Buffalo Courier-Express*. Their destination was the École Professionelle, later famous as "the little red schoolhouse," and they reported to Captain Butcher early on May 5. He told them the Germans were en route from Luneberg Heath and traveling by air. Lt. Gen. Walter Bedell Smith, SHAEF's chief of staff, had first decided not to permit correspondents to cover the surrender, if indeed it became a surrender at this point. Pawley and Matthews were to acquaint themselves with all the details and be prepared to brief the correspondents later.

Word came that the Germans had been forced down in Brussels by the weather and were coming the rest of the way by car. The wait was stretched out, and tension mounted. General Smith first selected the war room as the surrender site, but his negative attitude toward press attendance held firm. The orderly but electric calm was broken when the remarkable nose for news of *Life*'s Charles Wertenbaker put him first on the doorstep of the Reims schoolhouse and then, with that special ease of his, in General Eisenhower's outer office with the aides. Some stylish finesse was required to get Wertenbaker out of that office, but he was finally lured into the street and left there. Since he had always been most welcome on the premises before, no concrete wall had to fall on him to tell him something big was about to break.

He waited around and was rewarded for his patience. His hunch proved out, even though it availed him little.

About 5 P.M. on the fifth, von Friedeburg and Poleck, their uniforms in sharp contrast to those in Reims, drove up and stepped out of their car, hastily entering "the little red schoolhouse" where they were taken in tow by Maj. Gen. Kenneth W. D. Strong, the intelligence chief at SHAEF. Wertenbaker snapped his fingers in exultation, but he was not allowed to re-enter the building. He kept up his watchful vigil for a while, then suddenly decided he was working the wrong angle. He climbed in his vehicle and lammed for Paris with the footfeed on the floor. He was going to beat on General Allen's door.

After a brief exchange with the Germans, General Smith told them flatly that the terms still were "unconditional surrender." He heard them say that Grand Admiral Doenitz was greatly concerned about surrendering his troops to the Russians, but this drew no satisfaction, because General Smith considered it still open season on Germans, no matter where the armies of the Big Three found them. Von Friedeburg then said he did not have the authority to capitulate without further consultation with Doenitz and it was obvious that talks could get no further that day.

At this juncture Captain Butcher picked up the telephone, having made a fateful decision on his own. He called General Allen and instructed him to bring along a minimum press party. Almost immediately, the Signal Corps photographers [1] and sound men and designated pool representatives in Paris, who had been alerted, were told to hit the road. Captain Butcher then confronted the Chief of Staff, whose temper had been short before, and informed him that he had gone ahead to arrange for press coverage and had set aside the office directly below that of General Smith as a space for about a score of real, live reporters. Butcher was relieved to find the Chief of Staff congenially acquiescing. He not only agreed that it was all right for

---

[1] The photographic party included, in all, Col. Kirke B. Lawton, Lt. Leo Moore, Lt. H. W. Schmidt, Tech. Sgt. Jack M. Howell, Lt. Robert McWade, Lt. Robert C. Scrivner, Lt. Andrew G. Burt, Jr., Tech. Sgt. Harold Lee, Sgt. A. B. Masserlin, Corporals Charles Corn, Ardeen Miller, Roger Davis, and Privates First Class Albert N. Stephens and Bruce Chin. Later arrivals were Ralph Morse, of *Life*, for the U. S. still pool; Fred S. Skinner for the British still pool; Yves Naintre of the U. S. newsreel pool; and Ronie Reed for the British newsreel pool. The radio technicians were Lt. Col. Walter Brown and Capt. Ted Bergmann.

the correspondents to be in Reims, but said he would permit them to be in the room for the signing. The photographers had permission to snap the Germans entering and leaving the room, he added. This change of attitude was partly due to Smith's decision to have the first meeting with the Germans in his office, holding the discussions there. After the negotiations, the whole party could then go to the war room for the final act of signing. This made it easy for all equipment to be put in place and the room lighted for the photographers. General Eisenhower, on a swing down the corridor, saw the lights being tested in the war room and observed that the schoolhouse was taking on the atmosphere of a Hollywood studio. By the time this casual remark got around to his Chief of Staff on the morning of May 6, it had taken on the proportions of a criticism, and General Smith descended on Matthews with the speed of Halley's comet, and with about as much fire in his tail. He ordered Matthews to cut down to one silent cameraman and one photographer, and to take the microphone out of the room. After starting to comply, Matthews took this new development to Butcher, the great intercessionist, who waited until lunch to bring it to General Eisenhower's attention. The Supreme Commander said he had turned it all over to his Chief of Staff, and it was his picnic. Butcher edged back to General Smith and talked quietly and at length about how the removal of the microphone was in effect robbing history of an important event in world affairs. General Smith was not happy to reverse himself, but he finally permitted the restoration of one mike, which had to do double duty for radio and the sound-on-film camera.

Lt. Col. Thor Smith back in Paris had been exerting every kind of argument for two days and nights that the press coverage should center at Reims, rather than the Scribe. The relay of information from Matthews and Pawley, he felt, would not insure against the story breaking suddenly and badly, so he elatedly welcomed Butcher's decision to accept a "small" press party. The "Berlin list" was alerted, even though some names were now gone, and told to be at the Scribe prepared to move to an unannounced destination on short notice. Meantime, Charlie Wertenbaker was removing any doubt about the destination, if they went anywhere, because he had been busily telling his cronies about the eyeful he had had in Reims. The lobby was abuzz.

Barely had a C-47 transport been called for when the phone jangled and General Allen was told that the Germans would probably sign between 4 and 7 P.M. Hastily the SHAEF public-relations staff [2] assembled at the Scribe. The lobby of the Scribe was like a steam room in which all the pipes had been broken, and pressures were still mounting. The alert had leaked out, of course. Exchange Telegraph, the British news agency, was on the "Berlin list," but decided against the trip since this might be another alarm. Communications terminals from which press traffic could originate were scarce, and Reims was not one of them. Besides Exchange Telegraph knew how the news of events, no matter where they happened, had a way of breaking in Paris. Price Day, *Baltimore Sun,* was quick to grab at the opportunity, and talked Exchange Telegraph into letting him go as the ET representative. Australian Consolidated Press was not on the "Berlin list," so the Aussie correspondents drew lots and by this method got Osmar E. White for the pool to protect the "down under" continent. With the roars of a disappointed, lynch-spirited mob behind them, the selected war correspondents [3] and their SHAEF chaperons took off.

When the plane was in the air, and only then, General Allen gave the party a hint of what might be in store, and he voiced a pledge to which all of them would subscribe. "This group represents the press of the world," he said, "and the story is off-the-record until the heads of the governments have announced it. I, therefore, pledge each of you on your honor not to communicate the results of the conference, or the fact of its existence, until it is released on the order of Public Relations Division, SHAEF." Many of the correspondents on the plane took notes on this pledge, especially Edward Kennedy, AP, and Boyd Lewis, of the rival UP. No one objected. A C-47 is a noisy menace to talk, so there wasn't much, each man keeping his

[2] The complete SHAEF public-relations division list in Reims for the surrender, including those from Paris and those already at the SHAEF forward headquarters at Reims: Brig. Gen. Frank Allen, Col. George Warden, Group Captain G. W. Houghton, Lt. Col. Richard Merrick, Lt. Col. Thor Smith, Lt. Col. Reed Jordan, Capt. Harry Butcher, Capt. Don Davis, Lt. Col. S. R. Pawley and Lt. Col. Burrows Matthews.

[3] The correspondents selected for Reims included Edward Kennedy, AP; Boyd Lewis, UP; James L. Kilgallen, INS; H. C. Montague Taylor, Reuter's; Price Day, Exchange-Telegraph; Margaret Ecker, Canadian Press; Osmar E. White, Australian Press; Jean E. LaGrange, Agence Presse; Michael Litvin-Sedoy, Tass; Thomas Cadette, BBC; W. W. Chaplin, NBC; Charles Collingwood, CBS; Herbert M. Clark, Blue Network; Paul Manning, MBS; Gerald V. Clark, Canadian Broadcasting Corporation; Staff Sergeant Charles Kiley, Stars and Stripes; and Sgt. Ross D. Parry, Maple Leaf (Canada).

own counsel and plotting his moves to outwit the competition. The plane landed at Reims about 5 P.M. that Sunday afternoon, May 6.

Von Friedeburg had been in touch with Grand Admiral Doenitz, who was holding out with the remnant of his forces at Flensburg near the Danish border, and it was learned that a duly authorized German representative was being flown to Reims in the person of Colonel General Gustav Jodl, new chief of the German Army, accompanied by his aide, Major Wilhelm Oxenius. They had landed just ahead of the correspondents, who did not know if they would be permitted to see what was going on. They knew that Pawley and Matthews were there and that they might get only a briefing. The press was hustled into a small conference room where Pawley and Matthews brought them up to the present.

France has long revered the memory of the "taxicab army" of nearly 5,000 troops which rolled from Paris to the Marne to block a German drive in World War I, but it has erected no monuments to the second edition which was now converging on Reims. In all manner of wheezing vehicles, propelled by charcoal burners and gasoline, the correspondents who had been left behind in Paris began to straggle in. About twenty of them were already at the schoolhouse door demanding entry. Some came to the windows and Lewis, among others, handed hamburgers out to those who were hungry. General Allen's staff urged him to deny these "outsiders" any consideration. The "Berlin list" had been agreed to by the press, and any departure from it would put the Army in a controversial position. They said the world press was protected, that there was not room enough for all, and that any change in plan would merely create a whole new family of problems. The door held and the military police helped hold off the street claque.

In his frequent talks with the press inside the schoolhouse to keep them posted, and while they were taking notes, General Allen again emphasized that there could be no release of their eyewitness accounts until the heads of the Big Three nations had themselves announced the cessation of hostilities. It was known by then that General Eisenhower was trying to get approval for a release as soon as possible after the papers were signed.[4] Ironically, this worried some of the

---

[4] Matthews, Pawley, Butcher and Thor Smith were all strongly urging Generals Smith, Strong and Allen to advise the JCS that a long embargo on the surrender would not work.

press. Those who had a front seat might be beaten with the story
if it were pushed out promptly through Paris. Some now demanded
of General Allen that an embargo be placed on the story until *they*
could get back to Paris, whereupon the release could be made at a
"mutually agreeable" time—i.e., any time which would protect the
"Berlin list" by-liners and the Reims date line.The Reims schoolroom
debating society suddenly had more time to take counsel of their
anxieties when it was discovered that even Jodl lacked authority to
accept all of the Eisenhower surrender terms. This meant more messages to Flensburg and further instructions from Doenitz. Finally,
before the military chiefs and the press party, at 2 A.M. on May 7, Jodl
reached for the pen, then paused. "With this signature," he said
quietly, "the German people and armed forces are for better or for
worse delivered into the victors' hands. In this war, which has lasted
more than five years, both have achieved and suffered more than
perhaps any other people in the world."

The victors eyed him stonily, and heard his pen whisper across
the paper. The Germany of Adolf Hitler was at the mercy of its
conquerors. After him, General Smith added his signature, then
Maj. Gen. Ivan Suslaparov (U.S.S.R.) and General François Sevez
(France) affixed theirs. Jodl and von Friedeburg were then taken to
General Eisenhower, his first time to see them.[5] He asked if they
fully understood the terms to which they had just agreed, and whether
they would be carried out by Germany. They nodded.

The war in Europe, technically, was over, except for the need to
inform the scattered military forces of both sides to cease fire. This
posed the greatest problem for the Germans, with their official government crowded into a small nook of northern Schleswig-Holstein at
the base of the Danish peninsula of Jutland. Before General Bradley's
Army Group of forty-three U. S. divisions there were still pockets of

---

[5] According to Captain Harry Butcher, "After the Germans had been received by General Ike and had left his office, General Bull, the G-3, came in
to discuss the method of telling some 5,000,000 Allied combatants to stop
fighting at a given time. He suggested sending the message by radio and other
means to all units 'in the clear.' I suggested this would defeat the policy dictated
by the heads of government as to the time of announcement and would also
undercut the correspondents who had agreed to hold the story. As result the
messages from Allied Headquarters were sent in code. None of us foresaw that
the Germans would get on their own radio in Flensburg and broadcast their
capitulation 'in the clear.' Yet I doubt that the Germans could have reached all
their units in coded messages in those hectic hours."

Germans fighting along the 640-mile front, many fighting the Russians while trying desperately to back into American or British hands. Seventy U-boats were still loose in the Atlantic, twenty of them along the North American coast. In addition to whatever communications the German government could use, it was now up to the Allied navies everywhere to signal the submarines to surface and surrender. All this would take time.

The ink of the signatures now dry, General Allen went to General Eisenhower seeking an easing of restrictions on the release. Although the Supreme Commander favored the earliest possible breakthrough of the Big Three-imposed clamp, he had been commanded by the Combined Chiefs of Staff to stand aside until Truman, Churchill and Stalin had spoken. The General said to Allen: "These are my orders, and by God, they are yours, too."

Meanwhile there was a delay on the return of the press plane to Paris. Boyd Lewis turned to his typewriter and others followed suit. Already Lt. Col. Richard Merrick's censor stamp was being imprinted on copy, conditional only on the release time, which now promised to be 3 P.M., May 8. Boyd Lewis, Edward Kennedy and James L. Kilgallen of INS were the highly charged trio of the press party. Lewis knew there was only one way to be first and still work within the ground rules. His one area of decision was the distance from the landing strip at Orly into downtown Paris and the Scribe. If he could outrun the rest, with his story in shape to transmit, his copy would move first. When the correspondents finally went back to the C-47, Lewis made a dive for, and got, the seat nearest the door. Everyone tumbled to his strategy of being first out.

"As we landed," said Captain Don Davis, pilot of the C-47, "there were so many people in the tail, we came in almost like a pogo stick." At 7:30 A.M., the plane taxied up and the door nearly exploded from the competitive pressures within. Boyd Lewis calculated well and made his dash to the Scribe with a comfortable lead. With the ruthlessness of a man who plays to win, he not only filed his twenty-five-word flash, his 100-word urgent, and about 5,000 words of eyewitness copy, but he filed on all five of the transmitting outlets,[6] blocking all

---

[6] RCA, Mackay, Western Union, Press Wireless and Army Telex. Kennedy disagrees that this "blocked" him, saying, "By the end of the war, we had exceptionally good communications from the Scribe to New York ... with high-speed transmitters capable of sending up to 700 words per minute. The AP and

avenues in his favor. Jimmy Kilgallen, the aging Irishman, had thirty-
one pages of copy in his fists and a slight edge on Kennedy as they
sprinted from the curb to the Scribe door. To gain a little time,
Kilgallen threw his typewriter behind him which caused Kennedy to
stumble and lose a couple of steps at a crucial moment. By the time
Kennedy arrived, Kilgallen had duplicated Lewis' feat from the number two position. "That bird wasn't going to beat me," he said.
"There's something to be said for training on good hookers of rye."

There were immediate indications that the Russians were displeased with the Reims development and with the fact that the only
Russian general who participated was an obscure one. They were
pressing hard for a second surrender in Berlin. Much later, we learned
that, as far as the Russians were concerned, there never was a Reims
ceremony. Michael Litvin-Sedoy's story for Tass was never printed.
The streets outside the Scribe Hotel were full of reports of all kinds.
One was that General de Gaulle would soon address the French
people, another was that some French newspapers already had
accounts of Reims. As the hands of the clock went to three minutes
past 2 P.M., Count Ludwig Schwerin von Krosigh, foreign minister
of the Doenitz government, spoke over the Flensburg radio. He had
taken the air because the surrender terms demanded that German
troops "be informed by every possible means of the surrender and
directed to cease resistance." The British Ministry of Information
picked up the broadcast and made its report available to the press

---

other agencies had monitoring stations outside New York equipped to intercept messages addressed to them and transmit them instantly to their New York
offices. There were also several fast channels to London. SHAEF accorded
priority to AP, UP, and INS as general and spot-news agencies. On important
stories, first takes were sharply limited in length and were sent in rotation
among the three agencies. As a matter of fact, while the V-E day story was
awaiting release, all our stories were punched out by teletypesetter and the
tape was ready to be inserted in the high-speed transmitters. With such facilities
and rules, it is obvious that all three agencies would have simultaneous transmission when the story was released. I was well aware of this situation and was
somewhat puzzled by the scrambling of Kilgallen. I did not see Lewis en route
and did not know whether or not he had reached the Scribe before me. I lost
no time in getting to the Scribe because I did not know what might be developing there, but there was no reason to be concerned whether any of us was a
few minutes ahead or behind." (The fact remains, however, that even at 700
words a minute, with the pile ahead of Kennedy after the moving of the
"flashes" and "urgents," he would have been left behind in the color story
detail in the fevered competition.)

in London. BBC's quote of this announcement came into the Paris AP office, and Kennedy sat there as both New York and London cabled him asking about its authenticity.

Nearly four months before Jack Redding had asked a question about what kind of censorship existed to halt individual enterprise if there was a fast-breaking surrender development. He was assured there was no way to get the story through. "What's to prevent me if I put in a call to the Paris Military switchboard," he suggested, "ask for the direct line to London, give the phone number I want, and talk to anybody who answers about anything?" Couldn't happen, he was told.

When Kennedy confronted Lt. Col. Merrick, the SHAEF censor, with a sharp question about how the surrender could be a matter of military security any longer when the Germans had broadcast from Flensburg, Merrick said he had had no further instructions and that the embargo still held. Kennedy then issued an ultimatum: he was going to get the story out.[7] He accused Merrick of having let the story "leak," of having already turned the UP material loose, and raged against the military for having gotten off security and into political matters. Even when Merrick proved the charges about UP were untrue, Kennedy was still unsatisfied. Apparently he persuaded himself that Jodl's signature ended the war, even though he well knew that fighting would continue long after that signature and also knew that, even after the Flensburg broadcast, hours would pass before the word could find its way to the fighting troops.

[7] Ed Kennedy's version: "The only 'leak' I recall mentioning was the 'leak' of SHAEF through the Germans. I told Merrick I considered myself justified in sending the news for three reasons: (1) We had been assured—from the White House down—that there would be no more political censorship and this was admittedly political censorship; (2) We had been assured that censorship in Europe would be ended as soon as the war there was over and since I had seen the Germans surrender unconditionally, it was over, and (3) that since Flensburg was under Allied occupation, the German announcement had obviously been authorized by SHAEF. I informed Colonel Merrick that in view of these circumstances, I intended to send the story. It is a universal practice that when a story which is being held for release is inadvertently or deliberately released in advance of the time set by its source or by any news organization, other newspapers and agencies consider it then to be automatically and generally released and feel free to publish it without further delay. I followed this universally accepted practice. Any agreement is binding for all parties to it and it is obvious that the commitments made to us by the administration were as binding as our own commitments. The gag on the story was a violation . . . by the administration and by SHAEF, under orders from the administration."

On Kennedy's instructions, then, Morton Gudebrod in the AP office put in a call to London, following the very procedure forecast by Redding months before. When he had London on the line, he asked for the AP number, Central 1515. While this call was going through, Kennedy got his story ready. AP's own account says that Russell Lanstrom answered the phone. "This is Paris calling." The voice was extremely faint, but it conveyed the word that Germany had surrendered unconditionally at Reims. Lew Hawkins, who had been handed the phone by Lanstrom, wanted to know who was calling. Gudebrod identified himself, but Hawkins did not know him and on this kind of a story, he had to be sure. Kennedy then broke in. "This is Ed Kennedy," he said. "Lew, Germany surrendered unconditionally. That's official. Make the date line Reims, and get it out." Kennedy then dictated a bulletin in takes. By Eastern War Time, Count von Krosigh did his broadcast at 8:30 A.M., May 7. Kennedy's story was transmitted to New York at 9:27.

The AP had just gone through a severe shock a little more than a week before when Jack Bell's story out of San Francisco on April 28, on a tip by Senator Tom Connally, announced that Germany had surrendered unconditionally. No other wire service had carried the story, and President Truman reacted immediately by telling the White House press that he had checked with General Eisenhower and there was nothing to it. As a result, when Kennedy's story was received, New York's AP terminus was edgy. A quick huddle was called by AP's top echelon. Alan Gould finally okayed it when Ed Kennedy's by-line came in. Glen Babb, AP's foreign news editor, said that clinched it for him, too. At 9:35 the story was on the trunks, and twenty minutes later Nashville ran up the danger flag by saying neither UP nor INS was carrying anything yet. Nervousness increased in New York when none of the world capitals confirmed, while back in Paris, Kennedy turned to his staff and said, "Well, now let's see what happens. I may not be around here much longer." INS and UP were after their Paris correspondents quickly with service messages, and Lt. Col. Thor Smith was already coming to the conclusion that the story was from someone who had been at the surrender and that it was no ordinary leak of information but a "deliberate breach of faith."

My first inkling that something was sizzling along the Seine came in an urgent teletype message: "UNCLASSIFIED ASSOCIATED PRESS IS HEREBY SUSPENDED AND MAY NOT FILE TRAFFIC FROM THIS THEATER

UNTIL FURTHER ORDERS. REQUEST ARMY GROUPS TO ADVISE THEIR ARMIES OF THIS SUSPENSION PENDING INVESTIGATION. APPARENT BREACH OF CONFIDENCE AUTHENTICATED." The Ninth Army AP hands were stunned, Gallagher going quiet for a change, but Ken Dixon inclined to Kennedy's side. The ban on all AP correspondents held for six hours, then was lifted, but it was never pulled off Kennedy as long as he remained in Europe. Kent Cooper, general manager of AP in New York, reacted quickly to the ban, and a request for clarification came through to General Eisenhower. Cooper called up the time-honored gods, "freedom of the press" and "the right of the people to know," neither of which was involved in the transatlantic situation. Robert Bunnelle in London fanned the fire by asking for comments from some junketing Congressmen on censorship and suppression of news, but he cautioned New York to lay off mentioning Kennedy's use of the unauthorized phone, since it was taking the Army some time to find out how Kennedy had eluded the chokehold on his copy.

If there had been an uproar at the Scribe when the surrender itself was on, the place was now a steadily erupting geyser of wrath. Marshall Yarrow, Reuter's and Drew Middleton, *New York Times,* resented General Eisenhower's renewal of AP's privileges after six hours of restraint, contending this was an affront to all the agencies and correspondents who had abided by SHAEF's rules. The prevailing press contention was that AP should not be allowed to get out of its responsibilities by throwing all blame on the correspondent. Along with dozens of others, eight of the correspondents who had been at Reims signed a long, blistering protest directed to General Eisenhower about Kennedy and his conduct.

While the anger of his colleagues was being heaped upon Kennedy in Paris, and the tide running against him in the press camps, General George C. Marshall, the Army's Chief of Staff, was alarmed to see the bulk of the American press suggesting that Kennedy was being pilloried by the military! General Eisenhower received an urgent message: "It has been decided by the Chief of Staff that any statement on this matter should come from General Eisenhower. If statement made, it should come promptly as press and radio is featuring Associated Press story as great scoop and making martyr out of Kennedy as victim of unjustified withholding of news by your headquarters. Press generally is referring to the incident as the great snafu of war.

Nothing will be done on this end." General Eisenhower worked on a draft, while his chief of staff and Lt. Col. Thor Smith were with him. He decided that General Allen should release the SHAEF statement and gave the approved version to Colonel Smith to take back to Paris. He also replied to Kent Cooper, AP's general manager. Cooper came right back asking that Kennedy have the right to state his case and that AP's membership have all the facts instead of being asked to accept the "brief, unilateral, and undocumented statement contained in your reply." There was a challenge to the integrity of the Supreme Commander implied in Cooper's message, and he went further to wonder whether this action meant that military censorship was now going to move over to the political sphere in a Europe at peace. Although the AP ban was painful and incomprehensible to Cooper, he could not know about the mystery which confronted SHAEF as to how the news got out. But when Bunnelle's warning came through to keep mum about the phone call, and AP's interoffice message recapitulated names and incidents, it must have become clear in AP's New York headquarters that some chicanery had been involved. Hence, the whole of AP's informational web was getting a hard look.

All this underscored General Marshall's message, showing how strongly the American press must be lining up with Kennedy and indicating how distance and one side of the picture can change things, for only if Cooper were backed strongly by his AP membership would he have adopted such a challenging attitude. Kennedy's colleagues not only denounced him, they strongly endorsed General Allen's statement, approved by General Eisenhower, which gave the reasons for SHAEF's serious concern: the chance that the surrender arrangements would fall through, the danger of misunderstanding by the Russians who were still very much in the Big Three accords, and the possibility of a still-mounting casualty list after the signatures for lack of communications to German fighting units. The statement flatly stated that military security *was* involved. General Eisenhower's answer said in part: "After the meeting, and on his return to Paris, Kennedy arranged by unauthorized channels to transmit the whole story by telephone to the London office of the Associated Press for transmission to New York and immediate release. Kennedy admits his action and admits violation of his solemn commitment. His action placed me in position of violating a directive given to me. I have been informed the Associated Press appears to have taken the position of condoning and, in fact, praising this action of its representative when it actually was a self-admitted, deliberate breach of confidence. The Associated Press, therefore, takes the responsibility for clear violation of its word of honor to me as Supreme Commander of the Allied Forces in Europe, and as a representative of the U. S. who had undertaken a firm commitment for his government in connection with its allies. It has been one of the very few unfortunate experiences I have had with the press during my service as a commander." And then he added a final line which showed how close to the roots the Kennedy action had struck. "Up to now," General Eisenhower's statement ended, "I have felt free to take all correspondents into my confidence."

There was more, pro and con, but the AP switched from the demanding tone of Kent Cooper on the eighth to a statement on the tenth by AP president Robert McLean: "The Associated Press profoundly regrets the distribution on Monday of the report of the total surrender in Europe which investigation now clearly discloses was distributed in advance of authorization by Supreme Allied Headquarters. The whole, long, honorable record of the Associated Press is based on its high sense of responsibility as to the integrity and authenticity of the news and the observance of obligations voluntarily assumed. . . ." Kennedy's own agency had now turned against him as did all the professional newsmen in uniform who had sweated throughout the war to bring about a better, smoother working relationship between the military and the press. The Army public-relations staff which had worked out the arrangements for the last big act of the war in Europe were no novices. Some of them had far more experience than the correspondents. Had the American press adopted an attitude of "wait and see" on Kennedy's act, it would have left a more reasonable, mature picture of itself.

Kennedy was given his departure papers by SHAEF on May 17. Long after Kennedy arrived in New York and had had several vacations, Cooper wanted to wind up the affair for the benefit of all concerned by having Kennedy admit he was wrong. But Kennedy refused, turned on his heel, and the AP knew him no more.

As the serenity of V-E day overtook the Ninth Army press camp at the Elbe, there were only a few correspondents left. Most of them, after General Simpson's briefing, had gone to Paris. Wes Gallagher went from Ninth to Paris as acting bureau chief to replace Kennedy and to put his integrity into the breach. The Scribe's end of the war had been more wordy, violent and vituperative than the end of the conflict in Germany. It was perhaps significant that even though the real struggle ended in Central Germany, the last scrap of the press was fought in Paris, the city it had attained in force and had refused to leave.

Breaking Camp

It was all over officially at 0001, May 9, as the Army counted time, or one minute after midnight of May 8. General Bradley put it differently, writing "D plus 335" across the face of his well-worn map case. The Russians had another way of making it official by holding their own surrender in Berlin, when Field Marshal Keitel had to eat ceremonial crow for the propaganda agencies of the Soviet Union. The surrender table as the Russians rigged it in Berlin had Marshal Zhukov as head man, British Air Chief Marshal Tedder on his right, U. S. General Carl A. "Tooey" Spaatz on Zhukov's left, and to his left French General Delattre de Tassigny. Zhukov called the meeting to order and Field Marshal Keitel entered leading the German delegation, General P. F. Stumpf for the Luftwaffe, and the same Admiral von Friedeburg who had already been through the Reims affair. Zhukov had suffered from no compunctions about "Hollywoodizing" the Berlin surrender and nearly a hundred cameramen and writers recorded all aspects of the event for the Soviet Union propaganda mill.

When the war ended, my driver, Corporal Max O. Shepherd, reported that the speedometer on our jeep was standing at 24,981 miles, all rung up since we had made out the first trip ticket together in Clevedon. The Ninth Army press camp, which had started with Franklin Banker, AP, as its first correspondent, was now at the end of its road with the last correspondent signed in, Russell Hill, *New*

257

York Herald Tribune, who had taken the place of Seymour Freidin. Every day jeeps went out from the press camp to the air strip near Oschersleben. Outbound they were piled high with bedrolls and personal belongings, but the jeeps always came back empty. In Oschersleben the correspondents climbed aboard for Paris or London, never to return. In our first state of relaxation for months, the press camp actually luxuriated in each departure since it meant that much less work and that much more leisure for the military and civilian staffs.

With the Pacific war still going strong, Ninth Army headquarters was earmarked for transfer to that theater, partly because it had been one of the latest arrivals in Europe. There were local plans for the U. S. Second Armored and Eighty-second Airborne Divisions, now quiet in Magdeburg and Ludwigslust. The Eighty-second had had the final heady experience of seeing Lt. Gen. von Tippelskirch and his 145,000-man Twenty-first German Army surrender to it, including 2,008 trucks and cars, 109 half-tracks, 17 tanks, 197 armored vehicles, 89 trailers and two Hungarian cavalry divisions.[1] Captain Edward C. Lavelle heard from Paris that in SHAEF's last press conference correspondents from all Allied nations had made a matter of record their satisfaction with the way "SHAEF's field press censorship had done its job during the war." One evening we had a small decoration ceremony in the press room and there were medals to hand to Captain Lyman Anderson and Lieutenant George Fuller. There was no press contingent to view the quiet affair in the shadow of the crumpled and cracked operations map, on whose acetate facing so many wartime situations had been drawn.

The Russian ex-slave laborers showed us there would be nothing simple about settling the affairs of our international family. Some of them had been with us since Schloss Rheydt and had ridden happily east toward their homeland, but they now began to act strangely. They no longer were eager to get to the Elbe River and cross over to the Red Army on the east bank. Word was being circulated that there would be no welcome for them in Russia. They had worked for the Germans. It mattered not why or how. What was more, it was understood their association with the American Army did them no good, and my offers to give them certificates, or references, were refused. No documents, please! The Poles on the staff never had wanted

[1] In addition, there were more than 5,300 mistresses, wives, children and girl friends tagging along trying desperately to keep out of the hands of the Russians.

to return to their homeland, outspokenly declaring that, although there was a Poland in their hearts, the real Poland could not have survived first the Germans, and then the Russians. They even began side-stepping the Russians who were still with us. The Czechs took off to the south, the knowledge of Patton in Pilsen giving them assurance for the time being.

Diminutive Stacha—only four feet ten inches tall—a Polish twenty-six-year-old in charge of the laundry, was brought to me by Philippe Barres, the Gaullist editor of the *Paris Presse,* one of the late stayers. "If possible," he said, "I would like this girl to work for me in Paris. I will pay her and take care of her. My wife would also like to have her, and she does not want to go back to Poland." France had an open door at the time for male Poles who could take up residence in France. They were being encouraged to marry French women. But a Polish woman was another thing. "I cannot take her to France myself," said Barres, "but if she gets to France by any means, she will be welcome at my home. I will then try to get her a work permit." He was saying, in essence, that the uniform of the U. S. might still have some magic at the border which was tightening up, and it was up to me to abandon Stacha to her fate or to give her a new opportunity in France to pick up the thread of life.

The simplest of all closing-out activities was the removal of the Dutch Army guards. They were cited as surplus to our needs, returned to Brunswick and Ninth Army, and thence to their barracks in the Netherlands. But the van Egerschots, Willem and Yvonne, had no wish to return to their homeland. They preferred to go to France and seek further employment with the American forces in some capacity where their hotel knowledge and language facility would have a use.

One of the women in the kitchen livened up the lazy days of our postwar operation by announcing that she was pregnant. I took her in the jeep over the German hills to a field hospital in a tent near the Magdeburg *autobahn.* Yvonne went along as an interpreter, since the scullery maid could speak no English. When the jeep pulled up in front of the reception tent, I went inside.

"I need an obstetrician," I told the nurse lieutenant on duty.

"How dreadful for you!" she said. "Women all over the world will be revenged at last."

I explained that my concern was for a girl in the jeep outside, and she went to the tent flap and looked out.

"Which one?" she said.

"The one in the back seat. The other one is an interpreter."

"Has the interpreter been in attendance throughout these developments?" the nurse asked.

"All right, let's cut out this Fanny Brice business. Have you got an obstetrician here or not?" Still wearing an expression of amusement, she disappeared through the tent asking me to follow her. She presented me to a major and explained the predicament. A warm smile of anticipation spread over the major's face. "A pregnancy," he said. "Imagine! Me, I'm an obstetrician in civil life, but ever since I've been in the Army, all I've seen is trench foot or VD. Bring the lady in, by all means, bring the lady in. It will be a pleasure."

While the nurse went out to the jeep to bring the two women in, it was explained to the doctor that a certificate of pregnancy was all that was needed for the moment. With that in hand, it would be easier to confront the soldier responsible who could either marry the girl, or make promise of financial support over the required period of years cited in Army regulations covering such emergencies. The report was affirmative. "How the pregnancy survived a ride in that jeep over these cobblestone roads," said the major, "I'll never know." Back in the press camp, the soldier was not at all upset, as he had found the girl an agreeable, hard-working companion. He signed the forms without protest and arrangements for a marriage were in order.

The axis of the Ninth Army's advance had put it in an unusual position politically when the time came to divide up Germany. Ninth Army alone had to yield ground in two directions from the advances made by its troops and for which it had taken casualties. There was no one left to write about this, although it was an important reference point in years to come. The portions of Germany held east of Helmstedt to the Elbe, and south of the press camp at Klein Wanzleben—roughly the attainments of six American divisions—fell inside the North-South Yalta demarcation line. This region was to be under British jurisdiction until the Soviet Union's final deployments were made, at which time the British could turn it over to the Russians. The signal for this step was the arrival of Major Lindsay-Howe of the British Army, who drove in the Rabbethge gate one day in late May.

"How soon," he said, "do you plan to leave here?"

"Any day now—why?"

"This is the most likely-looking place I've seen about," he said. "How large is it?"

He was led around the premises and shown the extent and finer points of the Rabbethge mansion. He was quartering officer for a British military-government unit and, as soon as we cleared, wanted to move his colonel and the rest of the detachment in. "Who are all these civilians around here?" he asked. The story of our PW's and how we had brought them across Germany was told. All our attempts thus far to explain to them that they were free to go had had no effect, and they were still hanging on. "How do you feed them? Accounting for rations and all that?"

"We just report so many civilian employees and draw for them along with the rest of the military forces."

"Must be wonderful," he said, rubbing his chin in study. "We can't do that. Our ration count is very strict."

With the possibility that he could provide a benevolent solution for these people, I urged him to consider that the staff, already acquainted with the big place and trustworthy, could be very cheap help indeed. He was unconvinced until we approached the cellar and a flip of the keys in the door revealed the well-filled racks of wines. "Impossible!" he said. "Americans here and the bottles are still full!" [2]

"We'll make you a deal. We have a big trailer out there. We were going to load this stuff into it and take it back with us to Wiesbaden. If you'll take over the civilian help and care for them when we leave here, we'll leave the wine cellar. If your colonel will accept this proposition, when you come back, the key is yours." The major went to his car and said he would be back the next day with an answer.

The press camp pregnancy had necessitated that we give the soldier

[2] Since Wes Gallagher, AP, Vic Jones, *Boston Globe,* and Gordon Gammack, *Des Moines Tribune,* had been traveling with Second Armored Division, Maj. Gen. I. D. White's key-custodian, when he gave me one key to the Rabbethge wine cellar as they moved out, on the sly gave another to Gammack. When it came time to pick rooms, this trio, which was notorious for demanding the best, startled Captain Griffith by asking for a servant's-quarters layout in the basement. No sack of sand had to fall on anyone to know this was dictated by some unusual circumstances, but there were more than 10,000 bottles of wine in the racks so Griff let them have their fun. They couldn't make much of an inroad on the supply, no matter how hard they tried. One of Vic Jones's *Boston Globe* colleagues, Corporal Fortunato C. Rosa, once a rewrite man but now with an anti-aircraft unit, made regular calls and went out each time with bottles in his musette bag. But even with this, there was enough left to make Major Lindsay-Howe's eyeballs pop.

leave to return to the bride's homeland for the marriage. After the wedding, he was horrified to learn that he had been victimized. His bride had had a miscarriage as a result of her long trek homeward over Germany's rutted roads. To keep up the fiction, and to secure herself a husband, she had been married with a padding at her midriff! "Imagine havin' to send your folks a picture of a pillow for a grandson!" said the soldier, who had fled his bride.

Major Lindsay-Howe returned and wanted all the civilian staff to be called together in the courtyard so he could talk to them. He asked Yvonne and Willem to stand by as interpreters. The Russians, Poles and a few Dutch gathered around. Faces in that small circle mirrored all the expressions in the emotional gamut. There was an air of finality in this meeting. For half a year, we had all been together in common cause. The faces in that semicircle were really bound to us for only two reasons—we had been kind to them and had given them food, lodging and protection—but they had been a part of whatever we had achieved. Through the van Egerschots, Major Lindsay-Howe said he would like to have all of them stay and be employed by the British. There was a Tower of Babel conference among them, but agreement was quick and total. They knew we had to depart. The major said he would like to move in the next day, June 1, 1945. With much ceremony, I gave him the key to the wine cellar.

No farewell like this could go by without a party, and we had taken some of the cellar stock out of the racks for the occasion. Major Lindsay-Howe took the key, went down himself to check, and found there was little dent in the inventory he had been shown before, which continued to be a marvel to him. Everyone ate in the great dining room that night, and we had the last of the fresh meat from the ration dump. We had a sixteen-mm. movie projector and one feature starring Shirley Temple, entitled *Kiss and Tell*. With liberal dosages of the wine, it was a great success. The course was not straight for many when they headed off for bed at midnight, but it had been a happy farewell affair.

The British were scheduled to arrive at nine, and we were to clear at eight, so all we had was coffee to add to our K rations before hitting the road. The queen of the slave-labor contingent was Stacha, envied for her good fortune in the promise of employment in Paris, if we could get her over the border. She was all togged out in her ragged but well-washed best. The drivers went to their vehicles after saying their good-bys. At five minutes to eight, a line suddenly formed alongside my jeep, involving all the people to be left behind.

"They want to kiss your hand," said Yvonne, and at my look of dismay, she went on. "It's an old custom. It means they think you have been a good boss." And kiss it they did, every one of them.

The engines started. "Let's get outta here," said Griff gruffly as he saw the tears begin to well up in the D.P.'s eyes, men and women alike. Our same old cavalcade started on its last jaunt. There were five big trucks, stacked high. There were twenty jeeps, and behind them were trailers of all kinds, some GI, but some German equipment we had picked up along the way. Press Wireless, on the road more than a week before, had left its reminders in the three stark poles. The D.P.'s waved until we turned out of sight, leaving the nearest thing we had known to a home since Maastricht. We were in retreat from the Elbe, and there was sadness in this retreat for those who had been a part of the victory.

Our convoy was only one of thousands headed west as the victory was turned over to politicians and statesmen, and the carving up of Germany entered the final stages.

. . . TAKE 19 ————————————————

Meeting the Russian "Friends"

The P&PW Service Battalion, the catch-all designed in midwinter of 1943 at 20 Grosvenor Square in London, was holding a family reunion of sorts when our convoy arrived in Wiesbaden. Not since its equipment and men had first been assembled in Clevedon had it been all together, nor did it quite get together in Wiesbaden, either. It had been reassigned in part, shot up, clobbered in accidents, and some of it had been captured. Some of the original drivers were dead and buried in cemeteries back along the meandering way. On June 4 the turn-in was as nearly complete as it would ever be.

For myself, there was a new set of orders, assigning me to the First Allied Airborne Army. It had always been expected that the Allied entry into Berlin from the west would be made by a combined force of British and Americans. A ready-made headquarters for this was the First Allied Airborne Army, then lodged in the vicinity of Bielefeld, Germany, but with its rear echelon on the outskirts of Paris. The forward elements were on the main east-west *autobahn* about 200 miles west of Berlin. First Allied Airborne Army had never functioned as an army throughout the war. It had air-dropped one corps into the Netherlands where the men came under British command on the ground, and it used two of its divisions to jump the Rhine, these also coming under British command on the ground. As a headquarters, it had never had much respect shown it by its subordinate airborne divisions, and General Bradley was forever outrunning the drop zones suggested for its operations. It was now undergoing two developments as a headquarters, both of which suggested different and busier days ahead. One was that Lt. Gen. Lewis H. Brereton, its commander since midsummer, 1944, was leaving it to return to the U. S. and turning it over to Maj. Gen Floyd L. Parks, his chief of staff. The other was the withdrawal of its British officers and men and the absorption of headquarters, Berlin District, and with it the mission of being the U. S. contingent to occupy the American sector of the German capital. The American troops deployed forward into Halle on the Saale, while the British stayed in place in Bielefeld since it was on their main line toward Berlin and the British occupation zone. The Russians, known to be posting Berlin liberally with Communist propaganda while industriously running their fingers through the political and financial debris of the German metropolis, were in no rush to get on with the agreed division of that city into its separate chunks for postwar administration.

The public-relations setup of First Airborne Army, now shorn of its "Allied," contained a mobile convoy of seventeen trucks which consisted of both British and American commercial and Army radio transmitters. In command, for SHAEF, was Lt. Col. Jack Redding. General Parks was already in Berlin, but was being whisked about in a Russian car and seeing little more than the Russian escorts wanted him to see. He was about to inherit the American sector of Berlin and all its headaches, its politics, its intrigues, part of the city administration and the onrushing housekeeping problems of the Big Three Potsdam Conference. Berlin was now certain to attract a different kind of correspondent, because the political pundit was overtaking the chronicler of conflict.

For my portion of First Airborne Army activity, it was necessary to begin in Paris, since SHAEF's Public Relations Division was planning the press relations of Berlin. Although SHAEF, by drawing on the pool of talent now collecting from all field armies at Wiesbaden's Headquarters Twelfth Army Group, would provide the press-camp personnel, the actual support of the military and correspondent force would be the responsibility of First Airborne Army of which General Parks had made me the PRO. The certainty of reunion later in Berlin made my farewells easy as, with Stacha and the van Egerschots, I made ready to take the road to Paris.

"Do you feel like a smuggler?" Griff asked.

He was surveying the oddly costumed human cargo. Stacha was

wearing a helmet liner, which came all the way down to her nose, and a GI jacket with sleeves so long her hands never came out unless she pulled them up. Yvonne was in an Army field coat and her helmet had the silver bar of a first lieutenant. Willem had on a tattered Army combat jacket and wore the OD stocking cap normally used to cushion a helmet. All of them were in the back seat. If any of them were spoken to in English, they could hold their own, with the exception of Stacha, her sole acquaintance with the language being her ability to say, fairly clearly, "Jeez Chris', my achin' back!" which had been taught her somewhere along the way.

To clear the final hurdle of the border, without lengthy and possibly unsuccessful explanations, Griff was going to lead in his jeep and engage the border guard in conversation about where to turn off to get to an obscure French village. This would involve discussion over a map and pile up traffic. While this was going on, our driver was to pull out on Griff's right, keeping the jeep between him and the MP, whereupon I'd wave my valid orders to get us on through. If he chose to give us the go-ahead, well and good; if not, we would talk as required. The checkpoint was on the outskirts of Saarbrücken, and the town Griff would ask about was Puttelange. We stayed close together, and took a survey of the border site from the last point of vantage to be sure there was traffic ahead of us. We were relieved to see a queue of four vehicles already in line. One harassed MP was busy with the traffic moving toward France. The situation in our command car was slightly electric as Griff pulled up and asked directions to Puttelange. Luckily, the MP had not heard of it, so out came the map and they prepared to study it. The time had come.

Our command-car chauffeur swung out to the right, up even with the jeep, and called to the MP, showing my orders and saying he had to get "the last of the Ninth Army press camp on back to Paris as soon as possible." The MP looked up, and the girls waved at him. He grinned, beckoned us on, and the car rolled into France. Griff stayed on for further discussions, then caught up with us about two miles down the Route Nationale No. 3 as we were pulling full speed toward Metz. "You *are* a smuggler," he said. Opening some canned meats, we lunched by the roadside, which killed enough time for Griff to make Puttelange, in case the same MP noticed him on the return.

Late the next day, on the first anniversary of D-Day, Stacha was driven to the door of Philippe Barres, who set about getting her a work permit. The van Egerschots secured employment with the American Red Cross, and were told they would probably be assigned to run one of the Red Cross billets back in Wiesbaden from which they had just come. At any rate, from the bargain of the wine-cellar key in Klein Wanzleben to the running of the border at Saarbrücken, the future care and employment of the civilian staff of the defunct Ninth Army press camp had now been arranged. It was possible to turn to futures—the public-relations chores of First Airborne Army and the press-coverage setup for the Allied occupation of Berlin.

The Berlin planning set a ceiling of 150 on the number of correspondents of all kinds who would probably have to be cared for through the first month, after which it was expected the numbers would dwindle. It wasn't that the occupation of Berlin would be story enough for them, but the gamble was that they would be able to grab news bones thrown over the shoulders of the Big Three at their Potsdam conference. There was no promise of anything at this stage. The Russians had fixed the site as the Cecilienhof and were not yet letting the Americans approach the area. The press, as usual, was confident that the power of their numbers, pressure and proximity would overcome any barriers erected to keep them out.

Redding placed all equipment and personnel in Weimar as a staging point. He had put Captain Sam Brightman in charge of the Weimar gathering place, but Sam was joined immediately by tough, noisy, hard-swearing Captain James A. Griffith, our Ninth Army press-camp commandant, to whom Brightman tossed the administrative reins with alacrity. On June 10, the Paris contingent of the First Airborne Army took off for Halle, where my new staff was in place in a former Luftwaffe school, and included Captain Ross Evans, of New York City; and Lieutenants Neil Sharkey, of Marion, Ohio; Robert Schulberg, of Allentown, Pennsylvania; and trusty George Fuller.

In mid-June, the whole Weimar-Halle area was stirring. Planes were coming in from Paris each day with correspondents and landing at Weimar. As Weimar began to bulge, some of the press secured jeeps at the motor pool and came forward to Halle to ask questions about when we would set off. It was getting well into the second month since the surrender, and the Russians still barred the way to Berlin. The old Berlin hands were showing, most of them with a list of places to get to after they entered the city. There were Sigrid Schultz, *Chicago*

Tribune; Louis Lochner and Daniel DeLuce, AP; Pierre J. Huss, INS; Marcel Wallenstein, *Kansas City Star;* Henrik Ringsted, the Danish *Politiken,* and a string of others.

As General Parks talked in Berlin, there was a flurry of messages pouring back which led Colonel Ralph Swofford, the G-3, to draw up the initial movement order, to be put in motion June 22 with entry of the quartering party and a communications nucleus, including a survey officer to fix radio-transmitter sites. Shortly after this first group, cadres of the occupation forces—key men of the Second Armored Division—would go in, since on them would rest the policing of the American sector. The press was to come with the main body of troops. It was decided that in the first convoy, we would take one jeep with trailer for Redding, a communications officer, and myself, putting the entire seventeen-truck communications convoy in the next movement. As the press would come with the main body, it would give us two days to install. Before the deadline, we had Griff make a dry run from Weimar to Halle to get it timed, should there be a sudden call to hurry, a most improbable development considering how much time the Russians were taking.

Before sunrise, June 22, the parade ground of the Luftwaffe cadet school saw the first party collected. Everybody was booted and shined. Brig. Gen. Stuart Cutler, of Headquarters Command, was the over-all boss of the detachment, and Colonel Frank Howley, the Philadelphia advertising man destined to be military governor of Berlin, had a military-government unit with him. There was great contrast between old soldier Cutler and the polished Howley, the latter a dramatic, phrase-turning conversationalist, easy in the presence of the press and a sophisticate used to the marble halls of politics. In good order, as the sun came up, we started over the Saale River into the Russian zone of East Germany. For the moment the long delays of the in- scrutable Russians and their stubbornness faded. We were on the way. There was a real feeling of excitement, and the Russians all waved as we crossed over the bridge. But as the last vehicle in the column came into the Russian zone, the bridge was closed behind us and the head of the column was halted.

General Cutler and Colonel Howley, with a Russian officer, drove back down the convoy to the headquarters of the Russian commandant for the district. Word went down our column that the Soviet Union had saved a few bottles of vodka to honor their allies from the West.

Since all of us had gotten up rather early, we lolled back and dozed. Unlike the British and American sectors, there was very little movement of German civilians in the Russian zone. They were dead, desolate, or in hiding. An hour dragged by as a Russian officer in a lend-lease jeep counted all the way up to the head of the column, then counted back. Two hours went by before General Cutler and Howley returned, and Cutler was anything but a recently entertained dignitary. He was angry and asked that everyone assemble around him. He said the Russians had told him the convoy was bigger than agreed, that there were only supposed to be "thirty-six officers, 175 soldiers, and fifty vehicles" in the first party to enter Berlin. We didn't know where they came by the figures, but we were about double the number. "I can't get any clarification here," he said, "but Parks is up there in Berlin and he's expecting somebody today, so we'll have to cut down right here and half of us go back." This was a jarring note.

The whole Second Armored detail was clipped off and sent back. Our unit was so small it would not have mattered either way, but we decided to split so both ends of the line would know the story— Redding and the communications officer to continue, myself to return to Halle and come in with the convoy. By now, word had circulated that Americans were in the vicinity, and Germans came out of their houses to stand by. Russian soldiers were out to watch as well. Cutler and Howley went up and down the column, cutting a man here, a vehicle there, while bedrolls were unloaded and duffelbags thrown in the street. It was embarrassing, and the Germans were catching on, too, as one Ally enforced its will on the other. One German standing near me smiled knowingly as I hoisted my belongings into a returning jeep. "Russki strong!" he said. Hard to take was the fact that we had been instructed to get along, while they appeared to have orders only to obstruct. It was well after noon when the shrunken column, with Howley in command, passed through Landsberg, on over the Mulde River toward Berlin. The rest of us, with General Cutler, whose face was set like a storm cloud, went back to Halle.

The decision for our group to split had been a good one, however, because the signal from the advance party next day gave us news that they were not yet in Berlin. The Russian escort of Colonel Howley's contingent turned them off at the southwestern Berlin suburb of Babelsberg, once the home of UFA, the German film industry. It was here that Howley was told, unceremoniously, that he was not bound for Berlin. The Russian gave instructions. Babelsberg, Howley was told, would house the American delegation to the Big Three Conference, and Howley's detachment would now set about getting it ready. It was a day to fill the gorge of Howley, who had started out in the morning with a convoy of conquerors and wound up with a junket of janitors.

The press corps at Weimar was not treated to the sight of the returning portion of the stripped quartering party, so the story was never given the treatment it might have had. Should it have come to world attention at that time, it undoubedly would have alerted the West to the true nature of its position in Berlin. It was a week before a through movement into Berlin was organized and green-lighted by a sweating General Parks, whereupon Swofford produced an order calling for the convoy to roll on July 1. The main body, which would include the press, was to follow on July 3. The July 1 movement order put me at the head of seventeen communications trucks, which included both British and American vehicles. A radio phone call came from Redding before departure, asking that one important thing be reaffirmed to the correspondents before I pulled out. "Tell them," he said, "that the Army is providing them access and opportunity to cover the occupation of Berlin by the western Allies, and that's all. Being in Berlin is no guarantee that they will get within whistling distance of Potsdam. That's on a higher level than we can go." When relayed, this information fell on unbelieving, if not deaf ears.

From the U. S. point of view, President Truman's press secretary, Charles Ross, expected to cover Potsdam by taking the regular White House representatives of AP, UP and INS along for the entire trip. It would be treated like any other presidential day on the road. On the European side of the Atlantic, three weeks before President Truman was to clear Norfolk on the naval vessel bringing him to Antwerp, it was apparent to us all, from General Parks on down, that there would be nothing easy about the press arrangements at Potsdam. Our plans for their coverage of the entry and occupation of Berlin would bring them in two weeks ahead of the Big Three delegation, during which interval they would have ample time to brush up against the Russians.

The second column to start for Berlin made it all the way, although not without incident. The crayoned circle on my map showed that the press should be quartered in the general neighborhood of suburban

Zehlendorf-bahnhof West, a railroad station. Luckily this was one of the least battered parts of Berlin, and Redding had noted some high ground just south of the Berliner Strasse—the main artery of transportation into the American zone—which appeared to fit the radio-installation needs. Other than this, Redding had been able to do little more than locate the small hotel where we were to lodge for the night and plant himself at the *autobahn* overpass at the Zehlendorf outskirts where he was waiting to pick up our portion of the column and lead it in. Less than a mile out, I had checked the column and found it intact and in good shape, the seventeen communications trucks and ten jeeps all running at close interval. Almost at the edge of Zehlendorf, there was the sound of honked horns in the rear, a sign that the column had been broken. As the noise reached me at the head of the column, Griff came roaring up in his jeep from his tail-end position. "We're having Russki trouble again," he said. "General Cutler's back there. It's a helluva row."

"What this time?"

"It's those limey communications trucks. Two Russian majors have jumped us, and they won't let the British go any further. They say they're not supposed to be on this road—that the British are coming in further north."

"How far back are they?"

"It's about a half mile. Cutler's sore as hell. He said to me, 'Captain, what's your name? I want you as a witness. I've taken about enough off these ignorant bastards in the last few days. They may think they won the war, but if this keeps up, they'll also know how the next one started.' He sent me up to tell you to hold the rest of the convoy."

Redding took over the portion of the column still with me, and Griff and I turned back. By this time there were several more Russians, and the one who was causing the trouble was obviously drunk, but was swaying back and forth on his feet with gun in his hand. Not only was he being argued with by Cutler, but the newly arrived Russians were also against him and they shouldered him off the road. I waved the British drivers ahead, and to the extent of the seventeen communications trucks there was a semblance of an Allied parade up Berliner Strasse.

Redding turned to on the communications that afternoon, and it was my chore to find housing within the mapped goose egg given me by Swofford. As I turned into the lush suburb of Zehlendorf, Lt. Col.

Albert McCleery, with his German-speaking driver, headed into another area of Berlin for an address given him long ago. When he
came into the neighborhood and spotted the number, he could hardly
believe it as a slight, tired woman in her sixties came to the door. She
was terrified at the sight of a soldier.

"Frau von Loesch?" asked McCleery.

"Ja," she said nervously.

With the help of his driver, McCleery explained. A long time ago,
he said, Marlene Dietrich had asked him to come to this address and
find out if her mother still lived here.

"But Marlene," said Frau von Loesch, "is she still alive?" McCleery
assured her that she was alive, and in Paris.

"Nein, not Paris," said Frau von Loesch. "I have heard her broadcasting from London. I feared for her while London was being
bombed. I prayed every day that she be safe." McCleery looked at
her incredulously, thinking maybe she had been touched by her recent
ordeal, but Frau von Loesch's conviction stemmed from two kinds of
radio broadcasting, the last frantic exaggerations of Goebbels saying
that London was being wiped out and ABSIE's (American Broadcasting Station in England) airing of a regular recorded series by Marlene
called "Marlene Sings to Her Homeland." Frau von Loesch was finally
convinced that McCleery meant her no harm and that he would get
word to Marlene as quickly as possible. He also learned that the tired
old lady was nursing her ninety-five-year-old sick aunt. McCleery left
with assurance that Marlene would be coming to Berlin before long,
and that he would be back to see her.

My driver that day, Morris Cocking, of Wichita, Kansas, spun us
into Zehlendorf late that afternoon, and after we found a German
innkeeper who spoke English, we began the long ordeal of com-
mandeering houses. The checklist was short: General conditions good?
Roof intact? Beds and bedding on the premises? Running water?
Windows in?

The edict against fraternization was still in force. It was therefore
illegal to billet American troops with German families, and war correspondents still had quasi-military status. The houses where my
interpreter presented us were all being carefully kept. Their owners,
thankful that the war had spared them, were now distressed to learn
that the very nature of their property was about to cause its loss—just
because it had escaped bombing destruction. One had to adjust rapidly

in many situations during the war. Being illegal was one thing, but improvising quite another. So winking at the fraternization edict, we first evicted each family. Once they were on the lawn in front of their homes, the interpreter made them the following proposition quickly: "You understand that your house has been requisitioned for the Allied press by the American Army, and now is completely under control of that Army?"

"Ja," sadly.

"You further understand that the American Army will now have to hire some one from German labor sources to look after this property, to serve as housekeepers, yardkeepers, and chambermaids?"

"Ja," more sadly.

"You further understand that you will be allowed, under close supervision, to remove only very personal possessions, while all your household furnishings must remain?"

"Ja," completely resigned.

"Now . . . if the American Army were to employ you . . . allow you to live in the attic or basement of this house, it is believed you would take care of the place with more consideration than a stranger. If we were to employ you, in this fashion, would you keep to those assigned quarters except when your work requires you to be in other parts of the house?"

Each German face would speedily change from despair to delight. *"Ja, ja, JA!"*

In this manner we acquired and staffed simultaneously fifty-six individual residences in the afternoon and early evening of July 1, 1945. Problems are not completely solved with acquisitions, however, and are in fact only starting. Overseeing a section as widespread as this required a certain number of administrative buildings. The mess went into the small hotel, where it could be easily and quickly organized. Our search continued for something central for administrative purposes, and the quest brought me to a wooden gate nestled in a high, thick hedge fence.

"Reichsminister Walter Funk, he used to live here," the interpreter said. "Now, the Russian commandant." Reaching for the handle to open the gate, I was suddenly alone. The interpreter fled up the street and around the corner. It was early evening and completely quiet on the other side of the bushy growth. The gate swung in easily, and I stepped inside. There was a sudden thump in my back, accompanied by a curt order in a language then relatively new to me. Imperiousness of tone was unmistakable and there was a gun muzzle pressing my left kidney. As my hands went up, a quick glance to my left revealed a small Russian soldier. His eyes were aslant, his face typical of the Asiatic common in the Red Army. The eyes were cold, and he slammed the gate with his foot and prodded me with the gun in the direction of the house.

Entrance was up a flight of steps. Past the heavy door, a sharp right put me into a small room which was probably originally dedicated to the sun, or could even have been a library once. It was now barren, having been converted into a combination office and guard room. A half dozen Russian soldiers, presumably sentries like my sponsor, were lounging about. All of them began chiding my custodian and laughing at my discomfiture. His face never changed expression, and he kicked a chair into the middle of the room facing its only desk. Motioning me into it, he did not take my holstered gun, but insisted and actually helped me place my hands in plain sight on top of the desk. His manner indicated that he expected they would stay there. His seriousness was emphasized by the other guards who moved from the line of fire on the other side of me.

Managing a half turn to speak to the whole group, I asked if any-one spoke English. Not a very funny line, standing alone, it neverthe-less aroused a titter. Another try. Could they produce their command-ing officer? This brought on a belly laugh, coupled with much slapping of thighs and backs. The clock on the wall, there probably because it was too big to be carried off in any Red Army pocket, ticked away loudly. Beckoning for my guard to watch, a reach into my pocket brought out my "diplomatic ration," a pack of cigarettes. There was fast action as the guards swarmed out from the walls, and the cigarettes disappeared into mouths and pockets. Everyone lit up and the impasse was restored.

A long, trying hour passed, and no other solutions presented them-selves. It had become very dark outside when the door at my back swung open. Everyone in the room, judging from the stir and scraping of feet, jumped to attention. A Russian officer, barely five feet tall and almost half that width of shoulders, strode in. The reason for the delay was apparent. He was gouging his teeth with a small metal pick, and he belched comfortably twice before he showed himself aware of my presence by looking at me directly—and silently.

"Do you speak English?" I asked him.

He raised his hand tiredly, seemingly in a gesture of boredom, and looked vacantly out the window. I realized it was never a good idea to lose one's temper, particularly when somebody else held the gun. Again, the door at my back broke the strain. It came crashing open this time and a body banged into me, then fell sprawling over the commandant's desk. A blonde, obviously German girl had been shoved with great force into the room. Her hair fell down over her face, and when she straightened up painfully and brushed her hair back there was so much terror in her eyes it hid her natural beauty. The Russian spoke to her in halting, Slavic-larded German. She had trouble understanding him. Finally, she turned to say, "I speak some English. I interpret."

"Tell him I'm an American Army officer, a lieutenant colonel." She repeated it in German, and he talked.

"He say, what you want?"

"Tell him, as of today, this has become the American sector of Berlin. This area is being taken over by the American Army. When can he clear out of this house and grounds?"

The fear returned to her eyes. "You want I tell Russki get out?" When assured she had heard correctly, she began phrasing it in less abrupt terms, because it took her a long time to make the main points. The Russian's actions were mercurial. First he swept his hand the length of his desk, and at the edge it collided with his hat, knocking it into the corner of the room. Then he clapped both hands to his head, took one down, and pointed it at me as he loosed a barrage in his own tongue.

"Tell him to speak German, so you can tell me what he says."

As suddenly as it had begun, he quieted his tirade and addressed her again. "He says: He commandant Red Army here. Has no instructions about Americans. Likes house, lives here, won't go."

Tired by now of Russian intransigence, and thinking there would be no better time to bull it through, I rose to my feet in a gesture of departure. "Tell him the Americans are coming into this part of Berlin in great numbers. The American Second Armored Division, with 16,000 men, will be in this sector day after tomorrow. Tell him I am going to report his conduct to my highest authorities who will take it up with Marshal Zhukov. Ask him for his name for my report."

At the mention of Zhukov, everyone in the room started up and the officer was apprehensive. He questioned the girl closely about the Zhukov portion of my ultimatum, then waved us hastily out of the room, after which we walked unmolested to the street.

In the moonlight, the number 11 on the gate glinted. "My name . . . Irmegard Schmidt," the girl said to me, extending her hand timidly. "I . . . walking Argentinische Allee . . . soldier took my arm . . . asked 'Speak English?' . . . I say . . . 'Little' and he bring me here. . . . Was very frightened . . . *danke*." She half ran down the street, as if unbelieving that she had been in the clutches of the Red Army and had come off unscathed.

So did number 11 Sven-Hedin Strasse come to be discovered. The next day the Russian commandant and his staff were gone. By accident, we had found the "open-sesame" in dealing with recalcitrant Red Army members of the lower levels. Nobody ever wanted to be brought to the attention of Marshal Zhukov, and what was more any Russian would give ground rather than risk the threat of a report.

The radio stations went in, one by one, on July 2 and established their contacts with Paris, New York and London. Germans sidled up to Cocking in the jeep, and to me to ask, now that word had spread about the coming of the journalists to the district, whether the ones they knew would be among them—Sigrid Schultz, Louis Lochner, Pierre Huss? One wanted to know whether BBC's Richard Dimbleby or Edward R. Murrow of CBS would soon be there. "I'm anxious to see Dimbleby, or Murrow," he said in faultless English. "I have listened to both of them broadcast. When the bombs came to Berlin, we used to know how much flak went up. We wanted to know what it was like up there, so when Murrow and Dimbleby came on raids, we would tune in BBC and a station in Boston to hear them give their impressions. Very, very good, too."

The real show of the American occupation of Berlin was to take place on July 3, when the Second Armored Division was set to roll up the highway to the German capital. The hope was for an entrance in full military pomp, and the correspondents accompanying the column were instructed to stay in line. A preliminary reconnaissance of the Mulde River bridge, about which both Generals Parks and John W. "Pee-Wee" Collier, the Second's new commander, had misgivings, indicated it would not be strong enough to take the division's heavy equipment. It was the American wish to put in a floating ponton span, but the Russians resisted this as a reflection on their bridge-building ability. When the division did start across, about half of the first battalion made it when the Russians suddenly became worried, closed the bridge, and said it could not be used. Collier came raging into Berlin and confronted Parks in Babelsberg, just as he was concluding a meeting with a Russian major general representing Marshal Zhukov. Collier said his whole column was held up and that the Russians would let him neither use the bridge nor construct one of his own. It was nine o'clock at night, and Parks turned to the Russian general asking him if he could issue orders in Zhukov's name. He said he could, whereupon Parks pressed him to issue an order permitting the use of another bridge farther south. The Russian said he'd telegraph, but he was dealing with two determined Americans who were straining to hold their tempers. "You go with General Collier," said Parks firmly, helping usher him to the car, "and issue the orders in person." The Russian, not too happy, went along. His orders permitted the Second Armored to come on, but it had to make a 90-mile detour to get to the alternate bridge.

This broke the entry into Berlin into bits and pieces, not at all the formidable display desired, nor an entrance worthy of this great organization which had hammer-and-tonged its way through Africa and Europe. The correspondents forsook the column finally and came roaring in, following the markings of the press camp. They ran hither and yon, looking for the pick of houses and beds. The press wanted to know immediately if the U. S. and Great Britain had actually taken over their sectors from the Russians. Colonel Howley said they had, then had to take it back, because a ceremony for that very purpose was scheduled at the old Kaiser Wilhelm Kadettenschule, renamed the Adolf Hitler Barracks, on the Fourth of July. The Red flag was to come down, the U. S. flag go up. General Bradley would be there to make the acknowledgment to this gesture in which Marshal Zhukov was to participate. The military formation was to be a square U, the Russian Berlin Guards battalion, led by Major Vassily Demchenko,[1] on the left, and an honor battery of Second Armored's 90-mm. guns on the right, with a reviewing stand of notables at the bottom of the U.

---

[1] Major Demchenko was no casual choice to head this unit, nor were his men carelessly selected. The soldiers had to be six feet tall, had to have fought from Stalingrad to Berlin. Major Demchenko was the first man to cross the Dnieper River as the Germans were driven over it in retreat.

As the troops lined up that day, there was a busy Russian colonel on hand, with an interpreter constantly at his elbow. Five minutes before the ceremony, he called a council. He wanted to talk order of the ritual. Troops would be first called to attention. The reviewing party would take its place. The Russians would render honors to the Americans. It would be returned by the Americans in kind. The Russian representative would make a speech, which would be interpreted. The American commander would make his, which would be translated. Then the Russian national anthem, the American national anthem, and the salvo from the 90-mm. guns.

"But one thing we insist on," said the Russian colonel, "and that is the matter of the flag. The flag of the Soviet Union will not be lowered."

"It was our understanding," said the American interpreter, "that the Soviet flag comes down when the American flag goes up signaling the American assumption of occupation of this sector. . . ."

The Russian shook his head. "This ceremony has nothing to do with the occupation," he said blandly. "We Russians are only joining the celebration of the American holiday of Independence."

"You must lower the Russian flag," insisted the interpreter, "so it is known that this is the American zone."

"We will not lower the Russian flag while the Germans watch," the colonel said firmly.

"We took down our flag in Halle and in Magdeburg and many other places to make way for our Allies in the war according to the terms of our agreements on occupation boundaries. . . ."

"The flag of the Soviet Union stays up," said the colonel, and walked away.

Zhukov had sent in the Berlin Guards battalion as a gesture to General Bradley, but he sent only a brigadier general to represent him. The American members of the reviewing stand went through the ceremony with set faces, and the bulk of the press had filed the story in advance. To the world, then, it appeared that the American possession of its corner of Berlin was complete, but it was twelve full argumentative days before that statement was really true.

The Press Club of Berlin

Number 11 Sven-Hedin Strasse was a fairly spacious house set in equally roomy grounds on a shady byway of fashionable, suburban Zehlendorf. After my memorable clash with the Soviet Commandant, it had sentimental as well as practical value for me, if I could only hold on to it. When the Russians gave it up, and the Second Armored Division swarmed into Berlin, the most dangerous threats came from friendly quarters. High-ranking officers were coming to Berlin in droves, all of them looking for suitable places to live. Zehlendorf and Wannsee, the homes of the rich, were the most attractive hunting grounds, and the fact that number 11 Sven-Hedin Strasse had been good enough to attract the Russian Commandant had me worried. Steps would have to be taken to keep it squirreled away. Quietly, a crew of German laborers was recruited. Working behind the hedges and after hours, they were able to produce excellent and effective camouflage. Whole panes of glass were removed from the windows leaving only the jagged and broken ones and the debris of shattered glass on the floors. All of the cracked wallpaper was pulled loose to hang in tatters. Plumbing connections in bathtubs and sinks were tampered with to provide leaks and drips. Broken furniture was left on the bare floors, while good household appurtenances were carted off to storage. The sorriest of the draperies were left dangling askew, giving the whole house a haunted look.

This protective activity was well-timed. In all, eighteen generals drove up to the gate, ready to grab it for a Berlin home. Upon being

introduced to its plumbing horrors, its stenches, and its repair problems, each of them shook his head and went on. Finally, when there
was a chance to talk about it after more serious business had been
dealt with, General Parks approved my plans for use of the property
and put his own freeze on it.

A message came from Paris that Marlene Dietrich had orders permitting her to come to Berlin and that she would be landing around
noon one day. Hastily rounding up two military photographers [1] and
a jeep, we went to pick up Frau von Loesch and take her to Templehof
field. The old lady was beside herself with excitement, mostly because
Marlene was coming, but partly from the scene in her neighborhood
when the American jeep and soldiers came to get her. Making arrangements with the soldier who would park the plane, I placed Frau von
Loesch alone on the vast concrete apron, a slight, tired, expectant
figure who could hardly believe her famous daughter was in the aircraft slowly taxiing up. When the door swung open, Marlene, in her
famous USO uniform, looked out and waved, then dashed down
the steps, transformed from glamour girl extraordinary to long-lost
daughter. The hundreds of USO shows along the fronts of the world,
and the hundreds of times that Marlene had said, ". . . if you get to
Berlin, ask for Frau von Loesch," had produced this reunion at last.

As the Potsdam Conference drew closer, General Parks opened his
mail one morning and found that the Frankfurt courier had brought
him a carefully boxed American flag. Along with it came a set of
instructions. It was the flag which had been flying over the Capitol
the day Pearl Harbor was attacked. Through the flair for history
possessed by Congressman Maury Maverick, of Texas, the flag had
been removed after a resolution was passed by Congress that some day
it was to be flown in victory over each of the defeated Axis capitals.
General Mark Wayne Clark, the Fifth Army commander, had already
seen it through its ceremonial unfurling in Rome months before. Now
the old flag was on General Parks's desk in Berlin. "Got any ideas
as to the right occasion, or location?" he asked me. It seemed likely
to us both that the significance of the event would not be lost on
President Truman, and it was decided to postpone arrangements until

---

[1] I had already assigned these two Army cameramen to Billy Wilder, the
Paramount director-writer, who was shooting Berlin scenes for reconstruction
in Hollywood. Forming up in his mind then was *A Foreign Affair* (Paramount)
to star Jean Arthur, John Lund—and Marlene Dietrich.

he arrived, and then ask him if he would not want to be the means of focusing attention of the world press on this symbolic flag-raising. General Parks put the flag into his safe, saying he would like to see the President raise it in the forecourt of German anti-aircraft headquarters, now destined to be the Office of Military Government, U.S. (OMGUS).

Percy Knauth of *Life,* four days ahead of the Big Three arrivals, asked for some research help. "Any international conference," he said, "particularly one such as this, is bound to make great demands on the organizers to think of all the odd items which must be brought in. These statistical monstrosities have the makings of good side-bar features. I wonder if you could get up a handout for us listing all the things in way of food, beverage, care and entertainment of the delegations and staffs?" Captain Ross Evans was given the project, and a monumental one it was. It took a day and a half to complete it, but he finally brought it in, reading in order and in part: "30 vacuum cleaners, 20 lawn mowers, 100 bedside lamps, 3,000 linen sheets, 150 bottles of button polish, 500 ashtrays, 250 corkscrews, 250 bottle openers, 3,000 rolls of toilet paper, 20 electric refrigerators, 100 wastebaskets, 125 reams of writing paper, 250 ice bowls...." It went on and on, a shower of odd bits and pieces.

As this was being put on stencils for mimeograph, Lt. Col. Jack Redding once again had to remind the correspondents emphatically that there was no hope of entry into the Big Three compound, nor would any member of the official delegations come out to brief them. They could not even watch the arrivals at Gatow airfield, nor would they get any more information than the delegations chose to pass out after each day's proceedings. He could not even be sure there would be anything of this nature until we met the Presidential press secretary, Charles Ross. This won Redding yet another citation on his unpopularity plaque with the press corps, but such were the facts of life.

Our statistical release, with the help of a stencil-cutter's mistake, set the correspondents off in full chorus. When the typist came to the "250 ice bowls," he made an ever-so-slight miscue and hit the letter "m" lightly ahead of the word "ice." As his copy was being proofed, the reader was paying no attention to the original, but was only hastily reading through the stencil itself as he faced the light. The "m" showed through just enough for him to catch it. He mused a bit, still not referring to the original: "Mice bowls? Mice bowls? Hell, that's not right, it should be mouse bowls." He put this down, the correction fluid was applied, and dutifully typed in its place was "250 mouse bowls." The press corps, which might have started caustically with the bottle openers and corkscrews, skipped these and brought collective scorn to bear on the "250 mouse bowls." Some of their stories suggested that the entertainment evidently included a "circus of white mice" and went on to say it was no wonder the world press was denied Potsdam if such things were going on while the peace and future of the world were supposedly being decided.

This was the mood of the more than 100 correspondents of many nations on hand. They were all restricted to Berlin as Redding and I drew our own passes, okayed by the Big Three powers, allowing us to be on Gatow airfield for the welcoming ceremonies. Redding had the primary task of getting to Charles Ross, while I was assigned to pick up names, color, anecdotes and incidents which could be relayed to the press.

There was a rumor that President Truman wanted full and free coverage of the Big Three, but that he was bound by agreements to use official communiqués as the only avenue of news. This rumor, came close on the heels of the July Fourth debacle which the Americans had thought would mark their taking over of the occupation sector, but which the Russians had cunningly chosen to celebrate as our "Independence Day" in order to avoid hauling down their flag. The press also knew that the commanders of all units in the Second Armored Division, soon after they arrived, had been instructed to keep their guns loaded, their equipment under guard, and not to allow any Russian soldiers to crawl around tanks or big weapons or take any pictures of them at close range. The alternative was to shoot—and shoot to kill. The Second Armored had a well-established reputation for being efficient at that sort of thing, too.

This was a long two months after V-E Day, and slowly but steadily everyone's eyes were opening to the fact that the Russians were not only reluctant to see us in Berlin, but would overlook no chance to embarrass us. It had been fine for us to honor our agreements by giving up hundreds of square miles we had fought for and won east and west of the Elbe, but a few square blocks of Berlin were another matter. The press was in a mood to take off on this, and especially now that it was believed Truman's desire for a free press was being hamstrung by Stalin. Redding asked me, during this week before the conference, to lay on every conceivable kind of press meeting to keep hands from being too idle. I filled the pressroom rostrum with specialists on every topic from "art objects" to "Zehlendorf" and with intelligence officers and medics to talk on problems of Berlin. It was almost like old times when Tanya Long (Mrs. Ray Daniel), *New York Times,* took the medical officer apart for "shortage of screens to keep out the flies from the war correspondents' mess hall." Each of these talks merely stalled the press long enough to write a feature, then tempers flared up again.

When Redding and I arrived at Gatow at noon, July 15, the old airfield was a riot of color, and the flags were whipping in the slight breeze. The sun was bright and around Gatow were fields of waving, unharvested grain. The honor guards of British and American troops were there, temporarily at ease. There was another kind of guard around Gatow, too, symptomatic of things to come. Nowhere to be seen, but hidden in the high grass and grain at the edges of the airstrip, were three circles of Red Army soldiers. This may not have been the first appearance of the Iron Curtain, but several of the press from the West who tried to use enterprise and ingenuity to slip into this international circus ran up against these formidable gatekeepers.

With an election imminent, Churchill and Clement Attlee made of the British Lion a two-headed representation at Potsdam. Churchill was still the Prime Minister, and Attlee leader of His Majesty's loyal opposition, but the election made it desirable for both to sit at the conference table until results were known. The familiar, imperturbable Churchill went through the honor-guard inspection as soon as his plane landed and heard "God Save The King." The music faded as his car drove off. With him rode the great weight of an international reputation, a wartime phenomenon which made a resounding thump on the drum in contrast to the quiet man who was to take over leadership of the British people.

President Truman's plane was the seventh to land. By this time, the pattern of greeting was well established. To the fore each time came a hard knot of Russians, dressed in the pearl gray of their diplomatic corps. The leader of the delegation was a sharp-faced, strong-looking man, with hair that matched his uniform and an animated manner of talking. The men who hovered around him were of greater stature than he. One of them walked always on his right and acted as interpreter. For purposes of filling in my notes, it was necessary to have the name of this Soviet Union gladhander. Taking the time between planes, which were coming in fifteen minutes apart, I stepped up to the group, now standing in a circle to the side some distance away from the other nationals. "Could you tell me," I asked the interpreter, "the name of the head of your delegation?"

He spoke sharply in Russian. Simultaneously, two of the guards fell out and came up behind me on either side. The one on my left suddenly had my forearm at his neck, the point of my elbow back over his shoulder and my arm folded so tightly it could not be moved. On my right, a great weight descended on the holster which held my gun, and my right arm was across his body in a hard grip. There was an unmistakable pressure over my left kidney, and the interpreter, his chest against mine, sighted his gimlet eyes. His English was icy. "Why do you want to know?" he asked. The man I had sought information about was walking rapidly away, tagged by the other two bodyguards. It was all done so smoothly that even the closest onlookers were undisturbed. To them we only looked chummy. "I'm here to get information for the Allied press. It would be incomplete without the name of the leader of the Russian delegation."

The speed with which the protective web had been thrown about the delegation head proved the efficiency and wariness of the Soviet police, and their inability to trust anyone. There was, of course, no evidence of intrigue at Gatow. Every person there had been screened by every security test of three nations, including the Soviet Union, yet its representatives left nothing to chance. The interpreter barked again. The pressures melted away. My wrist was released, and my left arm slid off the Muscovite shoulder. The two who had helped pinion me departed rapidly. The manner of the interpreter now changed, and he smiled disarmingly. "He is V-y-s-h-i-n-s-k-y," he spelled it out, "Andrei Y. Vyshinsky, first deputy commissar for foreign affairs of the Soviet Union." He turned without another word and rejoined the delegation. He explained it all volubly to Vyshinsky, who nodded his head, watched me, and rubbed his chin reflectively. Then he, too, smiled—possibly with relief after the scare I had given him. His playmates had given me one, too.

President Truman's plane was now on the runway, and the honor guard of the Second Armored Division was lining up. Vyshinsky smoothed his coat and started slowly for the "Sacred Cow," the presidential aircraft. As the props stopped, the ramp was rolled up and President Truman stuck his head out of the door to wave. He had been in the presidential role long enough to know photographers would be set for, and need, that shot. Then the man from Independence came jauntily down to cross another threshold of the tumultuous era into which he had been catapulted. My business now was with Charles Ross. Redding was stationed with the honor guard to catch Ross there if I failed. The presidential party would have to halt there. More than 100 members of a disgruntled press, the pipeline to millions around the world, were awaiting what we could arrange, and they waited anxiously, fretfully in Zehlendorf. Ross, as if he knew what was coming, stuck his head out the door and looked around, in no hurry to descend. "Mr. Ross!" He looked down, then, as if in resignation, began his descent. President Truman's car was coming up. "Sir, there isn't much time here, but Colonel Redding and I are from the press camp in Berlin, where, as you probably know, there is great pressure to be included in the conference coverage. Could we meet you later somewhere?"

"Yes, of course," he agreed. "I understand I'm staying in the house with the President. Can you come there as soon as possible?" He headed for his seat in the motorcade. President Truman would not review the guard from his car, so stopped the procession and got down. This gave us a few minutes for Redding to meet Ross and confirm 5 P.M. that day as the best time for our conclave. Meantime, the Secret Service was having trouble with *Pravda* photographers, who, like the U. S. Signal Corps cameramen, were on Gatow with official sanction. *Pravda*'s men felt licensed to run through the honor guard ranks and squat at the feet of the President. The Secret Service collared two of them, then seat-of-the-pantsed them off, even though they shrieked that they were the privileged of *Pravda*. "I don't care if you're from the *Police Gazette,*" said the Secret Service husky. "Stand back!" And they stood back.

After a preliminary briefing of the press at Zehlendorf, Redding and I, to the tune of violent protests, returned to Babelsberg. The guards sent us to the third-floor office assigned to Ross. General Parks was paying his respects to the President and talking about the old flag, among other things. President Truman liked the idea of the OMGUS site, and was delighted to have the opportunity saved for him. Ross was in an uneasy position. He had a White House pool [2] which had been covering the presidential trip and his inclination was to let this group cover the conference but he realized their presence put them in a privileged position. He confirmed that the President favored opening the conference to the world press, but that international commitments would not permit it. Ross did not wish to journey into Berlin each day to see the press either, as he did not want any charges of spoon-feeding leveled at the U.S. delegation. The final agreement was that he would give a daily diary to Redding and keep him posted in advance on all scheduled movements of the President. This was a gesture to the Zehlendorf press corps, but nobody was foolish enough to believe it would be received with complete satisfaction. As Redding set off to wrestle with this one, I had my office working hard on stories and pictures for the home-town newspapers and radio stations of the U. S. This material was not big enough for the attention of the correspondents, but it was important to the 4,000 soldiers involved in the housekeeping for the American Big Three delegation. We did not want them to go unmentioned, and our mill ground out 4,737 stories and 1,421 pictures during the period of the talks. Back in America, judging from the play these received, not only were the potentates important at Potsdam, so were those who shaved a face, drove a truck, ran a switchboard, acted as a military policeman or guard, and, yes, even the man who burned rubbish and handled the garbage disposal.

President Truman made two important forays from the compound, one to inspect the Second Armored Division and have a look at the destruction of Berlin, and the other to raise the Pearl Harbor flag. The windup of the first tour took him to the shadow of Hitler's *Reichskanzlei* balcony, but much to the chagrin of the photographers, he would not walk around among the ruins to provide them with pictures. It remained for Churchill to do this, the old warrior stepping smartly around the whole area with the air of a man walking in a pigsty. Churchill's sense of drama never left him, and in what time there remained to him he was busily putting period to many a wartime paragraph. The old American flag was raised with President Truman, Secretary of War Henry Stimson and Generals Eisenhower and Patton

[2] The White House pool included Merriman Smith, UP; Ernest B. Vaccaro, AP; Robert Nixon, INS; Morgan Beatty, NBC; and Hugo Johnson and Al O'Eth of Paramount Newsreel.

in attendance. Truman used the occasion to add weight to the Big Three talks by disclaiming any desire on the part of the U. S. to extract territorial acquisitions from the vanquished. The flag,[3] as a result, became an even brighter badge of American ideals in the face of the international depredations of the Soviet Union.

Most interesting of the exchange visits of the heads of the delegations before the conference was the initial meeting of Truman and Stalin, to take place at Truman's residence. As the note-taker for briefing purposes, I was with the Secret Service at the front gate and had permission to move around to the rear when the pictures were taken on the veranda there. A half hour before Stalin's arrival, eight Russians in Red Army uniform came casually but fully armed down the street. Two of them went to the entrance and two to the exit to join the Secret Service. The other four went across the lawn to the rear. It was all done quietly, but the Secret Service man standing with me said he wouldn't bet "more than a plugged nickel that they were really soldiers." A quarter hour before time, the street became deathly still. All life and movement disappeared from it. The way was now clear. Suddenly, more than a block away, a huge, lumbering black Zis hove in sight. It rode its tires so heavily that the body must have been bristling with armor plate, and the glass of the windows was so thick it was grayish green. In front with the driver were two hard-faced men, and in what appeared to be the jump-seat section, his profile showing through the dense glass, sat Stalin, apparently alone. The Secret Service man said, "If your nose starts to run now, let it. Don't reach toward your hip pocket for a handkerchief. *We* are covered!" The car swung quietly into the semicircular drive. It was 11 A.M., July 17, the time for the first handshake of the little Georgian bandit who had grown so powerful, with the man who had come a long way from Missouri. At 5 P.M. that day, they were to sit down as heads of states to raise the curtain of Potsdam's conference.

President Truman was proposed as the presiding officer that afternoon. He urged four main agenda items: the formation of a Council

[3] In the spring of 1948, Maury Maverick noted that the banner had not yet returned to the Capitol. The White House directed that General Parks, then Chief of Public Information, take care of it, and as his special projects officer, it fell to me. That spring, carried by an honor guard made up of all the services, the old flag was borne to the Capitol steps where it was received by Senator Arthur Vandenberg and Congressman Joe Martin, who carefully took it inside where it is today enclosed in a glass case—surrounded by all our history.

of Foreign Ministers to get on with the peace treaties; the Allied Control Council to function at once handling Germany's government;
free elections as soon as possible for former satellite and occupied
countries; a quick peace treaty with Italy. Stalin put more into the
hopper than that—such as cutting up the German merchant fleet and
navy, reparations in general, trusteeships for the Soviet Union under
the United Nations charter, relations with the various Axis satellite
states, the Franco regime in Spain, the problems of Lebanon and
Syria and the Polish question. The conference was on at last, and
the arrangements between Ross and Redding provided at least a
limited pipeline to it.

Nobody knew for sure when he got there, or how he came, but
Stalin was always first each day at the Cecilienhof table. This caused
a bit of unrecorded drama. President Truman had included in his
Secret Service retinue his old first sergeant, Fred Canfil, then the
U.S. Marshal in Kansas City, Missouri. Canfil always led the Truman
procession, charging into the room like the first sergeant he never got
over being. At first sight of him each day, Stalin would rise and give
him a flourishing salute, which Canfil never failed to return with equal
flair. Several days had gone by before Canfil tumbled to the reason.
Stalin's henchmen, of course, had gone over the U.S. delegation list
to identify each of the Americans. Canfil was noted as "a U.S.
Marshal." Seeing that Canfil was a trusted Truman companion with
a front-running position in the President's protective arsenal, Stalin
fixed Canfil in his mind as a prairie-land equivalent of his own
Lavrenti P. Beria, who also ranked as a marshal. As such Stalin gave
Canfil full marks and honors. "This was probably the first time Stalin
ever saluted a sergeant," said Canfil, "and about time, too, considering
all the Communist gab about the common people."

The ultimatum to Japan and the final Potsdam communiqué put
an end to the discussions and the press ordeal in Berlin. Lieutenant
George Fuller read the communiqué for all four of the American radio
networks, after which he was followed by the individual commentators
for those networks—Roy Porter, NBC; Richard Hotellet, CBS; Donald
Coe, ABC; and Arthur Mann, Mutual. The affairs of the press in
Berlin now moved swiftly back to normal. The last of the wartime
evidences of alliance, the integrated press facilities, began to vanish.
British correspondents dropped out of the Zehlendorf area and trooped

over into the British zone, taking up quarters in the Hotel Am Zoo. The French press found housing in its own section, a sliver of land between the British and Russian sectors along the northern perimeter. Zehlendorf became a truly American quarter.

Now that the Potsdam conference had ended, the four nations in Berlin were expected to make a Victory March. Marshal Zhukov presided at a meeting of all the troop commanders in his imposing house. He was of considerably greater stature than a Berlin troop commander, but he was the monitor of every propaganda achievement which could be derived from Berlin. After the usual amenities, talk turned to the Victory March, and Zhukov made a sudden, flat statement, "The Russians will march first since they did the most to win the war." This was a stunner around the table for all but Maj. Gen. James M. Gavin, whose Eighty-second Airborne Division had recently replaced the Second Armored as the Berlin occupation force. He was polite, but there was no doubt about the fiber of his voice. "Marshal Zhukov," he said slowly, so the interpreter could pass every word, "I don't care anything about the order in which we march, but I will not be a party to fixing precedence in line by contribution to the winning of the war. Every nation fought its hardest and best. When I think of Berlin, I look back of me and see a long line of white crosses down through Italy and across Africa. Don't you tell *me* that you alone captured Berlin." Intransigence can work both ways. Marshal Zhukov had met an ex-newsboy from Mount Carmel, Pennsylvania, who used to fight much bigger boys to keep his corner. But keep it, he did—then and now.[4]

---

[4] The parade arrangements hassle started in a regular meeting of the Kommandatura, the four-power ruling body of Berlin, when the Russian member, Maj. Gen. Garbatkov stated that Zhukov had instructed him that the Russians or the Americans would march first. The British and French were quite naturally upset. This was one of the first overt dividing actions the Russians took at a high level in Berlin. Gavin tried counterproposals, such as drawing lots for place in line or marching in alphabetical order. Garbatkov demurred, and by obvious prearrangement took the whole group to Zhukov. The Russians did not want to follow the British, and were contemptuous of the French. The Marshal indicated places at a bare table and opened coldly by stating that the Russians had done such great things to get to Berlin, the rest of the Allies should respect this. It was then that Gavin delivered his thrust, adding that he would be willing to have the Eighty-second bring up the rear since no one would dare to say that "America had done the *least* to win the war." Russian generals had great respect for the Eighty-second from time of first contact when Corporal Dan Bost, of Detroit, Michigan, did his "bat man" free-fall act for Lt. Gen.

While all these bigger things were going on, my German labor crew had been reassembled and the nightmare interior of number 11 Sven-Hedin Strasse was being repaired. Wallpaper was replaced or repasted, the plumbing came under the clank of tools, and the broken furniture was burned in the back yard. Walther Funk's old sideboard buffet was pulled from the wall and relocated in what was to become the most popular part of the house—the bar. Requisitioning more furniture had been going on at the expense of Nazis who had lived richly in Zehlendorf. After our trucks had gone the rounds, number 11 Sven-Hedin Strasse even included a complete billiard room with a genuine Corot painting on the wall.

On the night of August 10, 1945, number 11 became the Press Club of Berlin. As it opened, the radio was crackling with bulletins from the other side of the world telling of Japan's inexorable movement toward capitulation. My membership card was number 1 in this unique establishment, which no one complained about too much, since the first entry into the place had been made by me—with a gun in my back. Some of the joiners thought this latter factor symbolic, because the membership was $25 a head and it was extracted from every war correspondent lured there just as he entered the door and before he had a chance to wet his palate or to look the prospects over. The Press Club of Berlin evolved from wartime experience of the military with correspondents. There were charges thrown at it of "highway robbery," "high-handedness" and "chicanery," but its intentions were entirely straightforward.

While a press camp had been the answer for an Army on the move, it was clear that it would now be wise to have a club-like arrangement, and General Parks had had this in mind when he put the real-estate freeze on the place. In a club of his own, the war correspondent could live fairly well at small fee.

But mere comfort of surroundings was never enough to keep the press happy. Any equivalent of their town pump, or popular meeting place to swap gossip, must have a bar, and the better it is kept stocked, the more popular the place. Mother Hubbard's cupboard was well-equipped by comparison to number 11 after two months of the

---

Tchepourkin, the famous Cossack general, right after the juncture of the forces. Dan held his free fall until below 300 feet. General Tchepourkin was so enraptured, he ran out to Bost, kissed him on both cheeks, and gave him his own Russian Guards Medal.

Russian commandant's residence, and the supply roads had been carrying only high-priority items for the Big Three. Berlin's alcoholic stores were scarce at best, and even to think of opening the Club without ample drink was to doom the enterprise to disaster. As the Big Three conference packed up, it seemed to us a good time to open the Press Club. The press corps needed some distraction, with all the news emphasis swinging to the Far East and leaving them marooned. The solution of our most acute problem came unexpectedly, when a friend who knew our plight called to say he had the task of disposing of all conference supplies in excess of requirements. "I've got lots of liquor," he said, "all first-class stuff. I either have to turn it over to the Berlin District supply office, or show withdrawal slips and money to cover. I have until August 17 to clear the accounts."

"How much money to take the liquor off your hands?"

He consulted his records. "If you take it all, it will cost about $3,200."

"What kind of names have to be on the vouchers?"

"High rank," he said, "and from the Big Three roster of Americans, but don't let that worry you. They'll all be gone when we settle up. The important thing is that I have $3,200 in hand August 17."

"You'll have it."

A covered truck was sent to Babelsberg immediately. It returned just as rapidly with a cellarful of aged, bonded and vintage liquors which would have gladdened the heart of the most finicky.

"What names did you draw this with?"

"He wanted rank," said the driver, Staff Sergeant George Trapper, an enterprising Californian who made the statement offhandedly, "so I drew half of this on a voucher signed George C. Marshall and for the rest of it I signed Harry S. Truman." There was a gasp at this announcement. It was now *extremely* imperative that we have the $3,200 on August 17.

Exactly forty-one days (to the hour) after the Russian had prodded me into number 11, the Press Club of Berlin opened its doors, with music, names, a basement of booze and promise of an interesting future. Jack Benny, Ingrid Bergman, Martha Tilton and Larry Adler, in Berlin with their USO show, were the best-known guests at the premiere. General Parks and General Gavin were cosigners on all the membership cards. Louis Lochner sat talking in a corner with Quentin Reynolds. The president of the Hearst Corporation, R. E.

"Dick" Berlin, and his associate, John W. Hanes, were there taking a break from their chase after the story of the Russian "acquisition" of the occupation money plates. Before detection the Russians had flooded the currency controls of the Western Allies in excess of agreed quotas, running up a potential $165,000,000 loss on the American taxpayer, had it all come up for redemption at Army finance offices.[5]

A German band [6] played one song over and over, a sunny tune called "Symphony," and it almost became the theme song of the Press Club. The piano player was Norbert Schultz, but his most famous composition went unplayed and unsung. Schultz had written the music to Hans Liep's lyrics of "Lili Marlene." He sold it originally for $65 to Apollo-Verlag, a music-publishing firm in Berlin, and a recording of it lay among the cobwebs of a Belgrade radio station until, after Yugoslavia's invasion by the Germans, the station was beamed to Rommel's Afrika Corps. Played as a filler one night, it attained phenomenal popularity. Montgomery's desert troops became even fonder of it than the Germans. From there, it went the rounds of the nations, and "Lili," who had first waited for Fritz at the barracks gate, was soon taking up with Tommy and GI Joe and then some. By the time Schultz put his fingers on the keyboard that night "Lili Marlene" was a money-making captive of the U. S. Alien Property Custodian and performance fees had credited $13,000 against Germany's war debts.[7]

[5] Says General Parks: "Actually the taxpayers did not lose anything because we took all the Russian marks which we had to redeem, bought German products with them and sold them in the PX to the soldiers of the American Occupation so that we could get our money back. This plate deal was a highly controversial one. I discovered it when my finance officer in Berlin came to me and told me he had sent back (to the U. S.) about $200,000 more than he had paid out to troops in the past month, the reason being that our men were selling the Russians watches, cameras, cigarettes and fountain pens for Russian-made marks. I immediately put an embargo on the amounts they could send home and reported the matter to SHAEF for correction because every plane coming into Berlin at the time was bringing watches, etc., to sell. . . . It came out that the plates had been given to the Russians over the protest of the Army, decision being made on a very high level." The Soviets piled tubs of this money on billet tables and allowed each Red Army soldier 4,000 marks when going on pass, each officer, 8,000. The exchange rate was pegged at ten cents to the mark.

[6] An American band jazzed it up on other nights, a crew from the Eighty-second's 505th Parachute Infantry which called itself "The Five Malfunctions," a combo which would have made Louis Armstrong lay back his ears and put down his horn.

[7] Ten years later, "Lili Marlene" had brought in a total of $40,000.

The head of the German civilian staff at the club was a prominent actor, with some American experience, Werner Fütterer. As Werner Bateman, he had played opposite Helen Hayes in her New York run of *Victoria Regina*. Returning home to Germany in 1939, Fütterer made propaganda movies for Dr. Josef Goebbels, because of which he did not remain long at the Press Club, but he was very much there at the opening. Two German film actresses came that night hoping for employment connections, Wini Markus and Ilse Werner. Ilse professed not to have been in the propaganda mill, but she was later trapped by an old German newsreel which showed her signing autographs for Wehrmacht troops in Paris. Throughout the evening, a hopeful strain was injected by the radio. The Japanese were seemingly responding rapidly to the Big Three ultimatum. But, in spite of all the festivity, there was a small, persistent undercurrent of uneasiness, with money as the root of it.

The membership tariff and the arbitrary rule of 100 per cent profit on all drinks raised first a hubbub and then a roar. All this was dictated by the August 17 day of reckoning, a week away, but to admit this in public might well have brought down the roof, as it certainly would have made a good story. We could only plead for patience and understanding—without offering any explanation. The black market was in full flower. The cigarette economy was being born with a flourish and at $100 a carton. A Mickey Mouse watch would bring $700 in Russian-printed occupation scrip. In this atmosphere of high finance, of barter and trade, nobody wanted to be taken for top bar prices, even if the drinks were good. But the first night's operation netted from all sources $1,817.00, and that $3,200 looked less far away.

Misgivings born of the complaints caused me early on that second day to requisition a lieutenant with some business experience, and Second Lieutenant Raymond Baile, who had once managed a chicken hatchery in Wichita, Kansas, joined us to get some quick, concise instructions. "There'll be all kinds of experts around here on how to mix a drink and run a floor show," I told him, "but you're here for one thing only. We are operating without an officers' club constitution and may have to do this for some time. We are not a legally constituted military club, but I want those records kept in such a way that they are unchallengeable. You tag every incoming nickel and every outgoing one."

This act later saved the necks of all of us. When Baile was told that we were backed only by a nod of approval from the Berlin District commander, had nothing in writing because of our haste in getting under way, and had further compounded this by the long gamble of signing vouchers with the names of the President of the United States and the Chief of Staff of its Army, he shuddered a little, but he took up the task as directed. On the morning of August 15, $3,200 was turned over to the Big Three accounting officer and those damning tabs were torn up like a fraternity-house mortgage. The books were clear, the cellar still held half the liquor, and we now had a quota system to stretch it out. Nightly we set out a bottle of each variety. Everyone drank his favorite early in the evening, then moved down the row until the supply for the night was exhausted. The liquors went first, the liqueurs last, a reverse order which occasionally produced stunning results. It is highly unlikely that former President Truman or General Marshall will ever be accused, but this is to set the records straight: *They* did not consume $3,200 worth of liquor at the Big Three talks, but the Berlin press did in their names! The 100 per cent markup stayed on, in order to produce a revolving fund with which we could operate in the future. Moaning about money clouded the fact that the Press Club of Berlin was maturing into the candle flame of Zehlendorf night life. It had music, lights and a natural, unrestrained gaiety in bold relief to the morbid atmosphere of the shattered metropolis. The people who frequented it were close to the day's news, and their talk was always lively and interesting.

The first meeting of the Allied Control Council took place in Berlin, and General Eisenhower chose to hold his press conference afterward at number 11. He came with Lt. Gen. Lucius Clay, military governor for the U. S. zone of Germany, and his wartime chief of staff, Lt. Gen. Walter B. Smith. The meeting had finished on a jocular note, at Montgomery's expense, when General Eisenhower, who had presided and had seen every motion passed by unanimous vote, said it was too bad that the whole meeting could not proceed along co-operative lines. He had wanted to propose before adjournment something which he felt would be heartily approved by everyone but the British member of the Council. Eisenhower's expression was bleak, French General Pierre Koenig's quizzical, Marshal Georgi Zhukov's puzzled, and Field Marshal Montgomery appeared almost to bridle. Pausing a moment,

General Eisenhower then said, "Let's go into the next room and have a drink."

With a smile still on his face when he drove up to the gate at number 11, Eisenhower looked over the grounds appraisingly. "Some foxhole, this," he remarked, then went in and faced the press. Afterwards he stayed around for a short ceremony in which I gave him a life membership in the club, saying, "Any time you come in the future, it's a signal that the drinks are on the house."

"Judging from what they normally cost us," Hank Wales remarked later, "the joint can sure as hell afford it."

A move for sterner measures in dealing with Nazi malefactors, especially those still in positions of governmental responsibility, began to get press attention. A letter from General Eisenhower, dated September 12, was delivered to Generals George S. Patton, Jr., and Geoffrey P. Keys. It dealt with the eradication of all vestiges of National Socialism from their sectors, saying in part, "Make particularly sure that all your subordinate commanders realize the discussional stage of this question is long past, and that any expressed opposition to the faithful execution of the order cannot be regarded leniently by me." Some of the old war correspondents, now rooting through the rubble of the Reich for political stories, felt that General Patton's stewardship in Bavaria might be out of line with the occupation statutes and the wishes of General Eisenhower. Among them were Carl Levin, *New York Herald Tribune;* Ray Daniel, *New York Times;* and Edward Morgan, *Chicago Daily News.* They converged on Patton's headquarters in Bad Tölz. Patton indicated he was not excited about the controversial appointments of Bavarian Minister President Friedrich Schaeffer because "this Nazi thing is just like a Democrat-Republican election fight." He was also quoted by Levin as saying that one of the first things he (Patton) had learned in military government was that "the 'outs' were coming around saying that the 'ins' were Nazis. More than half of the German people were Nazis, and you'd be in a hell of a fix if you tried to remove all party members. We've got to compromise with the devil a little bit to get things going before trying to get a simon-pure system."

When Levin's story was published on the morning of September 23, the reverberations were immediate and noisy. The *Stars and Stripes* was printed in the *Herald Tribune*'s Paris building, and had easy access to the story, so gave it a ride, too. This made the Patton incident jump to the attention of officialdom even before a playback from the U. S. The papers charged that "at least twenty Nazis were still in high positions" in the Bavarian provincial government, and there were generous implications that Patton was unfit for occupation command. On September 28, after driving to Frankfurt in answer to an urgent summons by General Eisenhower, Patton went immediately to the Supreme Commander's office and was closeted with him for two hours and a half. Both Maj. Gen. Clarence Adcock, the Eisenhower staff member for military government, and his deputy, Dr. Walter Dorn, were called into the conference. The correspondents hung around attentively. Eisenhower and Patton emerged from the session smiling and refused to comment. But seven days later the renowned combat leader was shifted from his beloved Third Army to a paper mill called Headquarters Fifteenth Army located in Bad Nauheim.

The word was passed to him on September 29, and he was ordered to take over the Fifteenth on October 7. It was a long, long way from the prankish insubordination of the WSM-NBC broadcast. There had been the famous face-slapping incident of Sicily, statements which had irked the British, and the wartime censor-stop on his comments, all of which had made him a problem child. Now, even though his battle achievements would never tarnish and would always inspire, the Patton saga was almost finished.[8]

The Press Club had a way of attracting, even manufacturing news. When Rudolph Dunbar, long-time correspondent of the Associated Negro Press, was announced as guest conductor of the Berlin Philharmonic Orchestra, it threw officers of OMGUS into a tizzy. They wanted desperately to cancel it, while most of us regarded it merely as an interesting expression of versatility among the correspondents. If

---

[8] Early in December, 1945, General Patton was injured in an automobile crash near Mannheim. He died twelve days later. In Heidelberg, his favorite song, Palestrina's "The Strife is O'er, the Battle Done" was sung over him in the Christ Protestant Episcopal church on December 23, but there was no eulogy. As German PW's were digging grave number 7,934 in Hamm cemetery, the body was placed on a special train for Luxembourg. Master Sergeant William J. Meeks, a Junction City, Kansas, Negro, was picked to drive the half-track carrying the casket to the burial ground the day before Christmas. Meeks was also the one who folded the flag which draped the coffin at the grave and reverently handed it to Mrs. Patton. Beside a Third Army private, John Pryzwara, of Detroit, who had been killed in the rolling Ardennes he had once described as "the worst tank country in the world," General George S. Patton, Jr., profane, tempestuous and colorful, was lowered to final rest. Carl Levin covered that story, too.

Dunbar's appearance were canceled by the military, on the other hand, it could quickly become something else and could provoke a minor political disaster. In the middle of the week before the concert, General Parks's driver came into the club and asked me outside. The General was parked in the shadows along the street and beckoned me into the back seat. He could not understand the reasoning behind the move to cancel when Berlin was in such a bright glare of the propaganda spotlight, and the Soviet Union was always set to make capital of any and every U. S. slip. As the boss of Berlin, he was going to let the concert go on and take the blame, if there was any. The program went ahead as scheduled, and there was no reverberation of any sort, other than favorable.

In the late fall of 1945, as the divisions which had fought in World War II were being disbanded, Army headquarters in Washington announced that only two airborne divisions would be retained in the postwar period—the Eleventh in the Far East, and the 101st. This was a shock [9] to the Eighty-second Airborne Division, formed in August, 1942, when the old Eighty-second Infantry Division had been split down the middle and one half had become the new Eighty-second, and the other the new 101st. The old Eighty-second had spawned Sergeant Alvin York and Jonathan Wainwright, hero of Corregidor, and the new one took off at a dead run to show the world its prowess. From the beginning, it had been a tug of war for prominence between the Eighty-second's resourceful commander, Maj. Gen. Matthew Ridgway, and the 101st's Maj. Gen. William C. Lee. The Eighty-second was first into battle, a full year before any other airborne

[9] The shock and funereal atmosphere which settled over the Eighty-second coincided with Marlene Dietrich's, when she was told in Paris that her mother was dying in Berlin. As soon as he could make arrangements, Bill Walton, now *Time*'s Paris bureau chief, escorted her to Berlin, and to the cemetery where her mother's coffin was already in an open grave. It had been taken there by four soldiers from the Eighty-second Airborne, who had also dug the accommodation for it. Great, yawning bomb craters were everywhere in the cemetery, the old tombstones leaning crazily or knocked down completely. Coffins blasted up from their original depths were perched at many angles, and from some of them, partially decomposed remains were protruding. The day was dull and gray, and a rain began to fall as the Lutheran service began. Marlene cried steadily. When she and Walton cast the symbolic earth on the coffin to signify the beginning of the burial, they both fled the macabre setting and never looked back. At least, Marlene had the assurance that her mother would stay buried because the war was over and no raining bombs would seek to wrench the dead from their rest.

division. The 101st lost Lee early in 1944, but was always as straight-line and orthodox as the Eighty-second was nervy and enterprising. At the Battle of the Bulge, when Sergeant Jimmy Cannon tagged the 101st "the battered bastards of Bastogne," the Eighty-second troopers were chiding them. "Why all the fuss about being surrounded?" they would ask. "How else does an airborne operation usually start? The trick is not to stay surrounded." This could and did lead to some spirited knuckling.

The decision fell almost as hard on a militant section of the press corps which was high on the Eighty-second, including William Walton, *Time,* who had jumped with the Eighty-second in Normandy; the articulate Charles Collingwood, of CBS; Martha Gellhorn, of *Collier's,* who had taken up the Eighty-second cause like a suffragette; and Judy Barden, of the *New York Sun* and NANA. Promptly from newspapers, magazines, and out of radio loud-speakers in America there came a steady stream of comment questioning the wisdom of letting the celebrated Eighty-second go down the military drain when its great record would be such an inspiration to the peacetime Army. The rooms and nooks of the Press Club of Berlin rattled with busy type-writers, and the results of this barrage appeared with ceaseless regularity in the Army headquarters. Suddenly General Jacob L. Devers reversed the decision.

General Gavin had been in England saying a diplomatic farewell to various British Lord Mayors in towns where the Eighty-second had been billeted. In late afternoon, we had taken off from London for Berlin, but the plane had been refused landing in the fogs at Tempelhof airdrome. Almost out of gas, our plane was led in by radar over the pierced-plank airstrip outside ruined Schweinfurt. Gavin wanted a call put in to Colonel Bob Wienecke, his chief of staff, to tell him we were safely down. He headed wearily for his cot, but Wienecke insisted on talking to him. When Gavin took the phone, he was a sad and disappointed general who had seen some of the finest fighting men of all time fall from Sicily to Northern Germany, and he thought their example would now repose in the dead archives —a paper cemetery more dreadful than the real ones. But a short conversation changed all this, the resurrection message having come through that day.

No sooner were we back in Berlin than Fuller, Schulberg and I were transferred to the Eighty-second, where with Sergeants Bill

Hancock, of San Leandro, California and Joe Ryan, of Johnstown, New York, plus twelve German stenographers, we began assembling a homecoming campaign for the Eighty-second which would make it hard to forget. Our goal was a packet for 1,927 radio stations and 786 brochures for newspapers over 10,000 circulation and containing in all 11,140 photos. We processed 9,137 names by home town, state and street address.

When the project was finished, the material filled thirty-six huge mailbags, which two trucks hauled away. The trucks started to move out at the same time the Eighty-second left Berlin. There was one last vindication of the press for its effort on behalf of the Eighty-second, and it came in the form of a terse message on the headquarters teletype in Reims: "The 82nd Airborne Division has been selected to make the Victory March up 5th Avenue in New York on January 12, 1946, representing all the troops of all services who fought in World War II."

But in the midst of this rousing success story, the price of whisky caught up with us. The blow fell just before I left Berlin. A letter addressed to the Commanding General, Berlin District, and signed by Ray Daniel, *New York Times,* requested an investigation of "the so-called *Press* Club of Berlin." Without warning, a board of six officers descended on the club, demanding "the books, if any," for an audit. Lieutenant Raymond Baile, who had worked unobtrusively but well in his hole-in-the-wall office, became the star of the show. The books were painstakingly checked, and, covering an operation of many weeks' duration, were found to be six cents off—in favor of the club. Shortly afterward, now that officers' clubs were being organized in Berlin, it became legitimate at last by Army order. Commenting on the investigation, one of the correspondents said: "Don't feel too badly about it. You know, if the press had been covering the incident of the adulterous woman brought before the Lord for stoning, it would have been the same. When He invited the sinless one to cast the first stone, had there been a guy there from the *Times,* he would have thrown one just to establish character." Into my records as a parting souvenir of the press when I left Berlin went an administrative reprimand for the manner of operation and financing, but into history and unquenchable memories of many went that unique institution born in the twilight of World War II—the Press Club of Berlin.

. . . WRAP-UP

Citations and Citizens

Yesterday it had been a great division. But on January 13, 1946, the Eighty-second Airborne Division was hundreds of small knots of men getting on trains bound for home. Their boots were shined as brightly as always, because an ingrained habit, like pride, is hard to break. Back of the Division were 316 days in frontline positions, or surrounded and outnumbered forward of those lines, and it had suffered 19,586 casualties for its steadfastness in the face of the enemy. The paratroopers had accumulated four Congressional Medals of Honor, 78 Distinguished Service Crosses, 894 Silver Stars, 2,478 Bronze Stars (with V for Valor on them) from the American Government, plus 91 decorations from the Netherlands, 42 from the British Empire, 74 from France, 39 from Belgium, and even 14 from the Soviet Union. Of the casualties, 2,665 were final and they stayed behind in the graveyards of Africa and Europe.

Maj. Gen. James M. Gavin, the man out front on the long walk up Fifth Avenue the day before, now looked numbly out of the window in his bare office at Camp Shanks, New York, and saw them go. Once, and it seemed like a thousand years ago though it was only 1942, I had reported to him in the sweltering 505th [1] Parachute Infan-

[1] The mascot of the 505th was a ninety-pound Boxer dog named Max, owned by Major Jim Gray of the Second Battalion. He had his own parachute, with special harness, and used to jump behind Lt. Clyde Russell, of Lincoln, Nebraska, who would yell smartly as they moved to the door: "Come on, Max!" Max always gave one bark, but the second would invariably turn into a "humph" when the opening shock hit him. The other paratroopers would talk

try headquarters at Fort Benning. He was a very serious lieutenant colonel, and he had an opening for an intelligence officer on his staff. He indicated his intention of putting me in that slot, saying he was sorry he could use none of my civilian experience. "The 505th is going to fight," he said in his low voice which masked great firmness, "and it won't need any publicity." This caused me to make a wholly facetious remark then which had now taken on an aura of supernatural insight, a statement that Gavin "might be the one to lead the victory parade someday" and that he would need a public-relations man then. There was an Irish twinkle in his eye at this absurdity, but he waved me out of the hut and off to work.

Yesterday, the Eighty-second had walked Fifth Avenue from Washington Arch to Eighty-sixth Street, and 4,000,000 of the citizens of New York turned out to watch, to cheer, and in some cases, to cry. Only twelve [2] of the original members of that Eighty-second were still around to carry on the cadence as an example for the living, and in memory of their dead. To the onlookers, there wasn't a noticeable hole in the ranks. As the public-relations officer for this spectacle, it had fallen to me to make good on that earlier lighthearted prophecy.

On this aftermath January 13, big, boisterous Lt. Col. Al Ireland, of Baltimore, Maryland; Colonel Robert Wienecke, of Glencoe, Illinois, and I stood soberly behind Gavin as he witnessed his pride and joy disintegrating into a mob of railway ticketholders. "I've got a month," he said, almost to himself. "Then we've got to start building it all back." All of us knew how hard that would be, faced as he was with postwar indifference and with fewer than 200 of yesterday's

---

to him on the way down reassuringly with "Wouldn't the girl dogs be proud of you now?" or "Ain't that a helluva first step?" and "Make a good downward pull before you hit." He made eight jumps, and the day Fox Movietone news sent Cameraman Al Waldron to shoot a sequence of him, he was changing sides of the street and was hit by a truck which broke his jaw and leg. The publicity which was carried on the injured " 'chuting canine" even brought him plastic splints from a Philadelphia specialist. He got well eventually, but never jumped again. Paratrooper recruiters used Max's story in many a plea for volunteers, saying the dog proved "it was more dangerous to walk across the road, than jump from a plane." Max evidently didn't believe it, because when the 505th loaded up with the Eighty-second for Africa, he disappeared. "Nothing dumb about that dog," said another 505er, Sergeant Jack Gavin (no relation to the General), also of Lincoln, Nebraska. Sergeant Gavin died in September, 1944, in the Netherlands airborne operation.

[2] There were more survivors, but they had gone home ahead as high-point men.

thousands having decided to return as regulars. Ireland was on the way to becoming a salesman. Wienecke was heading for his insurance agency in Chicago, and a job was waiting for me at Warner Brothers Studios in Hollywood. There was no indictment against us in Gavin's voice, even though we all had rail tickets in our pockets, too. He was only saying, with the same firmness of his earlier declaration, that "the 505th is going to fight," that he was going to remake the unit in its own image. Months later there was again an Eighty-second Airborne Division, ready to do all the things that its predecessor had.

One of the cornerstones in its reconstruction was a museum devoted to the Eighty-second's exploits. Under its roof, the long trek of the Eighty-second was mapped, its list of decorations posted, its battle actions described, and the walls were papered with clippings. There was a rule that no paratrooper fresh from jump school ever entered the division except through the magical doorway of this museum. Each new group was taken there by Gavin personally. He led them across the old battlegrounds—the Biazza ridge in Sicily, over the Salerno beaches aflame, neck deep through the inundations near the Merderet River in Normandy, to the Waal bridge of Nijmegen, and had them brace their feet before Liége in Belgium's Battle of the Bulge. He made them see the fearful, tattered remnants of Lt. Gen. von Tippelskirch's Twenty-first German Army surrendering near Ludwigslust, the triumphal arrival in Berlin, and finally, the march up Fifth Avenue. After this, he reached into the small box which held the division shoulder flashes with the double-A's (All-American) embroidered on them. Passing out one to each man, he said: "Now—*you* become a part of all this!" The effect on the fledgling paratroopers never varied. They walked out of the museum and into the future stronger, more determined, more fiercely proud than they had been when they first fell under the spell of the Eighty-second's battle-hardened past. On such things as this—pride in unit, or *esprit de corps,* as the field manuals reduce it to words—the Eighty-second was reborn and its integrity as a fighting unit has never been challenged. Its history has come in part from the typewriters and cameras of men like pioneering Jack Thompson, *Chicago Tribune;* William Walton, *Time;* Marshall Yarrow, Doon Campbell, and Robert Reuben, Reuter's; Chester Wilmot and Stanley Maxted, BBC; Phil Bucknell, *Stars and Stripes;* Robert Capa, *Life;* Leonard Mosley, Kemsley Newspapers; Robert Vermillion and Walter Cronkite, UP; Bill Boni, AP; Martha Gellhorn,

Collier's; Dick Tregaskis, INS, and many others who contributed to the file on the valor of airborne troops in general, and particularly underlining the personality and vitality of the Eighty-second. Without that final stand by the press in its behalf, there might be no Eighty-second today, because at the crucial time of decision, it was no longer in control of its own survival.

It is understandable that the Eighty-second uses the printed and broadcast word as a means of keeping its spirit alive and strong, Gavin having set the tone by becoming a firm believer in the role of the public-relations officer in war or peace. What a remarkable change this represented in the military service, and what a contrast to the attitude of the generation of the late Lt. Gen. Leslie J. McNair. The newer commanders in all the services have learned to appreciate the value of taking anonymity out of life in uniform, and in so doing have added to the battle potential of each unit. In all the wars up to 1939, there had not been anything like the citation of names and individual actions in print, broadcast and picture caption such as prevailed in World War II alone. It was an extension, in a new way, of the old Napoleonic thesis: "Give me some bright bits of metal and pieces of ribbon, and I will conquer the world." He didn't quite conquer it, though he shook it up pretty well, but the decorations and ribbons handed out by him are still cherished generations later in the homes of Frenchmen. Modern methods provided us with a way of recognizing individual accomplishments and recording them for the larger family of the community in which a man lives, has friends, relatives and a sphere of influence. Some editors treat their "military news" sections as dispose-alls, but those who do have never seen the expression on the face of a man in uniform when he gets a letter from home containing a newspaper item about him.

Once in a while, the cry against the "militarist" still goes up, but unthinkable as a military career once was, it is now equally improbable that any able-bodied man or woman will miss partnership with service life either in uniform or as a dependent. The media of information, while retaining the right to criticize and counsel, are growing increasingly aware of their responsibilities to report intelligently and constructively on the maintenance of a proper military posture keyed to generations of danger. A healthier understanding has resulted about the tremendous time lags in development of new weapons and the fact that it is no longer possible to put a lot of men into uniform swiftly and thus magically produce an effective military force. It is generally accepted that the only real menace to America today lies in surprise enemy air attack and that the only true air defense is one which keeps global war from starting. All this places a constant and grave responsibility on the military-information officer, who must keep the public actively interested and well versed about the forces bulwarked against any enemy's aggressive design.

He is constantly being chased up the Congressional budgetary tree, at a time when experience in handling military information is vital and that which is of public benefit should be encouraged into release. The crippling blows which have been dealt the military public-information field are often applauded in editorials for their "economy," the editorial writers not seeming to understand until too late that the "economy" is at their own expense. While it takes only diligence to provide the names and details of a plane crash, it takes far more specialized and thoughtful activity at the military source to keep pace with day-to-day public information needs and to heighten interest in efficiency and in better results inside the service for public and national security. In this area, the military is weak—this at a time when what we have to fight with this minute should be understood by everyone to be all we have to win with should we be hit.

Many an old war correspondent has been shelved because the pickings are slim for military reporting or analysis unless there's a war on. In some papers it is much easier to get a two-column head about someone who can remember the batting averages of the Brooklyn Dodgers in 1936 than it is to get the same space to explain what kind of diversionary trick the Russians are up to when they reduce their army by 640,000 soldiers in 1956.[3]

The greatest postwar gathering of correspondents under military auspices was the seaborne expedition to the lonely Pacific atoll to witness the explosion of an atomic bomb. The net result, tempered by the public attitudes of the time, did only a little to establish world understanding of our awesome future. A further delay in absorbing the full impact of the changes brought about by the atomic bomb and its

[3] Just before the death of Colonel Robert McCormick, he had his *Chicago Tribune* city desk give one of his special and most mature writers an assignment. "At the airport yesterday," the reporter was told, "the men's room was a mess. Get a photographer with you on it and start a campaign against dirty toilets in airports." Ex-paratrooper Jack Thompson was the reporter.

sinister sister weapons was caused by the North Korean decision to seek southward adventure. The old tactics were in use, the old public-relations officers called up, and the old by-liners were again on the front pages in big type. From the United Nations side, there were a few innovations like the appearance of jets, an early lack of censorship, and war correspondents armed with dinky sound-track cameras for something called TV. As if to prove that Hiroshima, Nagasaki and Bikini were only side shows and war was to remain forever conventional, when Edward R. Murrow and I lumbered into Korea together in July, 1950, the trip was made in a tired C-47 aircraft and our other flight cargo was twenty jugs of blood plasma—the same old ingredients of conflict we had known in the past. Bitter as was this struggle, though, Korea had some warmth of old-school-tie and family reunion in the military-war correspondent relationship. This potential seedling of World War III was held to orthodoxy by the United Nations' provision of about as many rules and umpires as actual warring participants, and coverage from a war correspondent point of view was confined to pattern, too.

Korea clouded the fact that a real World War III, besides being fought by forces in being where deployed at the time of hostilities, would be communicated to the people of the world by reporters in being and where they were working at the time of attack. This requires of the editor, as well as the military strategist, that he build a plan in the image of the deeds of the past and not necessarily in the same structures and forms. If it is not to be an all-encompassing "go for broke" conflict next time, and is only another peripheral action such as Korea was until throttled in truce talks, then there may be press camps again but the numbers of war correspondents will forever remain smaller than in World War II. Except for limited actions, the tidy line of the infantry—back of which lie snug headquarters, depots, dumps and assembly areas—and the concentrations of naval forces are gone forever. In the fast-moving battle picture presented by looming airborne devices with lethal warheads, surface troop dispersal and strong points are not enough. In the air is the area of decision.

No longer do we live in an America safe from recurring, rising tides of international irritations. This turbulence has traditionally swamped other more exposed countries, but any new flood tide would surely hit the North American continent first. America is the primary target. As a news story, the struggle to reduce it looms as the greatest "eye-witnesser" ever—should anyone be around to write or broadcast it.

From the editor's chair, any World War III is sure to be a "local story" in the beginning—and, maybe, for the duration. The war correspondent of the future will never have time to specialize after the fact of war, and should be keeping abreast of developments daily. When war breaks, he may be covering City Hall or the State Capitol where they are debating how much to support Civil Defense and the Ground Observer Corps. If an all-out attack comes, every reporter will be a war correspondent expected to cover what he may know only as a community catastrophe. William Howard Russell (1820-1907) had to go half a world away to find a war to write about and his war news usually appeared six weeks after the events. Today the strategist at the enemy's planning tables can thrust war an equal distance in hours. And he can smack it right into the front yard of the American citizen with the accuracy of the bike-borne newspaper carrier boy—an accuracy more terrifyingly eloquent and final than any words.

It is for this reason that every military activity, at home and abroad, now uses its public-information office to establish better relations with the citizen, and as long as the citizen has a role in this power-poised peace, or in the fight should it develop, no better chore will ever be performed than to give him the factual measure of his task, reminding him now and then of other men and women who have brought us to history's present. All of them in their time faced dilemmas which were staggering, too.

On the night of February 16, 1955, after I had searched for some three and one-half months for men now in obscurity, Ralph Edwards put his "This Is Your Life" around them for the NBC-TV network. It was a little more than a decade since Chester Finkhausen, of Payne, Ohio, had asked me in France during the Elster surrender to guess where we might all be "ten years from now." Neither of us could have imagined we would be participating in the reunion of the I&R platoon of the 329th Infantry Regiment on the stage of the El Capitan theater in Hollywood, and that it would be historic as the first reassembly of a whole military unit in the presence of 40,000,000 viewers. The most surprised, of course, was Lieutenant (now Captain) Samuel W. Magill, whose life it was. The tenseness of the capture of the 20,000 Germans was relived by us all, and it had some special significance. These platoon members, now coming into middle age, had started as ordinary American boys, and they took their strength and invincibility from dependence on each other. Even though the story was ten years old, the inspiration of it reached an incredibly vast audience. That night, after it was over, we were swapping stories. There was a lull and Donald Wilkinson, an old member of the platoon now living in Indianapolis, Indiana, came to sit with me. He told of a clipping he had from the Wellsville, Ohio, newspaper about his part in the big surrender. "I remember how you put your typewriter on the hood of your jeep," he said, "and stood there writing that story about me. I have it framed and it hangs on the wall at home."

To him, since it had been in his old home-town newspaper, it was better than a medal or citation. To the rest of us, war correspondent and public-relations man alike, the fact that he cherished and saved a ten-year-old clipping was our citation, too.

Acknowledgments

The late Douglas Southall Freeman, who delved into archives and old letters and records as much as anyone who ever lived, once told me that all it takes for a book is arrangement of the research materials in neat and orderly chronology, but this book also involved a lengthy search of another kind, a trailing of men and women still alive who had changed profession or gone into retirement.

There have not been many books about war correspondents. F. Lauriston Bullard's *Famous War Correspondents* was published in 1914, just as World War I began. Rupert Furneaux compiled *The First War Correspondent: William Howard Russell of the Times*. Dr. J. Cutler Andrews put together 813 interesting pages called *The North Reports the Civil War*. There are also more recent books, such as *They Saw It Happen,* by Louis L. Snyder and Richard B. Morris, and Cecil Woodham-Smith's *Florence Nightingale* and *The Reason Why*. All these helped put *Never a Shot in Anger* in perspective.

A great difference between wars is shown by comparing *My Experiences in the World War,* by General John J. Pershing, and Eisenhower's *Crusade in Europe*. Pershing was as indifferent as Eisenhower was alert to the values of the press. The creed of General Eisenhower is one with which every officer should familiarize himself when he is yet a lieutenant. No commander in the world's history had as many war correspondents to deal with as General Eisenhower, and no top commander was ever repaid more handsomely for respecting the integrity of war correspondents.

308

General Bradley's *A Soldier's Story* speaks of the ease with which the press moved in, out and about his headquarters. Captain Harry Butcher in *My Three Years With Eisenhower* often refers to developments among the correspondents.

The six volumes of Winston S. Churchill's wartime history contain many references to the press, not surprising, since he was a politician sensitive to what was being said and, besides, had been a war correspondent himself. Field Marshal the Viscount Montgomery of Alamein outstripped all other British high-rankers in his appreciation of the importance of "a happy press," and he devoted half his introduction to *Normandy to the Baltic,* to a forthright tribute to the wartime correspondents. Finally, Rear Admiral George P. Thompson's lamplit way through the dark life of the censor, *The Blue Pencil Admiral,* should be read by anyone interested in the press phase of World War II.

A book such as mine depends on numberless colloquies with old friends. I am heavily indebted to Edward Lavelle, now editor of the *West Hartford* (Connecticut) *News;* James A. Griffith, who preserved many of the salient documents; George Fuller, now of Daphne, Alabama; John Hanssen, of Colorado Springs, for his notes and assistance; Lt. Col. William Drake of Chillicothe, Missouri, who held the Third Army Press Camp together no matter how fast Patton wanted it moved; Charles Rhodes, of Malibu, California, who took great chances and got some of the war's best pictures; and Colonel Bertram Kalisch, of Astoria, Long Island, New York, who ranged all theaters of World War II before it was over, and kept notes and files; and thanks should go also to old Air Force colleagues: Lt. Col. William J. McGinty, Lt. Col. Charles Hinkle and Capt. James Sunderman, who helped and advised along the way.

Other military men gave valuable advice and information, including General of the Army Douglas MacArthur, the Army's first public-relations officer; Maj. Gen. Norman D. Cota, now retired in Bryn Mawr, Pennsylvania, who will always live in esteem of the war correspondents who knew him at St. Lô; Maj. Gen. Robert C. Macon; Colonel E. B. Crabill; and Captain Samuel W. Magill. Major General the Lord Burnham was helpful in locating British Empire correspondents and others, as was Brigadier Lionel Cross, now the Chief of Public Information at SHAPE in Paris. Commander Patrick Morgan, British Royal Navy, of H.M.S. *Dryad,* provided valuable data. Lt.

Gen. James M. Gavin, with his bright recall of exploits and men of the Eighty-second Airborne, was an excellent source. Thanks are also due Colonel William T. Ryder; Lt. Col. Walter C. Griscti; [1] Captain John James Briscoe, with a particular bow for his meticulous 182-page master's thesis, *The Kennedy Affair;* Maj. Gen. Frank Allen, now with the military Assistance Advisory Group in Rome, Italy, for his notes and leads; and Colonel Robert Allen Griffin, publisher of the *Monterey* (California) *Peninsula-Herald.* To my old boss, Lt. Gen. Floyd L. Parks, a special salute for patience, advice and criticism of parts of this book in manuscript form.

The files of the Overseas Press Club in New York were opened to me by Ruth Lloyd. The bound volumes of *Stars and Stripes,* European edition, in the Library of Congress, the wartime file of *Editor and Publisher,* and the press sections of *Time* and *Newsweek,* were especially productive, and the book, *Star-Spangled Radio,* written by old friends, Ed Kirby and Jack Harris, was good for certain verifications.

Garry Schumacher of the New York Giants publicity department recreated the scene in the Polo Grounds, and in England, Irene Henshall and Mrs. L. G. Loney pointed me to Burton-on-Trent and Mrs. Joan Tourt (née Ellis). To my wife, who saved the letter-a-day I wrote her throughout the war, I owe much for providing me with a makeshift diary. And to my tireless assistant during this book's preparation, Gladys Hartschen Ruiz, thanks are in order.

Everything mellows in time, but not so much as to dim the admonition of Lt. Col. J. B. L. "Jock" Lawrence in 1943, as we stood at the curb in Grosvenor Square. "As for newspaper guys, mind you," he said, "they don't like nuthin'. You gotta start with that." And in some cases, finish with it, too. When an answer to my queries came from Marshall Yarrow, now editor of the *Ottawa Citizen,* filling me in on certain D-Day horrors, he concluded grimly with, ". . . as I remember the incidents of June 6, 1944, I owe you little or no thanks for anything." His colleague, Robert Reuben, now running the Pen and Quill Restaurant in Manhattan Beach, California, first refused jocularly to answer the phone, saying, ". . . I don't think I should talk to this guy. I was having a drink one night in London, gabbing with

---

[1] Griscti, Colonel John M. Virden and I served as advance men for General Eisenhower's tour of NATO in January, 1951, and were involved in setting up the public-information establishments as they exist along SHAPE's perimeter today.

him, and before I knew it I was in parachute school." But they both did talk, as did many others, which was a great aid. In fact, as research was going on and many of the old war correspondents were polled, it was evident that time had soothed their feelings about censors, public-relations officers, the Army itself. Considering the historic accounts of mishandling in past wars, it has probably occurred to them all by now that war correspondents figured in more planning, and benefited from more high-level decisions on their behalf, than they cared to admit while the war was going on. To others who have not been mentioned, my gratitude for their contributions to the shape and substance of *Never a Shot in Anger*.

Colonel Barney Oldfield, USAF
HQ Continental Air Defense Command
Colorado Springs, Colorado

Appendix

* These names are taken from the official War Department records of accreditations for the World War II period. Many of the war correspondents changed jobs, and I have been dependent upon the War Department's choice of affiliations in my entries here. There are only a few of the many names of servicemen who were on the editorial rosters of the several editions of *Stars and Stripes,* bylines that were sometimes best known to front-line readers. The War Department does not include them in this set of archive material. Another group was left out, too—the short-timers who left their state-side desks and junketed to the war theaters for a quick look, who usually passed into, through, and out of any theater in less than a month. — Colonel Barney Oldfield.

Best, Cort, AC/Photo Division
Bettencourt, Sylvia de, Correio de Manha
Biben, Joseph H., Biben Publishing Company
Biddle, George, Life
Bienstock, Victor, Overseas News Agency
Bigart, Homer W., New York Herald Tribune
Billotte, William C., Jr., Omaha World-Herald
Binder, Carroll, Chicago Daily News
Bjornson, Bjorn, NBC
Black, John C., Gillette Publishing Company
Blackburn, Casper K., Seapower
Blair, Robert H., Fox Movietone News
Blakeslee, Howard W., Fox Movietone News
Blakeslee, Mrs. Victor, Collier's
Blay, John S., Yank
Boatner, Charles K., Fort Worth Star-Telegram
Bockhurst, John A., News of the Day
Boggs, William, Abbott Laboratories
Bogrod, Aaron, Time
Boguslav, David, Chicago Sun
Bolden, Frank E., Pittsburgh Courier
Bolling, Landrum, Beloit Daily News
Bongard, Nicholas, March of Time
Boni, William F., AP
Bonney, Teresa, Duell, Sloan & Pearce
Booth, W., Philadelphia Record
Bordaam, William, INS
Bordas, Walter, International News Photos
Boren, Wallace R., This Week
Borgstedt, Douglas H., Yank
Bostwick, Albert L., Veterans of Foreign Wars
Bottomley, C., Australian Dept. of Information
Bourchet, Rene, Ospecre Algerese
Bourges, Fernand A., Life
Bourke-White, Margaret, Time
Bovill, Oscar, Pathe-Gazette
Bow, Frank, Brush Moor Newspapers
Bowen, Lewis, American Red Cross
Bowerman, Waldo G., Engineering-News Record

Boyce, Ralph L., Yank
Boyle, Harold (Hal), AP
Boyle, John W., Time
Bracker, Milton, New York Times
Bracker, Virginia L., New York Times
Bradley, Holbrook, Baltimore Sun
Brady, Lloyd C., AP
Brag, Rubin, Diario Carioca
Braidwood, Nelson, London Telegraph
Bramley, George E., American Aviation
Brandao, Paul, Correio de Manha
Brandt, Bertram G., Acme Newspictures
Brandt, Frank M., Yank
Brandt, Raymond P., St. Louis Post-Dispatch
Branham, Leo, AP
Breese, Howard F., AP
Bregon, John, INS
Breimhurst, Donald W., Yank
Brennan, John C., Sydney Bulletin
Brennan, Peter, NBC
Brewer, Sam, New York Times
Bria, George C., AP
Briggs, Walter L., UP
Brigham, Daniel P., New York Times
Brines, Russell, AP
Bridgman, Julie, Liberty
Broch, Nathan, Aneta News Agency (Dutch)
Brock, Ray, New York Times
Broderick, Hugh, International News Photos
Brodie, Howard J., Yank
Brook, Alexander, Life
Brooks, Deton J., Chicago Defender
Brooks, Olive, INS
Brooks, William F., NBC
Brown, Arthur E., Chicago Herald-American
Brown, David, Reuters
Brown, Dickson, London News Chronicle
Brown, Harold P., Reuters
Brown, Harry, Yank
Brown, James E., INS
Brown, Norman E., Australian Dept. of Information
Brown, Robert E., UP

Browne, Barbara, Christian Science Monitor
Browne, Mallory, New York Times
Brumby, Robert M., MES
Bruto, Frank, AP
Bryan, W. Wright, Atlanta Journal
Bryant, Robert, International News Photos
Bryant, Vaughn M., AP
Buckley, Christopher T., Reuters
Buddy, Edward C., Pathe News
Bullard, Arthur E., American Red Cross
Bullitt, William C., Time
Buntin, William, INS
Burchett, Wilfred, London Daily Express
Burdette, Winston, CBS
Burke, James C., Liberty
Burke, James W., Esquire-Coronet
Burnham, L. B., UP
Burns, Douglas R., Australian Dept. of Information
Burns, Eugene, AP
Burns, George F., Yank
Burns, John T., AP
Burroughs, Edgar Rice, UP
Burroughs, Henry J., AP
Burrows, Ted, Yank
Burton, L. V., McGraw-Hill
Busch, Noel F., Time
Bush, Asahel, AP
Bushemi, John A., Yank
Butler, Eldon K., AP
Buttrose, C. O. G., Sydney Morning Herald
Byfield, Ernest L., Chicago Herald-American

Cafaliere, Nicholas, March of Time
Calabria, Frank J., March of Time
Calhoun, C. H., New York Times
Calhoun, Millard F., Time
Callender, Harold, New York Times
Calmer, Edgar M., CBS
Calvosa, Ulrich, Collier's
Camp, Helen, AP
Campbell, A. Doon, Reuters
Campbell, Edward L., AP
Cancellare, Frank, Acme Newspictures
Capa, Robert, Life

Caparelle, Peter L., Ring
Carley, John O., Memphis Commercial-Appeal
Carlisle, John M., Detroit News
Carnes, Disney C., Saturday Evening Post
Carpenter, Iris N., London Daily Herald
Carr, Milton L., UP
Carroll, Loren, Newsweek
Carroll, Peter J., AP
Carroll, Sidney, Esquire-Coronet
Carson, Lee, INS
Carter, Amon G., Fort Worth Star-Telegram
Carter, Archie N., McGraw-Hill
Carter, Arthur M., Afro-American Newspapers
Carty, William, Australian Dept. of Information
Case, Lewis S., Paramount News
Casey, Robert, Chicago Daily News
Cashman, John, INS
Cassidy, Henry C., NBC
Cassidy, James F., WLW
Cassidy, Morley, Philadelphia Bulletin
Caswell, Donald F., UP
Catledge, William T., New York Times
Cellario, Alberto, La Prensa
Chafin, Glenn M., Bell Syndicate
Chakales, Lawrence S., AP
Chamberlain, Charles W., AP
Chandra, P. T., India-Burma
Chang, C. B., Central News Agency
Chao, Sam, Reuters
Chapelle, Georgette M., Look
Chappelle, Minafox, American Home
Chaplin, William W., NBC
Chapman, Frank M., Acme Newspictures
Chapman, John F., McGraw-Hill
Chase, Milton, WLW
Chase, William T., AP
Cheng, Hawthorne, Chinese Ministry of Information
Chernoff, Howard L., West Virginia Network
Chester, John F., AP
Chickering, William H., Time
Childs, Marquis, St. Louis Post Dispatch

Chinigo, Michael, INS
Chipping, Chu, TaKanpPao
Chorlian, Edward, CBS
Clapper, Raymond, Scripps-Howard
Clark, Edgar, UP
Clark, Herbert, New York Herald Tribune
Clark, Katherine L., WCAU
Clark, Michael, The Nation
Clark, Richard, UP
Clark, William E., Life
Clarke, Edward T., Cleveland Press
Clarke, Philip C., AP
Clausen, John A., War Dept., Special Services
Clausen, Walter B., AP
Clayton, Bernard, Life
Clayton, Frederick, American Red Cross
Cleary, Ed J., McGraw-Hill
Clements, Olen W., AP
Clover, Robert, AP
Clurman, Robert O., AP
Cobbledick, Gordon, Cleveland Plain Dealer
Cochrane, Jacqueline, Liberty
Cochrane, Robert B., Baltimore Sun
Codel, Martin, American Red Cross
Coe, Donald G., ABC
Coffy, Patrick V., Yank
Coggins, Jack B., Yank
Cohen, Haskell P., Pittsburgh Courier
Cohn, Arthur E., INS
Cohn, David L., Houghton-Mifflin
Colburn, John H., AP
Colby, Carroll B., Popular Science
Coll, Ray, Honolulu Advertiser
Collingwood, Charles, CBS
Collins, Walter, UP
Combas, Guerra E., El Mundo
Combs, George H., WHN
Conefry, Walter, Scripps-Howard
Conger, Clinton B., UP
Coniff, Francis, INS
Coniston, Ralph A., Aneta News Agency (Dutch)
Considine, Robert B., INS
Coogan, James A., UP
Cook, Donald P., New York Herald Tribune
Cook, George J., Yank

Cook, Howard N., Life
Cook, Max B., Scripps-Howard
Cook, Zenas D., Newsweek
Cooke, David C., McBride Publishing Company
Cooke, Donald E., Yank
Cookman, Mary C., Ladies Home Journal
Cool, Robert N., AP
Cooper, Edward H., Christian Science Monitor
Corbellini, George, Yank
Cornell, Douglas, AP
Corsinia, Aralbo R., Petroleum Magazine
Cort, Horace W., AP
Corte, Charles, Acme Newspictures
Corum, Bill, King Features
Corwin, Norman L., CBS
Costa, Joseph C., New York Daily News
Courtenay, William, London Daily Sketch
Courtney, W. B., Collier's
Cowan, Howard S., AP
Cowan, Ruth B., AP
Cowles, Virginia, NANA
Coxe, George, Alfred Knopf
Coyne, Catherine, Boston Herald
Craig, Elizabeth M., Gannett Publishing Company
Craig, Thomas T., Life
Cranston, Paul F., Philadelphia Bulletin
Cravens, Kathryn, MBS
Crawford, Kenneth, Newsweek
Crider, John H., New York Times
Crocker, A. J., St. Paul Dispatch
Crockett, E. Harry, AP
Cromie, Robert A., Chicago Tribune
Cronkite, Walter L., UP
Crost, Lyn, Honolulu Star-Bulletin
Crotchett, Earl, Universal Newsreel
Crowther, Francis B., New York Times
Crozier, Thomas E., New York Herald Tribune
Crumpler, Hugh, UP
Cuddy, John M., UP
Cuhel, Frank J., MBS
Cumming, C., Christian Science Monitor

Doan, Donald P., AP
Dodd, Howell E., AP
Dolan, Leo V., INS
Donaghey, Donald, Philadelphia Bulletin
Donahue, Robert F., Pathe News
Donghi, Frank, Acme Newspictures
Dopking, Al, AP
Dored, John, Paramount News
Dorsey, George, Pathe News
Dorvillier, William, UP
Dos Passos, John, Life
Douglas, Wes, Chicago Sun
Douglass, Richard W., Yank
Dowling, John G., Chicago Sun
Downes, Donald C., Overseas News Agency
Downs, William R., CBS
Doyle, Robert J., Milwaukee Journal
Drake, Catherine, Readers Digest
Drake, Francis, Readers Digest
Dreier, Alexander, NBC
Driscoll, David E., MBS
Driscoll, Joseph, New York Herald Tribune
Driver, Roy A., Australian Dept. of Information
Drummond, J. Roscoe, Christian Science Monitor
Duga, Dennis L., Melbourne Age
Dunbar, Rudolph, Associated Negro Press
Duncan, Raymond E., Yank
Dunn, Francis W., Bell Aircraft
Dunn, William J., CBS
Durdin, F. Tillman, New York Times
Durdin, Margaret L., Time
Duret, Fernando L., El Universal
Durrance, Thomas D., Time
Durston, John H., New York Herald Tribune
Dynan, Joseph E., AP

Eager, Clifton C., Australian Press
Ebener, Charlotte, INS
Ecker, Allan B., Yank
Edmonds, James E., WLW
Edmundson, Charles F., Time
Edson, Peter, NEA
Edwards, Clyde D., CBS
Edwards, Herman F., Portland Oregonian

Edwards, Leonard, Australian Broadcasting Commission
Edwards, Reginald J., Australian Dept. of Information
Edwards, Webley, CBS
Eitington, Lee, Time
Ek, Carl, Passaic Herald-News
Ekins, Herbert R., WSYR
Elisofon, Eliot, Life
Ellison, Earl J., Look
Elliott, John, Australian Broadcasting Commission
Emeny, Stuart, London News Chronicle
Enell, George, American Red Cross
Engelke, Charles B., UP
Epstein, Clifford, Detroit News
Erickson, Wendell S., AP
Eunson, Robert C., AP
Evans, Druscilla, New York Post
Evans, Edward A., Scripps-Howard
Evans, Joe, New York Herald Tribune
Eyerman, J. R., Life

Fabinani, Henry, Paramount News
Fagans, Allen T., Newsweek
Falvey, William, New York Mirror
Faris, E. Barry, INS
Farnsworth, Clyde A., AP
Faron, Ward H., AP
Farr, Walter G., London Daily Mail
Fast, Howard, Esquire-Coronet
Faust, Frederick, Harper's
Faust, Hal, Chicago Tribune
Feder, Sydney A., AP
Feldman, Arthur S., Blue Network
Fendell, Jack D., CBS
Feng, Paul, Central News Agency
Fenger, Austin B., Associated Broadcasters
Fenwick, Robert W., Denver Post
Ferber, Edna, NANA
Ferris, Dillon J., Yank
Ferris, Jack, Newsweek
Fielder, Blaine P., Group 3, Australian Papers
Filan, Frank, AP
Finan, Elizabeth S., Harper's Bazaar
Finch, A. Percy, Reuters
Finch, Barbara M., Reuters
Finch, Edward, Time

Finnegan, Herbert A., Boston American

Fischer, Ernest G., AP

Fisher, Alan, PM

Fisher, William, Time

Fisk, James B., National Geographic

Fitchett, Ian G., London Daily Express

Fitzhenry, L. J., Brisbane Courier-Mail

Fitzpatrick, S. H., Australian Dept. of Information

Fitzsimmons, Thomas J., AP

Flaherty, Pat, NBC

Flaherty, Vincent X., Washington Times-Herald

Flanner, Janet, New Yorker

Fleeson, Doris, Woman's Home Companion

Fleischer, Jack M., Time

Fleming, Dewey L., Baltimore Sun

Fleming, James, CBS

Fleming, Thomas E., Yank

Florea, John T., Life

Fodor, Marcel W., Chicago Sun

Folkard, F. B., Group 3, Australian Papers

Folliard, Edward T., Washington Post

Folsom, Charles E., Boston Post

Folster, George T., Chicago Sun

Fonda, Dow H., AP

Foote, Mark, Booth Newspapers

Forbes, Ernest D., WFBM

Ford, Corey, Collier's

Forrest, Wilbur, New York Herald Tribune

Forsberg, Franklin S., Yank

Fort, Randolph L., AP

Forte, Aldo, UP

Foss, Kendall, New York Post

Foster, Cedric, Yankee Network

Foster, John, Aviation Magazine

Foster, Wilson K., NBC

Fowle, Farnsworth, CBS

Fowler, Homer Wick, Dallas Morning News

Frank, Gerold, Palcor News Agency

Frank, H. H., Overseas News Agency

Frank, June M., This Month

Frank, Stanley B., New York Post

Frankel, Lazarus, Billboard

Frankish, John F., UP

Frano, John J., Yank

Fraser, John G., Blue Network

Frazer, William L., Yank

Frazier, Benjamin W., Yank-Look

Frawley, Harry J., AP

Fredenthal, David, Life

Frederick, Pauline, Western Newspaper Union

Freeman, Beatrice, Magazine Digest

Freeman, Edward, Baltimore News-Post

Freidin, Seymour K., New York Herald Tribune

Frey, Robert L., UP

Friedman, Seymour, Yank

Frisby, Herbert M., Afro-American Newspapers

Frissell, Toni, free lance

Froendt, Antonio, Religious News Service

Frutchey, Fred, NBC

Frye, William F., AP

Fulton, William J., Chicago Tribune

Gaeth, Arthur, MBS

Gaige, Richard T., Yank

Gale, Jack F., UP

Gallagher, J. Wes, AP

Gallico, Paul, Cosmopolitan

Gammack, Gordon, Des Moines Register-Tribune

Gannett, Lewis, New York Herald Tribune

Garland, Robin, Saturday Evening Post

Garrison, Omar, Reuters

Gask, Roland, Newsweek

Gaskill, Betty, Liberty

Gaskill, Gordon, American

Gaston, Carl D., War Dept., Bureau of Public Relations

Geiger, Richard, AP

Geis, Bernard J., Esquire-Coronet

Gelder, Stuart, London Daily Express

George, Carl, WGAR

George, Collins, Pittsburgh Courier

Gercke, George, March of Time

Gercke, William F., Paramount News

Gervasi, Frank H., Collier's

Ghali, Paul, Chicago Daily News

Ghio, Robert A., Yank

Gilman, LaSelle, Honolulu Advertiser

Gilman, William, Baltimore Sun
Gilmore, Eddy L, AP
Gingrich, Arnold, Esquire-Coronet
Gingrich, Helen, Esquire-Coronet
Glosker, Anita, NANA
Glynn, Paul T., CBS
Goble, James B., Yank
Goldberg, Abraham I., AP
Goldstein, Sam, International News Photos
Goodwin, Joseph C., AP
Gopalan, J., Associated Press of India
Gorrell, Henry T., UP
Gorry, Charles P., AP
Goss, Frank B., CBS
Gottfried, Carl M., Time
Gottlieb, Sol S., International News Photos
Gould, Beatrice B., Ladies Home Journal
Gould, Randall, Shanghai Evening Post
Gowran, Clayton, Chicago Tribune
Graebner, Walter A., Time
Graffis, Herbert, Chicago Daily News
Graham, Frederick, New York Times
Graham-Barrow, C. R., Reuters
Grandin, Thomas B., Blue Network
Grant, Donald S., Look
Grant, Gordon N., Tampa Tribune
Grant, Herbert B., Chicago Times
Gratke, Charles E., Christian Science Monitor
Grauer, Benjamin F., NBC
Graves, Lemuel E., Norfolk Journal and Guide
Gray, Peyton, Afro-American News-papers
Gray, William P., Time
Green, Allen, Scripps-Howard
Green, Clinton H., New York Times
Green, Janet, Trans-Radio Press
Greene, Hamilton, American Legion Magazine
Greene, Roger D., AP
Greenhalgh, Robert F., Yank
Greenwald, Edwin B., AP
Greenwald, Sanford, News of the Day
Greer, Allen J., Buffalo Evening News
Gridley, Charles O., Chicago Sun
Griffin, Bulkley, Hartford Times
Griffin, Henry, AP

Griffin, John, AP
Grigg, Joseph, UP
Grim, George H., Minneapolis Star-Journal
Grossi, Daniel, AP
Groth, John A., Parade
Grover, Allen, Time
Grover, James A., Time
Grover, John, AP
Grover, Preston, AP
Grueson, Sidney, New York Times
Grumich, Charles A., AP
Grupp, George, Boating
Guard, Harold, UP
Gudebrod, Morton P., AP
Gwinn, John W., AP
Gunderson, Arthur R., UP
Gunn, Stanley E., Fort Worth Star-Telegram
Gunnison, Royal A., Collier's
Gunther, John, NANA
Guptill, Charles H., AP
Guth, Oscar A., UP

Haacker, Charles, Acme Newspic-tures
Haaker, Edwin, NBC
Haas, Saul, Portland Oregonian
Hackler, Victor, AP
Haden, Allen, Chicago Daily News
Haeger, Robert A., UP
Hager, Alice R., Skyways
Hahn, Willard C., St. Louis Post Dis-patch
Hailey, Foster B., New York Times
Hairland, Patrick, London News Chronicle
Hales, Samuel D., UP
Haley, Pope A., AP
Hall, Charles H., Springfield Repub-lican
Hall, Clarence, Link & Chaplain Mag-azine
Hall, Flem R., Fort Worth Star-Tele-gram
Halton, Matthew, Toronto Star
Hamburger, Edith I., Cleveland Press
Hamburger, Philip P., New Yorker
Hamm, Clarence L., AP
Hammond, Gilbert T., Boston Her-ald-Traveller
Hampson, Frederick E., AP

Handleman, Howard M., INS
Handler, Myer, UP
Hanley, Richard S., Yank
Hansen, Robert H., Look
Hanson, Ernest, Saturday Evening Post
Hardesty, Harriet C., UP
Hardy, Eugene J., Chilton Company
Hargest, William J., American Machinist
Hargrove, Charles R., Wall Street Journal
Harkness, Richard L., NBC
Harkraeder, Carleton, Newsweek
Harmatz, Herbert J., Reuters
Harmon, Dudley, UP
Harper, Robert S., Ohio State Journal
Harrington, Oliver W., Pittsburgh Courier
Harris, Harry L., AP
Harris, Reginald S., Australian Consolidated Press
Harris, Richard, UP
Harrison, A. Paul, UP
Harrison, Joseph G., Christian Science Monitor
Harrison, Paul L., NEA
Harrity, Richard, Yank
Harsch, Joseph C., Christian Science Monitor
Hartrich, Eugene, Chicago Sun
Hartt, Julian, INS
Hartzog, Hazel, UP
Hatch, Willard A., Acme Newspictures
Haugland, Vernon A., AP
Hauser, Ernest O., Saturday Evening Post
Haverstick, John M., Yank
Hawkes, George H., Group 4, Australian Papers
Hawkins, Eric E., New York Herald Tribune
Hawkins, Henry E., Reuters
Hawkins, Lewis, AP
Hawkslet, G. G. M., Group 4, Australian Papers
Haworth, William F., Yank
Hay, John, Yank
Haynes, Weston, American Red Cross
Healy, Thomas, New York Post

Hearst, Dorris L., New York Journal American
Hearst, Joseph, Chicago Tribune
Hearst, William R., INS
Heath, S. Burton, NEA
Heinz, Wilfred C., New York Sun
Heinzerling, Lynn L., AP
Heisler, Philip S., Baltimore Sun
Hellinger, Mark J., Hearst Newspapers
Hemery, Clement, INS
Hemingway, Ernest, Collier's
Hemingway, Martha Gellhorn, Collier's
Henderson, Ralph E., Readers Digest
Henle, Raymond Z., Pittsburgh Post-Gazette
Henry, Henry T., AP
Henry, James E., Reuters
Henry, John R., INS
Henry, Thomas R., Washington Star
Henry, William M., Los Angeles Times
Henshaw, Fred W., United States News
Hensley, Malcolm S., UP
Herald, George W., INS
Hercher, Wilmot W., AP
Herfort, Norman V., Pix Pictorial
Herlihy, Martin, Reuters
Herman, Arthur F., INS
Hermann, Leopold, AP
Hersey, John R., Time
Hershey, Burnet, Liberty
Hewlett, Frank, UP
Hicks, George, Blue Network
Hiett, Helen, Religious News Service
Higginbotham, W. R., UP
Higgins, Marguerite, New York Herald Tribune
High, Stanley, Readers Digest
Hightower, John M., AP
Hill, Carol, Collier's-Redbook
Hill, Ernie, Miami Herald
Hill, Gladwin A., New York Times
Hill, Max, NBC
Hill, Russell J., New York Herald Tribune
Hills, Lee O., Miami Herald
Himmelsbach, Gerard R., INS
Hinde, John, Australian Broadcasting Commission

Hindson, Curtis, Reuters
Hine, Alfred B., Yank
Hipple, William, Newsweek
Hirsch, Joseph, Abbott Laboratories
Hlavacek, John M., UP
Hoffman, Bernard, Time
Holburn, James, London Times
Holland, Gordon P., Group 5, Australian Papers
Hollenbeck, Don, NBC
Holles, Everett R., CBS
Hollingworth, Clare, Time
Holt, Carlyle H., Boston Globe
Hooley, John A., NBC, CBS, MBS, ABC
Horan, James D., G. P. Putnam's Sons
Hornaday, Mary, Christian Science Monitor
Horne, George F., New York Times
Horner, Durbin L., Yank
Hoskins, Francis T., MBS
Hostick, King V., Chicago Sun
Hottelet, Richard, CBS
Houle, Harry J., American Red Cross
Hovey, Graham, AP
Howard, Ralph, NBC
Howard, Rosemary, Newsweek
Howe, Quincy, CBS
Howland, William S., Simon & Schuster
Hoyt, Palmer, UP
Hubbard, Lucien, Simon & Schuster
Hughes, John B., The Oregonian
Huie, William B., American Mercury
Hull, Harwood, NBC
Hulls, Alan, Group 2, Australian Papers
Hume, Rita, INS
Humphreys, William J., New York Herald Tribune
Hunt, Frazier, Readers Digest
Hunt, John R., War Dept., Special Services
Hunter, Kent, INS
Hurd, Peter, Time
Hurd, Volney, Christian Science Monitor
Hurwitz, Hyman, Boston Globe
Huss, Pierre, INS
Hutch, Donald E., AP

Hutcheson, James M., AP
Hutton, Geoffrey, Melbourne Argus

Ichac, Pierre, Vainere
Ingraham, Herbert, Time
Irvin, George B., AP
Irwin, Theodore, Look
Isaacs, Harold, Newsweek
Isley, Charles C., Stauffer Publishing Company
Israels, Josef II, This Week

Jackson, William A., International News Photos
Jacobs, Ann L., Young America
Jacoby, Annalee, Time
Jacoby, Melville, Time
Jackett, S. T., Reuters
Jameson, Henry B., AP
Jandoli, Jerome B., INS
Janssen, Guthrie E., NBC
Jarrell, John W., INS
Jencks, Hugh I., UP
Jenkins, Burris A., New York Journal American
John, Elizabeth B., Cleveland News
Johnson, Albin E., INS
Johnson, Carol L., NEA
Johnson, Edd, Chicago Sun
Johnson, Hugo C., Paramount News
Johnson, John R., National Geographic
Johnson, Mac R., New York Herald Tribune
Johnson, Malcolm, New York Sun
Johnson, Vincent, Pittsburgh Post-Gazette
Johnson, William M., Afro-American Newspapers
Johnson, William W., Time
Johnston, George H., Group 1, Australian Papers
Johnston, Paul A., Yank
Johnston, Richard J., New York Times
Jones, Alexander, Washington Post
Jones, Edgar L., Atlantic Monthly
Jones, Edward F., Time
Jones, Edward V., AP
Jones, George, New York Times
Jones, George E., UP

Landau, Ida B., Overseas News Agency
Landry, Robert, Life
Landsberg, Morris, AP
Lane, Charles G., AP
Lang, Daniel, New Yorker
Lang, Will, Time
Laning, Edward, Life
Lanius, Charles, Trans-Radio Press
Lardner, John, NANA
Lauterbach, Richard E., Time
Lavelle, Elise, National Catholic News Service
Lawrence, William H., New York Times
Lawton, Fleetwood, NBC
Lea, Thomas C., Time
Leach, Paul R., Chicago Daily News
Leader, Anton, CBS
Lear, John W., Saturday Evening Post
Learned, Albe L., American Red Cross
Leavell, David, Fort Worth Press
Leavelle, Richard C., Chicago Tribune
Lecardeur, Maurice, Acme Newspictures
Lecoutre, Martha, Tri-Color
Lee, Clark, INS
Lee, J. Edgerton, INS
Lee, Paul K., AP
Legg, Frank G., Australian Broadcasting Commission
Leggett, Dudley, Australian Broadcasting Commission
Lehrman, Harold A., Argosy
Leimert, Walter H., CBS
Lennard, Wallace W., Australian Broadcasting Commission
Leonard, John, Reuters
Leonard, Reginald B., Group 3, Australian Papers
Lerner, Max, PM
Levin, Meyer, Overseas News Agency
Lewis, Boyd, NEA
Lewis, Ervin G., WLS
Lewis, Flora, AP
Lewis, Fulton, Jr., MBS
Lewis, Harley C., Acme Newspictures
Lewis, Morris, War Dept., Special Services
Larry Lesueur, CBS News

Lewis, Robert E., American Red Cross
Leyson, Burr W., Skyways
Lieb, Jack, News of the Day
Lieberman, Henry, New York Times
Liebling, Abbott J., New Yorker
Limpus, Lowell, New York Daily News
Lindley, Ernest K., Newsweek
Lindsley, James S., AP
Lippmann, Walter, New York Herald Tribune
Littell, Robert, Readers Digest
Litz, Leo M., Indianapolis News
Lloyd, Rhona, Philadelphia Evening News
Lochner, Louis P., AP
Lochridge, Mary P., Women's Home Companion
Lockett, Edward B., Time
Loeb, Charles H., Negro Newspaper Publishing Association
Loehwing, David A., UP
Logan, Walter F., UP
Long, James M., AP
Longmire, Carey, New York Post
Lopez, Andrew, Acme Newspictures
Lopez, Carlos F., Life
Loring, Paul S., Providence Journal
Loughlin, John, Group 1, Australian Papers
Loundagin, Nicholas F., Newsweek
Loveland, Reelif, Cleveland Plain Dealer
Lower, Elmer, Life
Lowry, Cynthia, AP
Lubell, Samuel, Saturday Evening Post
Lucas, Lenore V., Overseas News Agency
Lucas, W. E., London Daily Express
Luce, Henry R., Time
Luter, George W., Hawaii Magazine
Luter, John T., Time

Macauley, Thurston B., INS
MacBain, Alastair, Collier's
MacCartney, Robert R., Group 1, Australian Papers
MacCormac, Isabel, New York Times
MacCormac, John P., New York Times

McLemore, Henry, McNaught Syndicate
McMahon, Henry O., Washington Times-Herald
McManus, James L., Yank
McManus, Robert, Farm Journal
McMillen, Richard P., UP
McMurtry, Charles H., AP
McNeil, Marshall, Scripps-Howard
McNulty, Henry P., UP
McQuaid, Bernard J., Chicago Daily News
McWilliams, George, INS
Mechau, Frank A., Life
Mecklin, John M., Chicago Sun
Meier, G. Lawrence, MBS
Mejat, Francois, Pathe News
Mejat, Raymond, Pathe News
Melendez, Dorothy, Star Herald
Meltzer, Theodore, INS
Meyer, Ben F., AP
Meyer, Jane, Chicago Herald American
Meyer, Robert L., UP
Meyers, Debs, Yank
Meyers, George N., Yank
Michaelis, Ralph, Air News
Michie, Alan, Readers Digest
Middleton, Drew, New York Times
Miles, Frank F., American Legion
Miller, Graham, New York Daily News
Miller, Lee, Scripps-Howard
Miller, Lee (Mrs.), Conde-Nast
Miller, Lois Mattox, Readers Digest
Miller, Loye W., Scripps-Howard
Miller, Merle D., Yank
Miller, Robert C., UP
Miller, William J., Cleveland Press
Miller, Wiliam M., Look
Mills, Raymond, International News Photos
Miner, Charles S., New York Post
Mintzer, Leonidas, California State Guard
Misabe, C. R., UP
Mishael, Herbert, Melbourne Age
Mitchell, Bruce H., Life
Moats, Alice L. B., Collier's
Moe, M. Lorimer, Time
Moler, Murray, UP

Montrose, Sherman, Acme Newspictures
Moody, Blair, Detroit Free-Press
Moorad, George L., CBS
Moore, Charles M., London Daily Telegraph
Moore, Pugh, AP
Moore, Robert E. L., Trans-Radio Press
Moore, William T., Chicago Tribune
Moosa, Spencer, AP
Moran, Maurice, AP
Morde, Theodore A., Readers Digest
Morehouse, Ward, New York Sun
Morgan, Edward P., Chicago Daily News
Morgan, Ralph F., AAF
Morgan, Wilfred R., War Dept., Bureau of Public Relations
Morin, Relman G., AP
Moroso, John A., AP
Morphopoulos, Panos, Newsweek
Morris, Frank D., Collier's
Morris, Joe Alex, Collier's
Morris, John G., Life
Morris, John R., UP
Morrison, Chester, NBC
Morriss, Marion M., Yank
Morrow, Thomas, Chicago Tribune
Morse, Ralph, Life
Morton, Joseph, AP
Morton, Ralph S., AP
Most, Mel, AP
Mowrer, Edgar A., Chicago Daily News
Mowrer, Paul S., New York Post
Mowrer, Richard, Chicago Daily News
Muchmore, Gareth B., AP
Mueller, Merrill, NBC
Mueller, William A., Chicago Times
Muir, John, Whaley-Eaton Service
Muir, Malcolm, UP
Muller, Edwin, Readers Digest
Muller, Mary T., Readers Digest
Munn, Bruce, UP
Murdock, Barbara, Philadelphia Bulletin
Murphy, Charles J., Fortune
Murphy, William, Philadelphia Inquirer
Murray, James E., UP

Murray, William, Pathe News
Murray, William R., Yank
Murrow, Ed, CBS
Musel, Robert, UP
Muth, Russell A., Fox Movietone News
Muto, Frank, War Dept., Bureau of Public Relations
Mydans, Carl, Life
Mydans, Shelley, Life

Naintre, Yves, Paramount News
Navarro, Robert, March of Time
Neill, Franklin F., INS
Nesensohn, Carl D., Acme Newspictures
Nevin, Jack E., San Francisco Call Bulletin
Newhall, Scott, San Francisco Chronicle
Newman, Albert, Newsweek
Newman, Larry, INS
Newton, William, Scripps-Howard
Nichols, David M., Chicago Daily News
Nichols, Leslie A., MBS
Nixon, Robert G., INS
Noderer, Elvedore R., Chicago Tribune
Noel, Francis E., AP
Noli, Louis, AP
Norall, Frank V., CIAA
Nordness, Nedville, AP
Norgaard, Noland, AP
Norris, Frank C., Time
Norton, Howard M., Baltimore Sun
Norton, Taylor E., Time
Norwood, William R., Christian Science Monitor
Noyes, Newbold, Washington Evening Star
Nurenberger. Meyer J., Jewish Morning Journal
Nutter, Charles P., AP

O'Beirne, D. P., Reuters
O'Brien, Frank, AP
O'Brien, Mary H., Fawcett Publications
O'Connell, John, Bangor Daily News
O'Connell, John P., New York Daily News

O'Conner, James A., Group 1, Australian Papers
O'Connor, Eugene, American Red Cross
O'Donnell, James, Newsweek
Oechsner, Frederick, UP
Oeth, Alfred J., Paramount News
Offner, Philippa G., Life
O'Flaherty, Hal, Chicago Daily News
Oggel, Dean M., Yank
O'Keefe, Richard J., Philadelphia Inquirer
O'Kelly, Raymond, Reuters
O'Laughlin, John C., Army & Navy Journal
Olde, George, Springfield Newspapers
Oliphant, Homer N., Yank
Oliver, David R., Pathe News
Oliver, Frank, Reuters
Olsen, Alphonsus G., Melbourne Age-Sydney Sun
Olsen, R., Sydney Sun
Olson, Sidney, Time
Omelian, L. J., WLEU
O'Neill, James P., Yank
Opper, Frederick B., Blue Network
O'Quinn, Judson C., AP
O'Regan, Richard A., AP
O'Reilly, John D., New York Herald Tribune
O'Reilly, Martin L., Pathe News
Orro, David H., Chicago Defender
Osbiston, Francis, Group 4, Australian Papers
Osborne, John F., Time
O'Sullivan, J. Reilly, AP
Oswald, George, Universal Newsreel
Ottley, Roi V., PM
Ottoway, N., Group 3, Australian Papers
Oursler, William C., Fawcett Publications

Pacine, H. J., Group 2, Australian Papers
Packard, Eleanor C., UP
Packard, Nathaniel, UP
Packard, Reynolds, UP
Paine, Ralph D., Fortune
Painton, Frederick C., Readers Digest
Palmer, Frederick, NANA
Palmer, George J., AP

Palmer, Gretta Clark, Liberty
Palmer, Kyle, Los Angeles Times
Palmer, Mary B., Newsweek
Palyi, Melchoir, Booth Newspapers
Parier, Damien, Paramount News
Paris, Peter M., Yank
Parker, Fred, International News Photos
Parker, Jack D., WJIM
Parker, Pegge, American Weekly
Parker, Robert, WLW
Parr, William G., NBC
Parris, John A., AP
Parrott, L., New York Times
Parsons, Geoffrey, New York Herald Tribune
Pasley, Fred, New York Daily News
Patterson, Harry E., Daily Oklahoman
Paul, Herbert, Cowles Papers
Paul, Raymond A., Australian Broadcasting Commission
Paul, Richard H., Yank
Pawlak, Mason H., Yank
Peague, Harry H., American Red Cross
Pearson, Leon M., INS
Pepperburg, Ray L., American Illustrator
Percival, Jack, Group 5, Australian Papers
Perkins, Alice K., Fairchild Publications
Perkins, Bertram J., Fairchild Publications
Perlin, Bernard, Life
Perlman, David A., New York Herald Tribune
Perry, George S., Saturday Evening Post
Perryman, Charles R., News of the Day
Person, Kriston, Free Norwegian Press
Peterman, Ivan H., Philadelphia Inquirer
Peters, Harold A., Blue Network
Peters, Walter F., Yank
Peterson, Elmer, NBC
Peterson, Frederick, Group 3, Australian Papers
Peterson, George L., Minneapolis Star-Journal

Peterson, Ralph E., NBC
Pflaum, Irving, Chicago Times
Phelps, Winston, Providence Journal
Phillips, Cecil A. C., New York Times
Phillips, John, Time
Phillips, Martha E., Afro-American Newspapers
Phillips, William L., AP
Phipps, William E., AP
Pickens, William, Trans-Radio Press
Pignault, Charles, TAM
Pimper, John A., Yank
Pinkley, Virgil M., UP
Pinney, Roy, Liberty
Pitkin, Dwight L., AP
Pitman, Frank W., AP
Plachy, Frank, New York Journal of Commerce
Plambeck, Herbert, WOW
Platt, Warren C., National Petroleum News
Pleissner, Ogden M., Life
Polier, Dan A., Yank
Poling, Daniel, Philadelphia Record
Polk, Catherine, Los Angeles News
Polk, George, Los Angeles News
Poor, Henry V., U. S. Engineers
Poor, Peggy, New York Post
Poorbaugh, Earl R., INS
Pope, James S., Louisville Courier-Journal
Porter, K. R., Ziff Davis Publishing Company
Porter, Leroy P., NBC
Potter, Henry O., Group 3, Australian Papers
Potter, John P., Baltimore Sun
Poulos, Constantine, Overseas News Agency
Powell, Hickman, Popular Science
Powers, John H., Town & Country
Pratt, Fletcher, Harper's
Pratt, Melbourne, Group 5, Australian Papers
Preston, Hartwell L., Life
Prevost, Clifford A., Detroit Free Press
Prewett, Virginia, Chicago Sun
Pribichevich, Stoyan, Time
Price, Wesley, Saturday Evening Post
Priestly, Thomas A., Universal Newsreel

Roos, Leonard H., Pathe News
Root, Gordon, Southam Newspapers (Canada)
Roper, James E., UP
Rosen, Fred, Yank
Rosenthal, Joseph, AP
Ross, Nancy W., free lance
Rouzeau, Edgar T., Pittsburgh Courier
Rowe, William L., Pittsburgh Courier
Rucker, Joseph T., Paramount News
Rue, Larry, Chicago Tribune
Ruge, John A., Yank
Rundle, Walter G., UP
Russell, E. A., UP
Russell, Edmond A., New York Herald Tribune
Russell, Frank (Ted Malone), Blue Network
Russell, H. T., UP
Ryan, Cornelius, London Daily Telegraph
Ryan, Robert G., Yank

Sabin, Jesse, News of the Day
Saerchinger, Caesar, American Historical
Salisbury, Harrison, UP
Sample, Paul, Time
Sanders, Branan I., AP
Sann, Paul, New York Post
Santin, Miguel A., El Mundo
Sargint, H. J., NANA
Sasso, Arthur H., International News Photos
Satanomy, Edward, UP
Sayre, Joel G., New Yorker
Schalben, Orville, Milwaukee Journal
Schedler, Dean, AP
Scheer, Sam, International News Photos
Scherman, David, Life
Scherschel, Frank, Life
Schmidt, Dana A., UP
Schneider, Philip (Lt.), Leatherneck
Schuck, Hugh, New York Daily News
Schulman, Sammy, International News Photos
Schwartz, Robert, Yank
Scott, Burgess H., Yank
Scott, David W., Pathe News
Scott, John, Time

Seacrest, Joseph W., Nebraska State Journal
Seawood, Charles P., Acme Newspictures
Sebring, Lewis, New York Herald Tribune
Sedgwick, A. C., New York Times
Selle, Earl A., Honolulu Advertiser
Senick, Langdon, Fox Movietone News
Sevareid, Eric, CBS
Severyns, Marjorie, Time
Shadel, W. F., Rifleman & Infantry Journal
Shafer, Thomas, Acme Newspictures
Shapiro, Henry, UP
Shapiro, Lionel S., NANA
Shaplen, Robert M., Newsweek
Sharp, Roland H., Christian Science Monitor
Shaw, Albert E., Westminster Press
Shaw, Charles, CBS
Shaw, Jack, MBS
Shaw, John W., American Red Cross
Shaw, William, March of Time
Shaw, William D., Yank
Shayon, Robert, CBS
Sheahan, Joseph G., Chicago Tribune
Shean, Vincent, Newsweek
Sheean, James V., Redbook
Sheets, Millard O., Life
Shehan, Thomas F., Yank
Shelley, John D., WHO
Shenkel, William, Newsweek
Shepley, James R., Time
Shere, Samuel, Life
Sheridan, Martin, Boston Globe
Sherman, Dean F., Alaska Life
Sherman, Eugene, Los Angeles Times
Sherrod, Robert L., Time
Shippen, William H., Washington Evening Star
Shirer, William L., CBS
Shoemaker, Leslie, UP
Shoenbrun, David, Overseas News Agency
Shoop, Duke, Kansas City Star
Short, Gordon H., Australian Dept. of Information
Showers, Paul, Yank
Shrout, William C., Life
Shultz, Sigrid, Chicago Tribune

Stout, Wesley, Saturday Evening Post
Stowe, Leland S., Blue Network
Strand, William, Chicago Tribune
Stratton, Lloyd, AP
Strickler, Homer, New York Sun
Stringer, Elizabeth, UP
Stringer, William, Christian Science Monitor
Strock, George A., Life
Stromme, George L., Occidental Publishing Company
Strout, Richard L., Christian Science Monitor
Strozier, Fred L., AP
Struthers, I., Paramount News
Stumm, Loraine, London Daily Mirror
Sturdevant, Robert N., AP
Sturdy, Frank, Chicago Tribune
Stutler, Boyd B., American Legion
Sullivan, John V., Yank
Sullivan, Neil, Pathe News
Sulzberger, Cyrus L., New York Times
Summers, Harold J., Group 5, Australian Papers
Sunde, Tenold R., New York Daily News
Sutton, Donn, NEA
Suydam, Henry, Newark News
Sweeney, Don G., UP
Symontowne, Russ, New York Daily News

Tait, Jack M., New York Herald Tribune
Talbott, Sprague, Look
Taves, Brydon, UP
Taylor, Alexander, New York Post
Taylor, Henry, Scripps-Howard
Taylor, Robert, Newark Evening News
Teatsorth, Ralph C., UP
Telegian, Manual, Abbott Laboratories
Telford, Frank, Young & Rubicam
Tepling, Lloyd, UP
Terrell, John U., Newsweek
Terrell, Maurice E., Look
Terry, John B., Chicago Daily News
Tewkesbury, Richard, NBC
Thale, Jack A., Miami Herald

Thayer, Mary V., INS
Thomas, Bryon, Life
Thomas, Ed, UP
Thomas, Igor, Saturday Evening Post
Thomas, Lowell, NBC
Thompson, Charles H., UP
Thompson, Craig F., Time
Thompson, Fred, Readers Digest
Thompson, George F., Fox Movietone News
Thompson, J. Flynn, Time
Thompson, John H., Chicago Tribune
Thorndike, Joseph J., Life
Thorp, Gerald R., Chicago Daily News
Thusgaard, Carl, Acme Newspictures
Tighe, Dixie, INS
Tobin, Richard, New York Herald Tribune
Toles, Edward B., Chicago Defender
Tomara, Sonia, New York Herald Tribune
Tomlinson, Edward, Blue Network
Tondra, John A., Fox Movietone News
Travis, Roderick, Group 3, Australian Papers
Treanor, Thomas A., Los Angeles Times
Treat, Roger L., Washington Daily News
Tregaskis, Richard W., INS
Tremaine, Frank, UP
Troutman, Stanley, Acme Newspictures
Trumbull, Robert, New York Times
Tubbs, Vincent, Afro-American Newspapers
Tucker, George, AP
Tully, Andrew, Boston Traveller
Tupling, William L., UP
Turcott, Jack, New York Daily News
Turk, Raymond J., Cleveland News
Turnbull, James, Life
Turner, Ewart (Dr.), Religious News Service
Twitty, Tom, New York Herald Tribune
Tyree, William, UP

Uhl, Alexander H., PM
Ullman, Frederick, Pathe News

Vadeboncoeur, E. R., NBC
Van Atta, Lee, INS
Valens, Evans G., UP
Vanderbilt, Sanderson, Yank
Vandercook, John W., NBC
Vanderlip, Candace, INS
Vandivert, Margrethe, Time
Vandivert, William, Time
Van Sluys, C. J., Aneta
Vas Dias, Arnold, Aneta
Vaughn, Miles W., UP
Ventres, Fisko, Hartford Courant
Vermillion, Robert V., UP
Vern, Ike, Quick
Veysey, Arthur, Chicago Tribune
Vidner, Richard, New York Herald
    Tribune
Villanova, Anthony, Miami Herald
Vivian, Robert E., Reuters
Von Bovene, G. A., Aneta
Von Schmidt, Harold, Saturday Eve-
    ning Post

Waagenaar, Samuel, INS
Wade, William W., INS
Wadsworth, Horace A., Newsweek
Wagg, Alfred, Chicago Tribune
Wagner, Theodore, St. Louis Post
    Dispatch
Wahl, Jim M., NBC
Waite, Elmont, AP
Waldrop, Frank C., Washington
    Times-Herald
Wales, Henry G., Chicago Tribune
Walker, Charles L., Harper's
Walker, Gordon, Christian Science
    Monitor
Walker, Harrison H., National Geo-
    graphic
Walker, John H., Time
Walker, Milton E., New York Herald
    Tribune
Walker, Samuel, New York Post
Wall, Carl B., Readers Digest
Wallace, Ed R., NBC
Wallenstein, Marcel H., Kansas City
    Star
Walsh, Burke, Saturday Evening Post
Walsh, John B., National Catholic
    WC
Walters, John B., London Daily Mir-
    ror

Walton, William E., Time
Wang, George K., UP
Ward, Henry, Pittsburgh Press
Warden, William, AP
Waring, Gerald H., British United
    Press
Warner, Dennis, Melbourne Herald
Warner, Eugene P., American Red
    Cross
Warren, Mervyn, Group 3, Australian
    Papers
Waters, Enoc P., Chicago Defender
Watson, James B., BBC
Watson, Mark, Baltimore Sun
Watson, Paul R., Our Navy
Waugh, Irving C., WSM
Wear, Joseph R., Fort Worth Star
    Telegram
Weber, Thomas, Look
Wecksler, Abraham N., Conover
    Mast
Weil, Joseph, American Red Cross
Weisblatt, Franz, UP
Weisman, Al, Yank
Wellard, James, Chicago Times
Weller, George A., Chicago Daily
    News
Werner, Merle M., UP
Werner, Oscar L., AP
Wertenbaker, Charles, Time
Weston, Joe, Time
Weston, Mervyn C., Argus
Wheeler, Elliot R., AP
Wheeler, George, NBC
Wheeler, Herbert K., Chicago Times
Whipple, Sidney, Scripps-Howard
Whitcomb, Philip, Baltimore Sun
White, Elmont, AP
White, Frank, Indianapolis Star
White, Herbert K., AP
White, Leigh, Chicago Daily News
White, O. E. D., Group 2, Australian
    Papers
White, Theodore, Time
White, Walter, New York Post
White, William, New York Herald
    Tribune
White, William L., Readers Digest
White, William S., Time
Whitehead, Don F., AP
Whitehouse, Arthur G., Fawcett Pub-
    lications

Whiteleather, Melvin K., Philadelphia Evening Bulletin

Whitman, Howard J., New York Daily News

Whitney, Betsey C., Washington Times-Herald

Whitney, Peter D., San Francisco Chronicle

Wiant, Thoburn H., AP

Widdis, Edward C., AP

Wilcher, Lester, Cowles Newspapers

Wilcox, Richard L., Time

Wiley, Bonnie, AP

Wilhelm, Donald, Readers Digest

Wilhelm, John R., Reuters

Wilkes, Jack, Time

Wilkins, Ford, New York Times

Williams, Donald, Stars & Stripes

Williams, Emlyn J., Christian Science Monitor

Williams, Garth M., PM

Williams, Glenn A., AP

Williams, Gurney, Collier's

Williams, Henry L., Group 5, Australian Papers

Williams, Joseph F., INS

Williams, Larry W., War Dept., Bureau of Public Relations

Williams, Leonard W., Newark Evening News

Williams, Maynard O., National Geographic

Williams, Oswald M., Australian Broadcasting Commission

Williams, Thomas V., AP

Willicombe, Joseph, INS

Willis, Douglas, BBC

Wilson, Edmund, New Yorker

Wilson, Gill Robb, New York Herald Tribune

Wilson, Lon H., Yank

Wilson, Lyle, UP

Wilson, Richard L., Minneapolis Star-Journal

Wilson, Robert C., AP

Wilson, William C., UP

Winkler, Betty, Press Alliance

Winkler, Paul, INS

Winn, Mary Day, This Week

Winner, Howard, Pathe News

Winter, William, Overseas News Agency

Wittels, David G., Philadelphia Record

Wohl, Harry, St. Louis Star-Times

Wolfe, Henry C., This Week

Wolfe, Thomas, NEA

Wolfert, Ira, NANA

Wolff, Werner, Yank

Wong, N. H. S., News of the Day

Wood, Percy S., Chicago Tribune

Woodbury, Clarence M., American

Woodward, Stanley, New York Herald Tribune

Woolf, S. J., NEA

Worth, Edward S., AP

Wright, James, Paramount News

Wright, McQuown, UP

Yancey, Luther F., Afro-American Newspapers

Yap, Dioadado M., Bataan

Yarbrough, W. T., AP

Yates, Thom. Yank

Young, B. J., Group 4, Australian Papers

Young, Murray G., WHK

Young, Stanley, Cosmopolitan

Young, Thomas W., Guide Publishing Company

Youngman, Lawrence, Omaha World Herald

Zaimes, Charles J., American Red Cross

Zaimes, Margaret K., American Red Cross

Zayas, George, Collier's

Zegri, Amando, NBC

Zinder, Harry, Time